EARLY AND MODERN HISTORY

Wolfe County

KENTUCKY, 1860-1957

EARLY AND MODERN HISTORY

Wolfe County

KENTUCKY, 1860-1957

COMPILED BY

WOLFE COUNTY WOMAN'S CLUB

CAMPTON, KENTUCKY

Commonwealth Book Company
ST. MARTIN, OHIO

Copyright © 1957 by Wolfe County Woman's Club.
Copyright ©2019 by Commonwealth Book Company.
All Rights Reserved.
Printed in the United States of America.

ISBN: 978-1-948986-06-9

Wolfe County
by Berta K. Cecil

Wolfe County, the 110th formed in the state of Kentucky, was established in 1860, out of parts of Morgan, Breathitt, Owsley and Powell Counties and named in honor of Nathaniel Wolfe, then senator from the city of Louisville, Ky. When the first settlers came to what is now Wolfe County they found it densely covered with forests, abundant with wild game including the buffalo.

In 1950 the Agricultural census showed that Wolfe County had a population of 7,615 people, 230 square miles, 1189 farmers and 147,200 acres of land. This county has two main rivers, seven major creeks and many tributaries and the North Fork of the Kentucky River curves in and out of Wolfe County to the south; several main tributaries of this stream being in Wolfe County.

The main creeks are Lacy, Gillmore, Buck, Big Branch, Clifty, Laurel, and Stillwater; each of these having several tributaries, so you can see the county is well watered and has many acres of good bottom land.

Campton, the county seat, which had a population of 77 in 1870 has today a population of over 500 and has been the county seat since 1856. Hazel Green the second largest town in the county has a population of around 300 and Lee City about 125 residents.

It is said that Swift Creek silver mines camp was originally on the site of the present courthouse in Campton. As to the authenticity of this statement I cannot say, but legendary information is that Swift Silver mines is located somewhere in the labrynth of hills and the maze of canyons of Swift Creek, in Cumberland National Forest in Wolfe County, Ky., and if it could be located again the founder would be rich beyond his wildest calculations.

Many of the descendants of Wolfe Countians came from Virginia, which was only natural, as in 1779 Virginia covered the state of Kentucky; which later was divided into three counties, Fayette, Lincoln and Jefferson.

One of the earliest families of Wolfe County was Michael O'Hair, who came from Ireland about the beginning of 1800; moved his large family (13) children, to what is now known as Hazel Green but was Montgomery County. One of his daughters, Eleanor B., married William Trimble, who was born in 1787. Another daughter, Sibby B., married William Lacy, who was born in 1790. All four of these persons are buried in the Hazel Green Cemetery.

Other first families of Wolfe County are Andrew Pence, who paid taxes on 640 acres of land on both sides of Holly Creek in 1830,

EARLY AND MODERN HISTORY

which the deed books say he purchased for $125.00. John Holland, William and Ambrose Holland, had a deed for 2500 acres of land on Holly Creek for which they paid $150.00. Samuel Rose purchased 1000 acres for $150 betwixt Holly and the North Fork of Kentucky, Jeremiah Lovelace, 200 acres for $200 on Frozen, Nathan Gibbs, 1250 acres for $350 on Frozen; Samuel Henry Hurst, 1500 acres for $200 on Frozen. In each case the others listed here witnesses the deeds of the others. Most of this land lies in Wolfe and Breathitt counties.

Quite a few families came to Wolfe County from Lee County, Va., among them were the Elkins, Days, Richmonds, Hortons, Congletons and others. Many others came from Tazwell County, Va. Among these came the Cecils, Camples, Roses and others.

One of the first high schools to be established in Wolfe was Hazel Green Academy at Hazel Green in 1880. (See sketch of H.G.A. elsewhere in book). In the last 75 years hundreds of students have gone out to make themselves a place in the world, bearing high the standards of Christianity and Democracy learned in this institution.

Kentucky Wesleyan Academy, a branch of the Ky. Wesleyan College formerly at Winchester and later moved to Owensboro, was built in Campton about 1894 according to information supplied by J. L. West of Mt. Sterling, (now deceased). Mr. West was one of the founders of the school which was supported by the Methodist Church. E. E. Bishop was the first principal of this school. He came from Lincoln, Nebraska and later married Miss Mattie Quicksall of Morgan County.

Taylor Center, county judge of Wolfe at that time, took the contract and built the school. Burned a brick kiln and made the brick from the clay on top of the hill on which the school was erected, which was the same site as the one where the present Wolfe County High School is built.

Miss Grace Pepper, was a teacher in Wesleyan Academy at Campton. This school was later merged with the main school, Kentucky Wesleyan College at Winchester, then under the administration of E. H. Pierce at that time.

After Kentucky Wesleyan Branch school was discontinued in Campton, people took up subscriptions and ran the school by charging tuition, some say $4 per month per child. Later this became known as Campton graded school.

In 1934 this was changed from an independent school to Wolfe County High and Grade School. In 1954 many of the county schools were consolidated with this school and school busses put on to haul the children. Now most of the one-room county schools have been absorbed by either the consolidated school at Campton or the grade consolidated school at Hazel Green. Only those in the most inaccesible places for the school busses to reach are kept on in most instances.

The first courthouse established in Campton was about 1860. It was a log house which was later destroyed by fire in 1887. It was rebuilt, a large frame building being erected which was also destroyed by fire in 1913. The present courthouse of yellow brick was constructed in 1917 and dedicated. The present jail house was built in 1907.

The order of Masonic Lodge was established in Campton in 1872 and also the Eastern Star Lodge.

Samuel Hurst was a great land owner both in Wolfe and Breathitt counties. Kash was a familiar name back as early as 1840. About 1870 Robert Cecil moved to Baptist Fork of Stillwater from Tazwell County, Va., with his large family. His wife was Celia Sample prior to her marriage. They had eight children (See Cecil-Sample).

C. M. Hanks Sr., was the first to represent Wolfe County in the House of Representative in 1863-65. In 1779 when Virginia encompassed the state of Kentucky among the early settlers who came to Boonesboro, were two men whose descendants came to Wolfe and Morgan counties at an early date. These men signed the article which stated: "The members appeared every morning at the sound of the conch or beat of the drum to work in the field and others to guard those who worked.'" These two men were John Harper and Edward Williams.

John Harper's daughter, Lydia, married Fielding Hanks, who came to Kentucky and settled in Wolfe County about 1818. He and his wife are burried in the old grave yard on the hill back of the present First Church of God, in Campton. They came from Montgomery county. He was known for his love of hunting, which was his reason for coming to Wolfe County. It was Fielding's son, C. M. Hanks Sr. (his middle name was Cudmillion) who was the first representative from Wolfe County.

Around 1800 John Lacy, who came from Greenbriar County, Va., settled on what later was named Lacy Creek (being named for him) near Hazel Green in Wolfe County. He is buried in the Carson graveyard with this notation on his tombstone, "Born Dec. 1, 1764, died Jan. 19, 1844." The William Lacy who married Sibby O'Hair was his son.

Many of the families of the 1870's were: Combs, Elkins, Rose, Cecil, Wills, Kash, Mize, Shackelford, Kincaid, Tutt, Cox, Childers, Center, Sample, Byrd, Perkins, Edwards, Schaeffer, Gillespie, Cundiff, Cockrell, Stamper, Booth, Collier, Lindon, Catron, Barker, Miller, Terrill, and others which are still familiar today.

From an issue of the Campton Courier published in 1905 the following lists of officials was taken: W. B. Duff, attorney-at-law; C. C. Fulks, Attorney; A. D. Lykins, Attorney; L. T. Hovermale, Attorney; J. H. Stamper, Physician and Surgeon; J. R. Carroll, Physician and Surgeon; Ira G. Profitt, Physician and Surgeon; B. D. Cox, Physician and Surgeon, and W. G. Lockhart, Dentist.

In this issue the Courier short sketches are given of several important business people in the county at that time. Among those given are: Judge Center, who was at that time the Democratic nominee for county judge; S. B. Lovelace, who came to Campton in 1903 with an oil rig to drill oil wells in Wolfe County; Charles H. Buchanan, manufacturer of saddles, harness and shoes; "S. H. Rose, one of the most valuable and reliable citizens of Wolfe County, was born and reared at Stillwater. Born May 31, 1852." This article goes on to state that S. H. Rose had a store and grist mill at Stillwater, established in 1886 which he operated very successfully for many years.

John M. Rose and Co., conducts one of the largest general merchandising establishments in Hazel Green in 1905 and his partner at that time was Ed F. Cecil.

G. B. Rose and Roscoe Wells store, owned by Rose and operated by Wells at Stillwater, was operated in 1905. John W. Cox, a nominee for sheriff of Wolfe County in 1905. Ben Sewell, a candidate for state senator in 1905. Robert L. Carroll, a candidate for county court clerk in 1905. W. R. Catron, was a merchant in Campton in 1905.

In this same paper is a lengthy article about Captain William Hurst, in which it says he is reputed to be the county's wealthiest citizen at the time. Prof. William Cord, head of Hazel Green Academy in 1905. Also a lengthy article about the Farmers and Traders Bank, who had in 1905 as cashier, S. D. Drushall and C. F. Combs as his assistant.

During the Civil War Granville Evans and Aleck Duff operated a general store in Campton. At that time we have a record that states main street in Campton was the division line between Floyd and Fayette counties.

Churches

Being a religious people the early settlers of Wolfe County established a place of worship soon after settling in the county. Records shown the Old Primitive Baptist Church on Baptist Fork of Stillwater was organized by two preachers, William Lykins and Daniel Duff in 1837, almost 120 years ago. This was near the present site of the Baptist Post office. Abe Swango gave two acres for the church site. His son, Chap Swango, later established a Seminary school in the county on what is now known as Seminary Creek, this was before the Civil War. Seminary Creek is a tributary of Stillwater.

The Christian Church at Hazel Green was established in 1848. (See history elsewhere in book.)

The Swift's Camp Church was established in Campton about 1848. (See sketch in book under this title.)

The Methodist Church, Campton, was established in 1880 and the one at Hazel Green in 1885. (See seperate sketches of these churches in book elsewhere.)

The New Hope Baptist Church was organized at Stillwater in 1889, in the Trace Fork schoolhouse and chose James Wheeler as Moderator and J. C. Barker as Clerk; William L. Gevendon as Aid and P. H. Haney as Aid.

Early members of this church were: M. F. Linkous, Laura Stamper, Nancy Linkous, John M. Pelfrey, Jefferson D. Edwards, Samuel C. Rose, Otis B. Linkous, Mary E. Linkous, Nancy C. Rose, William I. Linkous, William H. Stamper, John F. Linkous, Powell Rose, Margaret Rose, Lizzie Rose, Lizzie Steel, Jeff M. Rose, Sarah B. Rose, Lisa Moore, Robert T. Rose, Martha Harmon and Jeff D. Rose.

In the fall of 1902, some gentlemen came to Wolfe County prospecting for oil we are told in the pages of the Wolfe County Courier of that date. In 1903 the work was begun on a well for J. S. Cable one mile west of Campton. This was the first drilled well in the county. It was completed in April and brought in about 20 barrels a day natural and 60 barrels a day after being shot. Due to the bad roads however no pipe line was laid until spring of 1904. Others having oil wells drilled in 1904 were: C. C. Williams, E. F. Duff, J. C. Lykins, James Napier, Quillins Heirs, James Campbell, A. C. Oliver, Elgin Trent, O. T. Asberry, G. W. Halsey, John Williams, Willie Roberts, and W. H. Roberts. Others followed until 58 successful oil wells were completed in the field in 1905.

In 1952 there was a re-awakening in the Oil interest in Wolfe County and it has continued over until the present time (1956) and some wells have been reported to come in with good production.

The First Water Mill

The first water mill to come to Wolfe County located in Morgan County, later Wolfe County, was located three miles below Hazel Green in 1810. It was owned by three brothers, John Cox, who came from Grayson County, and his two brothers, James Robertson Cox and Solomon Cox.

EARLY AND MODERN HISTORY

Railroads in Wolfe County

The O&K railroad ran across Wolfe County from the time of its construction in 1901 until discontinued in 1933. Work on the O&K railroad tracks was begun in 1889 in the month of October. The first run in the county started at Cannel City in Morgan and continued across Wolfe by way of Helechawa to Jackson in Breathitt County and was a distance of 27 miles. The first run was made on July 10, 1901. On July 21, 1910 the track was extended from Caney Creek to Licking River in Morgan County.

Cannel City station (now razed) owed its existance to the Kentucky Block Cannel Coal Co.

Experts judged the coal found in this region tops at the Chicago Fair. When the famous vein of coal ran out there was no sufficient reason for the existence of the Ohio and Kentucky railroad in Kentucky.

Helechawa, a depot in Wolfe County, was operated by Charlie Moore, for many years. This is not an Indian name as many people surmise but was coined by the O&K's first chief executive, for his daughter, made by taking the first four letters of her first name; the first two of her middle name; and the first two of her last name. Her name was Helen Chase Waldridge. W. Del Waldbridge was the first chief executive of the road, from New York; and the last one was Guy W. Leslie.

One fatality marred the O&K's safety record. Bud Parks was killed in a wreck one mile north of Frozen on January 19, 1910; when a combination coach and car left the rails. The last run of the line in Wolfe was on November 1, 1933.

Mountain Central Railroad (See sketch)

There are two orphanages in Wolfe County and you will find their sketches elsewhere in this book. Dessie Scott Children's Home and Bethany Orphanage.

Wolfe County Health Department

The Wolfe County Health Department was established in 1927 under the direction of Dr. John L. Cox. Dr. Cox was Health officer in Wolfe for 22 years. He retired about two years prior to his death in 1951.

Mrs. Rex Center is Health Nurse and has been since 1943. Miss Irene Spencer is Health Clerk and Victor Allen is Health Sanitarian in 1956.

The first Health Clerk in Wolfe County was Mrs. Corda Peery, who filled this position for 20 years until her death caused by spotted fever.

WOLFE COUNTY

The Wolfe County Health Department is a valuable asset to the county, has been, and continues to render a valuable service through its health programs.

In this year (1956) the local Health Department is cooperating with the State Health Department in a Human parasite program which promises to improve the health of all those children which are afflicted with "Worms."

The Hazel Green Hospital was operated by Dr. Hiram I. Blood from 1933 until 1953. "Dr. Blood's Hospital" as it was commonly called, was at first only an office with a nurse to assist him. Later it filled the whole second floor of the Boy's dormitory at H.G.A. and had 12 hospital beds, (one of them a pediatric bed), two nurses and other helpers. There was a fully equipped operating room, an x-ray room, and a very fine incubator for pre-mature babies.

In 1949, the last full year of operation for this hospital, there was an average of 4.7 patients per day, 56 babies delivered, 36 major operations and 34 minor ones performed. Dr. Blood was an indispensable man. For nearly twenty years he was ready to climb into his car or jeep or even to go on horseback in extreme case to visit the sick among the hills or in the hollows.

Dr. Blood was a fine Christian physician. He served faithfully and well in his role at the head of Hazel Green Hospital.

FIRST WHITE SETTLER
Submitted by Mrs. Mazie Cox Read of Cushing, Okla.

Nim Wills was the first white settler in Campton. When he came, the only sign of life was an old campfire where the courthouse now stands. So the settlement was named Campton (for Camp town).

The camp was believed to have been made by John Swift and his men, when they were searching for his silver. The nearby creek, which now runs through the town, was named "Swift Camp Creek" but is usually referred to as "Swift Creek."

THESE PAGES TAKEN FROM HISTORY OF KENTUCKY
by Richard M. Collins

Swift's Silver mine (already spoken of under both Carter and Josh Bell counties; see pp. 414-415) is too wonderful and fanciful to be confined to those counties; but needs must have a local habitation also in Wolfe County on Lower Devils Creek, six miles from Campton, the county seat (which is 30 miles from Mt. Sterling, L. Swift's name is carved on both rocks and trees by whom is not known.

EARLY AND MODERN HISTORY

In February 1871, then Cherokee Indians territory to Irvine, Estill County, Kentucky, thence about 15 miles to the farm of Jacobs Crabtree. One of the men, claimed to be the young chief, talked English and was well informed about minerals. The ofject of their journey was quite mysterious, except that it seemed to be connected with the time - out - of - mind tradition about Swift's Silver Mine. Leaving the squaw at Crabtree's the Indians followed up Little Sinken Creek to its source, crossed over to Big Sinken Creek and after riding for several miles hitched their horses. Then after warning white folks, who out of curiosity were following at a little distance, that they would turn back if followed further, disappeared in a thick underbrush. Late in the evening they returned to Crabtree's bearing upon their backs two buck skin sacks heavily laden. By these sacks one of the Indians kept watch all night, with revolver in hand, and in the morning the three departed on the return road to Irvine. The whites went immediately to the neighborhood visited by the Indians, but did not succeed in finding any minerals but iron ore.

Two caves, known as Ashy and Pone (or pot) caves are about a mile apart on Lower Devils Creek. In the latter, on a visit in 1871 were found 27 pots or cruciables about 1½ feet across and the same depth in three rows of nine each, and each about ½ barrell capacity. The road to it although unused for many years was plainly perceptible, being worn down 4 or 5 feet, and with trees apparently 100 to 125 years of age growing in it. A large deposit of sulphur in ore or rocks and deposits of iron and bismouth ore found near; but with the road being near to them.

Nathaniel Wolfe in honor of whom this county is named was a leading citizen and a member of the senate of Kentucky at the session at which it was formed. He was born in Richmond, Va., October 29, 1810, received a liberal education and was the first to graduate from the University of Virginia at Charlotville, his being the degree of M. A., studied law and entered upon the practice at Louisville, Ky.

Wolfe County, the 115th county formed in the state, was established in 1860, out of parts of Morgan, Breathitt, Powell and Owsley Counties and named in honor of Nathaniel Wolfe, then a state senator from the city of Louisville. It is situated in the central eastern portion of the state on the waters of Red River which runs from east to west through the county, while the North Fork of the Ky. River forms its southern boundry; is bounded on the north and east by Morgan; south and east by Breathitt; south by Lee and west by Lee and Powell counties. It contains an area of 170 sq. miles. Besides the above the streams are: Gilmore, Stillwater, Swift, Parched

Corn, Wolfe Pen Gilladie, Upper Devil and Lower Devil. The surface of the county generally is hilly and broken with some rich level ground along the river bottoms.

Corn is the principal product, but wheat, oats, hay and tobacco are raised, and cattle, hogs, horses, mules to a limited extent.

Towns — Campton, 29 miles from Ritchburg, Estill Co. 18 miles from Beattyville, Lee County, 37 miles from Richmond and 45 miles from Paris, Ky. incorporated March 17, 1870; population in 1870 — 67. Hazel Green, 10 miles from Campton, 58 miles from Hazard, Perry County, and 46 miles from Prestonsburg; Floyd County; incorporated in 1856; population in 1870 — 77

SWIFT'S MINE
by Margaret Carroll

Almost all communities have their legends. Some of Indian fighters, some of war heroes, others of some good woman who cared for the sick and the aged. Wolfe County has its legends. The one mentioned here is of John Swift of the lost Swift silver mine. It can hardly be borne out that John Swift was a myth, as he left maps and written instruments giving directions how to find the mine, the indications from the writings were that the ore was smelted near the mine.

Also early settlers confirmed the fact that he had his base camp on the creek which now bears his name. This is a beautiful spot for camps as it is surrounded by low hills, and on the bank of a free flowing clear sparkling creek. However, within a mile or so the terrain, through which the creek flows, completely changes. The ground becomes rough, steep, and barren. One pioneer of early times lived in his rude log house on the same spot now occupied by the Wolfe County Court House. Swift's base cam must have been close by for it is said on occasions the good woman of this family baked corn pone for Swift and his helper. Roughing it as these early travelers and hunters did, corn pone (bread made from corn meal with butter milk and eggs added) was quite a delicacy. Before Swift made his camp there seems to have been no recorded name for the creek. From tradition John Swift was a very affable person, full of energy, extensively traveled, and a fellow well met. The settlers, although few in numbers, began to call the creek Swift Camp Creek, the name it now bears.

His camp must have been ample, as far as a camp in the early days went. He also appeared to be a man of some means and quite an entertaining talker. He seems to have been able to keep these early pioneers in the dark as to where he worked and what he did when temporarily away from base camp on the creek. No one seems to know where Swift came from nor what he did and he often left

EARLY AND MODERN HISTORY

both the base camp and the country for long periods of time. The frequent coming and going from the camp, to what was afterwards reported to be a silver mine, would continue for some months. He would suddenly disappear from the country with his pack horse carrying a heavy load. Then after a short time he would show up just as suddenly as he had disappeared. His belongings were carried on a horse with a pack saddle, there being in these early times no roads, just trails, for the early settlers to follow. These trails were none too plain for a stranger to find his way and many were lost and delayed in finding their destination. Only an experienced traveler, like Swift, would have no difficulty in finding his way about. From tradition there appears to have been only Swift and one other man with him who made the trips to what is now known as Swift Camp Creek in Wolfe County (at this time Wolfe County had not been formed). It is not known for sure that this man with Swift was his partner or a hired hand, but was supposed to be a partner as he is said to have made more than one trip to Wolfe County with Swift. It is also thought that from maps and the instructions left by Swift that this second man must have been a partner with him in the silver mine and assisted him in mining and smeltering the ore. From stories handed down both men appeared to be in their middle ages, strong and healthy, and each time they disappeared from the country, it is thought, they took with them the melted ore on their pack horse. After being away for a few months they would again return to their base camp with their horse, always closed mouthed as to where they went or what they did. One acquainted with Swift Camp Creek knows of its ruggedness, its high cliffs, its narrow gorges, in places the bare faced rock walls extend from the waters edge many feet straight up into the air. Truly a rugged creek. The very place one would go to look for a silver vein. A splendid place for the modern novice to try out his Geiger Counter. The two with their pack horse weighted down left one day as was their usual custom, leaving no information with their neighbor, who lived on the Court House site, (their only neighbor) as to where they were going or when they would return.

As in the course of events the pioneer family expected after some months the return of the two with their pack horse.

Neither of them ever returned. Time went on and it was thought that they may have moved their camp to some new location. In fact no one was greatly interested in the two. In the frontier days there was not much news, and it traveled slowly, and the two were never directly heard from again. After a few years had gone by it was reported a small party appeared in eastern Kentucky. They said that they were looking for a silver mine which had been worked a few years before and that it belonged to one member of the party. There is no record of this party ever appearing on Swift

Camp creek. After spending some months in the search for the mine they returned to their homes finding no trace of the lost mine.

The story is told that a short ways out of base camp on their last journey, with their pack horse heavily loaded with smeltered ore, while crossing a fallen tree, the horse with its heavy load fell and broke a leg. The men disposed of the horse, buried their treasure and continued their journey expecting to return and retrieve their bullion. Fate seemed to be against them.

Soon afterwards the second man, or partner, took sick and died. John Swift also came down with a lingering illness. After a long siege of sickness he finally regained his health but his eye sight was gone. With his sightless eyes he gave a description of the country, its creeks, its rivers, and rough terrain where mine was located, and described the route to take to his base camp. This information was all recorded by friends who drew from his description a crude map of the creek, his camp, the location of the mine, also a map of the place where the bullion was buried. **Tradition says that he made** a second trip in search of his mine but being unable to see, the trip was made in vain.

Where is this silver mine? Where is this horse load of bullion buried? In years past there have been a number of persons to appear in Wolfe County searching for this lost treasure. They would have with them what was purported to be a copy of the original map giving instructions as to the location of the mine, describing the place where the bullion was buried. One in particular was a small middle aged man who said his name was Miner. He traveled up and down Swift Camp Creek and finally came to the conclusion the smeltered ore was buried on the point of a rock cliff some 30 or 40 feet above the level of Hiram's Branch and a few hundred yards from its junction with Swift Camp Creek. Another reason for his shaft location was that this must have been the route Swift traveled because the Indian Stair Steps were not cut in the rock by the Indians as they had no tools of metal with which to chip the stone. That these steps were cut by Swift to serve him in going to his mine and also returning to his base camp. (The steps were cut in the face of an inclined rock reaching up some ten or twelve feet, so chipped that the toe of the shoe fit in the cut made in the stone. These steps are used by the natives in following the trail of the right side of the creek.) It has been said that the location of the lost bullion came to him in a dream.

There on the point of the ridge on a bald rock he sunk a shaft some six or eight feet deep and about four feet square into the solid rock, but no bullion. Another of the mine hunters that came to Wolfe County might be mentioned was an elderly lady, a person above the average in intelligence. She had also a copy of the map and the instructions supposed to have been left by Swift as well as a map showing where the smeltered ore had been buried when the horse was destroyed. She spent some years, and also spent some money, looking for Swift's lost treasure. She lived as a hermit in the Callaboose section, her only companion being a small black and tan dog, and wherever she went the dog would always follow. She walked to Campton (walking was her custom) about once each week where she went to purchase her meager supplies and to get her mail. It is said that she too was a believer in dreams. She had a number of small excavations made here and there. The diggings are not on a large scale and most all of these excavations were on the waters of Swift Camp Creek. All were in vain.

CUMBERLAND FOREST
Compiled and written by Mrs. Roy Cecil through Research

Cumberland Forest in Wolfe County offers many and varied attractions to visitors of Eastern Kentucky.

Nature lovers will want to visit the portion of Cumberland National Forest in Wolfe which annually attracts thousands of tourists; and which supplies such magnificent views of God's great out-of-doors.

Between March 17, 1914 and 1929, the Forest Service examined most of Eastern Kentucky and finally settled on that which was locally known as the Cumberland Plateau for the establishment of its First National Forest in Kentucky.

Actual purchase of the land began in 1933, when a total of 189 acres were obtained. Between 1933 and 1948, The Forest Service examined, optioned and purchased and placed under administration 433,030 acres. The option was taken on an additional 23,000 acres in 1949 which was later purchased in that year, bringing the total in acres in the Forest preserve to 456,000.

Men who played an important part in getting this land into the Governments hand were H. G. Garrett, Crit Childers, Broadhead, and Floyd Day. Garrett and Broadhead sold 10,000 acres each to the Forest, Crit Childers sold 5,000 and Floyd Day sold 10,000 in Wolfe and adjoining counties.

14,178 Acres

Wolfe County has a total acreage of 14,178 acres in the Cumberland Forest. From sale of timber in this boundary this past school year the county received $651.70 as their part. This varies from year to year according to the amount of timber sold. Some years it is around a thousand dollars, for the county's share.

Traveling East over Highway No. 15 you will come to Pine Ridge picnic area which is planned especially for your comfort and enjoyment; with a shelter house, picnic tables, fireplaces, toilets and a fire tower from which you can obtain a view of the nearby gorges. Also one mile west of the tower you will find Tight Hollow, which has a pocket of virgin timber, mostly yellow popular; which is a sight to gladden anyone's heart.

Pine Ridge picnic area is about 2½ miles west of Pine Ridge proper where you turn north along Red River road to reach Sky Bridge, about six miles from the tower. This Red River road is a one-way graveled road (with turn outs for passing) which will lead you to Sky Bridge if you follow the direction signs along the way.

Sky Bridge

Sky Bridge is a natural arch of rock across a section of a ridge near its northern terminus. The ridge at this point is about 30 feet between cliffs and 600 feet long. The dimensions of the arch are 75 feet in length and 18 feet in height. From the top of the bridge an excellent vista is available to observe surrounding countryside; which is made up of wild gorges, deep canyons, Red River circling around the base of the cliff which forms a promontory at its terminus. Magnificent! Breath taking! and soul inspiring is the scenery you will find in this area. It would be a wonderful place for a retreat for anyone seeking food for the soul.

Many people like to camp in this area during the spring, summer and fall and fish in Red River. You will have to obtain a permit to build a fire in the Forest and also buy a state-wide fishing license to fish in the river. Both obstacles are easily overcome. Or if you prefer, there are two lovely, modern motels in the area of Pine Ridge where you can secure lodgings for nominal rates.

If you are one of those fortunate individuals who take their vacation in May or June you will see a sight that is really worth seeing if you visit the Sky Bridge area. The Mountain Laurel blooms first, usually in May and lasts about a month. The small bushes of satin like foliage with pink and white blossoms hug the mountain sides, transforming whole areas into a garden of beauty. The rhodendron blooms in June and July, according to the temperment of the season and is also a mass of pink and white blossoms; but the shrubs are larger than the Laurel shrubs and have a broader glossier leaf, which is permanently green, and very beautiful as well as the blossoms. They grow most anywhere in this area; along the streams, on the mountain sides or right out on the cliffs, where it is hard to imagine anything growing at all.

Wild Flowers

It is reported that Dr. McFarland of the University of Kentucky staff has said that there are more specie of wild flowers and grass-

EARLY AND MODERN HISTORY

es growing in this section of Wolfe County around Sky Bridge than anywhere else in the whole of the United States. Whether this is a fact or not, a great many varieties can be found there. Great purple beds of geranium, blue phlox, purple violets, wild iris, black eyes susans, trilliums, and that rare orchid like flower known as "Lady's Slipper" may be seen along the river bed and on the hilly lowlands blooming in wild profusion.

In the surrounding forest belts are such trees as: short leaf pine, pitch pine, white pine, hemlock, yellow popular, white oak, black oak, scarlet oak, walnut, chestnut oak, virginia pine, basswood, beech, buckeye, white ash, black gum, hickory, black birch, holly, wahoo, wild cucumber, tulip poplar, sugar maples, red maples, dogwood, red bud, sourwood, sumach, and willows and many others.

Old Tunnel

Red River gorge is from Sky Bridge down Red River and the gorge through the tunnel, (which is an old L&N railroad tunnel), to Route No. 15 at Nada. Wild beauties enhance your drive on every side as you view tall cliffs with curious formations; some like ancient castles, some with windows through which daylight can be seen, all of them fascinating. You'll enjoy to drive this road more than once a year or season. Thousands visit this spot annually. Those who visit this place once are seemingly mesmerized with its spell, they are impelled to return again and again.

A little known group of areas, "Wild Cat Hollow", "Rock Bridge," and "Hell's Kitchen", are accessable by walking a few miles. The Forest Service has cut a well defined trail into Rock Bridge and Wild Cat Hollow where may be seen a pocket of white pines standing a hundred feet tall.

Rock Bridge is a Natural stone archway over Swift Creek about four miles northwest of Campton as the crow flies. To reach it one must drive to Pine Ridge on Route No. 15 and take the Red River road north there, as if going to Sky Bridge, but as soon as you come to a branch road to the right, commonly known as "Lover's Lane" take it and follow it to its terminus. Then you will have to follow an Indian trail into Rock Bridge and Wild Cat Hollow. It is not advisable to make this trip without a guide as one can easily become lost in this vast wilderness.

Rock Bridge is enchanting! If you follow the Swift Creek up stream about 100 yards from the bridge you will come to Rock Bridge falls, a truly picturesque scene. On one side of the stream is Wild Cat Hollow and from this place you can see the gigantic white pines towering above you and at your feet a white strip of sand so enticing that it seems to invite you to sit and rest your weary legs and feed your soul on the beauties of God's great out-of-doors.

Silver Mines

Now you find yourself in the area that abounds with tales of the lost Silver Mines. Between Rock Bridge and Sky Bridge is supposed to be the place where Swift found such a rich silver mine that if it could be re-located it would make all of Kentucky rich. Below Rock Bridge and accessible only to the most hardy, is Hell's Kitchen, a place of high canyons, giant boulders, and frothing waters.

This area along Red River is all one of majestic beauty and can be viewed best from a boat. These canyons are created by sandstone cliffs 50 feet and 100 feet in height just below the plateau level, which has withstood the elements while the land below has eroded. These cliffs often meander miles without gaps or means of getting up or down. Several hundred feet below the sandstone cliffs are frequently found limestone cliffs of smaller size. A trip up one of these canyons is truly magnificent! Natural caves are common in this area, and waterfalls, springs, natural Rock bridges, or arches appear frequently. There are several in this area.

The forest is divided into six districts. In each district is a ranger in charge. Under him are two or three year round employees, consisting of Fire control Assistant, Dispatcher and Timber Sale Assistant (where the sale of timber justifies it). In addition he has five regular lookouts who man the fire tower six months out of the year. He has also about as many emergency lookouts who are used when necessary to supplement the work of the regular lookouts.

Seeing is believing. If you are planning a vacation where nature abounds and where you can drink your fill of natural beauty, then plan a trip through Cumberland Forest, especially in the part that runs through Wolfe, Powell, Menifee, Lee, Owsley and Breathitt counties. You will want to spend some time at Sky Bridge in Wolfe and also visit Rock Bridge, some time at Natural Bridge in Powell, visit Broke Leg Falls in Menifee and other spots of interest through out this vast area.

EL PARK HOTEL

Compiled by Mrs. Roy Cecil through information supplied by Mrs. Nora Horton

The first hotel to be operated at Torrent was built sometime between 1890 and 1896 and was operated by W. A. Byrd. This was soon after the "Big Tunnel" was cut through the hill connecting the L&N railroad with the Winchester-Lexington line on one side and the Jackson line on the other side of the hill. Later this hotel was destroyed by fire.

EARLY AND MODERN HISTORY

In 1896 the hotel site consisting of 15 acres was purchased by J. T. Day of Hazel Green and B. F. McCormick of Lexington and the El Park Hotel was built.

The new hotel was a large one with a big dining hall and kitchen and lobby taking up the whole first floor. The second floor was given over to the bedrooms. Along the entire length of the building was built a large hall which was used as a dance hall. On either side were bedrooms which rented for $8.00 per day.

It soon became a fashionable resort hotel and was especially recommended for hay fever victims. Things were really booming around Torrent until the depression struck in 1928 and the rooms in the hotel were usually full.

The place was staffed with colored servants and all of the waiters were required to wear immaculate white coats and caps.

Not one was hired unless he could credibly play some kind of a musical instrument. Then at night when the serving was done for the day they would assemble in the dance hall and play for the paying clientel to dance until the early hours of morning. Oh, those were the gay ninties!

Over week end excursions trains filled the hotel to over flowing and many of the cottages which were kept for rental. Not only did the "excursion trains" bring "week enders" who wined and dined sumptuously at El Park; but many nature lovers who came for a day's picnic only, bringing their picnic lunch in a basket with them.

When the train stopped the people swarmed off like flies and struck out for the woods. The day was spent in exploring caves, climbing mountains, wading streams, picking wild flowers or just lying under the trees or in the lush grasses listening to the droning of the bees or the singing of the lark and watching bright blue summer skies overhead.

Late in the afternoon the train returned and announced its arrival with a series of shrill blasts which rang up and down the valley. Suddenly the woods emptied itself of all its explorers, some of them the worse for wear with scratches from wild berry vines, and grass stains and dabbling in the water; but all happy and contented for the day spent in God's great mountain country where the air is pure and clean and where the birds call alluringly to their mates.

It was about 1915 an oil boom was started at Torrent which caused the hotel business to take on an added impetus. In fact El Park could not accommodate all those who requested rooms there.

It was about this time that the hotel decided to build a dance hall on top of the mountain overlooking the hotel below which nestled against the side of the hill. So a pavilion was constructed near the top along side the rock ledges in a sort of semi-circle for about a quarter of a mile in length.

These rock ledges are more like a room with one side open to the air; going back under the hillside for 20 or even 30 feet in some places. Here in this perfectly protected spot were constructed tiers of seats for persons to sit and watch the dances which took place every night; as long as the season was not too cold and while the moon rode on high to give light. Here too the "imported" orchestras were brought from Cincinnati for week ends and the merry makers had fun until the wee hours of morning, the valley ringing out with their revelry all through the night.

There were two ways in which you could ascend or descend the mountain from the dance pavillion. The better way was the one used most of course; it was built along the side of the hill with stone steps cut from the rocks and supplemented with wooden steps where needed.

The other way was called the "Squeeze way". This was a natural funnel running straight up the mountain side, created by erosion of wind and water upon the rocky sides of the mountain through the centuries. It was just wide enough for one human being to squeeze through and by bracing themselves spread eagle fashion against either side of the tunnel and pulling themselves up by shrubbery, they could make it from top to bottom or vice-versa. Needless, to say, only the most daring ever tried this way to go up or down the hill.

A hay fever association was organized in Lexington and they recommended a trip to El Park Hotel as a cure to the disease. Free of the deadly pollen which so disturbs hay fever addicts — overnight their troubles vanished like magic. No wonder they wanted to go to El Park.

Great herds of horses were kept for the guests to hire for riding. The horses were stabled under the great rock ledges. The water fell over the cliffs and made a waterfall; making plenty of fresh water for them to drink. Under the ledge it is warm in winter and cool in summer.

El Park Hotel was often used as a convention spot. It is reputed that about 1,000 persons could gather in this area where the tiers of seats were located. There was a most unique platform used for the speaker.

By means of a giant cable and pulley the platform was lowered from the top of the mountain to the level of the people's heads, some hundred feet below the top of the mountain and anchored there so the speaker could stand and speak to the crowd. The cliffs caught and held the sound of his voice until the reception was perfect. When the speaker finished his dissertation the pulley lowered the platform to the ground and the speaker got off, then it was again drawn to the top of the mountain where it was again anchored until needed.

Lula Day Kash inherited the Torrent property which included the El Park Hotel at the death of her father, J. T. Day, in 1921 and it continued to function as a hotel under a rented management until it was destroyed by fire in 1935. The Lula Day Kash heirs, Jesse D. Kash, Rowena Combs, and Dollie Wilson Reed, still own the hotel site at Torrent.

(Supplied by Mrs. Irene McLin Keller)
From Papers of Mr. Day

The Mountain Central railroad was built by Floyd Day in 1898. Its purpose was to carry timber from Floyd Days lumber camps in sections of Powell and Wolfe Counties to his mills. In 1903 it was to be abandoned (as the lumber had been finished) but when the people in Wolfe County heard this they got up a petition and asked Floyd Day to extend the line to Campton Junction for a passenger line and freight train. He consented to do this. It was in operation from 1903 until 1928 for this purpose.

This was a very narrow gage railroad and when the train went up some of the steepest hills it is reported by the old folks who lived during the time of its operation that one could get off behind the train and walk as fast as the train would go, especially if it were heavily loaded. But it served its purpose well enough to operate successfully for 25 years.

At hand is a leisurely report from S. A. Gabbard, Richmond, Ky., upon a singular incident remembered from days of yore.

"Some 15 or 20 years after the Civil War," Mr. Gabbard begins, "a veteran of the Rebel Army built himself a distillery just across the creek from the farm where I grew up. He made corn whiskey under the supervision of a gauger appointed by the government. He'd boil his mash during the week, then make his run over the week end.

"He was visited upon an occasion of one week end run by Dick McIntosh, a veteran of the Union Army, and Zeke Rose, a veteran of the Rebel Army. Dick had lost a leg during the war. He heard Zeke say to Dick: 'Dick, I'm the one who shot off your leg. You're getting a pension now, so I think you aught to set up a quart of whiskey.'

"Dick set up the quart of whiskey as suggested, but it did not last long. After a while, I heard Zeke speak to him again and say: 'Dick, if you'll set up another quart, I'll shoot off your other leg.' "

HISTORICAL DATA ON HAZEL GREEN, KY.
(Taken from old Records)

Hazel Green was established as a town in when the original plot was recorded on January 22, 1849. The original plot calls for 27 lots. The streets were named as follows: Main Street, Grassy Street and Church Street.

William Trimble deeded to the Trustees of the Christian Church of Hazel Green, Ky., a parcel of land adjoining the town of Hazel Green on December 8, 1849. The Trustees were William Lacy, Sr., Phillip Little and Harrison Swango. The first Christian Church bell was brought by ox wagon in 1868.

Hazel Green Academy was established in 1880. The first school building for Hazel Green Academy was built in 1885. The building was 30x50 feet. The first graduating class was in 1895. Pearre Hall was dedicated in 1902.

This is in all probability one of the most accurate accounts of the early history of Hazel Green Academy available being copied verbatum July 23, 1953 from a copy of the Hazel Green Herald, published September 12, 1907, edited by Spencer Cooper.

The History of Hazel Green Academy

W. O. Mize and Lou Mize whose interest in Hazel Green Academy has been incessant from its beginning and J. Taylor Day and Judge G. B. Swango were the four persons who were directly responsible for the school coming into being.

The year 1882 marked an important epoch in Eastern Kentucky known as "The Mountains," embracing that vast section of the state lying between the Pond Gap at the Virginia line on the east, and Montgomery, the county seat of which is Mt. Sterling, on the west; and from the mouth of the Big Sandy River, on the north, to the Tennessee line at Cumberland county, a southwest direction, a territory of approximately 20,000 square miles, fabulously rich in undeveloped coal, timber, iron, building stone, fire clay, salts, oil, gas, cement, etc., and inhabited by the purest Anglo-Saxon blood on the American continent. A people with rich, though dormant intellect, stoically awaiting the planting of seeds of education, and the march of capital to bring to light their mental power and hidden wealth. It was at the date mentioned, 1882, there was not a single educational institution in this territory nor was there even a common school system reaching mediocrity. Lexington, with the

EARLY AND MODERN HISTORY

State A. and M. College; Millersburg and Danville, with their schools, were the nearest points to which these people could send their children to be educated, and very, very few were able to bear the expense incident thereto. The outskirts were in touch; but within, unsurmountable obstacles prevented the "Mountaineer" from receiving the education his and her natural intellect was capable of grasping. Thus were conditions in the beginning of 1882, when a good sister, long praying for the good of her people, and whose heart went out in love to those whom she had been born and reared, first conceived the establishment of a school at Hazel Green, which would offer advantages for a better education to the young men and women of the mountains and be a fount of moral influence as well. With that aim in view and in conformity to the longing in her heart nurtured for years, she consulted with her husband and co-worker, who was then in the Kentucky senate, and suggested that a bill be passed chartering "The Hazel Green Academy" to be located at Hazel Green, in the geographical center of the "Eastern" section (known as the mountains) of the state.

The charter was granted and the movement received plaudit of the entire population; but when it became necessary to raise the finances to erect suitable buildings and carry the enterprise to a success, but two individuals, Judge T. Day and G. B. Swango, citizens of the town, were willing to unite with Senator W. O. Mize, who had chartered the school, in the erection of the buildings, which were completed in the fall of 1885.

A fall term was begun before the school building was completed, in the Masonic Hall, with N. B. Hays as principal, who put as much zeal and intelligence into his work then as in the office he now holds — Attorney General of Kentucky. Thus began the career of the institution conducted as a private enterprise, and its losses financially were borne cheerfully by the three movers until finally a provisional agreement was entered into whereby the school became a mission of the Kentucky Board of the C.W.B.M., and J. W. McGarvey, President of the College of Bible, and R. T. Matthews, of Lexington, with the proprietors, were created trustees.

About this time Mrs. Anna Shouse was elected State President, and to her neverceasing efforts in behalf of this mission is due much of its success. The Kentucky Christian Women's Board of Missions was then a "feeble folk". Our auxiliaries were few and weak. Those were days of trial, and but for the wise leadership of Mrs. Shouse, no doubt the work would have been a failure.

In 1888, through the liberality of the founders of the school and with the concurrence of the Kentucky Christian Woman's Board of Missions, Hazel Green Academy became the property of the National Christian Board of Missions. Prof. A. J. Ellett was principal of the school at this time, but failing health forced him to relinquish his chosen work; but Miss Emma Jenkins, of Georgetown, who was his assistant heroically conducted the school unaided until the close of the term.

The next year opened with A. F. Erb as Principal, who was in charge one year. Professor Wynne and wife succeeded him for a short time. Prof. Wm. H. Chord was employed and began work as principal in the fall of 1890, and remained at the head of the school until the fall of 1906, when he was succeeded by Rev. H. J. Derthick as President, with a faculty chosen for ability and recognized adaptability to the work, which has grown from a humble beginning until the matriculation for 1906-07 numbered 321, coming from various sections of the mountains — as bright a student body as can be found anywhere, and we may add, more earnest. Hazel Green has not been without its calamities. Twice the Academy Home has been destroyed by fire, the last fire occuring November 13, 1899. This, together with the fact that the old building was not adequate for the demands of the school, brought serious problems to the State and National officers. We could not abandon the field in which so much precious seed has been sown, and going forward demanded a large outlay for new buildings. After months of prayerful consideration and thorough investigations, these women, strong in faith, decided to erect a new building. The citizens of Hazel Green and vicinity purchased a beautiful campus of thirty acres and donated it to the Christian Women's Board of Missions. The new ten thousand dollar school building now crowns its summit, and stands as a "city set on a hill that cannot be hid," while near it is a commodious three story frame dormitory for girls, known as "The Sarah K. Yancey Home," erected at a cost of $7,000, and named in honor of the present State Secretary, whose labors have been incessant and earnest in behalf of the mission; and still, on Harrison Heights (named in honor of Mrs. Ida Harrison, President of the State Board), it is contemplated to erect a re-inforced concrete dormitory for the boys during this fall at a cost of $9,000, of which sum at this date the National Board has collected by donations and has on hand for the purpose some $6,500. All these buildings are heated and lighted by natural gas of superior quality.

Thus to date (1907) is the history of the "Hazel Green Academy", owned and operated by the Christian Women's Board of Missions, at the head of which organization is Mrs. Helen E. Moses (as National President), backed by 45,000 earnest members.

HISTORICAL SKETCH OF HAZEL GREEN ACADEMY
Taken from data in F.S.A. Year Book and information supplied by H.G.A.

Hazel Green Academy was founded in 1880. Three men, W. O. Mize, J. T. Day and G. B. Swango each gave $500 for the first building. When this building was finished it had cost $3,900. Before the completion of the building the school was opened in what was then known as the "Old Masonic Hall" with Professor N. B. Hays in charge, and subsequently continued in the new building from 1880 until the summer of 1886.

It was during this time that negotiations began with the Kentucky Members of the Executive Committee of Christian Woman's Board of Missions, who desired that a Mission should be started in the Mountains of their state. Elder John Rogers drew the attention of the ladies to the need and possibility of doing a good work in connection with the school and church at Hazel Green, and thus the negotiations began.

At the request of the members, the Executive Committee decided to undertake the work, and they directed the petitioners to the initiative enterprise. Accordingly, at the end of December, 1885, a sort of provisional arrangement was entered into, in which Professor J. W. McGarvey of Lexington, and the Rev. R. T. Matthews of Newport, Ky., acted with the proprietors of the Academy as a Board of trustees; and thus the school began to be managed by the Kentucky Members of the Committee.

They employed Professor A. F. Erb as principal, and Miss Emma Jenkins as assistant and work proceeded in a satisfactory manner for three terms of five months each, the last closing May 18, 1888.

From 1886 to 1890 the school was conducted by three different principals, namely, Prof. N. B. Hays, Prof. A. F. Erb and Prof. R. H. Winn.

In 1890 Prof. William R. Cord and wife of Mason County, Ky., were employed to take charge of the school, which charge they had until 1906.

The orginal buildings for the school were in the center of town located on Broadway street near Main. The first dormitory was located on Church street near the home of W. O. Mize, at a cost of $3,500 in the year 1891. The building was burned and another was built in its place. In the fall of 1899 fire destroyed the second dormitory. At this time the Women of Kentucky were urging the Women's Board to take charge of Morehead Academy and unite the two schools. On hearing this the citizens of Hazel Green came forward and made the offer of the beautiful grounds which constitute the present campus to the C.W.B.M.; if they would continue the school at Hazel Green. They agreed to do this and the land purchased was given the name of Harrison Heights in honor of Mrs. A. M. Harrison who was president of the Kentucky Board at that time. Another milestone was reached when in the year 1902 Pearre Hall was erected. The name was given to the hall in honor of Mrs.

Pearre who directed the plans and made the building possible.

At the National Convention of the C.W.B.M., at Chicago, 1893, the National Board assumed full control of the Academy. In 1894-95 an additional room was built to the old school building in which Mrs. W. H. Cord taught the Primary Department. The year 1895 witnessed the first class of graduates from Hazel Green Academy. Three in number: Ben F. Quicksall, John S. Adams and S. Monroe Nickell, a small but noted class.

The first dormitory for girls on Harrison Heights was dedicated in 1905, the name Yancey Hall being so named for Mrs. Sarah K. Yancey. This lovely three story building was destroyed by fire but another was erected to replace it. On the night of October 28, 1929, this building was also destroyed by fire. The original Yancey Hall was destroyed in 1915 and the second one built in 1917.

After much work and planning the old school building was converted into a Girl's Dormitory and a new administration building and also a new gymnasium were built from brick which were made right on the campus. Mrs. Q. C. Daniels played an important part up to this period, being the matron of the dormitory for many years, and all who ever spent any time in the halls will recall the delicious meals which she served.

Mr. Grant K. Lewis is due much praise as it was through his directions that $1,000 was obtained for the gymnasium and also was instrumental in getting a hospital on the campus. This latter was located on the second floor of the boys dormitory.

In 1906 the Rev. Henry J. Derthick of Berea, Ky., came to Hazel Green Academy as principal and served with splendid success until the year 1910 when he left to go to Livingston, Tenn. Brother M. O. Carter was principal for one year, 1910-11. Reverend James Thomas McGarvey of Lexington, Ky., became principal in 1912 and served until 1928. He was followed by Mr. Henry A. Stovall of Jackson, Miss., who is still principal. However during a leave of absence for Mr. Stovall, 1955-56, while he pursued his education at Peabody College, Nashville, Tenn., Mr. G. E. Breece, from Pasadena, Calif., served as principal. The Breeces will be leaving the middle of June, this year.

The hospital which was located on the second floor of the boys dormitory was operated by Dr. H. I. Blood from 1933 until discontinued in 1950. He was an indispensable man for almost 20 years which he served as physician and doctor to the community around Hazel Green. It was with great sorrow that his friends in Hazel Green learned of his tragic death in Arkansas where he was killed by a mail pouch thrown from a fast train.

EARLY AND MODERN HISTORY

Some of the other improvements are the rooms which have been excavated from under the school building and which are used partly for library space and partly for the kindergarten and one room is a store where the children can buy ice cream, soft drinks and candy.

A major undertaking for 1954-55 was sponsoring the Wolfe County bookmobile in cooperation with the county and state. The headquarters for the bookmobile is in the basement of the Academy (some of the newly excavated rooms there) and 36 schools are visited regularly nine months of the year from this central place.

Last summer in 1955, second week end in August, the school celebrated its 75th anniversary with a pageant which was both colorful and interesting. It was composed and presented by Mr. and Mrs. Goff Long, Milligan College, Tenn. This pageant portrayed the main events through the 75 years which the school has been giving service to the mountains.

Many changes have taken place through the years, most of them for the best. Many students have gone out into the world to make their mark after having received their diplomas from HGA, one of the oldest schools in the Eastern Kentucky mountain region.

HAZEL GREEN ACADEMY THROUGH THE YEARS

Needless to say there has been many changes at HGA between the years of 1907 and 1955, most of them for the best.

From a school with a few buildings, it has grown into a school with almost adequate housing for its needs. In addition to the administration building there are: The boys dormitory, Girls dormitory, Industrial Arts buildings, (A new ndustrial arts building is badly needed), Jot 'Em Down Store, Laundry, Principal's cottage, Building and Maintenance foreman cottage, and the gymnasium. There is a definite need for a teacherage or a group of teacher's cottages.

For the last quarter of a century the grades below the seventh have been eliminated at the Academy and only junior high school and four years of accredited high school work are now offered in the program of study.

In the past few years more and more the school is trying to build up community interests so that the school may become a community center in itself.

A major undertaking the past year was the sponsoring of the bookmobile project for Wolfe County in cooperation with county and state agencies. The long hours spent in cataloguing 3669 books, and the time, money and effort put forth to provide storage space for these books all seemed quite worthwhile when the school was told by the District Library supervisor that the set-up at Hazel Green indeed deserved meritorious comment.

In 1955 forty-one boys and girls received scholarships due to the interest and generosity of friends, and church organizations. A year's scholarship is $165.00.

Extra activities carried out in this year of 1955 under the sponsorship of the regular faculty and staff included interscholastic basketball with a schedule for daily practice, eighteen match games, and participation in a district and regional festival; a 4-H Club for boys and girls; A Conservation Club for boys and girls; A Glee Club with a membership of 75; A Pep Club, Y-Teens, two age groups; The Christian Youth Fellowship and the Chi Rho groups which meet once a week during the school year. Communities included a Parents Club with monthly meetings; Community Sings, once a month; and most of the faculty members participate in some of the clubs in the county such as Kiwanis, Wolfe County Woman's Club, Homemakers Club, and are also active in the Sunday School and Church work.

The summers at the Academy are almost if not more busy than the regular school year. Here is a calendar of events for the past summer.

June 4th — Advisory Board Meeting. This constitutes about two dozen individuals from all over the United States coming to the Academy and staying for three days discussing vital interests of the school.

June 5th — Executive Board meeting of Former Students Association.

July 3-9th — Eastern Kentucky Young People's Conference.
July 10-16th — Central Kentucky Young People's Conference.
July 19th — Masonic Rally including nine counties with a membership of 2500.

August 9-10th — Tour group enroute to World Convention in Canada.

August 12-14th — Home Coming at the Academy.
August 15-19th — C.Y.F. Planning Commission.
August 22-September 3rd — Folk Institute conducted by the University of Kentucky and the American Squares Magazine of New Jersey.

September 3-4th — State Guild Meet.
September 6th — Opening of Fall Term of School.
October 9th — All-day meeting for the Corner stone laying of

EARLY AND MODERN HISTORY

Christian Church.

October 22nd — Seventh District meeting of the Ky. Federation of Women's Clubs.

The presence of Mr. and Mrs. George E. Breece, who are giving two years of service to the Academy, is making possible a year's leave of absence for Mr. and Mrs. Stovall, who entered George Peabody College in Nashville, Tenn., in the fall of 1955. They are taking some extra curricular work which will better prepare them for the extra activities which will be a part of the school program in the future.

This year of 1955 is the 75th Anniversary of the Institution of Hazel Green Academy and it was properly celebrated with a pageant depicting the years of service for the school. Mr. Goff Long, a former student at the Academy wrote the pageant with the help of his wife and they directed it during the Home Coming on August 13th. Perhaps the largest crowd which has ever attended a Home Coming attended the last one.

Mr. and Mrs. Henry Stovall celebrated their 25th wedding anniversary in 1954 and during the annual home coming festivities they were given special recognition in behalf of the work they have done at the school and for their 25 years of consecutive service. The F.S.A. presented them with a beautiful silver service.

The teaching staff at Hazel Green Academy in the fall of 1955 was as follows: Mr. and Mrs. G. E. Breece, who are relieving the Stovalls, Charles E. Cecil, Mrs. Bobby Rose, Mrs. Martha Shemwell, Mrs. James I. Hollon Jr., Miss Marcia Barton, Miss Leona Hood, Mrs. A. T. Johnson, Pryce Tutt, Mrs. Pryce Tutt, and Mr. O'Donnell. Miss Rowena Combs has also joined the staff as assistant librarian.

Others on the H.G.A. staff are: James I. Hollon Jr., farm foreman; Mrs. Stella Smith, Mrs. Pearl Lacy, Mrs. Golden Byrd, M. C. Nickell, and Mrs. Elsie Smith.

WESLEYAN ACADEMY ESTABLISHED AT CAMPTON IN 1896 AS A BRANCH OF COLLEGE NOW AT OWENSBORO

(Information by Mrs. Bertie Catron and Rev. W. L. West)

School discontinued over dispute in 1912.

In the year 1896 Kentucky Wesleyan Academy was established in Campton, Wolfe County, Kentucky, on the present school site, with Rev. W. L. West, as the founder and president. This school was a branch of Wesleyan College then at Winchester and now at Owensboro, Ky. E. E. Bishop was the first principal of the school which comprised all of the elementary grades and high school. Being an accredited high school, students finishing at this institution could enter college without taking entrance examinations.

Some of the first teachers were: E. E. Bishop, Miss Mattie Quicksall of Hazel Green, who later became Mrs. E. E. Bishop; Prof. C. J. Nugent, Miss Daisy Pollock, the music teacher. Prof. Nugent and Miss Pollock later married while teaching there. Miss Grace G. Pepper, another teacher is still living and now makes her home in Germantown, Ohio.

Mr. and Mrs. E. E. Bishop operated a boarding house in connection with the school for students who did not live close enough to attend the school and stay at home. There was an average attendance of between 150 and 200 students.

The school was discontinued in 1912 or there about, when there arose a misunderstanding between the principal and a few of the local people, through no fault of his own; at which time they attempted to oust him from office. As a result Wesleyan College withdrew its support and the school was discontinued.

Columbus C. Hanks donated the five acre plot of land on which Kentucky Wesleyan Academy was built and on which the present Wolfe County High School now stands. He was the father of Mrs. Bertie Hanks Catron, who attended this school.

Miss Grace G. Pepper was the teacher of Mrs. Bertie Catron when she was in the fifth grade. Miss Pepper visited Campton in 1951 and she had with her some of the work her fifth grade students had done when she taught here.

Rev. West died last year while in his 90's.

SWANGO SPRINGS ONCE A FAMOUS RESORT

(For this article we are indebted to Mrs. Rose Conlee for information)

Nearly three quarters of a century ago, a lady who lived near the little village of Hazel Green, in Wolfe County, Kentucky decided to bathe a mangy dog in some water from a spring on her place. This lady was Mrs. Nancy Swango, wife of Harry Swango. She discovered a few days after having bathed the dog in the spring water that it was completely healed of its mange. She began to tell her neighbors about this remarkable discovery and some one suggested that she send off the sample to have it analyzed and this was done. It was found that the water contained a high percentage of minerals which were good for many diseases. Mr. and Mrs. Harmon Swango operated a boarding house for many years.

EARLY AND MODERN HISTORY

The news of the "find" continued to spread by word of mouth until a Mr. Rittenhouse heard of the springs and decided to purchase them and build a resort hotel near the spot. He purchased the land containing the Swango Springs and erected a large two story hotel near them.

It was a beautiful site for a hotel; in a lovely park like area on a wooded hillside, overlooking a peaceful valley. In about 1895 a hotel was constructed and soon became a famous resort for people from all over the United States and even foreign countries, it is said, came to drink of the healing stream of water.

In addition to the hotel Mr. Rittenhouse had a famous stable built and kept blooded horses for hire. Many people from the Blue Grass drove through to the springs in their carriages or buggies. For in those days there were no good roads into Hazel Green. Most people came into the village via the L and N railroad to Helechawa and thence by the mail hack into town.

The people who came to stay at the springs and drink the water came mostly in the spring, summer and early fall due to the conditions of the roads in the winter time. The people in the town of Hazel Green made many friends among these "Summer Boarders", as they were called.

There were parties given at the hotel to which the town folk were invited and many happy gatherings took place there.

In addition to the water that was drunk at the springs, much of it was shipped out via the railroad to all parts of the United States. This practice was kept up until about 1943, until the death of Mrs. Ellen Coldiron, who owned the springs at that time. The sale of spring water netted a goodly income over a period of a good many years.

About 1910 the Rittenhouse hotel was burned to the ground and a new hotel was not erected in its place. After that for many years the people continued to come and board out among the residents of Hazel Green or to stay at one of the two hotels which were in operation at that time.

The Lou Day hotel was on the Carl May corner facing towards Rodney Gillespie's present home site. After her death, Mrs. Emma Evans, her daughter, had the old hotel torn down. After it was gone, Mrs. Emma Evans and her daughter, Nellie, kept spring boarders and "over nighters" in their house.

On the site of the present Lockard store was the Hazel Green Hotel. It was built, owned and operated by J. T. Day. It was built about 1890 or 91. It did a flourishing business over a period of years. After J. T. Day's death it went to his daughter, Mrs. Lula

Day Kash, and it was sold after her death. The Cecil family also operated a hotel where the home of Dr. Beebe is presently located (formerly owned by Dr. H. I. Blood).

Every day or sometimes twice a day you could see a group of people walking towards the springs with water jug in hand. They would go to the springs and drink as much water as they wanted and then fill their jugs and take them home with them or rather back into the village. This went on until 1940 when the people began to come and take water home with them in jugs in their cars.

A few years after the Rittenhouse hotel was burned, Mr. Crockett Coldiron purchased the springs and sold the water until his death, then his wife carried on the business until her decease. After Mrs. Ellen Coldiron's death, her son-in-law, Glen McCoun and wife, bought the springs. He has not operated them in any way since he purchased them.

In addition to its worth as a healing water, the little park which surrounds the springs on the hillside overlooking the town of Hazel Green, was a favorite retreat for couples who were in love or thought they were. They would stroll out to the springs and back. There were many picnics held on this site through the years.

As recently as 1935 people came to board with Mr. and Mrs. C. S. Cecil in the village and drink the spring water. Some of them were so sick when they came they had to be carried into the house but when they left they were able to walk and looked fine.

FARMERS AND TRADERS BANK
(Taken from old records and newspaper clippings)

The first meeting of the stockholders of the bank was held on November 19, 1902 at which time the directors and officers were elected. This meeting was held in the county attorney's office and J. H. Stamper was elected as secretary to take the minutes.

The name "Farmers and Traders" was chosen at this time and has been proudly carried through the years, its name showing the kind of people whom it serves.

Directors named in 1902 were: J. N. Vaughn, J. H. Stamper, S. S. Combs, George Clark, G. W. Halsey, J. R. Elkins, J. T. Crain, S. G. Drushel and Lon Rogers.

G. W. Halsey was elected as the first president of the bank and S. S. Combs as the first vice-president and S. G. Drushel as cashier.

A. F. Byrd was appointed attorney for the bank at that time; later in July of 1907 Rose and Sample were employed as Bank attorneys.

EARLY AND MODERN HISTORY

The bank began operation in the brick building leased from Eustes and Firestein on January 15, 1903; and in August of the same year the building was purchased from the above mentioned parties for the sum of $3,000. The bank remained in this building until December 1906 when it was destroyed by fire.

On the following January 1, 1907, J. P. Brissey was elected as cashier to succeed Drushel who resigned and acted as cashier until January 1, 1910 when James Drake was elected in this capacity.

In January 1921 B. D. Rose was elected as president and served until January 1922 at which time W. S. Tutt was elected as president.

J. C. Lindon was elected as cashier on January 13, 1925 and served until April 29, 1933 and on May 6, 1933 Rush Evans was elected as cashier.

In August 1933 W. S. Tutt died and he was succeeded as president of the bank by W. G. Lockhart who served in this capacity until November 1937, when he died. Douglas Evans succeeded Lockhart as president, and served until 1944, when Omer G. Catron was elected as president number six of the bank. After serving one year, he resigned to be followed by George Holt, who served from December 1944 until 1952, when O. L. Miller succeeded him in this capacity. The bank is now operating with the following personnel:

O. L. Miller, president; James H. Dunn, vice-president; Riley Harris, 2nd vice-president; Charles E. Lindon, 3rd vice-president and also cashier; Reva Terrill and Vergie Pence, assistant cashiers.

Present directors are: Bertie L. Center, Riley Harris, Dr. James H. Dunn, Charles E. Lindon, Rosaline Emerick, China Lindon and O. L. Miller.

The Farmers and Traders Bank celebrated its 50th anniversary of service to the public in January, 1953.

The Farmers and Traders Bank has been steadily growing through the years and increasing its surplus and earnings until now it has over $78,000 in capitol and undivided profits, with deposits totaling $1,080,691.50 as of January 15, 1953.

Only eight presidents have served during the fifty years: G. W. Halsey, 1902-1921; B. D. Rose, 1921-1922; W. S. Tutt, 1922-1933; W. G. Lockard, 1933-1937; Douglas Evans, 1937-1944; Omer G. Catron, 1944-1945; George Holt, 1945-1952; and O. L. Miller, elected in 1952 and is still serving.

Only six cashiers have served in this capacity during the history of the bank: S. G. Drushel, 1903-1907; J. P. Brissey, 1907-1910; James

Drake, 1910-1925; J. C. Lindon, 1925-1933; Rush Evans, 1933-1944; and Charles E. Lindon was elected as cashier in 1944 and is still serving in this capacity in October 1955.

SWIFTS CAMP CHURCH
By Mrs. W. E. Bach

We a number of Regular Baptist meeting together at Swifts Camp in Morgan County, Kentucky, do Covenant together and Constitute a Church of Christ on the 8th of July, 1848.

Elder Wm. Boothe
Elder John D. Spencer

Members Names — Brethrens

Elder Henry H. Reynolds, Dismist by letter 1852; Henry Reynolds, excluded August 1859; C. M. Hanks; Elkahan Garrett, Dismist by letter 1851; James Cheatham, Dismist by letter 1849; William Spencer; John Wierman; John Spencer; John Wiet, Deceased September the 5th, 1854; Joseph McPherson, Senior, deseast — 1861; Joseph McPherson, junior, excluded — 1859 — Aug.; John Burchfield, excluded — 1859; Franklin Spencer, dismist; Elder James Wm more, Dismist by letter feb. 1860; Kenchenkely, Deseased; James U. Senter, diseast; William A. Tutt; Calip Campbell, Samuel Napier.

Names of the Male Members of Swifts Camp Church Jun 2 Saturday in 1866, pved jere

1. C. M. Hanks, 2. franklin Spencer, 3. John Wierman, 4. William A. Tutt, 5. Caleb Cammel, 7. Elder J. D. Spencer, 8. William Banks, 9. W. H. Tutt, 10. Wm. Ham, deseast 1877; Samuel Naper, James Drake, Thomas Tolston, Walter Buckhannen, Timoth Frier, William Banks, 1876, restored; Joseph Baley, 1876, by letter, desest 1878; Wms. Spencer, brot over; Calvin Wiatte.

Sisters names:

Lydia Hanks, Deseast 1861; Milla Ann Hanks, deseast 1862; Marthy Reynolds, Dismist by letter 1852; Mary Johnson, left the Bounds of the Church; Katharine Cheatham, Dismissed by letter 1849; Sarah Jane Garrett, Dismist by letter 1851; Sally Noble, Dismist by letter 1853; Luisa Spencer, Deseast May the 20th, 1853; Elizabeth Wierman, Dismist by letter; Nancy Wierman, Deceast July the 27th, 1851; Polly Reynolds, Dismist by letter; Judy Wills, Araminta Spencer, Jane Wiet, deseast; Rachel Caudle, 1851 Dismist by letter 1852; Loving McPherson, 1852, 1852; Sally Noble, 1854, Returned her leter in 1854; Rebecca Tolson, 1854; Sally Spencer, 1854; Nancy McPherson, 1855, left the bounds of the Church; Elizabeth Johnson, 1856; Jesten More, 1857, out of the bounds; Mary Ponder, 1857, same; Susan Ponder, 1857; Mariah Center, 59, same; Caroline Lutes, 59, same; Gemina Write Cox, 60; Elizabeth Tolson, 1861; Mary Tolson,

EARLY AND MODERN HISTORY

1861; Sousan Naper; Elisabeth Naper; Barby Ashly; Rebeca Cambell; Sary Conley, not in Bounds of Church; Anna Stamper; Margret Bomgarner; Zerilda Long; Sary Olinger; Martha Naper; Samira Spencer; Jane Yates; Mary Napper; Margaret Campbell.

"June the 1st Saturday in 1866'

1. Judy Wills, 2. Jane Wiett, 4. Rebecca tolson, 4. sary spencer, 5. elizabeth jones, 6. Susan ponder, 7. Jeston More, 8. Elisabeth tolson, 9. Mary Senters, 10. Susan Naper, 11. Elisa Naper, 12. Barba Ashly, 13. Rebeca Camil, 14. Sary lovely-1ste Wilson, 15. Any Stamper, 16. Marget Bumgarner, 17. Susanna Spenser, 18. Martha Napper, 19. Sussenda Spencer, 20. Jane Yats, 21. Mary Naper, 22. Margett Camel, 23. Elizebethe Wierman, 24. Nancy Oliner, 25. Nancy Wells, 26. Loucinda Eveans, 27. Sally Ann Duff, 28. Mary Elen Hanks, 29. Laura Ann Hanks, 30. Martha J. Hanks Cox, 31. Rebecca Spencer, 32. Louisa Spencer, Martha Wierman, Roseline Duff, Margrett E. King, Julyann Drake, Rachel Drake, Elisabeth Baley, Zerilda Wills by leter 1877, Eviline Wiatt, Cordelia Asbury.

Lydia Harper is my great-great-grandmother, Judy Wills is my grandmother, Zerilda Wills is my mother. (Mrs. Wm. E. Bach)

The above names found in the Old Church Book of the "Swifts Camp Creek Church, located in Wolfe County, Kentucky. Entries in this Book are from July 8, 1848 to May 3, 1887. Copier by Mrs. William Everett Bach, Lexington, Kentucky, from the Original Records. May 17, 1956.

PRESBYTERIAN CHURCH AT HAZEL GREEN, KENTUCKY

ORGANIZED JUNE 3, 1882

By Mrs. W. E. Bach

On Saturday, 27 May 1882, Revd. Edward O. Guerrant, Evangelist for the Synod of Kentucky, began a meeting in the Town of Hazel Green, Wolfe County, Ky. He was assisted by Mr. Joseph H. Hopper, Agent of the American Sunday School Union. There were only six Presbyterians in the county, at the time, four of whom resided in Hazel Green (Viz - Col. Robt. J. Samuel and his wife, Emma, her brother James Underwood and Sidney McLin) — and two residing at Campton — ten miles distant, (Viz - Prof. J. Roland Day and his wife.)

During a nine days meeting the following joined the Presbyterian Church: H. Clay Herndon and wife, Nannie; Thomas J. Cole, Jno. C. Day, James Underwood and Sidney McLin. Jno. C. Day was baptized on Monday, May 29, 1882. Col. and Mrs. R. J. Samuel; Sidney and Daniel Isom (colored). Col. and Mrs. Samuel united by letter from the Presbyterian Church at Marion, Ala.

June 1, 1882 — Mr. Green Trimble of Mt. Sterling generously donated the Presbyterians a beautiful lot upon which to erect a house of worship. We bought one adjoining it, from Mrs. Porter Lacy for $75. Col. Samuels and Dr. Guerrant gave their note for it, payable in sixty days.

Prof. J. Roland Day and wife, and Mrs. James Bise, Dr. Felix M. Thomas, Jno. A. Adams, Thomas J. Stevenson and wife, joined the Church.

Began Subscription for Church building.

June 3, 1882 — After prayer meeting the Congregation held a meeting and unanimously elected Col. R. J. Samuels, H. Clay Herndon to be the Elders of the Hazel Green Church, and Jno. A. Adams and Jno. C. Day to be deacons. Subscription to new church amounts to $505.00.

At this meeting the following came into the Church: Geo. Nelson Candler, Albert Burton, James P. Bise and John Robinson.

June 4th, 1882 — Col. R. J. Samuel and H. Clay Herndon installed to be Elders of the Hazel Green Presbyterian Church, and Jno. A. Adams and Jno. C. Day to be Deacons. Services held in Masonic Hall. On invitation three persons came forward to unite with the Church — Viz: Mrs. Fred Day, Mrs. Albert Burton and Mr. Jo. Blankenship.

After Sermon — the Communion of the Lords Supper was celebrated, the large congregation, of all the different denominations uniting.

June 4th: Mrs. John Adams, Mrs. Mary B. Sally, Mr. Burns Kash, Mrs. James Gilly, Mr. M. E. James, Mr. James Gilly, Miss Elizabeth Hogg (Col), Miss Martha Hogg (Col), Mr. Hiram Blankenship Jr., Miss Bell Robinson, Mr. Samuel Gilly, Mr. John D. Cruey. Dr. J. B. Taulbee and wife, Mollie E., A. J. Buskirk, Mr. G. B. Robinson, Mr. Asberry Robinson, Miss Mattie H. Willmore, Mr. C. H. Sally, Mr. R. H. Hale, Miss Milly Hogg (Col) and Miss Alice Samuel (Col).

Sunday, January 24, 1886, Spencer Cooper and Mrs. Sarah Cooper came into the Church from the First Presbyterian Church, Mt. Sterling. Rev. James Little came into the Church from Bethsalem Church on March 19, 1886. He conducted the Services on March 4, 1895 at which time J. T. Day and Lilly McLinn came forward and united with the Church.

July 27, 1891 — Rev. David M. Hawthorne of Abingdon Presbytery removed to Hazel Green and took charge of the Church.

Rev. J. Z. Haney, the preceding pastor, moved to Grayson in Carter County. On Sunday, August 23, 1891 — Dr. E. O. Guerrant received Miss Minnie Lou Day and Miss Amanda E. Wilson into the Church.

EARLY AND MODERN HISTORY

The Contract made and entered in for the building of the foundation for the Presbyterian Church was made on the 21st day of August, 1883. Erastus Brooks to lay the foundation as follows: 30 feet wide and 46 feet long and to be 8 inches above ground and to be sunk six inches in the ground.

It is interesting to note the names of the ones who made subscriptions to the building of this church:

W. H. Wilson, W. C. Coldiron, John Munsey, N. B. Graham, Jas. C. Swango, Jr., Farmer Adams, Dabid B. James, B. E. Roberts, John D. Rose, Sr., Quintus C. Daniel, Walter C. Daniel, A. Hooffman, John T. Bays, Isaac W. Mapel, A. Sidney McLin, J. P. Bise, J. B. Taulbee, A. F. Johnson, A. T. Day, Green Ward, J. A. Adams, T. J. Stephenson, Jr., B. T. Tyler, F. M. Thomas, Jas. M. Little, Burns Kash, W. S. Trimble, M. E. James, C. H. Sally, John D. Cruley, G. B. Robinson, Jas. Gilly, A. H. Lacy, R. D. Motley, F. B. Converse, R. H. Hale, Wm. A. Moore, W. B. Wooper, R. W. Cleland, Robt. J. Samuel, H. C. Herndon, James Underwood, Edw. O. Guerrant, G. B. Swango, J. G. Trimble, John C. M. Day, G. N. Candler, A. Porter Lacy, Floyd Day, D. S. Godsey, F. N. Day, J. H. Pieratt, Joseph Lee Wilson, Albert Burton, Robert E. Guick, W. T. Swango, and Wellington Payne.

On Saturday, the 1st day of October, 1910 Dr. Edward O. Guerrant visited Hazel Green and that evening he baptized Lillie Day McLin. He preached on Sabbath morning and night. In the afternoon of the Sabbath he baptized Hallie Day Bacn and Virginia Maurine Bach, the infant children of Mr. and Mrs. W. E. Bach. That night after the sermon Miss Virginia I. Day and Mary Roe McLin united with the church.

This church was sold several years ago and the money derived therefrom was spent in the Home Mission Field. The Old Church Bell which was used for many years as a Fire Bell as it could be heard for so far, was sent to the Highland College at Guerrant, Kentucky, by Mrs. F. N. Day, at the request of Dr. J. W. Tyler, who was at that time in charge of the Home Mission Work. This bell has been returned to Hazel Green, Kentucky by one of the former students of Hazel Green Academy, having purchased it from them and is now on the campus of Hazel Green Academy.

The Old Communion Set of six pieces which was made in 1737 was given to Mrs. F. N. Day, when the church was abandoned and is now in the possession of Mrs. William Everett Bach, Lexington, Kentucky.

Compiled by Mrs. William Everett Bach, Lexington, Kentucky, May 21, 1956.

HISTORY OF HAZEL GREEN CHRISTIAN CHURCH

(Compiled with the courteous assistance of Mrs. Carl Mize, supplied from records of W. O. Mize, Sr.)

Previous to 1848 Hazel Green was a Baptist Community consisting of two Baptist churches, one of which was located at the top of Rocky Hill and the other at the cemetery.

In the year 1848 a Christian minister by the name of John (Raccoon) Smith came to Hazel Green and held a revival in one of the Baptist churches. The Baptist congregation came in great numbers and presented themselves for membership with the Christian Church.

William Trimble then deeded land for the Christian Church on the corner of what is now owned by Capt. James I. Hollon in Hazel Green. On this location the first Christian Church was erected in 1849. Services were held there until 1882. The deed of the first Christian Church had the trustees names on it as follows: Phillip Little Sr., Harrison Swango and William Lacy Sr.

The first Sunday School was organized in the Christian Church in 1868 and the first prayer meeting was organized the same year. About that time Joe Nickell, the first minister of the church, held a great revival and the membership of the church was greatly increased.

During the Civil War the building was used by General Nelson's troops and was many times in grave peril of destruction.

About 1881 it was decided to obtain a new church site and build a new church. The lot on State Street in Hazel Green was obtained. The first elders of the new church were William Lacy Sr., Solomon Cox, and Joe Nickell. They were followed by Stephen Swango, Dr. J. M. Carter, Dr. J. B. Webe, W. O. Mize, J. M. Kash, J. T. Pieratt, Calvin Swango, Wm. H. Cord, H. J. Derthick, and M. O. Carter.

On June 15, 1882 the new Christian Church on State Street in Hazel Green was dedicated. The church bell was brought from Maysville by ox wagon and mounted — then rung all day. The pulpit was made by a Frenchman named George Rice, brought from Mt. Sterling by W. O. Mize to build his home. Materials from the woodwork in the Mize home were donated by Mr. Mize and made into the church pulpit by Rice. Mr. Mize also donated the first communion set, first chandeliers and the pulpit chairs.

Three brothers, John, Green and James Ward took the contract to build the church for $500. John Ward was the father of Mrs. Lou (Ward) Johnson.

EARLY AND MODERN HISTORY

From the year 1875 until 1890, the church had many noteworthy ministers, Overton Asbill, H. A. Lunsford, the Rev. Lewis, Jones Campbell, R. H. Winn, D. F. Fallen, A. F. Erb, D. G. Combs, and J. M. Downing. In 1890 William H. Cord became principal of the then new Hazel Green Academy and also pastor of the church. Among the elders and deacons of his pastorate were, William O. Mize, John M. Rose, John H. Rose, J. B. Davis, W. T. Caskey, John Pieratt, Fletcher McGuire, and C. Daniel. Under his ministry the C.W.B.M., now known as the Christian Women's Fellowship, was organized in the church and has been a continuous organization ever since. Mr. Cord served the church 18 years.

Brother Cord was followed by H. J. Dierthick, who served about four years. He is vividly recalled by older persons here for his intense love and interest in every person in the town. He often visited every home on a street in one afternoon and held a few words of prayer and as the occasion demanded went into the homes for special prayer, always hatless and with a Bible in his hand. He is still living and lovingly remembered by a large group here.

Following H. J. Dierthick, J. I. Carter and his brother, M. O. Carter, both teachers in the Academy, supplied as ministers of the church until the coming of Mr. MarGarvey.

In September of 1912 J. T. McGarvey became principal of HGA and at the same time it was understood that he became pastor of the church. Deaths and removals had greatly weakened the church membership and the C.W.F.M. Board assumed most of the payment of his salary.

Mr. McGarvey was the son of J. W. McGarvey, president of the College of Bible at that time. He therefore possessed a highly cultural background and was a scholar of the highest type. His sermons are still recalled as pure classics. He had a dignity and reverance in the pulpit that was most impressive. He had also a fine knowledge of music and a splendid tenor voice.

The church building at that time was in bad shape, the roof leaked, the seats were falling apart and new stoves were needed — who can forget the Sunday when most of the plaster from overhead fell on the audience? Through the efforts of a group of the women in the church some repairs were made. Miss Alice Hines obtained new pews and an individual communion service was introduced. In general the church made quite a forward step under Mr. McGarvey's leadership. During his pastorate, our country passed through World War I. Feeling was intense and no one was more outspoken than Mr. McGarvey. Miss Nancy Mapel, at that time secretary of the Red Cross Auxiliary, rang the church bell every day for victory. Mr. McGarvey served as pastor for sixteen years and resigned his work at Hazel Green to become financial agent for Transylvania College.

For the past thirty years the church has had as ministers men who have been teachers in the Academy, and none of whom served over two years with the exception of M. V. Roberts; until J. Ryan Nevius came to the church as a full-time minister in the spring of 1949 and served until October 1952, almost four years. Some of the pastors were students at the college of Bible, others missionary candidates waiting for appointments, and others full-time teachers who also served as church pastor. This latter list includes: J. T. Highfield, James Quinn, R. Q. Adams, Hugh T. Hollond, Wayne Testerman, Byron Spice, and Robert Shemwell who served until his death with cancer of the lungs in August, 1948.

In 1938-39 the church building had again fallen into a very bad state. A canvass was made for funds but not nearly enough was pledged to meet the need. Finally a church extension loan was secured and the building was rebuilt with a basement underneath for class rooms; and a central heating system. The new furnace nearly caused the loss of the building when it overheated. It was in flames when discovered by Bill Mize. Quick action on his part and that of others called in saved the building without much damage.

For help in solving all the problems of the church building we are greatly indebted to Henry A. Stovall, M. C. Nickell, and Dr. H. I. Blood. M. C. Nickell is a great grandson of Joe Nickell, the first pastor of the church.

Over the years the church has had and continues to have as guest speakers and leaders for our revival services, many of the most prominent persons in our brotherhood. In 1938 the membership of the church was about 130 with about 50 of these as resident members.

During the periods in the church history when the church was without a pastor the leaders in the Sunday School were instrumental in keeping the church alive.

Among those who served during the last 25 years in the capacity of Sunday School Superintendent are: Miss Irene McLin, (now Mrs. Wayne Keller); Mrs. R. F. Morgan, Mr. Stovall, Mrs. Roy Cecil, 1931-36; and again from 1949-52; Lawrence Howard Jr., William Earl Lacy, Mrs. Stovall, Danny Joe Howard, Mrs. Joe Nevius, and Mrs. Henry Stovall, again.

the town and give his entire time to the work of the church. Many

In 1946 the church felt that it needed a man who would live in long and earnest meetings were held. At last Wendell F. Taylor was employed and served until he lost his life by accidental electrocution on January 10, 1949 at 10:00 a. m. when his body came into contact with a live wire while trying to reclaim some light poles for use at the church.

His death was a real tragedy to the church. He had great plans afoot to broadcast the church services to the patients in the Hazel Green Hospital. The R.E.A. had given the church some abandoned poles if they would get them; Rev. Taylor and some of the school boys were trying to get a pole when the accident happened which took his life.

Rev. Taylor not only preached at Hazel Green but also served as pastor at Malaga and Salem. He was a native of Washington State.

Since the church serves the student body of Hazel Green Academy it has received many gifts from friends of the school. Words fail to express the deep gratitude of its membership to Mrs. Anna Scott Carter of Kansas City, Mo., long state secretary of the Women's Society of Missouri. She was instrumental in raising funds for the baptistry, pictures, pulpit, Bible, amplifier system and records, and the lovely new Hammond-Estey Organ.

Many men and women serving in the churches far and near and in other fields of usefulness found their start towards better living in the Hazel Green Christian Church. A long list could be compiled of those who are ministers, Sunday School teachers, missionaries, and prominent lay members. One name must be given, our own, Daisy McLin Huber, who with her husband, serves with such distinction in our brotherhood.

In 1948 the church celebrated its 100th Anniversary. A beautiful service was held at the church as a part of the annual Home Coming at which time the history of the church to that date was written and read by Mrs. Maude Martin Rose.

At the time of the 100th anniversary the church officials were: Henry A. Stovall, Dr. H. I. Blood, M. C. Nickell and Robert Shemwell, elders; there were four deacons and seven junior deacons, and five deaconesses: Mrs. Stovall, Mrs. Roy Cecil, Mrs. Martha Shemwell, Mrs. Dorsey C. Rose and Mrs. Scott McClure, the latter who served as secretary and treasurer of the church for many years.

The Hazel Green Christian Church had no regular pastor from the time of Rev. Taylor's death until Rev. Nevius came in the spring of 1949. However Dr. Gabriel Banks of Morehead College came and preached every other Sunday for several months during this time. Rev. Nevius preached his trial sermon on the last Sunday in March, 1949 and was hired as preacher soon afterwards. He moved about two weeks later. He served as pastor from April, 1949 until he resigned in the fall of October, 1952.

On Sunday morning, January 8, 1950 the church building was burned due to the over-heated furnace, which had almost caused the destruction of the building once before. But for the supreme efforts of those who went to the church that morning, all the furnishings of the church would have been destroyed by the fire. Not long had it been since the church was the recipient of a beautiful new communion service, and communion table, gifts from Curtis Rose, Dr. Courtney McGuire of Maysville and others. Everyone was so thankful that these lovely gifts were saved.

Rev. Nevius held services that morning after the fire had destroyed the church and thanks were rendered to God for what we had been able to save from the flames. A business meeting was called for that afternoon, January 8, 1950 in a classroom of the Academy. The group assembled there, elected a building committee, as follows: Henry A. Stovall, Dr. H. I. Blood, M. C. Nickell, Mrs. J. R. Nevius and Mrs. Roy Cecil. A Finance committee was also elected to raise funds for the new building: Mrs. Scott McClure, Mrs. Anna Scott Carter and Miss Roberta Lewis. Solicitations were begun almost at once for the new building. In the meantime it was decided to hold church and Sunday School in the administration building of the Academy, with the church in the chapel. This arrangement has continued until this time, 1957, and will continue until the new building is ready for use.

About a year after the old church building was razed by fire, the church membership held a business session after the morning services and voted to purchase a lot from Dr. Hiram Blood on highway No. 191 opposite the Cemetery, as the site for the new church building since the old site was not large enough for expansion of the church building. This lot was purchased and the old lot sold to Mr. and Mrs. Scott McClure as it joined their property.

On Sunday morning, October 26, 1952, Rev. Joe Nevius, tendered his resignation as pastor of the Hazel Green Christian Church; which was regretfully accepted by the church board. Rev. Nevius and his wife were both loyal workers in the church and community during his almost four years as pastor.

From October 1952 until September 1953 there was no regular pastor. The church membership is greatly indebted during this period of time to both Miss Margaret Finney, now a missionary in the Belgian Congo of Africa, and to Danny Joe Howard, a student at Transylvania College, for their untiring efforts in preparing and delivering sermons each Sunday. They took month about and there was no time that a service was not held in the church.

On September 16, 1953, Rev. Roy Miller was duly installed as pastor of the Hazel Green Christian Church with Danny Joe

EARLY AND MODERN HISTORY

Howard, past Superintendent of the Sunday School in charge of the service, assisted by Rev. Gilbert Counts of U.C.M.S. who made the address of the evening. Mr. Miller, with his bride of a few months, also participated in the service. Mr. and Mrs. Miller are preparing themselves for full time service in the mission fields.

Actual work began on the excavations for the new church in July, 1954, under the direction of M. C. Nickell with the work camp in charge of Mr. and Mrs. Robert Fudge of Oklahoma. All the excavating was finished during their six weeks stay and some of the concrete was poured for foundations. Then things came to a halt during the winter of 1954 to be resumed again in the summer of 1955. James Lynch of Stanton was hired to supervise the work on the church in the spring of 1955. Though the work did not progress as it was hoped, the laying of the corner stone was held on October 9, 1955 at which time a large crowd was present and a large offering was taken towards completion of the building.

Work was stopped after the laying of the corner stone until the fall of 1956 when it was resumed part of the time.

At this time, November 13, 1956 the steeple, donated by Mr. and Mrs. W. O. Mize of Jacksonville Beach, Fla., has been completed and erected on the building and is very lovely. It is of copper with a cross on top. There is still much work to be done on the church before it will be ready for occupancy.

The history of this church would not be complete without saying something about Mrs. James I. Hollon Jr., who has given so many years in service at the church as choir director and is at this time president of the CWF. Nor the fine group of boys and girls who contributed to the worship by singing in the two choirs. Mrs. James Stewart, Miss Marcia Barton, and Mrs. Charlotte Walter Sorrell, each of whom have contributed so much through their services as church organist or pianist.

At the present time the following persons are serving as elders in the church: Henry A. Stovall, M. C. Nickell, D. R. Graham, Ernie O'Donnell, Pryce Tutt and James Stewart. Deacons: James I. Hollon Jr., Carl Walter, E. T. Kash, Scott McGuire, Durward Amyx. Deaconess: Miss Leona Hood, who is also church treasurer, Mrs. Rodney Gillespie, Mrs. Stella Smith and Mrs. Carl Mize, who is chairman of the Board. Mrs. Roy Cecil is secretary of the Board and Clerk of the church. Rev. Paul Hartenberger came as pastor in the summer of 1956. He and his wife and family are a wonderful contribution to the church and community. It is hoped the new church can be dedicated in August, 1957.

WOLFE COUNTY

THE FIRST BAPTIST CHURCH IN CAMPTON

(Taken from old church records owned by Mrs. Mida Wyant and article written by Mrs. Hazel Booth.)

The First Baptist Church in Campton was at first a Primitive Baptist Church which was established in 1848. This was in a little log house near the home site of the late Judge W. C. Smith on Meadow Branch. This was when Wolfe County was still a part of Morgan County and the old road went right by the church house door.

In 1896 a large frame building was erected in Campton on the present church site. It became a missionary Baptist Church and practically all the members transferred their membership to this church.

The first pastor of the Primitive Baptist Church was Rev. Marion Spencer. C. M. Hanks, a grandfather of Mrs. Mida Wyant, also of C. M. Hanks Sr., both residents of Campton in this year 1957, was clerk of the church in 1848. Some of the charter members were: Boothe, Cheatum, Spencer, Gibbs, and Tutt.

The first pastor of the Missionary Baptist Church was John Miles Tolson and later Dr. G. M. Center, followed by Rev. Earl Morris. It was during his ministry that the new brick church was built and dedicated in 1944.

Pastors serving the Baptist Church at Campton since the ministry of Earl E. Morris, who was pastor for 10 or 12 years, include. Rev. Atlee Fortner, Sam Sloan, Shirl Davidson, Joseph Profitt, J. Edward Cunningham, and the present pastor, J. Robert Taylor (1957).

After the parsonage burned in 1950 the Cecil Rose property was bought on Plummer Street and used as a parsonage until Rev. Cunningham resigned as pastor in 1956. Recently this property was sold. A new pastorium, located on the church lot, has recently been completed.

The new church building completed in 1945, when Rev. Morris, was pastor, is now being used for educational purposes and kitchen and dining hall while a large new church has been erected and connected with the other building by a wing.

The new church, dedicated in September, 1956, will seat approximately 400 people, and has a baptistry, nurseries, adequate Sunday School rooms, and a modern heating system and rest rooms. The property all together is valued at $75,000. There are around 180 members of this church in 1957.

EARLY AND MODERN HISTORY

THE CAMPTON METHODIST CHURCH

The Campton Methodist Church was organized in 1884, under the direction and influence of a woman lovingly called "Aunt Mida Hanks", the wife of Cud Hanks, who is known as the father of Wolfe County and the originator of its name. Aunt Mida taught in a log building just back of where the old Methodist Church stood and where the First Church of God now stands and in this building and in her home, prayer meetings were held until a great need for a new building was felt, so with Aunt Mida's vision, the help of her husband, G. T. Center, Nick Fulks, and others, the church was built and dedicated in the year 1884 with Rev. Will Press Taulbee serving as their first pastor. Some of the first members of the church were Will Tyler, Deborah Tyler, Jane Hanks, Mahala Hanks, Nancy Center and G. T. Center. In September of that year, Rev. V. B. Daugherty, was assigned the pastorate. Some other pastors who have served were Will Tyler, L. T. Allison, J. R. Peeples, L. C. Dearmond, S. R. Mann, S. B. Godbey, Llewellyn Lee, Charles Cecil, David Sageser, C. M. Seale, John Bassett, J. H. Lewis, H. G. Murrell and the present pastor, Sewell Woodward Jr. During the pastorate of Rev. Llewellyn Lee, Aunt Hannah Moore, one of the church's most devout and faithful members took seriously ill and it was during this illness that the groundwork was laid for the future of the church when she made her final dedication of her earthly possessions which consisted of two houses and an acre of land to the Campton Methodist Church and the title was officially changed several years later while Rev. John Bassett was pastor. It was on this acre of land which Aunt Hannah had worked out by the "little" when she was a young woman, that many girls in Wolfe County and adjoining counties lived while they were getting their education, bringing her a small income and a great happiness in knowing she was helping others get an education which she had missed so much in her own life. Even when her health was failing and her hearing was poor, she always occupied "her corner" to witness for her Saviour.

In 1946 she received an inheritance from her brother, Johnny, whom she had believed dead many years but who had just recently died in California. News of his death was a shock from which she never fully recovered for the inheritance meant little to her compared with what his companionship might have been.

While Rev. C. M. Seale was pastor, which was a very short time, blueprints for the new building were obtained and submitted to the Building Committee: John White, H. B. Mullins, Fred Hanks, Omer Catron, Bertie Center and Bertie Catron.

Aunt Hannah passed away the last of May, 1948. During this same month, the church lost another jewel in the form of Cordelia Asbury Peery, who had served as pianist and song leader and like

Aunt Hannah was faithful to the uttermost. Following Aunt Hannah's funeral, the groundbreaking service for the new church was held and work was soon started under the supervision of J. P. Lawless Sr. The first service was held in the new building December 26, 1946 while Rev. J. H. Lewis was pastor and Rev. F. D. Rose was District Superintendent. This building is located on Plummer Street on the spot where Aunt Hannah's humble cottage stood and adjacent to it is the parsonage which was built soon after the church was built; both are built of red brick and each has its own central heating system.

Campton was once a three-church charge with Hazel Green and Bear Pen and at one time was affiliated with the Meadow Branch Church but for several years it has been a one-church charge. During the time when services were held only two Sundays a month in Campton, Sunday School was held each Sunday under the direction of the following superintendents: Betty Cannoy, H. B. Mullins, and Bertie Center and after it became a full-time charge, H. T. Carroll has served.

By meager living and self-denial, Aunt Hannah Moore left the Campton Methodist Church $5,400 in money, most of which had come from her brother's estate, her acre of land and two houses and a living memorial of a life well lived.

The latter part of 1956, the Campton church lost another beloved and faithful member, Mrs. Jane Carroll Allison and the early part of 1957, another beloved member, Mrs. Anna Lovelace, two of its oldest members. The present church stands not only as a memorial to Aunt Hannah, but to Aunt Mida Hanks and their faithful followers who have kept alive the first of Methodism started back in 1884.

Lillian Galbreath.

THE WOLFE COUNTY NEWS
by Berta K. Cecil, editor from 1946-1957

The Wolfe County News was established as the official county newspaper of Wolfe County, Ky., on November 15, 1944 with M. H. Holliday Jr., as publisher and owner and Mrs. Mazie Cox Read as the editor. Mrs. Read served as the very capable editor until she resigned to accept a teaching position in Oklahoma.

On December 24, 1945 Miss Lillian Galbreath became acting editor until Mr. Holliday could get someone else to take over the job, as she already had a full time job with FHA.

During the school year 1945-46 Mr. Holliday began consulting with Mrs. Roy Cecil, who was at that time a teacher at Hazel Green Academy, about becoming the editor of the News. She finally promised to give it a try when school was out in the spring. So on June

EARLY AND MODERN HISTORY

7, 1946, Mrs. Roy Cecil became editor of the Wolfe County News and has served in this capacity since that date.

One of the first things Mrs. Cecil did after becoming editor was to ask and receive permission to sell advertising space in the News in both Winchester and Mt. Sterling where so many of our good citizens go to trade. It was not long until a sound advertising program was worked out in both towns which has been profitable to all parties concerned ever since. Later Mrs. Cecil began to sell advertising space in West Liberty where she made a business trip once a month and later once a week. Later still Beattyville was included on her itinerary. Then when the Beattyville Enterprise and Owsley County News were included in the chain of papers owned under Holliday Publications, Mrs. Cecil traveled to Richmond, to sell space in three of the papers; namely, Owsley, Beattyville and Wolfe County papers. The paper has grown steadily in size and circulation through the years and we hope its contents have improved with the passing time. The paper which started as a tabloid size became a six column by twenty-one inch paper with four pages in the latter part of 1946.

On May 23, 1951 it became a standard size newspaper with eight columns in width and 21 inches in depth. This is sometimes four pages, sometimes 6, or 8 pages and even on special occasions has gone as high as 16 pages. But is usually 6 or 8 pages depending on the amount of advertising and news content available each week.

M. H. Holliday Jr., was at first sole owner of the Wolfe County News and Jackson Times and some of the other papers as added; but in 1952 Garvis Kincaid bought an interest in the papers. Later still, March 3, 1954 Mr. Kincaid bought out Mr. Holliday's interest in the chain of eight papers owned and published by Holliday Publications at that time, which, of course, included the Wolfe County News. The name of the firm was then changed to Eastern Kentucky Publishing Co., with David G. Collier as the capable publisher of all eight papers.

The circulation of the News is the largest at this time that it has ever been, around 1500 paid subscribers. It has long been the dream of Mrs. Cecil to push this circulation figure up into the neighborhood of 2000.

The Wolfe County News proudly serves the community of Wolfe and strives to publish the news in an unbiased way; always striving for the principles of truth and right.

THE HAZEL GREEN CEMETERY
by Mrs. W. E. Bach

In the fall of 1906 there were five women who sat around their loved ones graves in Hazel Green Cemetery which at that time was almost a forgotten spot. The Burial Plot was not fenced and therefore the roving animals had full sway. These women decided to do something about this and agreed to contribute one dollar each which they did to start a Fund for restoration and beautifying this Cemetery. On March 5, 1907 a complete organization was made at the Christian Church in Hazel Green and things began to happen.

These five women were: Mrs. Henry J. Derthick, Mrs. Fred N. Day, Mrs. W. W. Ringo, Mrs. W. O. Mize and Mrs. Nancy Cravens. The women added to this list on March 5th were: Mrs. M. O. Carter, Mrs. H. L. Atkinson, Mrs. Maude Kash, Mrs. Spencer Cooper and Mrs. J. H. Rose.

The first president was Mrs. H. J. Derthick, the first vice president was Mrs. M. O. Carter, the first secretary was Mrs. F. N. Day, the first treasurer was Mrs. Nannie Cravens, and the first Asst. treasurer was Mrs. W. W. Ringo.

Other names were added soon, among them were: Miss Lou Ward, Mrs. Tom Haddix, Mrs. George Rice, Mrs. J. T. Pieratt, Mrs. Bicknell, Mrs. W. T. Caskey, Mrs. M. V. Aoberts. Their first donations came from Mr. John C. M. Day, Winchester; Mrs. W. F. Horton, Mt. Sterling, and Mr. James S. Day, Midland, Texas.

Bazaars, ice cream suppers, chicken dinners were held to make money as well as quilts were made, rugs were woven, aprons made for the Bazaar, in fact many, many things were done to make money to beautify the Hazel Green Cemetery.

Mr. Frank Trimble, who was born in Hazel Green, Kentucky in 1840, and died in Memphis, Tennessee, October 12, 1915, did not forget his little Home Town of Hazel Green, for in his will he left to the Hazel Green Cemetery Association $1,000 for the maintenance of the cemetery. This $1,000 was received by Mrs. F. N. Day on January 15, 1917, together with $14.50 interest. Another sum of about the same amount was received at a later date. This sum was placed in Liberty Bonds and placed in a bank for safe keeping.

Not only did Mr. Trimble leave this nice sum for the Cemetery Maintenance but he also left a large sum to replace the Monuments to the different members of his family who were buried there. A handsome monument was placed at the graves of his father and mother, William and Eleanor (O'Hair) Trimble, and replaced several of the monuments to his brothers and sisters who are buried here.

EARLY AND MODERN HISTORY

Enough praise cannot be given the members of the Association for its good work.

Among the Presidents that I can name at this time are the following: Mrs. H. J. Derthick; Mrs. J. H. Rose, Mrs. George Wheeler. In 1912 Mrs. Ellen Pieratt was elected President with Mrs. F. N. Day as Vice-President; Miss Lou Ward, Secretary and Mrs. Sam Kash as Treasurer. Directors: Ellis Johnson, Dr. A. C. Nickell, Sam Kash, John H. Rose and Sam Kash. On January 2, 1913, Mrs. F. N. Day was elected President; Mrs. George Rice, Vice President; Miss Lou Ward, Secretary; and Mrs. S. H. Kash, Treasurer. Mrs. S. H. Kash, General Manager. On February 3, 1916 the following officers were elected: President, Mrs. F. N. Day; Mrs. Nannie M. Kash, Vice President; Mrs. E. A. Johnson (formerly Lou Ward), Secretary; Mrs. Carl Mize, Asst. Secretary; Mrs. S. H. Kash, Treasurer, and S. H. Kash, General Manager. S. H. Kash, Carl Mize and F. N. Day and E. A. Johnson were appointed on the Work Committee.

Mrs. Dorsey C. Rose was President for many years and I do not have the names of the officers who served with her.

Mrs. John Coldiron is the present President (1956).

I would pay tribute to every officer; every member and every friend of the Hazel Green Cemetery. It has become a place of Beauty and everyone who travels by it remarks how "Beautiful it is."

Written by Mrs. William Everett Bach (formerly Pearl Day) who is the daughter of Mr. and Mrs. Frederick N. Day. May 21, 1956.

SKETCH OF BETHANY CHILDREN'S HOME
(Compiled from information supplied by the Staff.)

Bethany Orphanage was begun in a windowless cabin, a product of the Civil War days, in June 1926, with Miss Marjorie Burt and her assistant, Miss Laura Wendland and three small orphan girls, in a spot about 13 miles from Campton and off Highway No. 15 four or five miles.

They came to Wolfe County at the invitation of three men who were anxious to have Sunday School for their children; and in answer to a need for the many orphan children; in the neighborhood.

Soon after they moved into the log cabin, Miss Burt made a trip to Chicago to attend the Commencement of the Chicago Evangelistic Institute, her Alma Mater, and to ask for a helper. She met a friend there, Miss Lina Miller, who had graduated in the class of 1924, and was also there for the Commencement. Miss Burt told her story to Miss Miller about the need of a helper to work with the orphans in Wolfe County, Kentucky. Miss Miller decided to join Miss Burt and leave her good job in Dixon, Ill.; but she came on a temporary basis. However she remained for 25 years, until her death in 1951 and became Miss Burt's "right hand" so to speak, as she filled the office of assistant Superintendent, carrying the load at home while Miss Burt was away as a Field representative.

As the family of orphans grew a modest building program was undertaken. A two-story school house with an attic, which housed the girl's dormitory. Then a store building, used for second hand clothing and also a post office, Bethany, which was established.

Bethany was named by the late president of the Chicago Evangelistic Institute, Mrs. Iva Durham Vennard, after the Bethany in the Bible, the place where Jesus loved to go. It was in October 1926, they moved into their new quarters. That fall the first boy came to stay at the home and there was no place for boys; so he slept in a barn.

The cabin was so inadequate that a new building was imperative. They had a prayer session which influenced Mr. and Mrs. Elof Peterson in far off Chicaga, to become concerned about this Bethany Orphanage in Wolfe County, Kentucky. Mrs. Peterson busied herself gathering supplies and they loaded up and came down to visit Bethany. At one glance it was evident to Mr. Peterson that they needed a building program underway. So he promised to return the next spring and bring carpenters and tools with him and construct a proper building for housing the children.

In the spring of 1927 he came with three car loads of men and supplies and "Faith Hall" was begun. It was completed and dedicated in the fall of '28 with an indebtedness of $5,000. In the fall of 1929 a Board of Trustees was organized and the place was incorporated.

The Board of Trustees has been very helpful in giving guidance and helpful suggestions to the heads of Bethany Orphanage. The present Board is made up of the following personnel: Dr. James DeWeerd, who is pastor of Cadle Tabernacle; Rev. Stanley Patterson, vice-president; Mrs. Ethel Olson, secretary; Miss Marjorie Burt, superintendent; Dr. Harry Jessop, Rev. Paul Huffman, Rev. John Lewis, Rev. Glen Rhoads, Mrs. J. R. Robbins, Rev. Stanley Patterson, Mr. Bufford Cadle, Mrs. Lona McGuire and Mr. Elof Peterson.

Over the period of thirty years, there have been over a thousand children fed at Faith Hall. At present there are 87 children housed and fed there.

EARLY AND MODERN HISTORY

On October 25, and 26, 1956, Bethany Orphanage celebrated their 30 years of service in the Mountains. At this time Memorial Cottage and also the new combination store and post office buildings were dedicated by Dr. James DeWeerd.

If you visit Bethany today you will find a small village in itself. There is a church which was dedicated for service in 1938 and which was redecorated and remodeled in 1951; a hospital dedicated in 1942, a brick, three-room school house, dedicated in 1946; Boys dormitory in 1948; Nursery in 1951; in addition to several cottages for workers; a pastor's residence, a farm of over 200 acres, where vegetables, corn, hay, are grown. Also where pigs, beeves, and cows are raised. Bethany strives to be self-supporting in so far as possible. But when they need something which they cannot supply they hold a session of prayer and God works with them and through his people to find a solution to their many problems.

A new dormitory for high school youths is under construction at this time. Up until a few years ago; Bethany did not try to keep their children after they reached the high school age; but now they have a program set up whereby they can keep the children and let them ride the county school bus to Wolfe County High School at Campton for their higher education. Thus the need of a proper housing unit for this youth group.

Bethany takes children of all age groups. Many of them come when only a few hours old. Besides caring for the children Bethany workers do an extensive community work. They maintain a store and sell staple groceries along with second hand clothing. Proceeds from same being turned into the Home and used for other expenses.

The Bethany post office serves 361 people and cares for the Orphanage mail. The farm is operated to help supply the needs of the Home. In addition they operate three churches at Bethany, Pence and Malaga. There and in other out-stations they conduct Sunday School and have church services. Weekly they conduct 32 Bible classes taught in various day schools and spend from forty to sixty minutes each place.

At least five of the children from the Home have completed their college training and received their degrees and followed vocations of their own choice. Many of the children have made outstanding marks in life. A few of the girls have taken up nursing. Many of the boys have gone into the Service of their country for Uncle Sam.

It is the aim of the Bethany Orphanage to lead boys and girls into the experience of Salvation and then to help to establish them firmly in the faith of the Lord Jesus Christ to the extent that it will be a stronghold for them along life's pathway.

WOLFE COUNTY

DESSIE SCOTT CHILDREN'S HOME

(Information furnished by Miss Esther Pushee.)

On Highway No. 15, five miles north of Campton, Wolfe County, is the Dessie Scott Children's Home; housed in the Girl's Dormitory of the former Alvan Drew School, and the brick building which was their school building. At the head of this home is the woman, known as Miss Esther Pushee, by whose efforts and the help of God, this home came into being.

Miss Pushee educated herself for foreign mission work but due to a heart murmur was not accepted for this fatiguing work. So she began looking about for mission work to do at home and thus began the Home first started at Little, Ky., in Breathitt County. This is a spot eight miles off the highway and in what was then known as almost insurmountable wilderness. But the mission was established and grew and thrived with perseverance on the part of the workers. In the fall of 1940 fire destroyed all the buildings and nine precious little ones with their house mother, who had been there only a month. Dessie Scott was trapped with the nine little ones, calling for help fell through a window. She and Dad Pushee were both taken to the hospital in Jackson, Ky. Next evening Dessie Scott died and so the name of the Home was changed to Dessie Scott in honor of the person who gave her life for others.

For twelve years the Dessie Scott Home thrived and grew in Breathitt County at Little; but it reached a stage where it was not adquate and it was too in-accessible to Miss Pushee heard about the buildings of the former Alvan Drew school being for sale in Wolfe County and came to look over the site. In the spring of 1950 the Lord made available the money to purchase one of the buildings which is now in use at Dessie Scott Children's Home.

At first the gilr's dormitory was bought and used as a combination dormitory for both boys and girls as well as a dining hall. This soon was filled to over-flowing and it was imperative to purchase another building. So the brick school building across the road was bought and this was made into a boy's dormitory where all the boys and some of their helpers are housed. This is called Shurlock Hall.

The Home is incorporated, licensed by the state, and operated on faith. When a need arises the whole family unites in prayer until the answer comes. Support comes in small part from board paid by relatives of the children; but mostly from gifts of money, clothing and food.

The present staff at the Home is composed of Miss Esther Pushee, Miss Louise Lee, Mr. and Mrs. Max Dunlap, Mr. and Mrs. Harold

Wurzbach, Miss Gertrude Strauch, Miss Deveda Granger, Miss Mae Brewer, Miss Marie Cintsman and Miss Gertrude Tucker.

The Board of Directors is as follows: Miss Esther Pushee, president; Miss Louise Lee, executive vice-president; Marie Clintsman, secretary and O. J. Cockerell, Attorney of Jackson; Board Members: Virgie Henry, Pine Ridge; W. H. Reynolds, Jackson; Mrs. Orville Booth, Campton; Mrs. Hobert Lykins, Pine Ridge; Rev. R. W. Battles, Orlando, Fla.; Herbert Spencer, Jackson; J. Phil Smith, Jackson; Estill Slone, Jackson, and Everett Bach, Lexington. Advisory Committee: Herbert Holbrook, Pine Ridge; Rev. G. E. Drushal, Lost Creek; Mrs. W. E. Bach, Lexington; Henrietta Liebknocht, Louisville; C. R. Cooper, Orlando, Fla.; G. C. Whipple, Binghampton, N. Y.; Mrs. R. Fortran, Endicott, N. Y.; Mrs. C. P. Shurlock, Pine Ridge; Tex McClintock, St. Louis, Mo.; Frank Widbin, St. Louis, Mo.; Virgil Carr, Mason City, Iowa; Dr. F. E. Massie, Lexington; Ray Roland, Winchester; Edgar Spencer, Pine Ridge, and Paul Letton, Winchester.

In 1954 Colonel Ray Rowland donated a 300 acre farm to the Home which has been named "Rowland Hills" in his honor. This farm has been a wonderful contribution to the Home for there is pastureland for the herd of cows which the Home keeps to supply their milk. The farm furnishes much of the produce which is used to help feed the children and the stock as well. It is a place where the older boys can find valuable training in work.

As this goes to press in the winter of 1957, the new nursery building is nearing completion at the Home. It will house both girls and boys through the ages, one to six years, and girls up to ten years, as well as four helpers. This has been a crying need at the Home for several years and the whole community rejoices with Miss Pushee and her staff as this project nears completion.

There are sixty children housed in the Dessie Scott Children's Home at this time in addition to almost a dozen helpers.

The Home had its beginning in January of 1934. Since that time hundreds of children have been cared for, educated, and taught to know and love the Lord Jesus Christ. Many of them are men and women of whom we can all be proud. Some have gone to Bible school, many have established fine Christian homes. There is no age when they are supposed to leave — it is to be home as long as they need it and wish it to be. All who will practice are given piano lessons. And for those who wish more than high school education, a way is provided.

WOLFE COUNTY HAD A "DR. COX" FOR THREE GENERATIONS

(by Mazie Cox Read)

"Dr. Cox" has a familiar ring in Wolfe County for it's had one for three generations.

The first was Dr. Jason Cox. He also served as a doctor in the Civil War. His son, Dr. Braxton D. Cox, followed in his footsteps, beginning practice in 1869 when he was 25 years of age. Likewise, his son, Dr. John L. Cox, served as a doctor in Wolfe County for many years and until his death.

Dr. John L. Cox was likewise carrying the tradition. His son, Nelson, was attending Medical school — to become a fourth generation "Dr. Cox" but death intervened.

LETTER TO MIRANDA TYRA

Copy of letter written to Mrs. Miranda Tyra, Campton, Ky., on August 9, 1947 by Sam E. Hager, R. No. 1, Brandenton, Fla.
My dear cousin:

Now you are surprised and wonder why I call you "cousin". Your mother, Dulcenia Combs Rose, wife of Robert Rose, and my mother were first cousins. Your mother was a daughter of my great-uncle, Henry Combs, who lived on Troublesome Creek in Breathitt County. My mother was Elmira Combs Hager, daughter of your great-uncle, William M. Combs, of Jackson, I think.

I think it was in September, 1887 or 1888 that I first saw Uncle Bob Rose and Aunt Dulcina and spent a night in their home along with my grandfather, William M. Combs. I was on my way to Millersburg, Ky., returning to college there. You might have been with your father and mother at that time.

Your husband was Boone Tyra, whom I knew. I last saw him in Campton a year or so before he died. I do not recall that I ever met you unless it was in your father's home as mentioned above.

My name is Samuel Eugene Hager, son of Rev. J. H. and Elmira Combs Hager. With my brother, Stewart Hager, I was left an orphan in the home of my mother's parents; upon her death in June 1871. We were reared by our grandparents.

You doubtless know that I was a Methodist Missionary in Japan a long time, over 47 years. I was retired by the Methodist Board of Missions on September 1, 1940 and came home to America and we built a home near Brandenton, Fla., only about 300 yards from the home of my brother, Stewart. We bought our land from him and

EARLY AND MODERN HISTORY

built on December 26, 1948-February 28, 1941.

For nearly 30 years I've been gathering information about the Combs family of Western Kentucky. Your first cousin, Anna Belle Combs, daughter of Sewell Combs, (your uncle) is now living in Richmond, Ky. I have corresponded with her for several years.

Sincerely,

Sam E. Hager.

HISTORY OF THE WOLFE COUNTY WOMAN'S CLUB
by Mrs. Robert Snowden

"Faith is never surprised at success". This statement is certainly true for our Woman's Club and our records and achievements will clearly show the fatiguing hours the women have given to our Club since it was organized.

The Wolfe County Woman's Club was first organized on Monday night, May 12, 1947, at 7:30 p. m. at the home of Mrs. E. E. Bach. There were twenty members present. The first officers were as follows: President, Mrs. A. P. McKenzie; Vice President, Miss Daisy Chambers; Recording Secretary, Mrs. E. K. Rose; Corr. Secretary, Mrs. J. W. Cable; and Treasurer, Miss Reva Terrill. The Club was aided by a very capable Miss Christine McGuire, representative of the Morgan County Woman's Club. She helped them with the constitution and with many other problems of a newly formed organization.

The Club was federated July 16, 1947. Now the hard work begins, but, oh, how we enjoy doing our part for the Club.

The officers elected for the Clubs second year are as follows: Miss Daisy Chambers, President; Mrs. James Cable, Vice President; Miss Reva Terrill, Recording Secretary; Mrs. Frank Rose, Corr. Secretary; and Mrs. Edward Bach, Treasurer. The first main project of the Club was to sponsor a playground for the Wolfe County High School grounds. Money was raised through various drives and projects. During this Club year the Powell County Woman's Club was organized through the help of the Woman's Club in Campton. Also a community beautification project was started for the Church grounds in Campton. There were also many other worthwhile projects during this administration.

The Wolfe County Woman's Club held its first meeting in their new Club House on Wednesday night, March 9, 1949.

The third Club year found the following officers elected to head the Club: Mrs. James Cable, President; Mrs. James I. Hollon, Vice President; Mrs. Martha Rose, Recording Secretary; Mrs. Reva Howard, Corr. Secretary; and Mrs. Elmer Clark, Treasurer. The main projects for the Club year 1949-1950, were a Community Health project and establishing a Club library.

The Woman's Club selected two major projects for the 1950-1951 Club year. These were to provide picnic tables for roadside parking areas, and to sponsor a kindergarten school for the Campton community. Officers elected to fill these terms are: Mrs. Reva Howard, President; Miss Reva Terrill, Vice President; Delmyra Shackelford, Recording Secretary; Mrs. Velma Rose, Treasurer; and Mrs. Ruby Terrill, Corr. Secretary. It was during this term that signs were erected to advertise Natural Bridge State Park.

On March 7, 1951, the following officers were elected for the Club year 1951-1952: Miss Reva Terrill, President; Miss Marcia Barton, Vice President; Mrs. Roy Cecil, Recording Secretary; Mrs. Elmer Clark, Corr. Secretary; and Mrs. E. E. Bach, Treasurer. The Club put on a circulation drive for the local newspaper, "The Wolfe County News." The Dental Clinic, of which the Woman's Club was co-sponsor, was a big success. The Club also donated $100 to the Dessie Scott Children's Home.

Officers for the Clubs sixth year were elected in March, 1952. Mrs. Roy Cecil, President; Mrs. Kathryn Rose, Vice President; Mrs. Forest Cable, Recording Secretary; Mrs. Cecil Rose, Treasurer; and Mrs. S. E. Pelfrey, Corr. Secretary. The Club voted to have a Community Betterment and Club House improvements for their main projects. The street signs seen on the Campton and Hazel Green streets are due to the hard-working crew of the Club headed by Mrs. Cecil. Also, the shrubs on the Courthouse lawn were bought during Mrs. Cecil's tenure in office.

Mrs. Mountie Lovelace was elected President of the Wolfe County Woman's Club for the year 1953-1954. Mrs. Elmer Clark, Vice President; Mrs. David Morris, 2nd Vice President; Mrs. Herbert Miller, Recording Secretary; Mrs. Margaret Smith, Corr. Secretary; and Mrs. Charles E. Lindon, Treasurer. There were forty-seven members at this time. Contributions to the Recreational Centers and Contributions to the Book Mobile were voted on as the Clubs main projects.

The History of Wolfe County, Kentucky, was started by the Club during the time Mrs. Lovelace served as President.

On March 6, 1954, Mrs. Roy Hanks was elected to the Presidency of the Woman's Club. Also elected were the following officers: Mrs. Herbert Miller, 1st Vice President; Mrs. David Morris, 2nd Vice President; Mrs. Forest Cable, Recording Secretary; Mrs. William J. Cox, Corr. Secretary; and Mrs. C. W. Murphy, Treasurer. Membership had dropped to forty-four at this time. The Club worked on the "Early and Modern History of Wolfe County." The Club

EARLY AND MODERN HISTORY

voted to compile a cook book of the favorite recipes of the local club members and friends in the county.

An honor came to our Club on October 23, 1954, when Mrs. E. E. Bach, was elected Recording Secretary of the Seventh District of Kentucky Federation of Women's Clubs at the District meeting in Prestonsburg.

The annual election of Officers for the ninth year was held March 2, 1955. The following officers were elected: Mrs. E. E. Bach, President; Mrs. Forest Cable, 1st Vice President; Mrs. J. Edward Cunningham, 2nd Vice President; Mrs. Paul Maddox, Recording Secretary; Miss Agnes Edwards, Treasurer; and Mrs. Mayo Ingram, Corr. Secretary. The Project Committee selected Community Improvement for the Clubs main project. The Club started a campaign for a new fire truck. It was October 22, 1955, that Wolfe County Woman's Club was hostess to the Seventh District. The meeting was deemed quite a success. The Club also sponsored the Diabetes Week detection drive.

The new officers selected to head the Clubs tenth year were as follows: Mrs. Robert C. Snowden, President; Mrs. W. P. Cecil, 1st Vice President; Mrs. Hays Pigman, 2nd Vice President; Mrs. Paul Maddox, Recording Secretary; Mrs. Charles Harris, Corr. Secretary;

and Miss Agnes Edwards, Treasurer. The Club voted to continue the drive for the fire truck, and to help the State Health Department with their new program of which Wolfe County has been chosen as a test area. The program is called "Growth and Development of Children in Wolfe County."

The Club has had one Talent show and is having another one November 19, 1956. Another order of Cook Books is in the hands of the publisher and will be ready for sale before too long. The Fire Truck was purchased on Friday, September 14, 1956, with money we had on hand in the fund set aside for this particular project. Other necessary equipment is being purchased to make the Fire Truck complete.

The Wolfe County Woman's Club from the very beginning of its existence has taken an active part in every drive that is carried on throughout each year. The Woman's Club has taken a big part in the County Fair held each Fall, having the Concession Stands. A Civil Defense Unit has also been organized through the cooperation of the Women's Club. Whenever we are called on to help, the club members do their part. The Club now has forty-six members.

The quotation "Faith is never surprised at success" certainly pertains to the Wolfe County Woman's Club.

WOLFE COUNTY

KENTUCKY — ORIGIN, FORMATION, GROWTH
by Clay Hollon

THE LAND area now known (1954) as the State of Kentucky, was, prior to 1584, claimed as part of Augusta County, Virginia; from 1584 to 1776, it was part of Fincastle County, Virginia; and from 1776 to 1780, it was designated as Kentucky County, Virginia. In 1780 the name Kentucky County was discontinued and the area divided into three counties, namely: Fayette, Jefferson and Lincoln. Then from 1784 to 1788, six additional counties were formed from these three counties, namely: 1784 Nelson, 1785 Bourbon, 1785 Mercer, 1785 Madison, 1788 Mason, 1788 Woodford. (See map). The above mentioned nine counties included all the area now known as the State of Kentucky which was formed in 1792, with the creation of eight new counties, namely: Christian, Clark, Greene, Hardin, Logan, Scott, Shelby, Washington. At this time the total population was about 73,677.

From 1793 to 1800, inclusive, twenty-five new counties were created, namely:

1793 Harrison, 1794 Campbell, 1794 Franklin, 1796 Bracken, 1796 Bullitt, 1796 Garrard, 1796 Montgomery, 1796 Warren, 1798 Barren, 1798 Boone, 1798 Cumberland, 1798 Fleming, 1798 Gallatin, 1798 Henderson, 1798 Henry, 1798 Jessamine, 1798 Livingston, 1798 Muhlenburg, 1798 Pendleton, 1798 Pulaski, 1799 Breckinridge, 1799 Floyd, 1799 Knox, 1799 Nicholas, 1800 Wayne.

From 1801 to 1912, inclusive, 78 more counties were created, namely: 1801 Adair, 1803 Greenup, 1806 Casey, 1806 Clay, 1806 Lewis, 1808 Estill, 1808 Hopkins, 1809 Caldwell, 1810 Butler, 1810 Grayson, 1810 Rockcastle, 1811 Bath, 1811 Union, 1815 Allen, 1815 Davies, 1818 Whitley, 1819 Harlan, 1819 Hart, 1819 Ohio, 1819 Owen, 1819 Simpson, 1819 Todd, 1820 Grant, 1820 Monroe, 1820 Perry, 1820 Trigg, 1821 Hickman, 1821 Lawrence, 1821 Pike, 1822 Calloway, 1822 Morgan, 1823 Graves, 1823 Meade, 1823 Oldham, 1824 McCracken, 1824 Spencer, 1825 Edmondson, 1825 Laurel, 1825 Russell, 1827 Anderson, 1829 Hancock, 1834 Marion, 1835 Clinton, 1836 Trimble, 1838 Carroll, 1838 Carter, 1839 Breathitt, 1840 Kenton, 1842 Crittendon, 1842 Boyle, 1842 Ballard, 1842 Letcher, 1842 Marshall, 1843 Johnson, 1843 Larue, 1843 Owsley, 1945 Fulton, 1848 Taylor, 1952 Powell, 1854 Lyon, 1854 McLean, 1856 Rowan, 1858 Jackson, 1860 Boyd, 1860 Magoffin, 1860 Metcalf, 1860 Webster, 1860 WOLFE, 1867 Bell, 1867 Robertson, 1869 Elliott, 1869 Menifee, 1870 Lee, 1870 Martin, 1878 Leslie, 1884 Knott, 1886 Carlyle and 1912 McCreary.

120 counties with a population of 2,907,000 in 1950.

EARLY AND MODERN HISTORY

KENTUCKY MOUNTAIN COUNTIES, YEAR FORMED AND POPULATION IN 1950

by Clay Hollon

1798 Cumberland, 9,000; 1798 Fleming, 12,000; 1798 Pulaski, 38,000; 1799 Floyd, 54,000; 1799 Knox, 30,000; 1800 Wayne, 16,000; 1801 Adair, 18,000; 1803 Greenup, 25,000; 1806 Casey, 17,000; 1806 Clay, 23,000; 1806 Lewis, 14,000; 1808 Estill, 15,000; 1810 Rockcastle, 14,000; 1811 Bath, 10,000; 1818 Whitley, 32,000; 1819 Harlan, 72,000; 1820 Monroe, 14,000; 1820 Perry, 47,000; 1821 Lawrence, 14,000; 1821 Pike, 81,000; 1822 Morgan, 14,000; 1825 Russell, 14,000; 1835 Clinton, 11,000; 1838 Carter, 23,000; 1839 Breathitt, 20,000; 1842 Letcher, 40,000; 1843 Johnson, 24,000; 1843 Laurel, 6,000; 1843 Owsley, 7,000; 1852 Powell, 7,000; 1856 Rowan, 13,000; 1858 Jackson, 13,000; 1860 Boyd, 50,000; 1860 Magoffin, 14,000; 1860 WOLFE, 8,000; 1867 Bell, 48,000; 1869 Elliott, 7,000; 1869 Menifee, 5,000; 1870 Lee, 9,000; 1870 Martin, 12,000; 1878 Leslie, 16,000; 1884 Knott, 20,000; 1912 McCreary, 17,000.

Kentucky has a land area of 40,198 square miles and over 400 square miles of water; and a population of 2,907,000 — an average of 71 persons per square mile.

The 43 mountain counties have an area of 15,387 square miles — about 37 percent of the state area — and a population of 833,000 — about 28½ percent of the state population, with an average of 53 persons per square mile.

WOLFE COUNTY has an area of 230 square miles — about 1½ percent of the mountain area, and a population of 8,000 — about 9½ percent of the mountain area population, and has an average of 35 persons per square mile.

The 77 non-mountain counties with an area of 25,200 square miles and a population of 2,074,000 have an average of about 82 persons per square mile.

EARLY FAMILIES OF WOLFE COUNTY
by Clay Hollon

Allem, Allison, Amyx, Arnett, Asbury, Athey, Baker, Banks, Bishop, Booth, Brashear, Brewer, Bryant, Burton, Bush, Byrd, Cable, Campbell, Carroll, Cassidy, Cecil, Center, Chapman, Childers, Cockerham, Collins, Combs, Coons, Congleton, Cox, Crane, Cundiff, Crawford, Cooper, Coldiron, Drake, Day, Dean, Duff, Dunn, Elkins, Evans, Faulkner, Fulks, Gibbs, Gillespie, Godfrey, Graham, Hall, Halsey, Hanks, Hatton, Horton, Hounshell, Hobbs, Hollon, Howe, Hurst, James, Jones, Johnson, Kash, Kincaid, King, Kidd, Lacey, Landsaw, Lincus, Little, Lovelace, Lykins, Lindon, Maddox, Mc-

Pherson, McNabb, McLin, Miller, Moore, Mize, Mullins, Murphy, Netherly, Nickell, O'Hair, Oliver, Oldfield, Osborne, Pence, Perkins, Peters, Pratt, Pieratt, Profitt, Puckett, Quillan, Roberts, Robinson, Rose, Sewell, Sherman, Shackelford, Shockey, Shull, Smith, Sparks, Spencer, Spradling, Stamper, Swango, Stewart, Steele, Sword, Taulbee, Terrill, Trent, Tutt, Tyra, Tyler, Tolson, Turner, Vancleve, Ward, Watkins, Wilson, Williams, and Wyatt.

ASBURY

George Asbury, born in 1802 in Virginia, married three times. By his first wife, Nancy, born in 1799, in Virginia, he had the following children: Catherine, who married A. J. Taylor; Thomas, who married Cordelia Tutt, daughter of Dr. William and Sarah Stamper Tutt. Their children were: William G.; Oliver T., who married Nancy Jane Patton. They had four children:

Maude, married William C. Smith. They had three children: Irene married Ben Durham, no children; Bill Oliver married Rowena Campbell. They have one child; Sally married Dallas Denniston. They had four children; Cordia Asbury married Andrew Thomas Peery. They had two children; Nancy Elizabeth married James LeRoy Catchings. They had four children; Maude Mae Peery, who finished business school and is Secretary for County Superintendent; James Porter Asbury married Mollie Phillips. They had three children. James Hobert, married; Tommie, Married and one child; Ollie, not married.

Bess Married McKinley Hobert Young. They had three children. Jimmy, married and three children; Wilda Lee; Francis Jane, married Benjamin Bailey and they had three children.
Audiline, Rosa Bell, Elizabeth G., and Iscy.

Alexander, who married Sibby Lacy. Mary, no information. Henry, no information. George Asbury also had children by his last marriage, names unknown to writer.

EARLY AND MODERN HISTORY

BYRD OF WOLFE COUNTY

(Information supplied by Mrs. Nora Byrd Horton)

Burd, Bird, or Byrd are all the same family. William Henry Harrison, our former president of the United States, married a Byrd.

William Byrd II, married in England where they were well to do and then came to Westover, Va., and settled on a large estate. He had a son, Henry Richard, who is the forefather of the Byrds of Wolfe County. He also had a daughter, who died of a broken heart. She was sent to England to study music and while there she fell in love with a commoner. When her father learned about this he went and brought her back to America.

Some time later, her father, William Byrd II, who raised fine thoroughbred horses, advertised in the English papers for a groom for his horses. A fine looking young man came to apply for the job and was accepted. Later he proved to be the man with whom his daughter had fallen in love in England and so he was dismissed. As for the daughter, she died of a broken heart.

Henry Richard, the son of William II, ran off when he was 16 and joined the Revolutionary Army. He was never big enough to carry a gun but hauled supplies with a wagon and team. He was behind Washington with supplies when Cornwallis surrendered to him.

Henry Byrd married a Baldwin. They settled in Tennessee.

1. John was his son. He married Ann Tutt, a daughter of Michael and Nancy Robinson Tutt.

2. Michael was their oldest son, who reared a family in Morgan County.

2. Sam was their second son, who reared a family in Morgan County.

2. Charles married Kathryn Long.
3. Clint Byrd married Ada Rose.
4. Osa Married a Wilson.
4. Mattie married a Nickell.
4. Emma married Riley Goss.
4. Steve married and lives at Lee City.
4. Bert never married.
4. Ada never married.
4. Sol never married.
4. Ora married John Cundiff.
4. Nola married Lacer Gevedon.
4. Charles died in infancy.

3. Boone Byrd, son of Charles and Kathryn Byrd married Lizzie Wallace.
4. Effie married Lonza Craft.
4. Willie married Golden Tipton.
5. Rex married and died.
4. Bruce never married.
3. Cynthia, daughter of Charles and Kathryn Byrd married Doc Miller.
4. Ollie married Lura Carroll.
5. Pauline died.
5. Kathleen married Thurston H. Strunk, Stearns, Ky.
5. (Billie) William R. married Sally M. Crume, they live in Grand Rapids, Mich.
5. Edison died young.
4. Edna Miller married Flave Cecil.
5. Charles Edward married Betty Norris.
6. A son.
5. Wilma Clay married Bobbie Rose.
6. Gary.
6. A girl.
3. George M. Byrd, son of Charles and Kathryn Byrd, married Eliza Morrow.
4. Lula married Robert Young.
5. Robert married Peggy. He is a graduate of U. of Ky. Majored in Science.
5. Charles Byrd Young was killed while piloting an aeroplane in World War II.
4. Ida married A. Thomas Rowe and they were connected with the Gospel Trumpet Co., in Anderson, Ind., for years, where he was business manager of all their publications and she was editor of the young peoples magazines.
5. One son, Tommie, who lost his life in Africa when a bomb exploded near where he was working on some telegraph wires. He was married but had no children.
4. Golden married Joe Rose.
5. Chester Clay was killed at Pearl Harbor when his ship, the Oklahoma, was bombed.
5. Harry Clyde married. He is a coach at Winchester. They have one child.
4. Loma taught for years. She is a University graduate. She married Stanley Myers and they live at Stanlo Farm near Owingsville, Ky.
4. Ruth Byrd died in infancy.
4. Byron married in California. He made Army his career. Lost his life in service of his country in World War II.
4. Orpha married Bill Stephens first. They had two children.
5. Billie, who married Jack Allen.

EARLY AND MODERN HISTORY

    6. Nancy.
    5. Jack is in the U. S. Army.
Orpha and Bill Stephens were divorced and she married David Cropp.
    4. Mabel married Oval Brumbaugh. Mabel is a teacher in the Winchester school system. She is a graduate of the Wesleyan College.
    4. Wendell married Ruth Sample. He graduated from Wesleyan College and from Anderson Seminary. He was a chaplain in the U. S. Army in Korean War when he lost his life due to a bomb explosion. He left his widow with one daughter, Wendy Lou.
    4. Cecil Kash Byrd holds his Phd. degree and works in the Lincoln Library in Bloomington, Ind. He married Esther Samples.
    5. Jean.
    5. Anne.
    3. Rozia L. Byrd, daughter of Charles and Kathryn Byrd, married W. H. Chambers.
    4. Katherine Chambers married Bruce Rose.
    5. Cecil married Martha Boothe.
    6. Rita Lee married Herschel Farmer.
    7. Mikey.
    5. Frank married Ruth Brown. They both teach.
    6. Jackie, a student at the University of Kentucky.
    4. Carrie Chambers married Roscoe Wells.
    5. Golden married Hendrix Allen.
    6. Hendrix Byrd Allen.
    5. Emmerson Wells married Alene Patton.
    6. Phyllis Glenn.
    5. John Wells married Ruby Combs.
    6. Sally.
    6. Rita.
    5. Rosalyn married Bill Alcorn.
    6. William Wells Alcorn.
    6. John Roscoe Alcorn.
    5. Pershing died young.
    5. Zuda Wells married Bob Marker.
    6. Robert Marker.
    6. Peggy.
    5. R. C., Junior married Elizabeth Wells. A daughter, Rose Lynn.
    5. Bill Jeff Wells married Thelma Taulbee. Children: Billie, Jr., Kathryn, Brenda, and Gary.
    5. Elizabeth Wells married John Kelly Hurst. They have three boys and one girl: Kelly Wells Hurst, Garrett, Carrie Sue, and Tommie.
    4. Zuda married Robert Rothman. Both now dead.
    5. Robert Chambers Rothman, a chaplain in Tokyo, Japan.

He married Rowena Worthman. They have one son: Robert Rothman III.

5. Richard Rothman is a young preacher and is unmarried in 1955.

3. Isom, son of Charles and Kate Byrd, married Luetta Gevedon.

4. Hettie Byrd married Bob Brashears. Several children, all in Wolfe County.

4. Carl Byrd married Emma Centers. Several children, all moved away.

4. Elmer married and moved out of county.

4. Victoria married Leonard Tutt. He died and she married again.

5. Paul Tutt.

4. Blanche married Charlie Horton.

4. Charlie Byrd married a Collins.

4. Floyd Byrd married and is now a preacher in Menifee County.

3. John Byrd, son of Charles and Kate Byrd, married Cinda Drake.

4. Bessie Byrd married Leonard Dennis.

5. Wendell married away.

4. Scott Byrd married twice. Child by first wife: Estill.

4. Reece Byrd married a Cope from Jackson, Ky. No children.

4. Russell married Maggie Centers.

5. Robert Byrd married a Long.

5. Blanche married John Moore.

4. Edna married a Hughes. A daughter.

2. William R. Byrd, son of John Byrd, married Mary (Polly) Stamper.

3. Ellen (now dead) married Vestine Stickley Drake.

4. Lina (and a twin that died at birth) never married, died when grown.

4. Rachel married a Collins and had two boys, then married Ben Gosney and had two girls.

4. William married Pearl Bolin — had two children, then married Cora Cox, No children by last marriage.

4. Robert Lee killed when thrown from a mule at 14 years of age.

4. Taylor married someone in Illinois.

5. A daughter, named Mary.

4. Jackson Byrd never married. He set a mark for the world's highest paraschute jumper in his time. He is now dead.

3. Jim Byrd, son of William R. Byrd, married Nancy McQuinn.

4. George Byrd married someone I do not know.

4. Jim Byrd married.

4. Tom married.

EARLY AND MODERN HISTORY

4. Martha Byrd married a Phillips.
4. Will Byrd married a Creech.
4. May be others.
3. William Anderson Byrd now dead. Married Emily J. Centers.
4. Norah L. married first time to Newton Horton. They had one son.
5. William Byrd Horton married Geneva Haden.
6. A girl, Emily Centers Horton.
4. Thomas Hendricks Byrd married Elizabeth Pratt.
5. Jean Logan Byrd married Cam Ballard.
6. Elizabeth Ballard.
6. Harriett Ballard.
6. Marcus Ballard.
5. Emily Centers married a teacher at Harvard College. They have twin boys.
5. (Twins) Ryland and Thomas Hendricks Byrd.
Ryland is a doctor and married a Guerrant. They have one child. T. Hendricks was killed in a car wreck.
5. Pratt Byrd married in Kentucky and took his wife to Germany while he was teaching Science there. They have one son born in Germany. William.
4. Lida Byrd, daughter of William Anderson Byrd and Emily J. Byrd, married Joe H. Gevedon.
5. Kendall Byrd Gevedon died at 29, unmarried.
5. Cantrell Raymond Gevedon died at about three years of age.
5. Ruby J. married Scott Rogers.
6. Two children.
4. Bertha, daughter of William A. and Emily J. Byrd, married Hobart Hoskins first. He was killed in a car accident. Then she married Burnice Brown. Three children by first husband.
5. Wilma is an airline stewardess. She attended Wesleyan College.
5. Hobart, Jr., married Carolyn Atchinson.
5. Kendal Byrd Hoskins, unmarried.
3. Robert Lee Byrd, son of William R. Byrd and Polly Stamper Byrd, married Emma Steel.
4. Shelby Byrd was killed in an elevator in Oklahoma when he was about 20 years of age. He was never married.
4. Katherine Byrd married a Lohman.
5. Two sons.
4. Mattie married Charlie Williams.
5. Robert Williams.
5. Charles Williams.
4. Lillie Byrd married Richmond Horton.
5. Hope.
5. Another girl and a son, Richmond, Jr.
4. Nellie Byrd never married.

3. Gillian Byrd, daughter of William R. and Polly Stamper Byrd, married John J. Tutt.

4. Luther Tutt married Carrie Centers. Two children by first wife. Married a second time, Mala Bailey, and had several children.

4. Ethel Tutt married a Canadian and they had one son.

4. Rolla Tutt (dead), married in Illinois and had four children.

4. Kelly Tutt married away.

4. Lillie Tutt married in Idaho. One child.

4. Daisy married away. No children.

4. Golden Tutt married and had one child. She is now dead.

3. Rosa Bell Byrd, daughter of William R. and Polly Stamper Byrd, married J. B. Hollon.

4. Earl died in infancy.

4. Twins (Lennie and Lydia, the latter died in infancy). Lennie married J. B. Land. Had one son, J. B. Land, Jr.

4. Russell Hollon never married.

4. Beckham married in Illinois and has one child.

4. Iva married a Hugh Nolan. They live in Oklahoma and have no children.

4. Ruth married a Condon.

4. Ted was burned to death in a fire in Campton about 1948.

3. Margaret, daughter of William R. and Polly Stamper Byrd, married Bruce Little. Both dead. No children.

3. Mary (dead), daughter of William R. and Polly Stamper Byrd, married Grant (Bud) Faulkner.

4. Two children died when infants.

4. George Faulkner grew up and married, but now dead.

4. Bruce Faulkner married away.

3. Charles T. Byrd, son of William R. and Polly Stamper Byrd, married Norah first. They had three girls and one boy. Then he went to Pasadena, Calif., where he married again. Had one daughter, Ellen, by last marriage. She is the youngest daughter of D. A. R. in America.

3. Emma, daughter of William R. and Polly S. Byrd, married a Stevens in Oklahoma.

4. Two daughters.

4. A son, Byrd Stevens.

3. Dr. Richard Byrd, son of William R. and Polly S. Byrd, married in Oklahoma. He is now dead. He left one daughter.

3. Tommie Byrd died at age of eight years.

3. Rebecca died at four years.

3. Mahala Byrd married in Oklahoma. Now dead.

Henry Byrd was the first person in the United States to start a Humane Society. After the Revolutionary War he gathered up all the old horses which had been turned loose to starve and fed them much to his wife's disgust. A old man came to him, a German, who was also interested in the care for old horses and agreed to help work and feed the stock for almost anything Byrd could pay him. Henry took him on but told him that he could not pay much as he was like everyone else, without much funds after the war. Several years later the old German man died and left his will. Henry Byrd was sole heir. He had saved up several thousand dollars and this was all turned over to Henry Byrd to help care for the old horses.

A. C. Byrd says that he was born in Hancock County, Tennessee on June 8, 1841 and that he was the son of John Byrd, who later moved to Morgan County, Kentucky in about 1845. A. C.'s grandfather's name was Henry Byrd and he came to Morgan County in about 1850 and made his home with his son, John, until the time of his death, which occurred in 1857 or 1858. A. C. Byrd's grandfather was a soldier in the Revolutionary War and he drew a pension as a soldier in the American Revolution.

2. Anderson Campbell Byrd, son of John Byrd, married Cinda Stamper.

3. Tilda Ann Byrd, married George Halsey.

4. Five children: Floyd, Cinda, Lillie, etc.

3. Anderson Floyd Byrd, son of Anderson Campbell Byrd, was a noted lawyer. He is now dead. He married Emma Elkins.

4. Carl Byrd married.

4. Bessie Byrd married a Rozelle (Colvert Rozelle). They had two children: Dan and Sam.

3. Mahala Byrd died when a young lady. Never married.

3. Sara married Ben Sewell.

4. Vergie Sewell.

4. Ben Sewell, Jr.

3. John Byrd, son of Anderson Campbell Byrd and Cinda Stamper Byrd, married Junie Spradlin.

3. Letcher Byrd married Millie Hanks.

4. Millie Byrd married away.

4. Floyd Byrd married away.

4. Ernest married away.

2. George Byrd, son of John Byrd, married Angeline Nickell. They had eight children: Rose Ellen, Willie, Alice, George Ann, Lillie, Nettie, George Curtis and Mallie.

3. Rose Ellen Byrd married Berry James. They lived at Hazel Green. No children. Both dead.

3. Willie married away and lives in Kansas.

3. Alice now dead. She married Tom Williams. They had several children and always lived in Middletown, Ohio.

3. George Ann, now dead, married Joe Lee Wilson. They had several children. They all live in Morrow, Ohio.

3. Lillie married James Cox. They made their home at Pine Ridge, Ky. James is now dead.

3. Children of Lillie Byrd Cox and James Cox were: Bill, now dead; Ray, now married and lives in Middletown, Ohio; Earl, is married and lives in Ohio; Maurine is married and lives in Ohio; Angeline married Herbert Rose. They live near Hazel Green where he is assistant postmaster.

5. Volney Herbert is married and lives in Franklin, Ohio.

5. Billie is in the U. S. Navy where he is a Lieutenant General.

4. Lucille was married, but she and her husband separated. They had two children. She and her children make their home with her mother at Pine Ridge.

4. Juanita is married and lives in Ohio.

4. Daisy married George Culbertson and they live at Salyersville.

3. Nettie, daughter of George and Angeline Byrd, died in her youth unmarried.

3. George Curtis married Jennie Taylor on Feb. 4, 1909. They had 12 children.

4. India, who married Clarence Murray. She operates a Beauty parlor in Middletown, Ohio where they live. They have no children.

4. Clinton married Dorothy Wellington and they live in Middletown, Ohio. No children.

4. Virginia married Earl McMann. They live in Middletown, Ohio. They have no children.

4. Chester married Viva Hall. He is a barber in Trenton, Ohio. They have two children: Jennie Lou and Phillip.

4. Leslie married Reva Gross. They have one son, Ronny. They live in Covington, Ky.

4. Christine is dead. She was married to Hillis Hendrix. They had one son, David.

4. Mary is at home with her parents, Mr. and Mrs. G. C. Byrd, in Campton.

4. Fred and Froy Byrd were twins. Fred married Lois Lawless and they make their home in Middletown, Ohio. Froy lives there also, but is unmarried.

4. Betty married Byron Johnson. They live in Jackson, Ky., where he operates a restaurant. One child, Patricia Ann.

4. Deloris married E. T. Kash, Jr. He is in the Medical Corps of the U. S. Army. He has his A. B. degree from the University of Kentucky. Deloris is a student at Lees College while E. T. gets his overseas duty performed.

3. Mallie, daughter of John Byrd and Angeline Nickell Byrd, married Bob Salle. She had two sons.

EARLY AND MODERN HISTORY

GABRIEL CONKLYN BANKS
Submitted by Gabriel C. Banks

Gabriel Conklyn Banks was born near Gillmore on May 31, 1892. His parents were William Harrison Banks and Denicey Jane (Lawson) Banks. Soon after the presen century began he moved with his father and two brothers to Fayetteville, Arkansas. In 1906 they returned to Gillmore and re-located on a farm adjoining the one they had sold a few years earlier.

At this time he attended the neighborhood school, helped about the farm, and worked at a nearby sawmill.

In September of the year he was sixteen, he pocketed the meagre proceeds from a crop he had raised that summer, shouldered a suitcase, and struck out for Hazel Green Academy. The low expenses at the school soon exhausted his funds, but those in charge of the institution made it possible for him to remain. At the end of the academic year he completed the prescribed ninth grade courses and took an examination on the eighth grade subjects, receiving a diploma. The second summer vacation the American Sunday School Union employed him to do organization work in Morgan and Wolfe Counties. By working in the summers and helping with the maintenance of the school plant while he was in school, he was able to continue his studies without interruption, graduating from the Academy with the class of 1912.

September following found him in Lexington, enrolled in Transylvania College. He was now a candidate for the ministry and it was not long until he was earning his expense money by serving small Central Kentucky churches as a student preacher. In addition to this he participated fully in campus activities, winning a few distinctions. Transylvania awarded him an A. B. degree in 1917.

The nation was at war and he shortly enlisted in Base Hospital No. 40. Before long he was overseas, first in England, later in France.

Although only an enlisted man, he spent much of this time abroad performing the work of a chaplain, having been petitioned by his comrades and authorized by the Colonel to act in this capacity. On his return from France, he entered the College of the Bible to engage in theological study. In 1921 he was graduated from that seminary.

That summer he married Opal Burkhardt of Crawfordsville, Indiana, and they were immediately commissioned by the United Christian Missionary Society to work in India. Ill health forced them to return to America two years later. There followed a brief pastorate in Terre Haute, Indiana. He then entered Yale University for further study, earning an advanced degree there in 1924.

Out of Yale, they located in Falmouth, Kentucky, serving the Christian Church two years. From Falmouth they moved to Maysville, Kentucky, where he continued as minister 10 years. During the last seven of this period, he was General Secretary of the Convention of Christian Churches in Kentucky.

In September of 1936 he left Maysville to accept a teaching position in the Department of English in Morehead State College. That position he still holds. During the war era he also ministered jointly to the Christian Churches of West Liberty and Salyersville. He has also attended the University of Chicago and George Peabody College for teachers.

He and Mrs. Banks are proud to claim three children: Mrs. Scott Schindel of Mt. Orab, Ohio; William Burkhardt Banks of Houston, Texas; and Mrs. David Helfrich, of Houston, Texas.

CHILDREN OF WILLIAM N. G. BARRON AND ANNIE BARRON
Contributed by Mrs. Molly Johnson Rowland

Clarinda Barron, 1824, Lee County Va., married J. W. Slemp.
Joseph Barron, 1826, Lee County Va., married Rebecca Pennington.

Hugh Barron, 1828, Lee County, Va., married Miss Walker.
Catherine Barron, 1829, Lee County, Va., married 1846, James D. Tyler.

John Barron, 1831, Lee County, Va., married Polina Ward.
Joe Annie Barron, 1833, Lee County, Va., married H. C. Slemp.
Mahala Barron, 1835, Lee County, Va., married James Roach.
Annie Barron, 1837, Lee County, Va., married James Gilley.
W. A. G. Barron, 1839, Lee County, Va., married Eliza Horton.
T. B. Barron, 1841, Lee County, Va., killed in War 1864.
J. K. P. Barron, 1844, Lee County, Va., married Rebecca Scotte.
Virginia Barron, 1849, Lee County, Va., married D. H. Bruce.
Parents of above children:

William N. G. Barron, Dec. 1, 1801-Jan. 1, 1865, Lee County, Va. Annie Barron, Aug. 18, 1804, Lee County, Va., Aug. 8, 1883, Lee County, Va. They were married August 8, 1823 at home in Lee County, Va.

Grandparents of above children: Joseph Barron, born 1769; Catherine Barron, born 1771. Randle Collier, born 1764; Catherine Collier, born 1771.

EARLY AND MODERN HISTORY

The great-grandfather, Aaron Collier, was born in 1740.
Children of John Tyler and Sarah Tyler.
Elizabeth Tyler, born in 1802.
Alfred Tyler, born 1804.
Charlotte Tyler, 1806.
Caroline Tyler, 1808.
Hanable Tyler, 1810.
Cliford Tyler, 1812, died Feb. 1895.
James S. Tyler, Jan. 28, 1814, died June 4, 1884.
Benjamin Tyler, born 1816, died 1892.

DEBORAH A. SWANGO TYLER-WILLIAM T. TYLER
Family records entered in their Bible by Deborah Tyler

Grandparents:
Fathers father — John H. Tyler, born 1780.
Fathers mother — Dorah Tyler, born 1784.
Mothers father — William G. Barron, born Dec. 1, 1801, died Jan. 1, 1885, Lee County, Va.

Mothers Mother — Anna Barron, born Aug. 16, 1804, died Aug. 8, 1883, Lee County, Va.

Parents:
Father — James S. Tyler, born Jan. 28, 1814, died June 11, 1884, Wolfe County, Ky.

Mother — Catherine Tyler, born Nov. 11, 1829, died May 3, 1908, Wolfe County, Ky. They were married on Nov. 29, 1946, Lee County, Virginia.

Children:
Clarida J. Tyler, Sept. 17, 1847, Lee County, Va. Married Nov. 1872, C. C. Hanks.

Hugh B. Tyler, May 14, 1850, Lee County, Va. Married 1875, Cammie E. Osborne.

William T. Tyler, Oct. 14, 1852, Lee County, Va. Married Dec. 29, 1872, Debby A. Johnson.

Annie B. Tyler, Sept. 8, 1855, Wise County, Va. Married April 1871, T. R. Horton.

Gale B. Tyler, April 17, 1858, Wise County, Va. Married 1886, Mattie Graham, died April 5, 1890.

Mahala Tyler, May 2, 1861, Wise County, Va. Married 1876, T. B. Hanks.

John B. Tyler, July 23, 1866, Lee County, Va. Married 1882, Laura Faulkner.

R. L. Tyler, July 23, 1866, Lee County, Va. Married 1888, Jane Allen.

Lawrence T. Tyler, April 23, 1869, Lee County Va., died Jan. 8, 1889.

Melvin Tyler, May 22, 1872, Wolfe County, Ky. Married 1890,

WOLFE COUNTY

Nannie Chambers.

Note: It is apparent that John J. and Sarah Tyler were also of Virginia since no location is given and the others are all from Virginia until the last child, which is born in Wolfe County, Ky in 1872. The names of all those marrying the children are all old Wolfe County names that I have heard my parents call and talk about during my early years. It is likely they were all married in Wolfe County and most of their families have grown up there.

The Barron record which follows does not say where the children married but some of them lived in Wolfe County. Anyway the names and dates may help to clear up some other records. The Will Tyler line appears in the Swango history.

BOOTH

The Booth family, according to records, first appeared in Wales of West Britain. Later, one of the more prosperous families moved to Southern England and settled down near the city of London.

From this family came William T. Booth, Sr., who because of persecution by the English Government under King George III, fled the country and sought refuge in the American Colonies. He and his family landed in New York City in the latter part of the Eighteenth Century. We next hear of them in Big Laurel, Virginia. Then eventually, in the Bear Pen section of Wolfe County where the Senior Booth settled and remained the balance of his days. His children scattered. John continued Westward and was never heard from again. Sarah, the youngest child, settled in Cowetta, Oklahoma where her children are still living. Elvina, another daughter, married and settled down in Lee County. Thomas married in Wolfe County but soon afterward moved to Johnson County, where his descendents are still living. Martin Booth, purchased some land in the Tar Ridge section, married and settled down there. Some of his grandchildren still live in the Torrent section. William Booth, Jr., the grandfather of the Booths, who now reside in the Campton and Lower Devils Creek section of Wolfe County, settled in the Booth Ridge area and remained there until his death. The old Homestead still remains.

Taylor Booth.

CARROLL FAMILY
Submitted by Mrs. Dora Bush

1. William Carroll came from Virginia to Kentucky and settled in what is now Wolfe County, but then was known as Owsley County back about the middle of the 1800's. He was married to Mary Ann Whisman by Elder John D. Spencer on Nov. 17, 1859. To this

EARLY AND MODERN HISTORY

union were born eleven children: Martha A. Carroll, who married Cyrus Kincaid. They had three children.

2. Mary E. Carroll married Joseph Spencer and to this union were born four children.

2. James D. Carroll who married Vina Spencer and to this union were born eleven children.

2. Sarah J. Carroll married Edward Kincaid and to this union were born 12 children.

2. Louvina Bell Carroll married Roby Cable of South Carolina and to this union were born seven children.

2. John F. Carroll married Linda Hall and to this union were born six children.

2. Delila Carroll married Robert Willis of Big Stone Gap, Va., and to this union were born three children.

2. Michael N. Carroll married Dora Spencer and to this union were born eight children.

2. Cyntha C. Carroll married James Spencer and to this union were born two children.

2. Emma C. Carroll married Henry Gentry and to this union were born seven children.

2. Maranda E. Carroll married Buckely Alexander and they had no children.

2. Martha A. Carroll married Cyrus Kincaid who had three children: Melvin Kincaid, who married Cinda Cable; Maye Kincaid, who married Uri Horton; Maeura Kincaid, who married James Bowman.

2. Mary E. Carroll married Joseph Spencer and they had four children: Della and Leila, both died in their teens; Annie Spencer married Horace Willaby; Rose Spencer married William Farmer.

2. James D. Carroll married Vina Spencer and they had eleven children.

3. Etta Carroll married Lewis Mitchell, no children, now dead.

3. W. H. Carroll married Mary Childers. They had two children.

4. Billie Agnes.

4. Margaret Ann.

3. Dora married John P. Bush. They reared four children. Dora died Oct. 25, 1956.

4. Children: Warren, Angus, Marvin, and Glenn.

3. Fred Carroll married Elizabeth Rose.

3. Ed Carroll married Lula Drake.

4. Wilma Jean.

3. Rose married Charles Kincaid. They had five children.

4. Children: Maxine married Robert Cable; Linnie married Oliver Treadway; Johnny, not married; Rita, not married; Sam, died in infancy.

3. Dudley Carroll married Fern Miller and they had one child: J. D. Carroll, serving in the Air Corps in 1954.

WOLFE COUNTY

3. Bob Carroll married Nellie Alexander and they had five children: Ralph married Dorotha Hollon; Hilda married Jack Grey; Rose married Clyde Edwards; Madge Carroll not married; Faye not married.
3. Lura married Alvan Hibbard and they had two children: Carl Hibbard married Cora Hobbs; Edith Hibbard married Lester Johnson.
3. Lester Carroll married Hattie Booth and they had two children: Betty and Bonnie, not married.
3. Ruby Carroll died in her 14th year.
2. Sarah J. Carroll married Edward Kincaid and they had 12 children:
3. Margaret Kincaid married Dr. John Williams and they had three children: Claude, Nettie and Glen Ray, not married.
3. Billie Kincaid married Lula Campbell and they had two children: Austin and Foster.
3. Charles Kincaid married Florence Barrett and they had three children: Clayton, Ursie May and Charles, Jr.
3. Flossie Kincaid married Dave Hogan and they had one child, which died.
3. Vina Kincaid married Leonard Toler and they had one child.
3. Beulah Kincaid married Rev. Robert Huff and they had one daughter.
3. Aubra Kincaid married and had two children(names not known).
3. Myles Kincaid married Lizzie Adams and they had five children (names not known).
3. Mary Kincaid married Glenn Flemings and they had four children.
3. Martha Kincaid married.
3. Chester Kincaid married.
3. Robert Kincaid married, name of wife and family not known.
2. Lavinna Bell Carroll married Roby Cable of South Carolina and they had eight children.
3. Will Cable married Cinda Lutes. (No children.)
3. Lula Cable married Grover Hobbs. (No children.)
3. Greely Cable married Lula Hobbs and they had two children.
3. Ethel Cable married Ed Honcer and they had one child.
3. Hattie Cable married Roy Hecker. (No children.)
3. Ruby and Courtney Cable both died when young.
3. Smally Cable married Belle Taylor and they had three children.
3. Edith married.
2. John F. Carroll, son of William Carroll and Mary Ann Whisman, married Linda Hall and they had six children: Colman, Willie, James and Brack. Never lived in Wolfe County.
2. Delila Carroll, daughter of William Carroll and Mary Ann

Whisman Carroll, married Robert Willis and they had three children. They lived in Big Stone Gap, Va. Oscar (deceased); Nettie, married a Mr. Gilmer of Virginia; and Earl is married also.

2. Michael N. Carroll married Dora Spencer and they had eight children:

3. Georgeann married Martin Treadway and they had four children: Elmo Treadway, not married; Edward Treadway, married; Elizabeth married a Mr. McGuire from Beattyville, Ky.; Della Carroll married a Mr. Sorrel.

3. Charlie Carroll married Edna Crowe. They had one child which is deceased.

3. Susetta Carroll married Gay Spencer.

3. Mildred Carroll married Asa Davis and they had one daughter, Carol.

3. Nellie Carroll married Bill Nappier.

3. Courtney Carroll was killed in a car accident.

3. Bill Carroll married, but his wife died.

2. Cynthia Carroll, daughter of William Carroll and Mary Ann Whisman Carroll, married James Spencer and they had two children.

3. Susan Spencer married Herbert Hull and they had two children, Garnett and Bobbie.

3. Callie married Ova Morrison and they had seven children: Fred Morrison, Helen Morrison, Joann Morrison, Everett Morrison, three deceased, do not know names.

2. Emma C. Carroll married Henry Gentry and they had eight children: Green, Mary J., Annabell, Frank, Bill, Charlie, Roxie, and Nettie Pearl. (Do not know anything about their families.)

This information supplied by Mrs. Jane Carroll Allison, August 1954:

John Carroll and Hester Elkins Carroll established their family in Wolfe County when it was a young county. Their children were: John Richmond Carroll, Robert Carroll and Rosie Carroll.

2. John Richmond Carroll, born June 11, 1868, on Bear Pen in Wolfe County, Ky., died May 1, 1923. He was a graduate doctor of the Louisville Medical School and practiced nearly 34 years, most of it in Wolfe County.

Dr. Carroll married Lula J. Smith, daughter of S. B. Smith and Miranda Combs Smith. They had six children, four of which grew to be adults: Loura, who married Ollie Miller; Billie Miller; Kathleen.

3. John Sam Carroll, who married Ruth Kean and they live in Texas. Two sons.

3. Bernice Marvin, born Oct. 4, 1894, was in World War I, died Jan. 20, 1936.

3. Allene married Jim Wireman, who later died.

4. A daughter, Jean, who married.

5. Two children after her marriage.
2. Robert Carroll married Maggie Smith. first, and second, Christine Gibson.
3. Children by first marriage.
3. Courtney, died unmarried; Wallace. married; Beatrice married, now dead; Evalena married Paul Lawless. Three children.
4. Louise married Bill Cunningham.
4. Paul, Jr., married Mary Thelma Catron.
4. Joyce married Fred Byrd.

CECIL AND SAMPLE RELATED FAMILIES
Submitted by Steve Samples

Lucinda Catherine Sample, born at Sword's Creek, Virginia, February 14, 1828, married James M. Cecil, born near Tazewell, Virginia, March 17, 1820.

In 1858 they and their family moved to Morgan County, Kentucky and purchased a farm about two miles southeast of Ezell, where they lived until their deaths.

Their children, according to my information, were:
1. Charles Cecil, who married Mollie Spradling, both now deceased. The children of Charles and wife were Henry, who married Carrie Swango, daughter of A. B. Swango, Forrest Fullet Cecil, (recently deceased) who married Myrtle Johnson, a twin of Pearl Johnson Davis, and Myrtle and Catherine, one of whom married Estill D. Williams, now residing at Ashland, Kentucky, and the other married another Mr. Williams, now deceased, and she resides also at Ashland, Kentucky.

Charles Cecil and wife lived on a farm in Morgan County, Kentucky and reared their family there, but later moved to Hazel Green, Kentucky and remained their until their deaths. He told me that the descendents of James Sample of Virginia were related to the one time Chief Justice Fuller of the U. S. Supreme Court. That may have been correct, as Steven Fuller, who married a Gibson in Russell County, Virginia, was the father of Celia Fuller. first wife of the said James Sample.

2. Maggie Cecil Carter, wife of Perry Carter, both now deceased, and mother of Will Carter, now deceased, and Chess Carter. The Carters reared their sons on a farm in Morgan County, Kentucky. Perry Carter was called "Judge" Carter and might have been at one time county judge of Morgan County, Kentucky, though as to that I have forgotten.

3. Angeline Cecil, who married James Cecil, a distant relative, both now deceased, the parents of Ora Cecil, who married Ova

Kash of Ezel, Kentucky, both now deceased, and also parents of Orville Cecil. Ora was one of sister Bertha's most loved relatives and was a deservedly popular girl. She and her husband located in Kansas and reared their family there. Orville went with his parents from Hazel Green where they lived for a few years, to Mt. Sterling, Kentucky, and continued to live in Montgomery County and Clark County. Angeline and her husband took care of her parents in their old age and purchased the old home place and after the death of her parents, sold the place and moved to Hazel Green.

4. Whit Cecil, who married Cora Kendall, and with his wife and their only child, Etta May, resided at West Liberty, Kentucky until late in life when they moved to Nicholasville, Kentucky, or its vicinity. Etta May married Stanley Womack of West Liberty. Whit was a successful merchant and owner and operator of a popular hotel at West Liberty and accumulated considerable wealth.

5. Mattie Cecil, who married Willis Henry, both now deceased. They were the parents of Mrs. Elizabeth Henry Hanna, widow of a former circuit judge of the Morgan County district. Elizabeth has for a number of years resided at Leesville, Florida. She has one son residing at Frankfort, Kentucky. Dr. O. P. Henry, now deceased, and two brothers, whose names I do not presently recall, were the other children of Mattie Cecil Henry and husband. During the early years of their wedded life the Henrys lived near West Liberty, Kentucky, but later moved to a farm purchased by them near Mt. Sterling, Kentucky.

6. William Cecil, who married Betty Oakley. They were the parents of Raleigh Cecil, and lived until their respective deaths on their farm on Grassy Creek in Morgan County, Kentucky.

7. Robert Cecil, who spent a number of years on the West Coast but later returned to Kentucky and married Clark Long. He and his wife are both dead.

8. Mary Belle, who married Floyd Clark and resided with him in their home at Sword's Creek, Virginia. They were the parents of only one child, a son, who was living at Sword's Creek, Virginia the last account I had of him. It is my recollection he was named for his father.

9. Kate, who married John Smith Nickell, who was his 3rd wife. Both are deceased. They were the parents of Clay Wade Nickell, now a successful travelling salesman. The Nickells continued to reside until after the death of the husband at the beautiful Cockrell home in Morgan County, Kentucky about one mile from Ezel.

This old home was a one-and-one-half or two-story residence built of hewn or sawed logs very smoothly planed and carefully notched or dovetailed. The home could scarcely be seen from the road because so completely encircled by closely growing white pine trees. This was indeed a wondrous home, built about the time of or shortly after Civil War days.

Uncle James Cecil and Aunt Catherine were model Christian citizens. Both were dignified, well-dressed and gave their all to their family, church and community. They brought with them to Kentucky and established in their home the best traditions of the Old Dominion State. It was through my acquaintance with them and their descendants and Cecil relatives that I got the idea that the Cecil family in America was and is a family with much above the average of pride, and which has not lost caste or dignity after immigration to America with the colony of Lord Cecil Calvert, a relative.

Henry L. Sample, born in Russell County, Virginia, December 30, 1836, died on Laurel Creek in Wolfe County, Kentucky; married Mary Clark of Virginia, and who died on Laurel Creek in Wolfe County, Kentucky.

Henry was a full brother of my grandfather, Steve G. Sample, but did not come to Kentucky until several years after the immigration of Steve and family and James M. Cecil and family in 1858. He and his wife acquired their farm on Laurel Creek in Wolfe County about a mile, as I recall, to the West of the Brewer store on the highway from Campton to Hazel Green. I visited in their home on one or more occasion and as I remember it it was pretty well surrounded by pine and spruce and other forest trees and rock cliffs were in the immediate vicinity.

The children of Henry and Mary were:
1. Ellen, who married Berry Nickell, son of Rev. James Nichell, an early minister of the Christian Church. Raleigh was their oldest child and they reared a number of other children, and later moved to Ohio where they lived until death.

2. Laura Sample, died while single.

3. Frank Sample, who as an old bachelor married Rettie Johnson, daughter of Frank Johnson. After Rettie's death he married a Mrs. McGuire and after her death married the widow of Ned Duff, who was the mother of Roscoe Little by a former marriage. Frank was during most of the time he was single the coroner of Wolfe County, Kentucky, which office gave him the privilege of carrying a pistol, making arrests, and serving civil processes. On one or more occassions he spent the night in the home of my parents and he and I roomed together on those occasions. The pistol he car-

ried was, I believe, the largest I ever saw. It is not to be implied that he was a fighting man or overbearing in his conduct, for he was not that type. After the first marriage he lived for a number of years on Lacey's Creek near the Sebron Trimble home and kept a country store. He later moved into Hazel Green, and carried on a mercantile business there.

4. George Sample, who married Nannie Brown, a daughter of James Brown and Pollie Rose Brown. They lived on a small farm near Pine Ridge, Kentucky and educated their children in the Pine Ridge Academy. One of their daughters, a Mrs. Henry, is postmaster at Pine Ridge and her mother resides, part time at least, with her. George has been dead a number of years.

5. Nannie, who married Tom Center. They became the parents of a number of children and lived in Powell County, Kentucky. Nannie assisted in our home for some weeks on the occasion of the birth of my sister, Sarah Alice.

6. Rhoda, who married Scott Coldiron, a neighbor boy.
7. Rebecca, who married Walker Lowe. Rhoda and Rebecca were twins.
8. Dora, who married John Nickell and after his death married Dan Davidson.
9. Lou, who married Mort Pieratt. Lou is now deceased.
10. Callie, who married a son of John Nickell.
11. Celia, who married Sewell C. Rose and later married a second time but I do not have the name of the second husband.

Uncle Henry Sample and wife were very reputable people in the community where they lived. His health was poor from the time he came from Virginia to Kntucky until his death.

James Frank Sample, born May 22, 1832, married Ollie Goodwin, only daughter of Samuel Goodwin and wife, Elizabeth Goodwin, at Ezel, Kentucky. Both are now deceased. Their children, according to the incomplete record which I have, were:

1. Emma, who married George Pack, who was reared by John D. and Rebecca Sample Henry. Emma now resides in Indiana.
2. Frank.
3. Asa.
4. Celia, who married Nelson Strode Haggard.
5. Ollie Sample.
6. Winifred Sample.
7. Anne Sample.

As shown, my record as to this family is entirely incomplete. I knew Emma as a girl very well, and about two years ago renewed acquaintance with her and one of her sisters at one of the annual meetings of ex-students of Hazel Green Academy. I have also on one or more comparatively recent occasions met Anne, who as I recall married a Mr. Spencer. She resides at or near Winchester, Kentucky and is noted as an outstanding golf player. I also met her daughter a few years ago but do not recall her married name. One of the sons of Uncle Frank and wife was called Bill Sample and was an outstanding football player on the Carnegie Tech football team a number of years ago. After the deaths of their parents most of these children immigrated into Ohio and succeeded in life because of their several abilities and worthiness. Their father was an old bachelor at the time of his marriage to their mother, a very young woman. He had spent most of his life in the West, including the Territory of New Mexico, and when he returned and visited his kin at the near Ezel, Kentucky he was exceedingly well dressed, and carried visible evidences of success while living in the West. Under those circumstances he won the confidence and love of the young Ollie Goodwin, a daughter of Sam Goodwin, who in turn was the step-son of the elder Steve Gibson Sample, brother of Frank. Writing to me from Bridgeport, Texas, May 18, 1947, Julia Cecil John, born March 6, 1868, a daughter of Russell Cecil of Virginia, referring to Uncle Frank Sample and his wife Ollie, had this to say:

"It is very strange to say, but just before your letter came, I lay awake one night, quite a long time, as I often do, and suddenly I remembered Uncle Frank Sample, a large man, rather pompous looking, and considered quite wealthy, and his very young wife, who when asked why she married such an old man, replied, — 'It is better to be an old man's darling, than a young man's slave.' I have wondered why that should stick in my memory, but I was very young, and young people remember many odd things."

Uncle Frank acquired a farm not far from Ezel, Kentucky, but advanced age with its penalties had caught up with him and it is easy to understand that in the rearing of a large family whatever wealth he had acquired in the West pretty well vanished before his death and left the survivors of his family faced with the necessity of making their own way in the world.

Larkin J. Sample, born of James Sample and second wife Elizabeth Herndon Sample, June 30, 1840. He married, according to my information, a Miss Clark and they resided near Sword's Creek, Va., until their deaths. I have been twice to their former home there and in 1951 went with my brother, Denzil, and brother-in-law, W. W. Quicksall, and a Mr. Hale, postmaster at Sword's Creek, to their cemetery on a flat-topped hill overlooking the old home. A short distance from the home was the old everlflowing spring of cold water shedded and used as a milkhouse. Uncle Larkin was a tall, slender man, well-dressed and dignified in appearance, as were his wife, his son, Granville, and his daughter, Alice, and her sister, whose name I have forgotten, on the occasion of their visit with Kentucky relatives sometime in the late 1890's. They had driven through in a two-seated carriage drawn by two nice horses. Besides the children above named, they had a son, Lafayette Sample, who married Rachel Thompson, already mentioned by me in this article. A list of the heirs of Lafayette W. Sample as given by E. D. Sample, his son and administrator, under date of January 31, 1925, was as follows:

Rachel, age 64, Honaker, Virginia, wife; E. W. Sample, age 36, Cleveland, Ohio, son; E. D. Sample, age 35, Honaker, Virginia, son; H. L. Sample, age 30, Marengo, Ohio, son; L. J. Sample, age 26, Welch, W. Virginia, son; Nancy Sample, age 24, Honaker, Virginia, daughter; S. N. Sample, age 21, Honaker, Virginia, son; Irene Sample, age 10, Honaker, Virginia, granddaughter.

Under date of June 18, 1937 it was my privilege to meet Estill D. Sample and Luther J. Sample, at that time operating a service station at Honaker, Virginia. Nancy Sample, mentioned as one of the children of Lafayette, married R. L. Preas and it was in her home at Honaker, Virginia where I met her mother, Rachel Thompson Sample, about 1951, and it was one of the above named sons of Lafayette and Rachel who was sheriff of Russell County in 1951.

Elbert Sample, son of James Sample and his second wife, Elizabeth Herndon Sample, married Salina Clark and in the latter part of the 19th century moved from Virginia to Wolfe County, Kentucky. As I recall, they lived on Laurel Creek until late in the 1890's, when they moved to near Mt. Sterling, Kentucky and engaged in dairying and later purchased a home near Rothwell in Menifee County, Kentucky where they resided until their deaths. Aunt Salina travelled some selling household necessities by retail to customers. Uncle Elbert lived to an advanced age and in his later years suffered from a facial skin affection. He was in every sense of the word a gentleman and he and his wife did all in their power for their fine group of children, who were:

1. Willie Sample, who married Alice McCormick by whom he had one daughter. After the death of his first wife he married Lou Emma Wells and resided with her in Middletown, Ohio.

2. Henry Sample, who married a daughter of Joe Cobb and wife, the latter being a daughter of James Nickell, a minister in the Christian Church and a first cousin of my mother. Henry and wife resided for a number of years at Middletown, Ohio, later in Lexington, Kentucky, and now reside in Deland, Florida. It has been my privilege while visiting my sister, Sarah, to visit with Cousins

WOLFE COUNTY

Henry and wife at Deland on at least two different occasions.

3. Zeola, who after obtaining a good education, including one or more terms at Bowling Green Normal School, Bowling Green, Kentucky, married a Mr. Tabor of Rothwell, Kentucky, now deceased, and is the mother of five or six children. I should remember the number because Zeola and one daughter and son-in-law recently stopped for a few minutes to visit with me at my office in Edna, Texas, while they were on their way for a short vacation in Mexico City. Before that short visit I had not seen Zeola for more than fifty years. She made an enviable reputation as a student at Southern Normal School prior to my going there in January, 1905, as disclosed to me by Dr. H. H. Cherry and many others upon my being introduced to them and answering their inquiries that I was a close relative of hers. Zeola for many years has resided at Winchester, Kentucky.

4. Bertha, whose first husband was named Littleton and who after his death married Dr. Faulkner of Mt. Sterling, Kentucky. She and her husband have spent a portion of this past winter in Deland, Florida, where her brother, Henry, and my sister, Sarah, both reside.

5. Elizabeth, who married my cousin and most intimate companion of my boyhood days, Curtis O. Rose, now deceased. They were the parents of four fine children, Maurice, who died as a little boy; Joseph Powell Rose, a commissioned officer since World War II in the U. S. Army; Mary Elizabeth, married and living in the West, and Curtis O., Jr.

Celia L. Sample, daughter of James Sample and his second wife, Elizabeth Herndon Sample, born June 9, 1842, married Robert M. Cecil, born September 3, 1842.

Robert M. Cecil was a son of Samuel W. Cecil and his second wife, Nancy Correll Cecil, therefore a half brother of James M. Cecil and Louisa Cecil Sample, both hereinbefore referred to; so that there were two of the Cecil brothers residing in Tazewell County, Virginia, who married Sample sisters residing in Russell County, Virginia, and one Cecil sister who married a Sample, brother of James M. and Robert M. Cecil. Celia Sample Cecil and husband, Robert M. Cecil, came from Virginia to Kentucky at a later date than 1858, several years later, as I have always understood. They purchased a farm on Stillwater Creek in Wolfe County, Kentucky, and there reared a large family, most, if not all of whom had been born in Virginia. They were both fine Christian characters. Aunt Celia had a fine sense of humor and enjoyed telling and listening to humorous facts. I do not have in my files the dates of their deaths nor much record information that might be put into this brief article. I can only write from memory, not too much to be trusted in giving genealogical data.

According to my information and recollection they were the parents of the following children, to-wit:

Robert Mitchell Cecil and Celia Sample Cecil and their descendants.

Robert Mitchell Cecil, son of Sam Cecil, was born in Tazewell County, Virginia in 1841. He was united in marriage to Celia Sample while they lived in Virginia. They moved to Baptist Fork of Stillwater in Wolfe County, Kentucky when their second son, Sam, was about 12 years of age. They had the following children, Frank, Sam, Tom, John, Nanny, Lou, Ella, Molly and Maggie.

1. Frank Cecil married a Chaney. They had several children, all born in Menifee County where they settled and lived until Frank's death.

2. Russell Cecil was their oldest son.
2. Ethel.
2. Flossie was another daughter. There may have been others.

1. Sam married Lula Rose and to this union were born two sons, Charles Hogg and Roy Mitchell.

2. Charles Hogg Cecil was graduated from Hazel Green Academy and from the University of Ky. in engineering. He accepted a position with Bethelem Steel and worked himself up to a nice position, which he held for about 20 years. He resigned to become vice president of North Western Steel in Sterling, Ill., after he and his wife, Mary (Stager) Cecil, moved to Sterling after her mother's death. Mary Stager is the daughter of Mr. and Mrs. John Stager of Sterling, Ill. and a talented musician. They had two sons:

3. Robert, who is at this time (1956) a sophomore in high school.
3. Charles Hogg, Jr., a student in the eighth grade.

Charles resigned his position with North Western Steel to go into business for himself. He established the Cecil Fuel Oil Co. in Sterling in the winter of '55 and he died of a heart attack on Jan. 19, 1955, soon afterwards and was buried in Sterling, Ill.

2. Roy Mitchell Cecil, attended HGA and Sweeney Auto School in Kansas City, Mo. where he graduated. After which he returned to Hazel Green and was in the Garage business for about 15 years. Then he sold his business and took up farming. He married Berta Kelly Cecil, a Texan, while he was in Kansas City, Mo. and they had three children: Alene, Mary Jo and Charles Kelly.

3. Alene finished high school at HGA and attended Eastern State Teacher's College, Richmond, Ky. and also Fugazzue Business school in Lexington. She worked at Lexington Signal Depot, Lexington, all during World War II. Then she returned to college at Eastern

then taught school. She married Arthur Seesholtz, from Newark, Ohio, who is a graduate of Eastern. They taught together several years, then went to DeLand, Fla., in the summer of 1956, where they purchased a third interest in Florida Military School and he is the Dean of boys and basketball coach and she is the secretary of the school. Sold interest in school and moved to Orlando, 1957.

3. Mary Jo Cecil, second child of Roy and Berta Cecil died of diptheria at 19 months.

3. Charles Kelly Cecil, the only son of Roy and Berta Cecil, graduated from HGA, attended Centre College at Danville one year, enlisted in the Army. Then married Betty Jo Lowe, daughter of Mr. and Mrs. Shelby Lowe of Stanton, in 1955. He served two years in the U. S. Army. They have one child, Barbara Ann, born July 17, 1956. Charles hopes to finish his college training when he is discharged from the Army.

1. Tom married twice. He married sisters. He had children by only the first one. After her death he married A. Peck the first time and Fannie Peck the second time.

2. Courtney married in Fayette County where he lives with several children.

2. Ida married John Wood and they live in Danville, Ky., where her husband is a building contractor.

3. They have three sons, Harold, Cecil and another boy, all of whom are married and live in Danville.

2. Ethel married a Peck. They have two or three children. They live in Ohio some place.

2. Eunice married Chester Evans.

2. Ora is married and lives away some place.

2. Albert and Russell, the youngest sons, both married in Lexington, Ky., and make their homes there.

1. John married Clara Brown and they had two sons and four daughters before he died. She is now dead, also.

2. Estill, the oldest son, died with typhoid fever when 16 years of age. His father died soon afterwards with the same disease.

2. Bertha married Mort Campbell. They had one son and one daughter.

3. Alton was a pilot in the U. S. Air Corps during World War II. He lost his life while on a mission over the Adriatic Sea. He was 19 years of age at the time.

3. Reva married James Cochran. They live in Lebanon, Ohio and have two children. Terri, age 3, and Stevie, age about one year.

2. Arthur married Anna DeHart. They make their home in Lebanon, Ohio where he is oil distributor for Sohio. They have two children.

3. Phyllis is the only daughter of Arthur and Anna Cecil. She is a graduate of Ohio State University and teaches at Columbus, Ohio. She married Junior Elbon, who has his O. S. and M. A. degrees from Columbus University. They have no children.

3. Arthur, Jr. (Buddy) is a youth in his teens. He is in high school.

2. Eulah married Oscar Green Kelly. She was graduated from Lees Junior College, Jackson, Ky., and attended some college in Ohio. She teaches in the grades in Lebanon, Ohio, and has been doing so for several years. Her husband, O. G. Kelly, is owner of the "Ideal Barbershop" on Broadway in Middletown, Ohio. They have two sons.

3. Robert Cecil Kelly is a senior in high school at Lebanon, Ohio. He is very active in the Boy Scouts. He is Junior Assistant Scout Master for troop 31, Lebanon. He is also chief of the "Order of Arrows". He attended the Scout Jamboree in California in 1953.

3. Gary Lee Kelly is the younger son of O. G. and Eulah Kelly. He is a student in high school in Lebanon, Ohio. He is a talented artist and has won recognition on some of his school drawings. He is also active in the Scouts.

2. Fern Cecil married Ford McClain. They have no children. Fern was graduated from Lees College. Her husband works at Armco Steel in Middletown, Ohio and they make their home in Lebanon, Ohio.

2. Virgil married Thomas Rooks. They live in Ohio and have five children.

1. Lou married a Neff. They had one child, who died in his early years. They made their home at Maytown, Ky., and both died there.

1. Nannie married John Wallace and they made their home in and around Lexington. They had eight children. Will, Frank, Brach, Elmer, Robert, Eunice, Mat and Verta.

2. Will married a Lovelace. They had several children.

2. Frank, second son of Nannie Cecil and John Wallace, married Clara Blankenship. He is now deceased. They had some children.

2. Brack married a Lykins. They never lived in Wolfe County.

2. Elmer married in Lexington where they have their home. He also married a Lykins, a sister to Brack's wife.

2. Robert married in Lexington.

2. Eunice married in Lexington.

2. Mattie married a Sams.

2. Verta married a Bridges.

1. Ella Cecil married Hiram Long. They moved away to Clark County where they both died.

2. Sam, now dead. He married away.

2. Lillie Bell married a Bailey and they live in Winchester. Have several children.

2. Kate married a Jewell and they live in Winchester and have several children.

2. Cecil is unmarried. He made the Army his career and is now retired.

2. Ernie is married and lives in Middletown, Ohio. He has two sons.

2. Ova made an artist and paints all the time. He is married and they live in Florida.

2. Celia married a Laycock. They live in Cincinnati, Ohio. They have one son.

2. Eula died in her early twenties. She worked in a bank prior to her illness.

1. Molly married Joe Brown. They had eight children: Ethel, Fronis, and twins, Roy Martin and Troy Mitchell, Nora, Mattie, Arlie and Dorsey.

2. Ethel married Garrett Childers. They have one son.

3. Gerald Keith, who is in the U. S. Navy with his base in California. He was graduated from Wolfe County High School prior to his entrance into the Navy. Garrett, his father is Conservation officer for wildlife in Wolfe County and has been for several years. They live at Zachariah, Ky.

2. Fronia, married Milan Latham. They live in Cincinnati, Ohio and have three children: Shirley, 18; Kenneth, 17; and Barbara Lee, 16 years old.

2. Roy Martin, one of the twins, married Robena Patrick. They have four children.

3. Arnold, 25, is married to a Miss DeHart. They live in Middletown, Ohio and have one daughter.

3. Sandra Jo is 19 and works in Indiana.

3. Darwin is in high school.

3. Linda is about 8 years old and in school.

2. Troy Mitchell, the other twin, married Betty Mann. He is now deceased. They had one son.

3. Troy Brown, Jr. He married a German girl while stationed in Germany with the Army of occupation. They have a small son. Troy is studying in an Art school in Cincinnati, Ohio where they live.

2. Nora Bailey married Edgar Bailey. They live in Franklin, Ohio and have two daughters.

3. Faye, 17, in high school.

3. Mary Ann, 9, in school. Mary Ann has an unusual singing voice. People are already predicting that she will go far with her voice.

2. Mattie married Homer Sorrell. They live in Middletown, Ohio. They have five children.

3. Wanda, who married Arthur Hounshell.

4. Becky Jo, a baby.

3. Lavonne, married Richard Henderson.

3. Patricia is 17 and at home and in school.
3. Johnnie Joe is in first year of high school.
3. Dale is in grade school.
2. Arlie married Vergie Johnson. They have three children.
3. Joan married Donald Gross.
3. Harold Joseph and Robert Daniel are twins. They are teenagers and in high school.
2. Dorsey was the youngest child of Joe and Molly Brown, (both of whom are now deceased). Dorsey married Izola Fandlin and they live in St. Petersburg, Fla.
3. Dorsey Milburn, Jr., is their only child.
1. Maggie Cecil married Otis Linkous and they had ten children. They moved to Ohio. Carl, Grace married Ed Russell, Bessie married Clayton Stamper and they have two children, Edna married a Spink, Ova married in Ohio, Troy married a Stamper and they live at Maytown, Ky., Gladys, Mabel, Ora (dead), Albert. All of their children married away from Wolfe County save the first two daughters and Troy.

John M. Cecil and Clara Brown Cecil had six children.

1. Estill, who died of typhoid fever at sixteen.

I was better acquainted with Sam Cecil in the later years of his life than with any of his brothers or sisters. He was for many years in the mercantile business with his father-in-law, Silas Rose, at Stillwater Bridge in Wolfe County and they later moved to Hazel Green where he was active in business for several years and where he resided at the time of his death. He had a great deal of information as to the family histories, the Sample and Cecil families of Virginia and Kentucky and enjoyed joking with his friends and associates.

I am not certain that I remember Frank Cecil above named or any of his family. I knew all the other children of Aunt Celia and Uncle Bob and regarded them all as well raised and excellent descendants of worthy parents.

Nancy Sample, daughter of James Sample and his second wife, Elizabeth, was born at the old James Sample home in Russell County, Virginia, married Shade Ratliff and they made their home in West Virginia not far from the Virginia State line.

I recall that during the 1890's she and one or possibly two daughters visited in the home of my parents in Wolfe County, Kentucky. I have no data concerning their family after that time, but remember that they were well-dressed, possessed of fine manners and we were happy to have them visit us in our home.

Sofia Elizabeth Sample, daughter of James Sample and second wife, Elizabeth Herndon Sample, born March 16, 1844, married Isaiah Drake Hurt. They resided and reared a large family at Gardner, Virginia. There were 13 children of this union, three of whom died at birth. Isaiah Drake Hurt died at the age of 80 years and his wife at the age of 82 years. Two of the sons whom I have met are Charles, who until recently was in the mercantile business at Honaker, Virginia, and now resides in Lakeland, Florida; and Elbert Sevier Hurt, whose wife was a Miss Cora Greer, and who now lives with his wife at Daytona Beach, Florida. Elbert S. Hurt was born December 9, 1881 and Charles is older. Elbert and wife reared four children. One of them, a daughter, is the wife of John Kimble, who has a fine position with the Texas Eastman Corporation at Longview, Texas. The youngest daughter of Elbert and wife, Cora, is married and her husband is in business at Daytona Beach, Florida. I am not presently advised as to the residences of the other two children of Elbert and wife, both adults. Elbert reared his family at Kingsport, Tennessee, where he was district sales manager for many years for Fuller Brush Company. He still owns his modern home there, but upon retiring last year moved with his wife to his present southern home at Daytona Beach, Florida.

Robert Hurt was the oldest child of Sofia Elizabeth Hurt and husband and died about a year ago at the age of 85 years.

The youngest son of Sofia Elizabeth Hurt and husband, for 39 years a railroad conductor out of Cincinnati, Ohio, has retired and he and his wife live in St. Petersburg, Florida.

Both Charles Hurt and Elbert Hurt are men of fine personal habits and appearance and were good businessmen. The wife of Elbert and her youngest daughter, the only other two of the Hurt family whom I have met, are highly cultured and possessed of fine personalities. Elbert visited me in my home at Edna, Texas, a few years ago on the occasion of a meeting in Houston, Texas, of executives and salesmen of Fuller Brush Company.

Thus concludes a hurriedly prepared sketch of the Samples of Morgan and Wolfe Counties, Kentucky, and of some of their Sample relatives living or who have lived elsewhere.

In conclusion I will say that prior to the beginning of the present century the name was generally spelled "S-a-m-p-l-e-s", but in the early years of this century I began dropping the last "s" from the former spelling of the name and have continued that practice, correctly or incorrectly, to the present time, and so far as I know all others of the family are likewise leaving off the last letter from the former spelling of the name.

I will add this further statement that I have never known of one of our name serving time in a penal institution.

With due apologies to the Woman's Club of Wolfe County, Kentucky, for whom this history was written, because of any unintentional errors included in the article, this ends several days work which to me has been pleasant.

—Steve Gibson Sample.

EARLY AND MODERN HISTORY

CHAMBERS
(Information by Mrs. Kate Rose)

Elisha Chambers was a Primitive Baptist preacher and the father of Elijah Chambers. Elijah married a Morrow and was the father of five sons and three daughters.
3. Gidian, who married a daughter of Bob Rose.
3. William married a daughter of Bob Rose, also.
3. Jack married Mary Bowman.
3. Elisha married Elizabeth Hurst.
3. Joseph married Polly Rose, daughter of Powell Rose.
4. Boone, now buried on Kash's Knob in Montgomery County.
3. Polly married John Rose, then after he died, Clabe Gabbard.
4. America, the daughter of the first union.
4. Several children by the second union.
3. Lydia married a Hampton. No children.
3. Sarah, third daughter of Elijah Chambers, married Alex Strong, brother of Captain Bill Strong. They reared a large family.

THE CHILDER'S FAMILY
(Compiled by Mrs. W. E. Bach, Lexington, Ky., from data in her files and data furnished by Z. N. Childers, Bradenton, Florida.)

Matt Childers married Nancy Lovelace — they are buried over in Flat Woods. Matt Childers was the son of William Childers, and a Miss Breeding.

Children of Matt Childers and his wife, Nancy Lovelace:
Gillie Ann; Marion who married a Sites; Jerry; Jane; Elizably married Billy Hurst; Logan married Elizabeth Haddix; Hoy married Adline Taulbee; Savannah; Hardin married 1st a Miss Bach, 2nd: a Miss McIntosh; Martha married Billie Lawson; Jonathan married Fannie Miller. Hoy Childers who married Adeline Taulbee had the following children:

1. Richard married a Buchannan; Nannie married Tom Anderson-Pearl; Blaine M. Maud Carson, Lexie, Ky.; Zola Alice M. Howard Vest; Rutha M. a Henry; Taylor; Mickell; Mag; Dell.

William Logan Childers, son of Matt Childers and wife, Nancy Lovelace; had the following children:
1. Harlan, B. 1883 Married Ealah Little — daughter of Harry and Evaline Little — Home — Charleston, W. Va. One daughter Evolun Clark.
2. Iola B. 1885 M. Jim Lindon — Children: Elmer Lindon (all deceased).
3. Howard Childers, B. 1886 married Mary Bell Arnett (Dau. of Phillip Arnett) Ch: Jewell Waters; Opal Parsons.
4. John B. 1890 married Lucy Gillispie (dau. of Columbus and

Belle Nickell Gillispie — Ch: Ova, Maurine. After Lucy's death he married Grace Nickell (dau. of Bruce and Linda Wilson Nickell — Ch: Dorthy Ponjetti; Alice Rogers. John's home in Winchester, Ky.

5. Zephaniah B. 1893 M. Ethel Oldfield, B. 1892 (Dau. of Daniel Boone and Sara (Wilson) Oldfield. Ch: Alvin R. Childers M. Marie Haney, Madge M. Bruce Walters; L. T. Childers, Bradenton, Fla.

6. David Lee B. 1897 M. Grace Watson: Ch. Jack; James Conrod, Youngstown, Ohio.

7. Wm. E. B. 1902 D. 1955 — M. Eliza Schaeffer: Ch. Garrett; Jean.

William Logan Childers, born in 1858, died 1942. Married Elizabeth Haddix, born 1860, died 1922.

Children:

1. Harlan, born 1883, married Calah Little, daughter of Harry and Evaline Little. Home in Charleston, W. Va.

C. Evolyn Clark.

2. Iola, born in 1885. Married Jim Lindon.

C. Elmer Lindon (all deceased).

3. Howard, born in 1886. Married Mary Bell Arnett, daughter of Phillip Arnett.

C. Jewell Waters and Opal Parsons.

4. John, born in 1890. Married Lucy Gillispie, daughter of Columbus and Belle Nickell Gillispie.

C. Ova, Maurine, after Lucy's death he married Grace Nickell, daughter of Bruce and Linda Wilson Nickell.

C. Dorthy Ponyetti, Alice Rogers.

John's home in Winchester, Ky.

5. Zephaneah, born in 1893, married Ethel Oldfield, born in 1892. Daughter of Daniel Boone and Sara Wilson Oldfield.

C. Alvin R. Childers, married Marie Haney. Madge married Bruce Walters. L. T. Childers, Bradenton, Fla.

6. David Lee, born in 1897, married Grace Watson.

C. Jack, James Conrod, Youngstown, Ohio.

7. Wm. E., born in 1902, died 1955. Married Eliza Schaeffer.

C. Garrett and Jean.

COLLIER

(by Mrs. Taylor Booth)

John Collier left Wise, Virginia when a young man. He settled in Wolfe County and married Louisa Shoemaker. They reared 10 children, of whom the only survivor is Mrs. Mary Whisman, R. 1, Beattyville.

Collier was a farmer and Baptist preacher. He blazed trails over the wilderness that is now Wolfe County, in an effort to teach people the Christian faith. He is still remembered for the extreme stand he took against whiskey, and he came to be known as "the whiskey-fighting Baptist."

Some of the oldest people in Wolfe County may still remember the "June Tide", a deluge the like of which has not been seen before or since. It came to be referred to as the "flood that John Collier prayed down" because it had swept away so many moonshine stills as it rampaged across fields and bottoms. He died at the age of 56.

Wolfe Countians who are grandchildren of John Collier include: Mrs. Hazel Booth, Mrs. Roxie Netherly, Austin Collier, Lester Collier, Wilson Alexander, Mrs. Logan Booth, Mrs. Callie Bryant, Mrs. Delphia McQuinn, Jesse Collier and Mrs. Lawrence Bailey.

CREECH-CENTER
(Contributed by Mrs. Ransaline Creech Center)

Eliga Creech and Nancy Coldiron were married about 1859 in Wise County, West Virginia. To this union were born 12 children. The first two children died at birth, then Rausaline was born on August 25, 1865; who later married G. M. Center.

Polly, who married D. B. Center.

Don Creech and Alph Creech.

Susan, who married George Trent.

Evaline, who married George Long.

Lucy, who married Tilden Pelfrey first, then Jess Adams.

Mag, who married Mat Childers.

Frank (now deceased).

Eliza, who married Curt Grose. This was the family of the late Eliga and Nancy Creech.

Rausaline Creech, daughter of Mr. and Mrs. Eliga Creech, was married to Dr. G. M. Center, better known as "Old Doctor Center", in 1881. To this union were born 12 children, eight of whom were reared to adult-hood and were married and had families of their own.

Willie Center died at eight months.

Cora Center died at five months.

Clayton Center died at 64 in August 1949, having reared a large family of his own.

Porter Center died in 1952 at the age of 63.

Ella, who married J. B. Tutt of Lexington.

Dan Center of Berea, who is married and has a family.

Viola married S. E. Shackelford of Middletown, Ohio.
Eliza died at the age of six.
Mae, who married B. W. Rayner of Dayton.
Dorsey died at one year of age.
Bertha married M. R. Lovelace of Campton.
Carma married Carl Buchholzer of Dayton.
Clayton Center married Zerilda Sewell and had four children, later married again and had several children by his second wife.
Children of first wife were: Daisy, who married Willie Taylor; Dorsey Center, Hobart Center, and Sewell Center, the latter is deceased.
Porter Center married Judy Cox and to them were born six children.
Mildred, who married Randal Leach, they have two children.
Marvin (Pete) married Thelma Jacobs and they have one son, Tommy.
Herbert, who married Fern Day and they have two children.
Ruth, who married Bill Belden and they have two children.
Mattie, who married Jack Nester and they have three daughters.
Virginia, who married Ricky Kotter. They had one son.

Ella Center Tutt Family

Ella Center was married to J. B. Tutt and they have five sons.
Pryce, who married Kathleen McLin and they have one son, Lynn Alan.
Bert, who married Ruth Clark and they have one daughter, Faith Carol.
Harold, who married Marceilla Tyra and they have a daughter, Judy.
Marion, who married Oleta Risner and they have a daughter.
Bobby, who married Geneva Mulcahy and they have a son.

Dan Center Family

Dan Center married Ruth Tutt and they had five children. Bernice, who married D. B. Robinson and they have two sons.
Vivian, who married and had two sons.
Mabel, who married and had two sons.
D. H., Jr., who married and had one son and one daughter.
Luther Willis, single and in Service in Korea.

Viola Center Shackelford

Viola was married to Sam Shackelford and had a son, Lawrence E. Shackelford, who married Grace Whitt and they had a son and daughter.
Viola also has a daughter, Virginia, who married Richard Hogan, and they have a son.

Mae Center

Mae Center married B. W. Rayner and they have two daughters:

Miki, who married Herman Shapirro and they have an adopted daughter. Marceille, who married Harry Bloomer and they have a daughter.

Bertha Lovelace Center

Bertha Center married Mountie R. Lovelace and they have a son, Ralph Lee, who married Allene Hollon and to this union was born a son. Bertha and Mountie also have a daughter, Viola Mae, who married Everett E. Holt and they have a daughter.

Carma Center

Carma Center married Carl Buchholzer and they have a daughter, Joan, who married.

(Contributed by Miss Anna Bell Combs)

Solomon Cox was born in Grayson County, Virginia, Dec. 24, 1795. He came to Kentucky at the age of 17 years and settled in Bath County where at an early age he was married to Ann Sexton. This marriage was blessed with four children before his wife died in 1821. Two years later Bro. Cox married Louisa Trimble. In July 1832, he joined the Christian Church under the teachings of "Raccoon" John Smith, and as warm friends, near neighbors and colaborers, they were together for several years.

A man of remarkable energy and strict integrity, he was employed by the authorities in 1834 to take charge of and construct a section of the state road, leading east for 50 miles out of Mt. Sterling; through what was then stretches of mountain woods. The labor was quickly and faithfully performed. From that date until many years later he was engaged in driving stock to the southern markets. In 1847 he moved from Bath County and settled in Morgan County near Hazel Green. About 1850 he was elected as elder in the Congregation of the Hazel Green Church, and until his death through a period of 31 years, faithfully discharged the duties of that high and noble office.

As a citizen in the prime of life, during the days when civilization was struggling for existance in the wilderness of Kentucky, as a terror to lawlessness, he did more to civilize in his day the communities of Bath, Montgomery, and Morgan counties than any other man living during this period.

Mr. Cox was survived by his wife, Mrs. Louisa Trimble Cox. He was the father of Ellen Pieratt, who was the father of Henry F. Pieratt's mother.

Mr. Cox and his second wife, Louisa Trimble Cox, were the parents of 11 children.

Dave Hogg, who was county court clerk of Wolfe County four terms, was married four times. It is reported that he wrote his own marriage licenses every time. One of his wives was Sallie Rose, and his last wife was Matilda Murphy. David Hogg went to Oklahoma in 1892. At the same time, Isaac Elkins and Dr. Jim Tutt went, too. The latter two came back later to Wolfe County.

Rev. J. T. Pieratt used to preach around Campton. He preached at the Napier School house above Campton. That was in the 1890's as my mother died in 1893.

The same block where the bank now stands was burned in 1887, Miss Anna Bell Comb's father owned the hotel then which was in the middle of the block and on the corner where her father's brick store was located, was where a Mr. Tutt lived.

THE COX FAMILY OF WOLFE COUNTY, KY.
(by Mrs. W. E. Bach)

John Cox, born in 1785, with his wife, Judith Sexton, of French Ancestry, came from Virginia, to Eastern Kentucky, about 1800. He is the first one to own a water mill in Morgan County, (now Wolfe), and has been known since as "The Cox's Mill" settlement. They had the following children:

James Cox, who married Anna Hanks.

William Cox, who married Cynthia Reid.

Cynthia Cox, who married Emmanuel Price Lewis.

Darinda Cox, who married James Stamper.

Dr. Benjamin Franklin Cox, who married 1st Zarilda Allington and 2nd Malinda McCormick.

Elizabeth Cox, who married Thomas Pieratt.

Ann Cox, who married Arch Day.

So this would make the descendants of the Hanks, Reid, Lewis, Stamper, Allington (Ellington) and Pieratts and Days related to this Cox family.

John Cox was buried on his Trundle Bed, as per his request, and my mother (Zarilda Wills Day) remembered being at his funeral and remembering him as asleep in his bed. He and his wife, Judith Sexton Cox are both buried at the "Cox's Mill Graveyard" three miles below Hazel Green. His grave is covered with a large stone as they use to do. She is buried by his side.

Their children are given above and they had many descendants in this county. I cannot give all of the children at this time but will follow with the children of James Cox, who married Anna Hanks, and who are my own ancestors:

James Cox married Anna Hanks and had the following children:
1. Judah (or Judith), who married Jordan Wills.
2. Andrew Jackson Cox married Matilda Stamper first and Rebecca Hall second.
3. Joshua Cox married.
4. Fielding Cox married Mattie Catron.
5. John Cox married Jane Catron.
6. Lydia Cox married McKinley Brown.
7. Nancy Cox married Allie Landrum.

The first John Cox who married Judith Sexton and came from Virginia, had two brothers who also came to Kentucky. Solomon Cox who married 1st. Ann Sexton and 2nd Louisa Trimble: Solomon Cox was born in 1795 and died in 1881. His children were: Lou Cox who married Allen T. Day; Ellen Cox who married Rev. Jim Tom Pieratt; Wes. W. Cox, married Elizabeth Nickell; Henry Cox. Another brother, James Robertson Cox, came to Kentucky from Va., and went on to Kansas or Missouri.

John Cox — the first to come to Kentucky, was given two Slaves by his father, before leaving Virginia. Their names were London and Barney Cox. I have heard my mother (Zarilda Wills Day) tell of knowing both of them and how they helped at her great-grandfather's mill which was "The Cox's Mill". During the War Between the States — she was left at Home as the oldest child as her father, Jordan Wills, served in the Confederate Army with General John Hunt Morgan, and she being the oldest child was often sent to mill to get her corn ground in to meal. She would always be helped on and off her horse by one of these Slaves. I have a copy of a wonderful will which "London Cox" made before his death.

James Cox and four of his sons served in the Confederate Army during the Civil War.

William Cox (known as Uncle Billy) married Cynthia Reid of Morgan County. They were the parents of the following: 1. Milt Cox, married Jane Perry; 2. George Cox, married Mattie Hanks (known as Aunt Matt); 3. John Jeff Cox married Jennie Redmond; 4. Tom Cox married Phoebe Jane Nickell; 5. Elizabeth Cox married Jim Rose (she was his second wife); 6. Mary (Mollie) married Tom Rose; 7. Judah Cox married John Ward (Parents of Lou Ward Johnson), also Henry C. Ward; 8. Jane Cox married Jim Wheatley; 9. Emily Cox married Richard Wells.

Dr. Benjamin Franklin Cox married Malinda McCormick and had the following children: 1. Morrison Cox; 2. New Cox.

Darinda Cox married James C. Stamper and had the following children: 1. Tom Stamper married Elizabeth Clark; 2. Rosslyn

Stamper never married; 3. Sarah Stamper married Pete Wills; 4. L. G. Stamper married Lou Lawson; 5. George Stamper married Mary Asberry.

Elizabeth Cox married Thomas Pieratt and had the following children: 1. Elizabeth Pieratt married George Lockard; 2. Columbus Pieratt married Gillie Nickell; 3. Darrinda Pieratt married Isaac Rose.

Cynthia Cox married Emanuel Price Lewis: children: 1. John Lewis. (There may have been more children, I do not know.)

Ann Cox married Archibald Day. Children: 1. Judge B. F. Day married 1st, Belle Greenwade, 2nd, Sweet Cassidy; William T. Day married Maggie Hawsley or (Spawlsey); John C. Morgan Day married Sarah E. Collingsworth; Sarilda Ann Day married Boone Stamper; Perlina Day married H. C. Lacy; James C. B. Day married Lily Hovermale; Judah Day married James H. Bowlin; Jefferson Day; Sarah C. Day married someone; Mary A. Day married J. Brown; Robert Allen Day married Fanny Patrick.

The names I have underscored are all the children of John Cox and Judith Sexton.

I would like to add that there are many by the name of Cox in both Morgan and Wolfe County, Kentucky, and after many years of research — I am unable to find the connection between two or three distinct families. For instance — there were two "John Coxes" who came early to Morgan County, Ky., and in the article written up a few years ago they have so many similar names that it makes me believe they are of the same family back a few generations. I have much data in my files on the Cox families and their connections but time does not allow me to write more about them now. I will be glad to contact anyone who is interested in this family.

(Mrs. William Everett Bach, 165 Bell Court West, Lexington, Ky.)

THE LIFE OF DR. BRAXTON D. COX FROM BIRTH UP TO HIS DEATH IN CAMPTON, FEB. 7, 1917
(by Mrs. Katherine Riggs)

Dr. Braxton D. Cox was born on March 15, 1844 in Owsley County, Kentucky. His parents came from old Virginia in a covered wagon not long before Braxton's birth. He was the son of Dr. Braxton Jason Cox and Lydia Cox. In 1861, when they were beating drums calling volunteers for the Civil War, Braxton D. Cox, 17 years of age, walked up and volunteered in Company G, 8th Regiment of the Kentucky Infantry. He went through many hard battles on Lookout Mountain, at Chicamauga and other points. On the 20th of September, 1863, in the evening of the last day of the fight at

Chicamauga, Braxton was wounded, his collar bone was broken and his right ankle dislocated. Two days after the others in the 8th regiment reached their quarters or camp in Chattanooga, Cox was brought to camp unable to travel or to be on duty for several months. On August 17, 1865, he received an honorable discharge from the Service.

He came to Wolfe County, Kentucky, 16 miles from what is now Campton, to what is now called Big Andy. He bought a farm of 300 acres, all in woodland. He cut timber, rived boards, and built himself a log house on this farm, just a one room cabin, 18x18 feet, with a stone chimney dobbed with clay mud and a wood fire place.

In the year 1869, he was united in marriage to Miss Elizabeth Spencer of Lee County, Kentucky, from the place which is now called St. Helens. She was the daughter of Goolie and Phoebe Ann Spencer. They started their married life on the farm in the little log cabin. Elizabeth proved a real good wife and helpmate. They worked, prospered and finally built a nice big farm house, sealed and weatherboarded it, and painted it white. To this union were born nine children.

In 1886, Mr. Cox went to Louisville and attended medical college until he received his doctor's diploma. His wife and children worked on the farm. They raised corn, oats, hay, potatoes, and all kinds of garden produce, as well as cattle, horses, sheep, chickens, and had lots of things to sell.

When he went to Louisville they were pulling street cars with mules. While he was still there in College they got electricity. He saw the first electric street car start. He said everyone was thrilled to see something like that running without some animal pulling it.

He came home with his medical diploma and began practicing medicine in 1889. Following his return from Louisville, two more sons were born in the family. They reared ten of their children to adulthood, and all had married but the two younger sons when they left the farm and moved to Campton in 1904.

All who knew him said he was one among the best citizens and doctors that Wolfe County ever had. On Feb. 7, 1917, Dr. Cox died at his home in Campton; leaving to mourn his wife, Elizabeth Spencer Cox; four daughters, Mrs. Loucretia Holmes of Congress, Ohio; Mrs. Rose Profitt, Slade; Mrs. Florence Profitt, and Mrs. Katherine Reynolds, both of Campton; five sons, Sherman, Brack, Dr. John L., Samp, and Stewart Cox; and 44 grandchildren. At this date, (Dec. 1954) all of his children have passed away except Mrs. Rose Profitt, Mrs. Katherine Reynolds Riggs, and Sampson D. Cox. He was the grandfather of Mr. W. H. Reynolds of Jackson, Ky. and Mr. James

B. Reynolds and Mr. J. T. Reynolds, both of Lexington.

(Given by Katherine Riggs of Campton, who has all those old dates given by her father. She also has his discharge papers from the Army and the old deed to the farm he bought in 1865.)

THE CRUEY FAMILY
(by Mrs. Salley Cruey Miley)

My grandparents and parents moved from Virginia to Kentucky when I was a little girl a little more than three years of age. The caravan consisted of two old fashioned covered wagons drawn by four horses. I still remember each horse's name. When we reached the Big Sandy River, that was a sight for me to see as I had never seen a big river before. The folks climbed out of the wagon (fourteen in all). The women stayed on the bank, as we had to cross by ferry. I watched every movement that was made.

They ferried one team across at a time. Unhitched from the wagon, a man would stand at the head of each horse holding them by the bridle, in order to keep them calm. The teams were landed safely, rehitched and ready for the women and children to be ferried over at last. I enjoyed that very much.

We landed in a little town called Hazel Green. My father bought a farm a mile out. One day a farm hand gave me a nickel. The first money I had ever owned in my life. I had heard the older folks talking about putting their money in the bank and letting it grow. So, I got a hoe and planted my nickel in a little clay bank, in front of our home.

I could visualize in my childish mind, a tree, large and beautiful, and hanging full of shining nickels instead of leaves.

And it was going to be my business to see that no one pulled any nickels off the tree. I kept watch for sometime, but nothing happened. Finally when I realized my mistake, I got a hoe and tried to find my nickel. But no luck.

I am now an octogenarian, and my nickel is still in the old clay bank.

Sallie Cruey Miley, 608 N. Washington St., Ardmore, Okla.

EARLY AND MODERN HISTORY

CONGLETON'S

(Submitted by Mrs. Lee Congleton)

Lexington, Kentucky, Sept. 13, 1924

Mr. Joe Congleton
Barbourville, Ky.
Dear Joe:

I have your letter 3rd inst. inquiring about the data I have been securing with a view to learning the origin of our family, or rather the place of their original settlement in this country and the movements or distribution of the descendants thereafter as far as possible; also the effort to connect up the different branches by tracing them back to their source. In this effort, which has been done mostly by correspondence with relatives, securing records through genealogists and the examination of historical records in the libraries, I have accumulated a file of papers which pretty well fill one of these paper file boxes used for filing letters, and which file I would be pleased to have you or any of your family examine at any time. In brief, the facts which I have gathered are as follows:

About the year 1730 William Congleton was granted a patent covering a plantation on the Pamlico river in Beaufort county, North Carolina, by the English Government. This plantation lies about two miles from the present town of Washington, N. C. and is owned by direct descendants of William Congleton who possess the original land grant or patent. (I have not yet secured the exact date of this paper but hope to do so soon.) The next record is the purchase by William Congleton in September 1731 of 520 acres, apparently adjoining the first grant, from Edward Ward. Other land deeds follow in the record. Then in July 1755 the will of William Congleton is recorded, in which he bequeaths three plantations and other property to his children, James, William, John, Henry, David Abraham and Elizabeth and Sarah, his wife. Then follows a large number of deeds, wills and other records of the doings of the many members of the family down almost to the present time.

The son William (let us say William II), who was doubtless born about 1740, and who was about fifteen years old at the time of the death of his father, has grown up, married and lives near his relatives; has three sons, John, born in 1767; James, born April 27, 1769, and William III, born in 1771; and four daughters, Agnes, Jean, Mary and Elizabeth. His wife was named Jean. This William II, having heard of the glowing reports of the lands that were being settled in central Kentucky by hundreds of his neighbors and friends, about the year 1790 or perhaps several years earlier, decides to take his young family and cast his fortune in that land. The route taken in those days by the pioneers who settled Kentucky was by wagons through the Old Wilderness Trail into central Kentucky. We have no record of this trip, but we have no doubt this common route was followed by our ancestors. The final place of settlement was a farm on Boone Creek in the eastern part of Bourbon county and about three miles from the little town of Little Rock, and perhaps a little farther north than North Middletown.

The first record of date that we have of the family in Bourbon County is the birth of a daughter to Polly, wife of James Congleton, on February 10, 1791. John has a son, William W., who was born in 1788, but we don't know whether his birth was before the family left North Carolina or after they came to Kentucky. Also two daughters, Elizabeth and Mary. The next record of data is the marriage of William III to Martha Ellison of Bourbon County on August 24, 1792.

A daughter, Fanny, was born in 1794; Jenny, 1795; and Polly, 1798. We know Fanny as the wife of Joseph Swearengin of Louisville in later years.

John, the oldest son, died in 1796 and his will and the sales of property and settlement of his estate is all of record in Bourbon County. After his death a son was born to his widow named John. This young son was the progenitor of a family of our name at Terre Haute, Indiana. William W., the oldest son of John, lived all his life on the old farm in Bourbon County and died there in 1831 at the age of 43 years. He married Mary Rule in 1807 and had four sons and four daughters: John Newton, William Henry, Columbus and Franklin, America, wife of Milton G. Caldwell, Margaret (Champ), Elizabeth (Colliver) and another who died a young girl.

John Newton Congleton, the oldest son of William W., born 1808 and died 1868, was a farmer and leading citizen of Montgomery County and died on his farm about one mile from Mt. Sterling on Lexington Pike. His tombstone is in the Mt. Sterling Cemetery and bears this inscription on his tombstone:

"He lived in deeds, not in years; in thoughts, not breaths; in feelings, not in figures on a dial. He most lives who thinks most, feels noblest, acts best and dying leaves noble deeds of love and kindness, ever to glitter the brightest jewels in fond memories."

William Henry, Columbus and Franklin went to Nicholas County where the first two lived on their farms, Columbus moving to Illinois where many of his descendants live, some have gone farther West, many of whom I have had correspondence with. A daughter of William Henry married Dr. Brown of Winchester, Ky., and Dr. Isaac Brown is the only descendant. Franklin Congleton was for many years a banker of Carlisle. His daughter married Horace Taylor of that city and Frank Congleton is the only descendant. Many children of the three daughters live in Nicholas County. I visited Mrs. Maggie Wilson, daughter of America Congleton Caldwell, in Nicholas County at the old home of Milton G. Caldwell, she being the first one of that branch of the family I had ever seen.

You will notice that I traced the descendants of the oldest son, John. I will tell you about the next son, James, who lived on his farm somewhere near the father, brothers and sisters. About the time of the great religious revival that spread over Kentucky with the preaching of the Campbells and Barton W. Stone (a meeting held by Stone in 1801 at Cane Ridge, Bourbon County, was attended by 20,000 people) there followed a new sect known as the Shakers, with able preachers and a new plea, founding colonies in the state, as you know. One of these was Shakertown near High Bridge, and our kinsman, James Congleton, and his family, his wife, Polly, was born in Iredel County, N. C. in 1766; sons, John, born in 1792; James, born in 1794; Jenny, born in 1791; Peggy, born in 1795; Polly, born in 1800; Cyrene, born in 1801; and Lucinda in 1806, all sold all they had and joined this Mercer County Colony. The Shakers were a wonderful people in culture and art and architecture as shown by their buildings there now as well as their thrift and industry marking their works. (Perhaps you have heard your Uncle Thomas Congleton tell of a visit he made to see Cyrene once in the eighteen-sixties while running logs down the river to Frankfort.)

We come to the third son, William III of this family who was the father of our race, yours and mine. You have noticed that he married in Bourbon County and had three daughters by his first wife, Martha Ellison. We do not know what year it was, but he left Bourbon County, pushed farther to the westward and made his home near the mouth of Green River and not far from Evansville, Ind.

Some of our older relatives believed he lived on the Indiana side of the Ohio for a time at least. But while here he became a widower with three small daughters. He met and married Margaret Wilcox. On March 5, 1801 William IV was born to them there. Then came John, 1803, Isaac, March 12, 1805; Martha, 1807; Samuel, 1811; Elizabeth born August 23, 1814, and James in 1823. After the family went to Eastern Kentucky.

I remember when I was a boy, seven or eight years old (I was nine when grandfather William (IV) died in 1889,) hearing grandfather tell about seeing the first steam boat that ever went down the Ohio river. It created great excitement among the peoples. I now find in Collins History of Kentucky, page 356, a record of this historic occurrence. This was the steamer Orleans on its way from Pittsburg to Natchez, Miss., and it reached Louisville in October, 1811.

But William III, having lived about fourteen or fifteen years at that place concluded to seek another place in which to live, and about the year 1813 he provides himself with a trusty gun, and all the usual equipment of the pioneer hunter, bids his family goodbye with the advice that when he has found a desirable location he will send for them; then he starts through the forests to Eastern Kentucky. It was no doubt months before word came to the family on Green River near Evansville (or thereabouts) that the father and husband had found their home on Red River in Wolfe County (then Floyd County, I believe). The lands which he took up there lie at the mouth of Buck Creek and comprised at the time a large boundary, including the Old Sand Fields in the river end there, and the higher lands across the river. We do not know how the family was advised as to the way to reach the new home; neither do we know who accompanied them on the journey. But the trip was carefully detailed and planned for the wife and children. The mother then got together those household effects which would be most useful to them and her five small children, ranging in ages from one year to twelve years, bid goodbye to her relatives and friends — which in those days meant the last farewell, usually — took passage on a keel boat and started on her journey to her husband and new home. The route up the Ohio River to Maysville, and then across country perhaps through Mt. Sterling, and eastward through what is now Frenchburg to Red River. This was a long and trying journey by slow boat and difficult land travel of several hundred miles, requiring several weeks time. The method of travel from Maysville we do not know, but the settlers were taking up lands and forming settlements at distances of few miles even after leaving the level country, and we can easily imagine friendly settlers aiding the mother and small children. It is most probable that the father had already built the log cabin that was to be their home for a time, before their arrival. At any rate, the location of that home is now marked only by the chimney rocks piled up at the edge of a present corn field. The grave yard is on the river bluff a few hundred feet away, well preserved in a small underbrush. A few years later a new and larger house was built several hundred yards west of the original cabin, and that was the home known to the older children of William IV and Isaac, your great-grandfather, where they visited during the lifetime of their grandparents. William III died about the year 1850 at a ripe old age, and the grandmother, Margaret Wilcox Congleton, died there four or five years later at an age of nearly eighty years. A number of old people still living remember "Granny Congleton" when they were children. James, the youngest son, lived with his mother unmarried during her lifetime, and for many years after her death the old farm was known as the James

EARLY AND MODERN HISTORY

Congleton Farm. Two years ago (1922) I made a rough survey of the lands there, showing the location of the river and the mouth of Buck Creek and the location of the original home, the graves, and the later home which is also marked only by chimney mounds, and the present frame house by the side of the last old home site, now owned by Mrs. Leborn Lykins.

Now, Joe, perhaps it is enough for me to say that my grandfather William IV and your great-grandfather, Isaac, worked together a few years near Beattyville where Uncle Isaac married Delilah Brandenburg, and their children reside in Lee and Estill Counties. Our branch of the family lived in Wolfe and Powell. In later years many of us have gone westward and some to the far west.

I failed to say in the earlier record here that William II, the father of the Kentucky Congletons, died in 1811, and I have copied which names all his children as given above. I visited the old farm in Bourbon County two years ago and copied the names and dates from the headstones in the family cemetery, which is surrounded by a stone wall built by Franklin Congleton. It is the family of William W. only, and it is not certain that his father, John, who died in 1796, and his grandfather, John, who died in 1811, lie there — apparently not. Those graves must be in the adjoining lands of theirs. I cannot say.

Joe, I had wished to write you more, but I think I shall rest now and hope that I may sometime find the time to write up my data in a better form, beginning much earlier than the Colonial days 1730 and dwell more upon the contemporary history along with the dates.

You will observe that our family came over here during the Indian days, but unfortunately we have been given no written record of their trying days in the early settlement period. Also, our family suffered through the bad lands laws enacted by Virginia. This makes another difficult chapter; but they lived that their children might enjoy better days. It is a great story when properly handled.

I hope that you will visit me soon and look over my file.

Your cousin, W. T. Congleton.

This letter was submitted to Mrs. Roy Cecil for inclusion in the Early and Modern Histories of Wolfe County by Mrs. Lee Congleton, widow of the late Lee Congleton of Lexington. Mr. Lee Congleton's first wife, Cora, was the daughter of Thomas and Jane Richmond Morton. After her death Mr. Congleton married Miss Adeline Wells, daughter of Mrs. James Cable. The last Mrs. Lee Congleton is a half-sister of C. E. Cable of Campton, Ky.

WOLFE COUNTY

FAMILY OF FREDERICK N. DAY
(by Mrs. W. E. Bach)

Frederick Newington Day, born in Lee County, Virginia, March 12, 1844, came to Campton, Wolfe County, with his brother, Colonel Lexington Morgan Day, in the fall of 1871. They had a General Mercantile Store, known as "Day Bros." Frederick (better known in later years as Uncle Fred) met and married "Zarilda Wills" the daughter of Jordan Wills, who was living with her cousin, George Cox and wife, going to school in Campton. They were married on November 12, 1872 in the home of George Cox and wife, who was Mattie (Hanks) Cox, both of them cousins of the bride, by Rev. John D. Spencer, Baptist minister.

They continued in the mercantile business in Campton until after their third child, Minnie Lou, was born — then moving to a farm which later became the town of Daysboro — named Dayton but there being another postoffice by the name of Dayton in Kentucky, they changed it to Daysboro. Lexington Morgan Day moved to Beattyville, Lee County, Ky., with his wife, Callie (Richmond) Day, where he practiced law and reared their family there. Many families now own the tract of land where Day Bros. once owned.

Frederick did not like farming and went to work for Mr. Floyd Day in his store in Hazel Green, about 1880, later J. T. Day & Co. Their two children, born in Daysboro, were Robert Bruce and Edward Owings Day. They moved to Hazel Green in March 1882, when Ed was only three months old. They first lived where the R. J. McLin Home is now and later moved to the hill where Spencer Cooper later lived and where their son, Thomas Jonathan Jackson, better known as (Stonewall Jackson Day) was born March 16, 1885, later they bought the Robert J. Samuels home on Broadway where they lived until 1918 and where their last two children, Emma Pearl and Virginia Inez Day, were born. They sold this home in 1918 to Dr. A. C. Nickell, and moved to Winchester, Ky., then selling their home there and moved to Lexington, Kentucky in 1922, where Uncle Fred died in 1923 and Aunt Rilda in 1946.

Frederick Newington Day was born March 12, 1844 in Lee County, Va. Married November 12, 1872 to Zarilda Wills. Their children were:

Willie Lee Day, born August 1, 1873. Married Minnie Belle Howard. Children 4:

1. Lillian May Day died in infancy.
2. Beatrice Inez Day.
3. Carroll Anderson Day, born March 2, 1900, died Dec. 26, 1926, age 26. She died in Portland, Oregon and was buried at Mt. Sterling, Ky.

James South Day married Hallie Cowden of Midland, Texas. He was born February 15, 1875. Married December 31, 1903. Died September 21, 1921 in San Antonio, Texas, buried there. No children.

Minnie Lou Day married Elza H. James. She was born January 27, 1878. Died October 7, 1901. Buried at Hazel Green, Ky. No children. She was married June 9, 1901.

Robert Bruce Day never married. He was born September 14, 1880. Died February 4, 1905. Buried in the Hazel Green Cemetery.

Dr. Edward Owings Day married Dorothy Bolling. He was born December 15, 1882. Married July 4, 1925. Died July 18, 1949. Buried at Little Rock, Arkansas. Children, 1: Dorothy Edwin Day.

Stonewall Jackson Day (better known as Tony). Born March 16, 1885. Died December 12, 1887. Age two and one-half years. Buried in the Hazel Green Cemetery.

Emma Pearl Day married William Everett Bach. She was born June 18, 1887. Married December 26, 1905. Children: 3. Hallie Day Bach, Virginia Maurine Bach, and William Everett Bach, Jr.

Hallie Day Bach was born November 2, 1906. She married Wm. O. Blackburn, born July 12, 1906. They had three children:

Patricia Yvonne Blackburn, born January 17, 1935.
Barbara Ann Blackburn, born October 25, 1937.
William Everett Blackburn, born July 18, 1943.

Virginia Maurine Bach was born May 4, 1910. She married Oliver Lee Steele, Jr. They had one child.

Virginia Lee Steele, born January 2, 1927. She married John Harvey, Jr. They had three children:

John Harvey, III, born November 19, 1950.
Martha Leigh Harvey, born April 30, 1952.
Ann Edmonson Harvey, born May 5, 1955.

Frederick Newington Day was a merchant all of his life — he came from a family of merchants. He ran away at the age of 17 years and joined the Confederate Army in Scott County, Va. He enlisted in Company D, 64th Virginia Regiment. He was captured at Cumberland Gap with eighteen hundred other soldiers and marched to Lexington, Ky., by the way of Camp Dick Robinson, to Lexington, where he was placed on the train for Chicago, Illinois, and placed in the Camp Douglas Prison. He was released and arrived in Virginia, the night Abraham Lincoln was killed. He loved the Cause of the Confederacy and almost worshipped Robert E. Lee and Stonewall Jackson. In fact he loved his Mother State of Virginia. That is made plain by the names he gave his children. His brother, Lexington Morgan Day was also in the Confederate Army. They returned after the War between the States and owned a merchandise store in Hansonville, Va., coming from there to Campton,

WOLFE COUNTY

Ky., in 1871. His grandfather, Joseph Day, built the first Courthouse in Hillsboro, Carroll County, Va., where he died in 1856. Joseph Day's father, John Day and wife, came from Pennsylvania.

Aunt Rilda, as she was known, taught school before her marriage and the first school she taught in Wolfe County, she got $27.00 for a three months school, with which she bought her a side-saddle. After coming to Hazel Green, her great theme was to educate her children. She was a dressmaker — having learned the art by cutting her own patterns by candle light and sometimes by burning a torch. She had a millinery store in Hazel Green and burned the midnight oil many nights in her work — then going to a sick bed to help some neighbor or friend. Father (F. N. Day) belonged to the Methodist Church, having joined when only nine years of age, in Southwest Virginia, later going into the Maxwell Street Presbyterian Church, in Lexington, Ky. Mother was a member of the Old Seminary Baptist Church, which she joined at the age of 12 years, later going into the Swifts Camp Creek Baptist Church, where her name is on record as transferring to in 1877. Her mother, Judith (Cox) Wills, and her great-grandmother, Lydia (Harper) Hanks, belonged to this church. Later mother moved to Hazel Green and in 1882 Dr. Edward Owings Guerrant, came from Wilmore, Ky., and organized the Presbyterian Church in Hazel Green, Ky., and mother was one of the Organizing Members, where her membership remained until the church was sold and abandoned. She later went into the Maxwell Street Presbyterian Church in Lexington, Ky., where she and father both belonged at their death.

Mother (Mrs. F. N. Day) was one of five women who organized "The Hazel Green Cemetery Association" at Hazel Green, Ky., which is now considered one of the most beautiful cemeteries in Eastern Kentucky. Both she and father with my sister, Minnie Lou (Day) James, and my two brothers, Robert Bruce and Stonewall Jackson Day, lie buried, as well as my mother's parents, Jordan and Judith (Cox) Wills, are buried near the family lot.

My mother (Zarilda Wills Day) was the daughter of Jordan Wills and Judith (Cox) Wills; Jordan Wills was the son of Thomas Wills and Mariah Swango. Thomas Wills was the son of William Wills, Jr., and his wife, Mary (Polly-Ballard) Wills; William Wills, Jr., was the son of William Wills, Sr., and his wife, Elizabeth. They came from Albemarle County, Va., about 1790 to Clark and Montgomery County, Kentucky. William Wills, Sr., and his wife, Elizabeth, are buried in Clark County, Ky. William Wills, Jr. and his wife, Mary, are buried in the Old Wills Graveyard near Mt. Sterling, Ky.

Judith Cox, who married Jordan Wills, was the daughter of James Cox and his wife, Anne Hanks (daughter of Fielding Hanks and

EARLY AND MODERN HISTORY

Lydia Harper). Fielding Hanks was the son of Abraham Hanks and Sarah Harper. Lydia Harper was the daughter of John Harper and wife, Mary Ann. They came from Prince William County, Va., at a very early date in Kentucky history.

James Cox was the son of John Cox and Judith Sexton; John Cox was the son of James Cox and wife, Elizabeth; James Cox was the son of John Cox and Margaret Davis. The latter two are buried in Asheville, North Carolina and James Cox and his wife, Elizabeth, are buried in Grayson County, Va. John Cox and wife, Judith Sexton, are buried in the Old Cox Graveyard near the Old Cox's Mill, which was the first one erected in Morgan County, Ky. Judith Sexton was the daughter of Benjamin Franklin Sexton and his wife, Comfort Smith, of Maryland. Benjamin Sexton's parents were Joseph Sexton of (England) and his wife, was, Mary Lee, of (France). They came to America at a very early date and settled in Maryland, later Benjamin Sexton married Comfort Smith in Maryland and came on to Virginia where Judith was born in 1782 and on into Clark-Bath and Morgan Counties, Ky.

(The above article is compiled by Mrs. William Everett Bach, formerly Pearl Day, of Hazel Green, Ky. She has gathered and compiled this from her personal files.)

Artical of Agreement

By and between Zarilda Wills of the County of Wolfe and State of Kentucky of the first Part and W. J. David B. Bowen D. Rose Trustees of Common School District No. 10 for said County of the Second Part Witnesseth that for an In consideration of the Amount of School Funds drawn from the State aforesaid for said Dist. No. 10 the Party of the first Part Binds myself to teach a five Months Common School in Dist. 22 Days to month 5 Days in Each week the said Zarilda Wills binds herself to teach the Elements of a Plain english language to Wit — Spelling Reading & Writing Arethmetic & English Grammer and history to the best of her Skill and ability Also binds herself to Adopt a Good Sisterm of Rules in said School we the trustees of the Second Part binds Ourselves to Pay Said Zarilda Wills of the first Part the Sum of $110.00 Payable when the Money Drawn for the Dist. Given under our hands this Day 1870.

(This article was given to me by my mother, Mrs. Frederick Newington Day "Zarilda Wills", and I have copied it exactly as it is in the original. —Mrs. William Everett Bach "Pearl Day".)

WOLFE COUNTY

THE DUNN FAMILY OF WOLFE COUNTY
(Submitted by Dr. James H. Dunn)

The Dunns first came from Ireland and England. John Dunn was from Ireland. George Dunn was from England. George came to New York and John settled in West Virginia.

George had seven boys and one of them came to Kentucky. Andy was the one who came to Kentucky. Andy John Dunn settled in Wolfe County, Ky. He made his home at Stillwater and had the following sons: William, George, Andy, Isaac, Tom, Bill and Sam.

1. Bill moved to Fayette County.

1. George settled in Wolfe County and is now deceased. He had six sons and two daughters:

2. Jerry, Elijah, R. A. Dunn made a preacher and preached the gospel for many years prior to his death, Billie, James H. married Callie Taulbee in 1907. They have four daughters.

James H. Dunn made a doctor and has been practicing in Wolfe County for many years.

3. Pearl Edna Dunn married Edward E. Bach, an attorney. Pearl Edna has been a teacher in the Wolfe County Schools for several years. She is very community minded and served as head of the Cancer drive in Wolfe County three years, always going over the top in the goal. She is serving as president of the Wolfe County Woman's Club, 1955-56.

4. Joyce Bach married David Adams and they have one son.

4. Marilyn Bach is a senior at Hazel Green Academy in 1955.

3. Alma Dunn married Graydon Taulbee and they have two children. He works in the Welfare Department at Campton and she is a teacher in the Wolfe County Schools.

4. Sonny attends Hazel Green Academy.

4. Patty is a child in grade school at Campton.

3. Thelma Dunn married Earl Kirk. She is also a teacher. They live in Lexington, Ky.

3. Ruby married Bernice Wilson and they have one child and live in New Castle, Indiana. — Teacher

2. William O'Hair Dunn.

2. Elizabeth married Henry Bradley.

2. Belle married Elijah Patrick.

The Dunns of America have been characterized in general, by their generosity, tolerance, and independence. Strong of body, mind and personality, they have been leaders in many fields of endeavor.

EARLY AND MODERN HISTORY

Members of the family have been praticulary outstanding as soldiers, public officials, lawyers, educators, physicians and business leaders.

(The first and last paragraphs of this family history were taken from a paper prepared by Media Research Bureau, Washington, D. C. The rest was given by Dr. James H. Dunn of Campton, Ky.)

THE EVANS FAMILY WHO SETTLED IN WOLFE COUNTY
(Through information given by Mrs. Ruth Athey, Harris Arnett and others.)

Granville Evans and Pattie Drake were married and had the following children. Lela, John, Douglas and Emma.

1. Lela Evans married Alfred (Bud) Horton and they had five children: Alpha, John, Myrtle and Buford.

2. Alpha married James Galbreath and they had three daughters.

2. John Evans.

2. Myrtle Evans (deceased).

2. Nora.

2. Buford.

1. John Evans, second child of Granville and Pattie Evans married Emma Day and had four daughters: Lillie, Lula, Nella and Mattie. (See the Allen T. Day family).

1. Douglas, third child of Granville and Pattie Evans, married Lou Ellen Creech, November 25, 1888 and to this union were born three children: Rush Evans, born Sept. 30, 1889; Ruth, born Nov. 7, 1891; Hazel, born Jan. 26, 1896.

2. Rush married Elizabeth Coons and they had no children. He is now deceased. He served as cashier of the Farmers and Traders Bank, Campton for several years.

2. Ruth Evans married George Athey and they had one daughter, Mattie.

3. Mattie married Rev. T. W. Farmer, who is a minister in the Church of God.

3. They had one son, Herschel, who married Rita Lee Rose, daughter of Cecil and Martha Rose. They had one son, Mikey. Herschel is a graduate pilot and flies commercial air planes.

2. Hazel married Clarence Bush. She is now deceased. They had one son, Rex.

3. Rex Bush married in Louisville. They had one son, Bobbie Evans Bush.

1. Emma Evans, daughter of Granville, married Elonso Sherman and they had five children: Hettie and Hattie (twins), Gladys, Ray, Sterling married in Dayton. Ohio and they had three children.

2. Nora Sherman married Harris Arnett and they had eight

children: Rondal, Victor, Maurice, Mildred, Kathleen, Austin and Jean, Charles.
  3. Rondal married and they had one child, Loretta.
  4. Loretta married a Spaulding.
  3. Victor married and had two children: Louise and Rex.
  3. Maurice Arnett (unmarried).
  3. Mildred Arnett married Otis Birchfield and they had three children.
  3. Kathleen married Earl Pelfrey, no children.
  3. Austin (unmarried).
  3. Jean married Roger H. Smith. No children. They live in Cincinnati where they are both employed.
  3. Charles married at Frenchburg.

THE GOSNEY FAMILY
(This article submitted by Mrs. Mazie Cox Read of Cushing, Okla.)

In the year 1877, Charles Humphrey Gosney, a native of Grants Lick in Butler County, Ky., came to Wolfe County on a hunting expedition. He stopped at a farm home to ask permission to hunt on their land. A young lady answered the door. It must have been love at first sight, for they were soon married. This young lady was Melissa Jane Tutt, a local schoolmarm.

Melissa, the eldest child of Thomas Kelly and Leodica Stamper Tutt, was born February 14, 1855. They had seven other children: Tilda, T. K., Belle, Rosa, Sarah, and two who died in childhood, Cinda and Breckenridge. T. K. died this year at the age of 92. Their youngest daughter is still living. She is Mrs. Sarah Phillips, age 82, of Hazel Green. Mrs. Tutt died in 1891 and Mr. Tutt a few years later.

Thomas Kelly Tutt, who had come to Wolfe County from up in the mountains, at one time owned one-third of all the land from Stillwater Creek to Red River. He paid for the land by cutting the timber and floating it (except oak) to Clay City. From this land, he gave each of his children a farm as a wedding present, and they all lived within a radius of a few miles for many years.

The community in which they lived was Bethel and it was on their land that the first church was built, as well as the first schoolhouse.

The nearest postoffice was Spradling, which was near the old Spradling Bridge. In later years, the community was awarded a postoffice and it was called Gosneyville. C. H. Gosney was the first postmaster.

C. H. and Melissa Gosney were the parents of eleven children.

They were: Ben, Susannah Belle, who died in infancy in 1880; Jim, Pearl, Charlie, Sullivan, Inez, Sarah, Woodie, and Maymee. Six are still living.

Mr. Gosney, known to many as "Trojan", worked most of his life as a blacksmith and provided a good living for his family.

He sold the farm and moved to Berea so the children could go to school. When they returned to Wolfe County, they built a home in Campton. He served as member of the Board of Education. He was also a member of the Jr. O.U.A.M.

He went to Oklahoma during the oil boom in 1912 and had a shop in Cushing, but he soon returned to Campton. He went to Oklahoma again in 1916 and again returned to Campton. It was here he died in 1929. Mrs. Gosney died the following year.

There are no Gosneys left in Wolfe County, but three of their grandchildren still live here.

THE HANKS FAMILY OF WOLFE COUNTY, KENTUCKY

(Compiled by Mrs. William Everett Bach of Lexington, Ky. and Adin Baber of Paris, Ill. Both are descendants of this family.)

Members of the Hanks family were on the James River in Virginia as early as 1618; the history of the Hanks branch of Wolfe County really begins with the establishment of Fort Boonesborough and the settlement of Kentucky, including Montgomery County, and the counties created from it. Abraham Hanks of Fauquier County, Virginia, was one of four companions whom William Calk brought into Kentucky, the spring of 1775, after Richard Henderson made his famous purchase of land from the Cherokees.

Calk's famous Journal has many references to Abraham Hanks, the last entry being that "Abraham turned back." He turned back only to help clear the way through Powell Valley; then came on in to Boonesborough in time to help survey the town and to plant corn.

Abraham purchased an option on land, from Calk on Slate Creek; but Abraham never got to make use of the land. He returned to Virginia, and remained there, altho two or three of his brothers and all his children eventually lived in Kentucky. One of his probable brothers, was Peter Hanks, a Revolutionary War Veteran, who had fought on the frontier of western Pennsylvania. He came from North Carolina, with his sons and daughters and settled on Slate Creek.

His son, Peter, Jr., was later killed at the Battle of Tippecanoe, and the widow, Isabella, and her children went to Texas, where descendants now live. William, another son, was a Baptist minister, and removed to Gibson County, Indiana, where he established churches. There was Absalom and Samuel and John. John remained on the Spencer Fork of Slate Creek, and died there. A daughter of old Peter, Ruth, married Hubbard Marshall, a son of Humphrey Marshall, a noted early Kentuckian.

But it is more with the Hankses of Wolfe County, the descendants of Abraham Hanks, we are interested in. William Calk and John Harper came to Slate Creek to spy out good land, and Harper settled on Harper Ridge near Morgan's Station. Abraham Hanks married Sarah Harper. The Harpers were of Prince William County, Virginia. The couple had several children, among whom were Abraham Jr., Fielding and George, who came into the Slate Creek area, and as neighbors to Peter Hanks family. There was also a James Hanks and it is tradition that he and Fielding were "mighty hunters."

Abraham Hanks, Jr., went to Hardin County, and seems to be untraceable. His widow and children finally removed to Edgar County, Illinois. Fielding and George, both married sisters, Lydia and Sibby Harper, respectively, daughters of old John Harper. George died in 1813 and his widow married and, with her children, went to Putnam County, Indiana, more about Fielding later.

These men had two older brothers, William and Luke, who went to Western Kentucky; William settled first on Green River in then Hardin County and later removed to Breckinridge County, where Luke came from Tennessee and joined him, and where descendants of both now live.

Abraham and Sarah Harper Hanks also had three daughters, who came into this area at an early date. They were: Sarah, Polly and Nancy. Their parents died and left them to be orphans. Sarah went to live with the Ringo family; Polly was with a family in Mercer County; and Nancy was with the Berry family. Sarah later married a cousin James Hanks, who went to the War of 1812, and did not return. Polly Hanks had six children, one of whom, Sophie, lived for a time in the Tom Lincoln's home in Indiana. Sophie married and went to Iron Mountain, Missouri; left many descendants there. Her mother, Polly, later followed Sophie and died about 1855.

Nancy went south to be with the Berry family. She was married in the home of Richard Berry, Jr. He later moved to Montgomery County but did not stay long; he removed to Missouri. Sarah Hanks married second, Andrew Varvell; they later went to Illinois, where some of the children of Fielding visited them. Fielding was noted for owning some of the best and most fertile land on Slate Creek. He later sold out and removed to the Red River, and settled in Wolfe County, Ky.

Fielding Hanks, who had been born in Virginia in 1784, began paying taxes in Montgomery County in 1805, and after he was married. He married Lydia, as aforesaid, and Jordan Hanks was the first child; His first wife was Lydia Combs. The second child was William, born in 1806, married Louisa Hall; 3rd: Lucinda, born in 1808, married, 1st, Joel Chambers, and 2nd, Henry Evans. 4th: Annie Hanks, born 1810, married James Cox, she lived to the age of 97 years. She died on Christmas Eve of 1904 near Hazel Green. They were blessed with the following children: John Cox, Fielding Cox, both of them married into the Catron family; Lydia Cox married J. K. Brown; Andrew Jackson Cox married Rebecca Hall; Nancy Cox married Allie B. Landrum; and Judith Cox married Jordan Wills.

Jordan and Judith Cox Wills were the parents of nine children: many descendants of this Cox family are to be found in Wolfe County. It is a large and well known family. One of the Wills daughters, Zarilda, married Frederick Newington Day, of Lee County, Virginia; they were the parents of eight children; one of them Emma Pearl Day, who is now Mrs. William Everett Bach, of Lexington, a noted and professional Genealogist and who is prominent in the State Work of the DAR and the United Daughters of the Confederacy. More data on the Day family will be found in this book.

The other children of Jordan Wills and Judith Cox Wills are as follows: Emma Wills, who married Sebron Trimble; Elizabeth, who married W. F. Horton; Clara, who married Jefferson Sexton; Belle, who married H. C. Salley; Ada, who married C. F. Kash; Robert Wills, who married Sarah Childers; Lucinda, who died at age of 12; Jane, who married Alex Nickell. Many descendants of this family live in Wolfe and Morgan Counties.

The most outstanding child of Fielding Hanks in a civic way was the son, born in 1814, and given the name of Cuthbert Million Hanks. He lived a long and useful life; died in 1892. His first wife was Millie Ann Garrett, and they were blessed with 12 children, viz: William Finley, who married Emma Swango; Rosaline, who married W. H. P. Duff, and lived at Campton; Sarah Elizabeth, married Harvey Spradling; they went to Liberty, Casey County, Ky.; Allen Barnes died as a young man; Christopher Columbus, of whom more later; Mary Ellen marred Thomas Collingsworth; Laura Ann marred Henry F. Horton, and their daughter, Mida Wyant, now resides in Campton; Martha Jane married George W. Cox; Thomas Boone, married Mahala Tyler, and reared a large family; Nancy Urbana, also named for the usual Nancy in the Hanks families, married Charles S. Guy and they went to live in Weldon, DeWitt County, Illinois, later returning to Winchester, Ky. They were accompanied to Weldon, Ill., by her sister, Lucy Caroline, who had married Charles L. Townsend. There was also a Cuthbert, Jr., who married Eliza Horton. Cuthbert Million Hanks, Sr., married the second time to Armida E. Hackney, and they were blessed with four children: one son, died in infancy; Milly Adoline, who married Frank Stamper; Lydia Ruth married Arthur Lykins. Dora Lee Hanks, who was not married, became a rather famous school teacher and, late in life, was interviewed several times on subjects pertaining to Wolfe County, and the Hanks family.

She stated, for publication, that Fielding Hanks, her grandfather, was the first settler in what is now Campton; and constructed the first house, a log one. That was in 1818, when her father, Cuthbert Million, was only four years old. Fielding and his wife, Lydia, both died in 1861, and are buried in the Old Cemetery, behind the Old Methodist Church grounds.

Cuthbert Million Hanks, like his brother, Andrew Jackson, made several trips to Illinois to visit kinfolks. He was known to them by his nickname of "Cud" Hanks. He became one of the largest land owners of Wolfe County. He was elected to the House of Representatives, during the troubled times of the Civil War, from 1863 to 1865 inclusive. It was during this active period of his life that he was instrumental in having Wolfe County established; he donated the site for the jail and courthouse; and was Sheriff. For long he was locally known as "The Father of Wolfe County."

The sixth child of Fielding and Lydia Hanks was Andrew Jackson, born in 1816, married Katherine Wilson the first time and his second wife was Sue Kemper. Andrew was a farmer and stockman; resided near Howard's Mill; during the Civil War he imported hogs from Illinois, where he made several trips, and visited kinfolks there. He retired in the 1890's; went to Lynn County, Missouri, where he died.

Nancy Hanks, named for her aunt, was born in 1818; married Allan Day; they resided in what became Morgan County.

George Hanks, named for his uncle, George, who had been much with his parents, Fielding, was born in 1820; married Jamima Wireman. He was drowned in 1857.

Louisa Hanks married a man named William Spencer. She died from a snake bite.

Lydia Hanks, the youngest child and daughter, married a Meadows.

THE HAMMOND FAMILY IN WOLFE COUNTY

The name of this family is spelled in several different ways; as, Haman, Hamman, Hammon, Hammons, Hammond, etc., as in the case of many pioneer family names.

The original member of this family in America was Phillip Hammon, who left his home in the German Palatinate, a part of Bavaria lying west of the Rhine and in the region of the present cities of Speyer and Ludwigshafen. With a Peter Hammon, relation unknown, and other emigrants, he came northward down the Rhine, spent some time at Rotterdam or Amsterdam in Holland, and then, by way of England, and on to America, landing from the English ship, "Crawford" at Philadelphia. There he took the oath of allegiance to the British Government on October 16, 1772.

Philip Hammon soon moved on westward to Greenbriar County, Virginia, now Monroe County, West Virginia, where he married (1779) Christiana Cook, daughter of Valentine Cook. He became an active member of the pioneer community and served several years as a soldier and scout in the Indian wars (Dunmore's War). When the Revolution came on he enlisted in the cause of independence and spent several years as a Revolutionary soldier, giving nine years altogether to these military services.

After the war Philip and Christiana moved to Owsley (Montgomery, Wolfe) County, Kentucky, where they had a family of 12 children: John, 8-19-1781; Nancy, 11-19-83; Polly, 8-4-85; James, 8-26-87; Elizabeth, 11-23-90; Sally, 12-23-92; Cela, 4-13-94; William, 6-26-96; Elijah and Jesse (twins), 1-31-99; Philip Jr., 8-28-01; and Valentine, 1802.

In 1821 the parents and several of the surviving children moved to Jackson County, Alabama where the father died on August 3, 1832 and the mother died on January 28, 1842. The son, James, who later became administrator of his father's estate, returned to Montgomery (Wolfe) County, Kentucky, and all the other surviving sons and daughters returned to Kentucky before or soon after the death of the parents.

While it seems certain that all the surviving sons and daughters of Philip Hammon spent their remaining years in Wolfe or its neighboring counties, it is certain that the oldest surviving son at the time of his father's death, James Hammon, did so. On his return from Alabama in 1822 James settled in Montgomery, now Wolfe County, in the area just west of the present town of Campton, Ky. He had married to Miss Susan Evans on October 27, 1817, and they had three small children when they started the journey to Alabama. Their third child and eldest son, Silas Milton Hammon, who was to become the grandfather of the writer of these paragraphs, was born on January 28, 1821.

James and Susan Hammon had eleven children: Angeline, 8-9-1818; Maryer, 9-25-19; Silas, 1-28-21; Mahala, 8-27-22; James, 1-25-24; John, 8-2-25; Philip, 12-12-27; Jackson, 1-6-30; Margarette, 1-12-33; Malinda, 4-20-35; and Lucinda, 2-27-40.

About one mile west of Campton, Ky., there come down from the south a small narrow valley with its narrow rocky and creek-bottom road. These are known today as "Bearpen Hollow" and "Bearpen Road." A mile or a few miles up this hollow James Hammon and doubtless some brothers and certainly his sons, built and set traps and caught bears. In this way the road and the creek and the hollow got their names.

The last home of James Hammon in the area was located across the valley to the north of Sandy Ridge Road, within half a mile of the present Highway No. 15. While living there the eldest son, Silas, reached his middle twenties. Father James and son, Silas, built a splendid 30x30 log house on the exact site of the present modern residence of Mr. Steve Rose at the point where Bearpen Road turns eastward toward Campton. Here Silas and his part indian bride, Louisa D. Faulkner, started housekeeping.

But, the same urge and drive and love of freedom and adventure and accomplishment that brought great-great-grandfather Philip down the Rhine and across the Atlantic has carried the children, grandchildren, and great-grandchildren of these hardy folk on in every direction and helped to place the family name in some spelling or others in practically every telephone directory in the United States, each one making his modest or pretentious mark or impression on the region where he lived.

(Contributed by Mr. Wm. A. Hammond, Xenia, Ohio. Written November 29, 1956.)

HOLLON AND RELATED FAMILIES IN WOLFE COUNTY
(by Clay Hollon)

John Hollon (son of William Hollon and wife Rebecca) was the progenitor of the Hollons in the area known since 1860, as Wolfe County, Ky. He was the first permanent settler in that county, having settled on Holly Creek in the year 1804. It is not known when he first arrived, nor how long he had been here prior to 1804. He had already purchased a large tract of land on Holly Creek, and presumably, had built a cabin, cleared land and planted crops, and sometime during 1804 went to North Carolina to fetch as his wife,

EARLY AND MODERN HISTORY

Charity Brewer, born in North Carolina, Sept. 24, 1777. John was born in Virginia April 24, 1777. Marriage is recorded in County Clerk's office at Prestonburg, Floyd County, Ky. They never remov- from that home on Holly Creek. John died there Nov. 25, 1854, aged 77 years. Charity also died there in 1874, aged 97 years.

They had nine children:

1. Rebecca, born June 10, 1806, married Andrew Pence.
2. William, born April 4, 1808, married Candus Short.
3. Fannie, born Jan. 29, 1810, married a Sexton.
4. Ambrose, born June 13, 1812, married Happy Jones.
5. Lucinda, born Oct. 30, 1813, married G. Wash. Swango.
6. Phoebe, born Aug. 25, 1815, married a Jones.
7. Jackson, born April 14, 1817, married Sallie Wright.
8. Hiram, born Nov. 20, 1818, married Mary Jones.
9. John, Jr., born July 9, 1820, married Polly Gibbs.

Rebecca Hollon (first child of John and Charity) born June 10, 1806, died Mar. 31, 1887; married Aug. 2, 1823, Andrew Pence, born Dec. 11, 1798, died Aug. 4, 1878. They had eleven children: (1) Jane; (2) Henry; (3) Felix; (4) Angie; (5) Cithy; (6) Katie; (7) Cinda; (8) Joab; (9) Jack; (10) Charity; (11) Fannie.

Henry Pence (second child of Andrew and Rebecca) died Dec. 18, 1903; married Jane Pelfrey. They had eight children: (1) Melissa; (2) Caroline; (3) Cithy; (4) Scott; (5) Logan; (6) Nathan, born May 8, 1886; (7) Angie; (8) Emily.

Nathan Pence (sixth child of Henry and Jane Pelfrey) born May 8, 1886, died Jan. 25, 1954, married Clara E. Taylor, born Nov. 9, 1888. They had eight children: (1) Mabel, born Sept. 30, 1907; (2) Lenix, born May 15, 1909; (3) Henry, born Dec. 13, 1911; (4) Ernest, born Sept. 1, 1914; (5) Earl, born Nov. 28, 1916; (6) Archie, born Aug. 7, 1919, died infant; (7) Mollie Edith, born April 3, 1923; (8) Edna Marcia, born April 25, 1927.

Mabel Pence (first child of Nathan and Clara E. Taylor) married April 23, 1922, Claude Raymond Hammonds, born April 4, 1907. They had three children: (1) Claude Raymond, Jr., born July 12, 1929; (2) Helen, born Sept. 19, 1933, who married Dec. 9, 1952, Claude Royce Dusina and had one child, Connie Royce Dusina, born Sept. 6, 1953; (3) Maxine, born March 14, 1935.

Lenix Pence (second child of Nathan and Clara E. Taylor) married Sept. 29, 1934, Deloria Ash and had two children: Lowell, born June 6, 1936, and Mary Lou, born Sept. 20, 1948.

Henry Pence (third child of Nathan and Clara E. Taylor) married April 7, 1943, Sylvia Moore. They had no children.

Ernest Pence (fourth child of Nathan and Clara E. Taylor) married Sept. 23, 1935, Mildred Laymon and had five children: (1) Gail, born Jan. 14, 1937; (2) Louise, born May 22, 1938; (3) Kenneth, born Feb. 8, 1941; (4) Leonard, born Feb. 16, 1943; (5) Keith, born Aug. 16, 1949.

Earl Pence (fifth child of Nathan and Clara E. Taylor) married April 26, 1941, Bertha Thompson and had six children: (1) Clara Alice, born Nov. 3, 1941; (2) Constance Ann, born Jan. 7, 1944; (3) Earl, Jr., born April 21, 1945; (4) Ernest, born Feb. 8, 1947; (5) Steve Nathan, born Sept. 8, 1948; (6) David H., born Jan. 26, 1953.

Mollie Edith Pence (seventh child of Nathan and Clara E. Taylor) married Dec. 31, 1950, James Thorne and had two children: James Lenix, born Aug. 23, 1952; Lu Ann, born Dec. 15, 1953.

Edna Marcia Pence (eighth child of Nathan and Clara E. Taylor) married Oct. 1, 1947, Lige Bailey, and had two children: Gary Lee, born May 2, 1948; Sherry Lynn, born Jan. 16, 1952.

Felix Pence (third child of Andrew and Rebecca) born Jan. 25, 1851, died May 5, 1915; married Elizabeth Gibbs, born July 16, 1854, died Nov. 18, 1932. They had ten children: (1) Jack, born Dec. 14, 1871, died May 31, 1900; (2) William, born July 6, 1873; (3) Johnnie, born May 1, 1875, died Feb. 27, 1942; (4) Sarah Belle, born Oct. 7, 1877; (5) Sam, born June 23, 1880; (6) Minnie, born June 6, 1882, died May 17, 1921; (7) Taylor, born Oct. 8, 1884; (8) Bruce, born Oct. 19, 1886; (9) Kelly, born May 15, 1890, died April 21, 1926; (10) Ealy, born Aug. 23, 1898.

William Pence (second child of Felix and Elizabeth Gibbs) married Rebecca Spencer, born March 4, 1884, died April 22, 1917. They had five children: (1) Roy, born May 17, 1904; (2) Dale, born Nov. 3, 1905; (3) Ada, born Dec. 17, 1907; (5) Ercie, born July 12, 1910; (5) Lelia, born March 12, 1912; married second, Nancy Sewell, and had one child: Vergie, born Dec. 2, 1919.

Dale Pence (second child of William and Rebecca Spencer) married Nellie Pence and had four children: (1) Earl, born March 22, 1928, died Aug. 9, 1934; (2) Paul, born Jan. 9, 1934; (3) Cecil, born Dec. 18, 1938, died infant; (4) Opal, born March 10, 1940.

Vergie Pence (only child of William and Nancy Sewell) did not marry.

Katie Pence (sixth child of Andrew and Rebecca) married John Banks. They had seven children: (1) Henry; (2) Andy; (3) John; (4) Hale; (5) Margaret; (6) Sanford; (7) Rene; all dead by 1953.

Cinda Pence (seventh child of Andrew and Rebecca) married William Tyra. They had eight children: (1) Dudley; (2) Sam; (3) Caro-

EARLY AND MODERN HISTORY

line; (4) Sarah; (5) Mary; (6) Bill; (7) Ebb; (8) Johnnie.

Joab Pence (eighth child of Andrew and Rebecca) married Vina Landsaw. They had eight children: (1) Leander; (2) Susan; (3) Will; (4) Taylor; (5) Sam; (6) Georgeann; (7) Felix; (8) Martitia.

Jack Pence (ninth child of Andrew and Rebecca) married Susan Landsaw. They had nine children: (1) John; (2) George; (3) Malissa; (4) Daniel Boone, born Jan. 4, 1860, still living in 1954; married Hattie McDonald; (5) Polly; (6) Sally; (7) Jack; (8) Lou; (9) Newton.

Charity Pence (tenth child of Andrew and Rebecca) married James Tomlin. They had two children: Tom and Link.

William Hollon (second child of John and Charity) married Candus Short, born North Carolina 1810. They had six children: (1) Preston, born Nov. 25, 1834, died Jan. 29, 1918; (2) Nelson, born 1842; (3 and 4) Mahala and Kelson, twins, born 1844; Mahala married a Terrill; (5) Lucin 1850, married a Cockrell.

Preston Hollon (first child of William and Candus Short) married (by Joe Nickels) April 20, 1856, Martha, born in Morgan Co. Sept. 17, 1837, died Oct. 2, 1917. They had nine children: (1) Nelson, born Sept. 6, 1857; (2) Isaac, born Oct. 3, 1859, died Feb. 21, 1947; (3) William, born July 4, 1863; (4) Miles, born Oct. 7, 1833; (5) John, born 1867; (6) Wilson, born June 9, 1869; (7) Elizabeth, born Sept. 6, 1872; (8 and 9) Abraham (or Absolom) and Andrew, twins, born Jan. 20, 1874.

Fannie Hollon (third child of John and Charity) born Jan. 29, 1810, married a Sexton, and moved to Greene County, Ind.

Esther Richmond (sixth child of Isaac and Esther Louisa) born Lee Co., Va., 1815, died Wolfe Co., Ky., 1865, married Jeremiah E. Elkins, born Va., 1816, died Wolfe Co., Ky., 1898. They came from Lee Co., Va. to Wolfe Co., Ky., in 1851. They had twelve children: (1) Johnathan R., born Lee Co., Va., 1835, married first, Fanny Hollon, married second, Susan Hondshul. (2) Clarinda, born Lee Co., Va., 1836, married first, John T. Moore, married second, John J. Swetman. (3) Mary C., born Lee Co., Va., 1838, married Isaac Murphy. (4) Esther, born Lee Co., Va., 1840, married first, Jonathan Carroll, married second, Elijah Collins. (5) William F., born Lee Co., Va., 1844, married first, Minerva Cassidy, married second, Polly Rose. (6) Preston, born Lee Co., Va., 1847, married Mary Ann Murphy. (7) Andrew, born Lee Co., Va., 1849, died 1888. (8) Isaac, born Wolfe Co., Ky., 1853, married Laura Kathryn Cecil. (9) James B., born Wolfe Co., Ky., 1855, married Sarah Rose. (10) Caroline, born Wolfe Co., Ky., 1857, married James Buchanan Hollon. (11) Louisa C., born Wolfe Co., Ky., 1861, married John Weeden Congleton. (12) Emma, born Wolfe Co., Ky., 1865, married A. Floyd Byrd.

WOLFE COUNTY

Jeremiah married second, Sarah Oakley, and had two children: (1) Fanny, born 1872, married Rev. William Brashear. (2) William Richmond, born 1874, married Dora Rose.

Jonathan Richmond Elkins (first child of Jeremiah and Esther) born Lee County, Virginia, 1835, died in Wolfe County, Kentucky in 1914; married first, Fanny Hollon, daughter of Hiram, son of John, Sr.; married second, Susan Hondshul. Had no children.

Clarinda E. Elkins (second child of Jeremiah and Esther) born in Lee County, Virginia in 1836, died in Bath County, Kentucky in 1914; married first John T. Moore and had one child, John T., Jr. born 1862; married second John J. Swetman, born 1811, died 1898. They had three children: (1) Mary Alice; (2) Paulina Charlotte; (3) Robert R.

Mary Alice Swetman (first child of John J. and Clarinda) born Feb. 4, 1868, married Dec. 22, 1892, Ben M. Arnold, born May 18, 1862. They had four children: (1) Joe T.; (2) Clara Ann; (3) Nettie Bell; (4) Lucile Rose.

Paulina Charlotte Swetman (second child of John J. and Clarinda) born Oct. 6, 1871, died Feb. 10, 1937; married W. W. Rogers, and had six children: (1) Benjamin Harrison, born March 11, 1892, died April 16, 1915; (2) Norman Mildred, born Aug. 17, 1893, died Sept. 1, 1908; (3) Elizabeth Clay, born May 7, 1896, married Harry Dorsey of Ashland, Ky.; (4) Clarinda Alice, born March 8, 1899, married Carey Thomas Watson of Flemingsburg, Ky.; (5) Addie S., born Aug. 18, 1907, married James Mulroney of Fleming Co., Ky.; (6) John Warren, born Sept. 17, 1910 (Aurora, Colo.).

Robert R. Swetman (third child of John J. and Clarinda) born June 26, 1874, married Nannie B. Jones, and had two children: (1) John F., born 1897; (2) William Wayne, born 1900.

Joe T. Arnold (first child of Ben M. and Mary Alice) born Feb. 8, 1894, married Ruth Donohue, and had three children: (1) Annette; (2) Mary Jo; (3) Morgan Lacy, born May 5, 1934.

Clara Ann Arnold (second child of Ben M. and Mary Alice) born Oct. 10, 1897 (unmarried).

Nettie Belle Arnold (third child of Ben M. and Mary Alice) born Oct. 3, 1901, married Wm. Kincaid, and had two children: (1) Ann Douglas, born Nov. 19, 1930, married James W. Ingram; (2) William Arnold, born May 2, 1933.

Lucile Rose Arnold (fourth child of Ben M. and Mary Alice) born Nov. 2, 1908 (unmarried).

Annette Arnold (first child of Joe T. and Ruth) born June 5, 1924, married Leon Stevens, and had three children: (1) Rose Ann, born Dec. 24, 1946; (2) Leon, Jr., born March 7, 1949; died infant; (3) Dale Edwards, born April 1, 1950.

Mary Jo Arnold (second child of Joe T. and Ruth) born Aug. 19, 1929, married James Tyree.

Mary C. Elkins (third child of Jeremiah and Esther) born in Lee County, Virginia in 1838, died in Morgan County, Kentucky, Jan. 10, 1891; married Isaac Murphy who died Nov. 8, 1896.

Esther Elkins (fourth child of Jeremiah and Esther) born Lee County, Virginia in 1840, died Wolfe County, Kentucky in 1904; married first, Jonathan Carroll, and had three children: (1) Jonathan, Jr.; (2) Robert L.; (3) Rosa, born May 1873, died Oct. 4, 1930.

Jonathan Carroll, Jr. (first child of Jonathan and Esther) was a Psysician, died May 1, 1928; married Jane Smith, born Nov. 23, 1887, and had three children: (1) Sam, (2) Lura, (3) Arlene.

Robert L. Carroll (second child of Jonathan and Esther) married Maggie Smith, and had four children: (1) Courtney, born Jan. 6, 1892; (2) Beatrice; (3) Wallis; (4) Evaline.

Sam Carroll (first child of Jonathan and Jane) born June 10, 1892, married Ruth Keene, and had three children: (1) Sam, Jr.; (2) Allene; (3) Gene.

Lura Carroll (second child of Jonathan and Jane) born March 11, 1898, married a Miller, and had two children: (1) Billy; (2) Kathleen.

Arlene Carroll (third child of Jonathan and Jane) born Jan. 12, 1903, married Jim Wireman, and had two children: (1) Jean; (2) Jack.

Beatrice Carroll (second child of Robert and Maggie) born June 28, 1894, married Homer Bay, and had no children.

Wallis Carroll (third child of Robert and Maggie) born Dec. 7, 1897, married Irene Goldman, and had five children: (1) Margaret; (2) Audrey; (3) Diana; (4) Bobby; (5) Carol Mae.

Evaline Carroll (fourth child of Robert and Maggie) born June 4, 1899, married James P. Lawless, born June 8, 1892, and had three children: (1) James P. Jr.; (2) Betty Louise; (3) Oneda Joyce.

Esther Elkins Carroll, married second, Elijah Collins, born 1850, died 1944, aged 94 years. They had two children: (1) William, born 1877, died 1945; (2) Lou, born 1879.

William Collins (first child of Elijah and Esther married first Sylvia Hays, and had one child. Mother and child died. He married second, Rinda Rose, and had two children: (1) William Omer; (2) Sterling.

William Omer Collins (first child of William and Rinda) born 1916, died 1952, married Susie and had one child, Donnie, born in 1940.

Lou Collins (second child of Elijah and Esther) born 1879, married Samuel H. Rose, born 1874, and had two children: (1) Dewey, born 1898, married Ann Center, and had no children; (2) Beech, born 1903.

Beech Rose (second child of Samuel H. and Lou) born 1903, married Ora Kash, and had three children: (1) Cecil Kash, born 1925; (2) Wilfred, born 1927; (3) Justin, born 1938.

William F. Elkins (fifth child of Jeremiah and Esther) born Lee County, Virginia in 1844, died in Oklahoma, 1930; married first Minerva Cassidy, daughter of Thomas and Louisa Richmond Cassidy, and had four children: (1) Molly; (2) Jonathan R.; (3) Lizzie; (4) Howard Henderson.

Molly Elkins (first child of William F. and Minerva) was born in Wolfe County, Kentucky.

Kelson Hollon, son of William Hollon and Candus Short Hollon married Rosaline Terrill during the Civil War.

1. Melvine married Lewis King.
2. Will Henry King married Flossie Goud, they had one child.
2. Jane King married Kelly Haddix, they had one child.
2. Ellen King never married.
1. Nannie Hollon married Arberry Gibbs. They had seven children.
2. Richard Gibbs married Rebecca Hollon. Had one child.
2. Kelse Gibbs married Pearl Brewer Carson. Had one child.
2. Walter Gibbs married Lillie Dalton. Had four children.
2. Herbert Gibbs married away and they had several children.
2. Clayton Gibbs married Rose Robinson Byrd. No children.
2. Mary Gibbs married Jim Tester. Had one child.
2. Young Gibbs married a Profitt. Had one child.
1. Bell Hollon married Jim Profitt and they had seven children.
2. Fred Profitt married Pearl Dunn, died in 1950. Two children.
2. Bertha Profitt married Bill Hatton. No children.
2. Bessie Profitt married Henry Combs. Four children.
2. Ira Goff Profitt married Nannie Brewer.
3. Adopted daughter, Carmic Simpkins married an Ingram.
3. Dorothy Mae Star.
3. One son, Russell Profitt. Russell married Mildred Wright and had one child.
2. Mort Profitt married Edna Campbell and had six children.

EARLY AND MODERN HISTORY

    2. Shelton married Bonnie Dunn. Had two children.
    2. Millie married Pearl Campbell, a minister, who lives in Baltimore, Md. Had one child.
    1. Catron Hollon married Clara Elkins, they had four children.
    2. Grace Hollon, now dead, married Vernon Christopher. One child.
    2. Kelse Hollon married at Clay City, now dead.
    2. Letcher Hollon married in New York, had one child.
    2. Stanley Hollon married at Clay City, now dead. Had two children.
    1. Emma Hollon married Jeff Patton and they had four children.
    2. Nannie Patton married a Rose first, then Bob Hollon. Had two children by the first marriage and several by the second.
    2. Courtney Patton married a Tolson, daughter of Boone Tolson. Had four children.
    2. Kelson Patton married a Moore. Several children.
    2. John Frank Patton died at the age of 10 years.
    1. William Preston Hollon married Elizabeth Murphy. They had three children.
    2. Daisy Hollon married a Powers and they had two children.
    2. Lennox, a young man unmarried.
    2. George Hollon married twice. First Miranda Terrill and they had one child. Second a woman in Tennessee and they had two children.
    1. Isaac Hollon married Georgia Ann Dunn. They had three children.
    2. Oldham married Maxine Brewer. They had three children.
    2. Nolan married and moved away to Hillsboro, Ohio.
    2. Jasper Elkins married and lives in Indiana.
    1. Martha Hollon married Isaac Elkins. They had two children.
    2. Clay Wade Elkins married away.
    2. Jasper Elkins married and lives in Indiana.

Lucinda Hollon (fifth child of John and Charity) born Oct. 30, 1813, married George Washington Swango, born June 7, 1811. They had thirteen children: (1) Abraham, born March 23, 1831, died infant; (2) Andrew, born Nov. 13, 1833, married Rhoda Ingram; (3) Fanny, born Jan. 3, 1835, married James Rose; (4) Stephen, born May 1, 1837, died Feb. 12, 1913, married June 6, 1859, Sarah Jane Shackelford, born June 1840, died Feb. 19, 1897; (5) Green, born June 11, 1839, married first, Rhoda Clark, married second Elitha Brashears; (6) John, born April 10, 1841, died 1925, married Sarah Lewis; (7) William, born July 19, 1843, married Polly Smith; (8) Ambrose, born Dec. 10, 1845, married Nancy Gibbs; (9) Jane, born Nov. 29, 1847, married William Lawson; (10) Caroline, born Sept. 14, 1849, married Henry Shockey; (11) Hiram, born July 9, 1851, married first Sarah Shockey, married second, Nancy Ratcliff; (12) Harrison, born Jan. 15, 1854, died Oct. 21, 1934, married first, Mary Hobbs, married second, Elitha Brashears Swango (widow of his brother Green); (13) Samuel, born July 26, 1856, married first, Ellen Hobbs, married second, Catherine Taylor.

Phoebe Hollon (sixth child of John and Charity) born Aug. 25, 1815, married a Jones, and had a son, John, born Oct. 6, 1830.

Jackson Hollon (seventh child of John and Charity) born April 14, 1817, married Sallie Wright. They had sixteen children: (1) Elisha, married Sallie Bryant; (2) Martin, married Rosilla King; (3) John, married Arminia Gibbs; (4) Ambrose, married Clarinda Hollon; (5) Elcain, married Martha Campbell; (6) Hiram, married Charlotte Sparks; (7) Marshall, married Nancy Kidd; (8) Dennis, married Elizabeth Childers; (9) Good Larkin, born 1843, married Mary Elkins; (10) A. Jackson, born 1856, died 1934, married Sarah Taulbee; (11) Robinson Crusoe, born May 1, 1866, died Dec. 27, 1953, married Laura Fulks; (12) Rhoda, born 1868; (13) Jane, married Harvey Gillespie; (14) Betsie, married Hiram Bryant; (15) Charlotte, married George Faulkner; (16) Rebecca, married A. L. Taulbee.

Hiram Hollon (eighth child of John and Charity) born Nov. 20, 1818, married Mary Jones, born in North Carolina in 1822. They had three children: (1) Raney, born Aug. 25, 1840; (2) Cephas, born Sept. 11, 1842, married Nancy, born 1849; (3) Fanny, born May 26, 1843, married Jonathan R. Elkins.

John Hollon, Jr. (ninth and youngest child of John and Charity) born July 9, 1820, died 1904, married Polly Gibbs, born in Morgan County, Ky., 1820, died in 1902. They had fifteen children: (1) Betsey, born 1837, married John H. Terrill; (2) George Washington, born Jan. 27, 1840, died April 23, 1923, married Orpha Rebecca Baker, born in Lee County, Va., Sept. 10, 1842, died July 9, 1937; (3) Nathan, born 1842, died 1880-1 (killed by lightning in the courthouse in Campton), married Amanda Ellen Baker, born in Lee County, Va., in 1844, died 1920; (4) Charity, born 1843, died 1907, married Dec. 27, 1866, Sam Henry Hurst, born 1843, died 1930; (5) Phillip, died young; (6) Lucinda, born 1849, died 1929, married March 4, 1867, James A. Sewell (son of Joseph Sewell and wife Nancy Thompson) born 1837, died 1912; (7) John D., born 1850, died 1923, married Elizabeth Chambers (daughter of Bill and wife Rebecca Rose); (8) Jackson, born 1852, married Caroline Shockey, born 1854; (9) William, born 1854, died April 8, 1927, married Comfort Terrill; (10) Fanny, born 1855, died 1941, married Stanford Reed (Dock) Perkins; (11) Hannah, born 1856; (12) James Buchanan, born 1857, died 1942, married first Caroline Elkins, born 1857, died 1891, married second, Rosa Belle Byrd, born 1868, died 1941; (13) Henry, born 1858; (14) Dock, born 1860, died 1937, married first, Judy Terrill, married second, Isabelle Spaulding; (15) Zerilda Jane, born

March 30, 1862, died July 7, 1896, married Nov. 30, 1880, Green B. Brewer.

George Hollon (son of William and Rebecca Hollon) born in Virginia in 1884, married Elizabeth, born in Virginia 1792. They lived in Ashe County, N. C. from 1810 to 1818-19, then moved to Wolfe County, Ky. They had nine children: (1) Sally, born in Ashe Co., N. C., in 1810, married David Banks; (2) Denica, born in Ashe Co., N. C., in 1817, married Moses Vires; (3) James, born in Wolfe Co., Ky., in 1819, married Elizabeth, born in Va. 1813; (4) Phoebe, born in Ky., 1820, married Feb. 1833, W. M. Banks; (5) Elizabeth, born in Ky., 1824, married Jack Watkins, Jr.; (6) Celia, born in Ky., 1827, married Preston Watkins; (7) Simon, born in Ky., 1830, married Nancy Banks, born in Ky., 1829; (8) Nancy, born in Ky., 1833, married Sam Taulbee; (9) Vardamon, born in Ky., 1837, married Celia Noble.

Sally Hollon (first child of George and Elizabeth) born in Ashe County, N. C. in 1810, married David Banks. They had a daughter, Elizabeth, born in 1854.

Denica Hollon (second child of George and Elizabeth) born in Ashe County, N. C. in 1817, married Oct. 19, 1835, Moses Vires, born in Franklin County, Va., 1813. They had twelve children: (1) James, born 1835, married Elizabeth Hollon; (2) John, born 1837, married Emaline; (3) Elizabeth, born 1839, married Elisha Terry; (4) Nancy, born 1841; (5) Randolph, born 1843, married Elizabeth; (6) Sarah Jane, born 1845; (7) Elmeada, born 1847; (8) Lauranie, born May 16, 1850, died July 27, 1933, married John Henry Elkins; (9) America, born 1852; (10) Moses, born 1854, married Oct. 31, 1876, Mary Robinson; (11) Nicey, born 1856; (12) Prudence, born 1858, married Nov. 23, 1875, Greenville Cundiff.

James Hollon (third child of George and Elizabeth) born in Ky. 1819, married Elizabeth, born in Virginia in 1813. They had six children: (1) Andrew J., born 1843; (2) Paulina, born 1845; (3) William "Black Bill", born 1848, married Betsey "Lizzy" Birchfield; (4) Rebecca, born 1849, married Isam Brewer; (5) James, born 1854; (6) Mary, born 1868.

Simon Hollon (seventh child of George and Elizabeth) born 1830, married Nancy Banks, born 1829. They had seven children: (1) Sanford, born 1851; (2) Silva, born 1855; (3) Clarinda, born 1857; (4) Littleton, born in 1860; (5) Meredith, born 1862; (6) George, born 1864; (7) Dave, born 1867.

Vardamon Hollon (ninth and youngest child of George and Elizabeth) born 1837, married Celia Noble, born 1830. They had three children: (1) William, born 1851; (2) James, born 1856; (3) Elizabeth, born 1859.

WOLFE COUNTY

CLAY HOLLON
4418 N. Monitor Ave., Chicago 30, Illinois

January 19, 1956

Mrs. Roy M. Cecil,
Campton, Ky.
Dear Mrs. Cecil:

Am enclosing family records of the first three generations of Hollons who were among the first to settle in Wolfe County; the descendants of John and George Hollon.

To add the fourth or more generations would mean several hundred more names, and would require more space which would be out of porportion to the total space you are contemplating for your history book.

Hoping this will be a satisfactory contribution, and that you are making good progress with your project, I am

Sincerely yours,
Clay Hollon.

REV. JOHNNY BARKER FAMILY CONTRIBUTES TO WOLFE COUNTY
(Contributed by Mrs. Marion Horton)

Among the early families of Wolfe County which contributed a valuable heritage to the citizens of this county was the Rev. Johnny Barker family of Stillwater, Ky.

John C. Barker was born on Grassy Creek in Morgan County and he taught in the public schools until he became a Baptist minister, which calling he followed until his death. He married Arzelia Rose of Stillwater, Ky. and they settled in Wolfe County at Stillwater and lived for sometime in the old Rose homeplace where Arzelia was born.

Arzelia was the daughter of William Rose and Nancy (Williams) Rose. It was said that Nancy was a direct descendant of Roger Williams, who established the colony of Rhode Island.

William or "Uncle Billy" ran a grist mill just below the Stillwater bridge and owned several hundred acres of land. Later this land was all divided among his children. Gilliann Buchanan and Arzelia Barker, his daughters lived on their part of the inherited land until they died.

There is a small cave which is located just east of the Stillwater church house (up the branch) where the Rose's hid their meat and

EARLY AND MODERN HISTORY

valuables during the Civil War. The soldiers took the horses and some grain from Billy Rose's home. During the Civil War while the men folk were away fighting, the wives gathered their children in a house, near where Jim Linkous now lives, for the night. This was a secluded spot heavily wooded. They were afraid to stay alone at night because of night prowlers and they would make no light in their houses save the light from the fire place.

Arzelia's sister, Sally, was a school teacher and owned a lovely saddle horse which she rode back and forth to school. One morning the soldiers rode up to the barn to take what they wished and Sally saw them putting the bridel on her horse. So, boldly she started to the barn. Her mother (Nancy) pleaded with her not to go, thinking they might dare to harm her. But Sally was dauntless and confronted the soldiers. She said: "Now look here gentlemen, you surely wouldn't take a lady's horse that she rides to school. You are soldiers, yet there must be some gentlemen left in you."

They looked at one another sheepishly then took the other horses and left while Sally stood holding her horse by its bridle and petting it. When Sally returned to the house after putting her horse back in its accustomed stall; her mother said, "Sally, you are a brave girl. You out-smarted those soldiers."

William Henry Barker and Angeline Gevedon were married in Morgan County. He was a Veteran of the Civil War. Born to this union were six children.

1. Johnny, who grew to manhood and later married Arzelia Rose.
1. Mary, who married Henry.
1. Tom, whom married Bessie Caudill.
1. Willie, who was a school teacher for over half a century and later was Superintendent of Morgan County school system, married a Miss McGuire.
1. George went out west and married there.
1. Dudley died unmarried. He was cashier of the bank at Cannel City for many years.

Johnny Barker, son of William Henry Barker and Angeline Gevedon, married Arzelia Rose and they made their home on Stillwater on land that she inherited. Born to this union were six children:
2. Elmer Powell, who married Mary Wynne Hampton and they settled near Winchester, Ky. Elmer taught school for several years, after he was graduated from the University of Kentucky, then later became a traveling salesman for school text books.
3. They had two children, Anne Wynne, who was graduated from the University of Kentucky where she majored in music, and is teaching music in the city schools of Winchester in 1954-55.

3. Johnny, a son, in his teens, who is a student in Winchester school. He was named for his grandfather, Rev. Johnny Barker.

2. Harold Barker married Avariel Horton and they moved to Michigan after their first four children were born. Harold worked in the oil fields for many years.

3. Adrian, eldest of Harold and Avariel Barker's children, was graduated from College where he majored in engineering. He is a mining engineer. He is married and has three children.

3. Gerald Barker, second son of Harold and Avariel Barker, also was graduated from college in Michigan. He is coach at Kalamazoo, Michigan where he lives with his wife and two children.

3. Patricia, first daughter of Harold and Avariel Barker, married John Payne, after she graduated from high school.

3. Richard Harold finished high school and went to work at Ford's plant in Detroit. He is married.

3. Jack was graduated from high school in June, 1954.

3. William, called "Billy", was a high school boy in 1954.

2. Luna Dell, first daughter of Rev. Johnny Barker and Arzelia Rose Barker, married Marion L. Horton and they lived in Wolfe and Lee Counties of Kentucky for several years while he worked in the oil fields. After their first two children were born they moved to Middletown, Ohio where they have lived since that time. Marion has a good position with Armco Steel Plant where he still works.

3. Mabel, oldest daughter of Marion and Luna Dell Horton, was graduated from high school and then married Robert (Happy) V. Campbell. They have four children.

4. Gerald, 12 years of age, Lynda, 9, Richard 7, and Nancy, 3 in 1954.

3. Kathleen, second daughter of Marion and Luna Dell Horton, attended Miami University at Oxford, Ohio. While there she met her future husband, William E. Burch. They were married his last semester in school, where he was also graduated. He was in the U. S. Navy for six years as a Lieutenant. During this time his headquarters were in Europe for the last two and one-half years of his service. Kathleen joined him over there for the last 18 months and they had many interesting trips over the continent.

3. Donald L. Horton is a graduate of Miami University, also, and went into the service in 1954, shortly after he married Kathryn Ann Bahl, who is also a graduate of Miami University.

2. Garland Barker, second son of Johnnie Barker and Arzelia Barker, was unmarried when this information was collected in 1954. He served in the Army during World War II and is presently working out of Detroit, Michigan delivering trailors over the United States and into Canada.

2. Genola Barker, second daughter of Johnnie Barker and Arzelia Barker, married Wilmer Hieronymus and they have two sons, Jimmy and Tommie. They live in Dearborn, Michigan. Wilmer is a

graduate of the University of Kentucky and holds an important position with Ford Motors in the engineering department. Their two boys are both young and in school.

2. Rodney Barker, the baby of the Johnny Barker family, married Jean Cable. They have three children, Marvin, Mary, and Gary. Marvin was 17 and Mary 16, and Gary 12, in 1954. Rodney works in the advertising department at Armco Steel in Middletown, Ohio. where they live.

FIRST HOLLON TO SETTLE IN WOLFE COUNTY
(Submitted through the courtesy of Captain James I. Hollon of Hazel Green.)

John Hollon, Sr., is thought to have been the first settler in Wolfe County. He built a house on Swango Fork of Stillwater. His wife was Charity Brewer Hollon.

Rebecca Hollon, who married a Pence, Andrew Pence, was the first child born in Wolfe County in 1802. William Hollon was born in 1804. John Hollon, Jr., youngest son of pioneer John Hollon, Sr., was father of J. B. (Buchanan) Hollon, who was county court clerk of Wolfe County several times; the first time in 1890.

John Buchanan Hollon was the father of Captain James I. Hollon of Hazel Green and several other sons and daughters.

The original name of the Demira Bella Dit Von Hollon came from Belgium. They settled in England about 1300 when Phillipa Van Halen married King Edward III of England, from English Royalty, the present generation of Hollons in Wolfe County originated.

About one-fourth of Wolfe County at one time belonged to the pioneer John Hollon, Sr., who operated a fur and trading post.

THE HURSTS OF WOLFE COUNTY
(Taken from "The Hurst of Shenandoah" by permission of the copyright owner.)

The Hursts of Wolfe County are traced back through the book. "The Hursts of Shenandoah" compiled by J. C. Hurst of Lexington and are shown in this same book to be descendants of three brothers, William, James and John Hurst, who came to the Shenandoah Valley from Buckinghamshire, England about 1730. They settled in Virginia and later migrated to Kentucky and other parts of the United States.

Since this book will deal with many illustrious families which settled in Wolfe County during the early 1800's, we can only give a brief account of each family here.

Samuel Hurst was married to Sally Landsaw in 1825, whose home was on Stillwater Creek in Wolfe County in 1826. Samuel was the son of Henry and Elizabeth Hurst and the grandson of "Mill Creek" John Hurst and Nancy Nunn Hurst. Though Samuel sought his bride in Wolfe County, he went back to Breathitt County to settle near his father on Quicksand.

However, after the death of his mother, Elizabeth, who was buried in Breathitt County, Samuel moved into Wolfe County in 1836 on lands purchased on Stillwater Creek. Later his father, Henry, moved here on the same farm and he and his widowed daughter, Elizabeth Childers, kept house in a log cabin at the head of Bets Branch (named for her). She was locally known as "Bets" Childers. Henry continued to live in Wolfe County until 1842 when his daughter, Elizabeth, married a second time to Absolom Haney, who took her to his home at the mouth of Haney's Branch on Grassy Creek in Morgan County. Henry lived there until his death in 1844.

Harmon Hurst, eldest son of Henry Hurst and Elizabeth Kiser Hurst, was born in Russell County, Va., on Aug. 23, 1785 and died in Buchanan County, Mo., Nov. 24, 1872. Harmon married Francis Haddix on August 14, 1815 and one of their daughters, Elizabeth, married James Landsaw, who lived in Wolfe County. The children of Elizabeth Landsaw, for the most part, migrated to Missouri where their grandparents, Harmon and Francis Hurst, lived many years and died at a ripe old age.

In 1827 records show that Elisha, third son of Henry and Elizabeth Kiser Hurst, moved to Stillwater (then Morgan County) later Wolfe County.

4. Mary E., daughter of Mary A. and William Taulbee, born in 1865, and died in May 1950, in Oklahoma. Married B. F. Patrick. They had five sons, Breck, John, Bryce and Clarence Patrick and one daughter, Gertie Patrick.

4. Martha R., born to Mary A. and William Taulbee, 1867 and died in 1870.

4. Eliza B., born to Mary A. and William Taulbee in 1869 and died in 1922, married Frank Lacy. They had five sons, Homer, William R., Samuel H., Bedford and Paul; also four daughters, Stella, Hannah, Elizabeth and Jessie.

4. Miles K., born to Mary A. and William Taulbee, 1871 and died in 1924, married Lora Crawley. They had five sons, William P., Arthur, Miles K. Jr., Joseph and Allen Taulbee.

4. Weston C. Taulbee, born to Mary A. and William Taulbee, 1875, still living in Dec. 1954, married Sana Tyra. Their home was in Hazel Green, Ky. for many years, after which they moved to Clay City, where the wife died, then W. C. broke up house-keeping. They had three sons: William H., Robert and Henry B. Taulbee; also five daughters: Mary Anita, who married a Salyer; Lena Lane, who married Jesse Vancleve; Ruth, who married E. L. Miller; Esther, who married and Regina, who married Elwood Center.

This land was known as the Franklin patent and is now on Highway No. 15. The last assessment against Elisha Hurst was in 1829.

In the fall of 1829, he and his wife and children left Stillwater Creek in a covered wagon bound for Illinois. The next we hear of him he is living at Big Creek in Edgar County, Ill.

Esther Hurst, eldest daughter of Henry and Elizabeth Hurst, was born in Russell County, Va., 1794 and died in Wolfe County, April 13, 1887. She was married to Andrew Wilson Jr., on Feb. 12, 1819 and her husband was the son of Andrew Wilson Sr., and Mary Nickell Wilson.

To Esther and Andrew were born four sons and three daughters: Frank Preston, James R., Samuel H., Richard M.; America, Mary A. (Polly) and Elizabeth.

Andrew and Esther moved to Wolfe County about 1841 where they purchased land on the forks of Red River at what is now known as Helechawa and there they remained until their death.

America, their daughter, married Samuel Haddix, (Who was a brother of Harmon Hurst's wife), and they made their home on Gilmore Creek in Wolfe County. America and Samuel Haddix had three sons and six daughters: Menifee, who married twice, first to Emiline Little and then to Elizabeth Vest;

Pauline, who married George Little. Caroline who married Elsberry Little. Rosaline who married Andrew Lindon. Henry who married Vina Little. Esther married William Lindon. Andy married Nancy Vest. Mary (Polly), who married William Fugate, and Elizabeth, who married Logan Childers.

Frank Preston, son of Esther and Andrew Wilson, was born on July 10, 1823, and died on Jan. 7, 1862. He was married to Louis Trimble, 1831, who died in 1922. Preston and Louisa made their home in Wolfe County on Red River. They are buried in the Hazel Green Cemetery. They had four sons and two daughters: Henry, who married Adeline Johnson; Asbury, who died early; Howard, who married Elizabeth Tipton, and Elvin, who was shot and killed in Pauhiska, Okla.; Rose, who married Floyd Stevens, and Elizabeth, who married Joe Stevens.

WOLFE COUNTY

Samuel Henry Hurst, son of Esther and Andrew Wilson, was born on Nov. 18, 1827, and died April 25, 1902. He married Polly Ann Nickell. Sam Henry inherited his father's farm at the forks of Red River in Wolfe County, where he resided until his death. He was a prominent and highly respected man in the community in which he lived; being elected to serve as sheriff of Wolfe County four years.

Samuel Henry Hurst and his wife, Polly Ann Nickell Hurst, had two children: America, who married twice, first to George M. Fairchilds and second to S. C. Alexander, and Gilliann, who married J. B. Hollon.

Mary A. (Polly), daughter of Esther and Andrew Wilson, was born on March 6, 1831 in Breathitt County and died in Wolfe County on Red River on August 16, 1916. She was married to William Taulbee, Sept. 9, 1848. Their home was at Adele, Ky., a few miles above the home of her brother, Samuel H. Wilson. The husband, William Taulbee, was a soldier in the Mexican War and was elected and served four years in the Kentucky Senate. To them were born 12 children, seven sons and five daughters as follows:

John A. Taulbee, born in Wolfe County in 1849, died in 1827, in Temple, Texas. He was a psysician and practiced his profession for many years in Hazel Green, Ky. He married Mary Cope, daughter of Calloway Cope, Breathitt County, in 1938. To them were born seven children: Ida L., Sabina A., Edward O., Callie L., Martin L., Lisle M., and William B. Taulbee.

William Preston, son of Mary A. and William Taulbee, was born in 1851 and died in 1890. He was married to Emma Oney. He was a prominent politician and an orator of some note. In 1886 he was elected to Congress from the 10th district of Kentucky, defeating his Republican opponent and kinsman, W. L. Hurst. He was re-elected and was a member at the time of his death. He was shot and killed on the steps leading from the East corridor of the House of Representatives, in Washington, D. C. by Charles Kincaid of Danville, Ky.; who was a correspondent for the Louisville Times. The trouble arose over an article Kincaid had written for his paper. Taulbee is said to have pulled Kincaid's ear where upon he shot him. Kincaid was tried and acquitted. William P. and his wife and five sons: James H., John H., Joseph F., William H., and Edgar W.

4. Nancy Esther, daughter of Mary A. and William Taulbee, was born in 1854 and died in 1933. She married Bryce Hammonds and they had one son, Logan, and one daughter, Clara L.

4. Samuel Henry, son of Mary A. and William Taulbee, was born in 1856 and died in 1906. He married Ellen Davis in 1938. He was a farmer and lived on Red River. He had two sons, George C. and Russell B. and two daughters, Mary H. and Blanche.

EARLY AND MODERN HISTORY

4. J. Breckenridge, born 1858 and died in 1929, married first to Mollie Patrick. He was a prominent physician and practiced in Mt. Sterling, Ky., until his death. He had two sons, Woodson H. Taulbee and Rowland S. Taulbee and also two daughters, Esther and Bertie Taulbee. He married a second time to Edith Bear and they had one son, Kelly L. Taulbee.

4. Clarinda Lane, daughter of Mary A. and William Taulbee, was born Jan. 13, 1860 and married John Holliday. No children.

4. James Menifee, son of Mary A. and William Taulbee, born in 1863 and died in 1937. He married Maude Combs. He was a physician and moved to Texas and had one son, Paul Taulbee.

4. Elizabeth, daughter of Esther and Andrew Wilson, was born Oct. 7, 1834 and died Jan. 8, 1909. She married William R. Davis. Their home was on Red River in Wolfe County and he lived to be over a hundred years old.

Children of Elizabeth and William R. Davis are as follows: James Andrew, married Elizabeth Henry; Esther C., who married Peter E. Gullett; Henry Wise, who never married; America E., who married T. Harlan Nickell; and Mary Louise, who married John A. Prather.

5. Children of America E. Davis Nickell and T. Harlan Nickell were: Boyd, Martie, John T., and Dennis T. Nickell.

4. Richard Menifee, son of Esther and Andrew Wilson, was born on Quicksand Creek in 1836, died on Red River in Wolfe County, Ky., Jan. 30, 1922. He married Clarinda Lykins, May 5, 1856 after which he made his home on Red River except for a short period during the Civil War, when he moved to Mt. Sterling.

Children of Richard Menifee Wilson and Clarinda Lykins Wilson were:

5. Harlan, America, Frank Preston, who married Nancy A. Nickell and Andrew and Jackson.

4. John Washington, son of Elizabeth and Elisha Childers, was born on Quicksand Creek in Breathitt County, Kentucky, Sept. 1, 1825 and died in Hazel Green, in 1921 after he had passed his 96th birthday. He married Julia Landsaw, youngest daughter of William Landsaw. They lived on Stillwater Creek, an inheritance of the wife from her father, until 1957; after which he purchased a tract of land in Morgan County. He also purchased a tract of land on what is known as "Dry Ridge" in Menifee County where he lived until during the Civil War when he moved to Mt. Sterling. After the war he moved back to his farm on Dry Ridge and lived there until his death. Children of John Washington Childers and his wife, Julia Landsaw Childers, were:

5. Samuel Henry Childers, who married Jane Collins.

5. Richard Apperson Childers, who married twice, first to Al-

media Tutt and second to Ella Hill.

    5. Rudolphus, who married Elizabeth Nickell.
    5. Dulcenia, died in 1872, never married.
    5. Elizabeth, who married L. C. McGuire.
    5. Archibald, who married Dora McGuire.
    5. Lyle, who married twice, first to Jefferson Oakley and second to Owen Lawson.

    4. Archibald, son of Elizabeth and Elisha Chambers, was born in Breathitt County in 1828 and was married to Mahalah Byrd in 1827. They lived in Wolfe County until after the outbreak of the Civil War. He took an active part in behalf of the Union and on account of local conditions he moved his family to Harrison County as a matter of safety. After the death of his first wife, he married Mellissia Jones. To this union were born ten children:

    5. Lourany, who married Lee Andrew Patrick.
    5. William E., who married Alice Hutton.
    5. Elisha M., who married Zerilda Nickell.
    5. Elizabeth Ann, who died at the age of three years.
    5. John W., who married three times: first to Lucy Hutchinson, second to Bettie Eave, and third to Jennie Terry.
    5. Jane, who never married.
    5. Rinda Ann, who married James Knox.
    5. Matilda, who married S. J. Roberts.
    5. Frances E., who married John W. Knox.
    5. George Byrd Childers, who married Elizabeth Rose.

SAMUEL HENRY HURST

Samuel Henry Hurst, fourth son of Henry and Elizabeth Kiser Hurst, was born in Russell County, Va., Sept. 9, 1799 and died on Stillwater Creek, Wolfe County, Ky., on Dec. 1, 1888. Samuel Henry Hurst was married to Sally Landsaw, who lived near the Fork of Stillwater Creek in Wolfe County.

After he came to Frozen Creek, he continued to buy land and he soon owned practically all of the Nickell and Hursts Forks to the Wolfe County line. Later he began to buy land on Stillwater and within a few years he owned nearly all the land from the Breathitt county line down to the mouth of Murphy Fork, making a total of perhaps 8,000 acres of land.

In 1836 he decided to move to his Stillwater land in Wolfe County, a distance of about six miles from his Frozen Creek residence. He built a large two-story log house with all the necessary outbuildings at the mouth of Pryor Branch of Lacy Fork.

To Samuel and Sally were born four sons and four daughters: Andrew Kiser, William L., Elizabeth, Esther, Daniel D., Dulcenie. Henry C., and Emily Jane, the last four of which were born on Stillwater in Wolfe County.

2. Andrew K., his oldest son was being prepared for the medical profession, but before he was ready to begin practicing he was stricken with typhoid fever and died in July 1847, at the age of 21 years and was buried on the hill above the family residence.

On August 8, 1853, the wife, Sally, died and was buried beside her son, Andrew. Samuel never married again. He kept his family all together until they were grown or married and he and his daughter, Emily Jane, and her husband, continued to live together after her marriage, until Samuel's death.

Everything went along in the regular way in the Hurst family until the outbreak of the Civil War. Samuel owned a number of slaves and with them carried on a successful farming business for that time and section of the country.

Since the people of Wolfe County were very much divided as to sympathies during the Civil War, some being in favor of the South and some in sympathy of the North, with the majority perhaps, siding with the rebellion. Samuel Hurst and his sons were in sympathy with the Union. But they thought they could keep quiet about it. Later, however, the sons joined the conflict on the side of the Union and due to their visiting their father under cover of darkness, the Rebels became suspicious of them.

On May 5, 1862, Samuel received word that his son, William, had been wounded in a fight with Confederate soldiers on the head of Red River. He immediately started out to see him and arrived soon after dark. During the night, after receiving re-inforcements the Rebels, who had been repulsed, returned and made prisoners of both Samuel and his son, William. They were taken to Libby prison in Richmond, Va. where they were held for six months and then discharged.

After being released from prison, Samuel returned to his home on Stillwater, Nov. 30, 1862, where he found his daughter, and family trying to exist as best as they could. However, some of his livestock and even some of the furniture had been taken over by the Rebel Guerrillas. He kept himself concealed as best he could but the news of his return soon leaked out and he had to be on the dodge continually. He was soon convinced that he could not live where he was so he went to Mt. Sterling which was in the hands of the Union forces where he stayed until March of 1864; then he rented a farm near there and came back and moved his family to it with the aid of the Army escort. He continued to live in Mnotgomery County until the close of the war when he moved back to Stillwater, Wolfe County.

Although he had lost much property during the war he again boldly took up the burden of life and was soon on the road to success.

In 1867, his daughter, Emily Jane, married Alfred C. Kash, who afterwards made his home with his father-in-law. In 1868 his other daughter, Esther, married Zera Welch, who made her home in Powell County. Sometime after Samuel moved from his old homestead and located one mile down the creek where he remained until his death in 1888.

In the meantime he divided his lands among his children with the exception of about 350 acres where he made his home. This was given to his daughter, Jane, by the terms of his will.

Samuel was a very religious man and a faithful member of the Hardshell Baptist Church. Immediately upon moving to Stillwater, he had Rev. Duff, come to Stillwater and organize what is still known as "The Stillwater Baptist Church." He was always an active member and continued to go there until his death.

William L. Hurst, son of Samuel H. and Sally Landsaw Hurst, was born on Quicksand, Breathitt County, Dec. 5, 1829 and died in Campton, Oct. 14, 1920. He was married to Isabella Duff on Oct. 4, 1877 by Rev. William Tutt. Isabella was a daughter of Henry C. and Mahalah Strong Duff. To this union were born five children, namely: J. Caessar, Minnie, Nellie, Hannibal, and Sally. William moved to Stillwater, Wolfe County, with his father, when he was seven years of age.

There were no schools in that part of the country and practically no teachers. A few years later his father went to Virginia and employed Jefferson Johnson, a teacher of some note, to come to his home and teach his two older sons. There was no vacation in this school and only two pupils who studied six days a week. After two years and one month of continuous school, save for Sundays, the teacher announced that he had taught the boys all he knew.

Samuel had selected the profession of physician for Andrew and that of a lawyer for William. About the year 1844 the father secured for the latter a position in the Circuit Court Clerk's Office at Irvine, Ky., and accompanied him there on horse back and saw that he was safely settled in his job and gave him the money necessary to pay his frugal expenses. As clerk he was furnished bed and board as compensation for his work but he received no salary. He was doing his work as part of his education. While there he acquired a good knowledge of legal forms and court procedure and he had access to law books which were around the court house. He utilized all his spare time in study. After spending three years there he felt he had learned all he could there, so he returned home to study some elementary books he had acquired. After studying at home for about two years he went to West Liberty, Ky., where he apprenticed himself to Robert Burns, a prominent attorney under whom he studied during the years 1851 and 1852; then he took the bar examinations and passed with a good grade and secured his license to practice law.

He went to Jackson and established an office where he soon built up a goodly law practice not only in Breathitt but in adjoining counties. He soon owned considerable property on Main Street and around town. He continued with a good business until after the Civil War broke out when he had to leave Breathitt.

When he returned to Jackson after the war he found his negro slaves gone, and most of his houses burned by guerrillas. He again took up his law practice but did not rebuild his home; but stayed at the hotel. Breathitt County, after the war was in a terrible state Feuds broke out and killings were ordinary affairs of the day.

After the close of the war he established his legal residence at Campton, Ky., and on May 29, 1878, he and his wife went to housekeeping at the head of Stillwater in Wolfe County, where all his children were born.

In 1883 he moved his family from Stillwater to Campton in order to educate his children. He owned a large farm at the edge of town on which he built a large brick residence and also a brick office in town. In 1895 he decided to retire from active practice and this he gradually did.

When William L. Hurst retired he owned about 6,000 acres of land and had saved up considerable money and had other property as well. He had accumulated a large library in addition to his law books and he now spent most of his time reading and looking after his lands. He received a Federal pension due to the loss of an eye during the Civil War. He always took an active interest in politics and attended practically all Republican state and district conventions and was a delegate to at least two National conventions.

He was elected for the state at large when James A. Garfield was elected president. He was the nominee of the Republican party for congress at the old 10th district in the year 1886; but was defeated by his second cousin, W. P. Taulbee, by about a 700 majority.

On January 1, 1916 the greatest blow of his life came when his son, Hannibal, was shot and killed while attending a dance at the

WOLFE COUNTY

Masonic Hall in Jackson, Ky. The son was a successful business man, 30 years of age, and held in high esteem by all who knew him. He nor his wife ever fully recovered from the blow. Though he lived to be almost 91 years of age.

At the time of his passing Circuit Court was in session in Wolfe County with Judge D. W. Gardner, present and presiding. They immediately suspended all business and the officers of the court and members of the Bar held a special meeting in his honor. After a number of talks were made eulogizing him they passed a group of resolutions in commemoration of his useful and colorful career.

They were formed by a committee formed by S. Monroe Nickell, G. B. Stamper, J. M. Tester, E. C. Hyden, and W. B. Duff and duly signed by S. Monroe Nickell, chairman of the committee, and other members, D. W. Gardner, chairman of the Bar meeting and J. C. Lindon, secretary.

After William L. Hurst's death his widow purchased a home at 642 Central Ave., Lexington, Ky., where she moved with her family and lived until her death in 1936.

Children of William L. Hurst and Isabella Duff Hurst, were: J. Caesar, born 1878, and who married June Hatton, October 1, 1939.

Minnie, born July 12, 1860, married July 1, 1914, to Dr. H. L. Biggs.

Nellie, born March 11, 1882, married D. B. Redwine, August 19, 1901.

Elsie, born Feb. 23, 1903, married W. G. Bush, 1923.

Isabell, born April 2, 1908, married Jan. 15, 1935, to William Jobe.

Haanibal, born June 1, 1884, died January 2, 1916, never married.

Sally, born June 9, 1886, married twice, first to Albert R. Marshall who died May 23, 1937 and second time to John M. Reed, in March, 1940.

William L. Hurst served with the Army during the Civil War and supported the Union. He was made a captain with 100 men under him in the early part of 1862, soon afterwards when coming back to Wolfe County to scout around and pick up more recruits, on May 5, 1862 he was engaged in battle with some Rebel soldiers near what is now known as Lee City; where Wm. L. Hurst was shot through the right eye and also in the shoulder.

During the early evening after the battle his father, Samuel Hurst, came to see him and refused to leave him. Soon afterwards they were surrounded by Rebel soldiers and taken prisoners. They were taken by horseback over the mountains to Abington, Va., and lodged there as prisoners after the most terrible suffering. They were placed in a dungeon and kept a month. They had no bed clothing and Wm. writes in a letter that he used his shoes for a pillow. From thence they were moved to Richmond, Va., where they were imprisoned for nine days and fed with small rations of bread and water. They were offered their freedom if they would join the Confederate Army but upon refusing were marched from the prison to a tobacco warehouse on the south side of the St. James River. They were kept in the tobacco house for one month and given very bad treatment after which they were removed to the (infamous) Libby prison where they stayed in close confinement until released in October of that same year.

Libby prison was originally a warehouse which was converted into a prison. There was no furniture and the prisoners slept on the floor. The window in the room had no glass, just an open space. Orders were given that no prisoner was to be allowed to get close enough to the window to look out. One day a commotion occurred just outside the window and a Colonel, who occupied the same room with Sam and William Hurst was unthoughtful enough and the guard shot him dead. His body was allowed to lay in the room with the other prisoners for many hours to impress upon them that they meant what they said about not looking out the window.

William Hurst and his father underwent terrible suffering while in the prison the complete details of which are reported in a copy of Caesar Hurst's book, "The Hurst of Shendoah", from which this information was gleaned with the permission of the author.

In 1849 at a political gathering in Hazel Green, Samuel Hurst engaged in a fight with John Gibbs over a dispute over a tract of land. They were fighting with their fists and when Hurst seemed to be winning, Mason Gibbs, son of John Gibbs, attacked Samuel from the rear. William Hurst immediately rushed into the affray and stabbed Mason with a knife, making a serious wound from which he lingered for sometime near death; but finally recovered. In the meantime a warrant was issued for Hurst; but before the arrest could be made, he left the state and went to Russell County, Virginia, where he visited with his kinfolks, the Kisers, till Gibbs recovered and his father got the matter settled in court. He then returned to Wolfe County to study law.

Elizabeth Hurst Chambers

Elizabeth, eldest daughter of Samuel H. and Sally Landsaw Hurst, was born at Quicksand, Breathitt County, January 28, 1831 and died March 12, 1908, married Oct. 23, 1851 to Elisha Chambers whose father was Elijah Chambers and whose grandfather was Elisha Chambers, Sr. Their home during their whole married life was on Stillwater Creek in Wolfe County, Ky.

To Elizabeth and Elisha were born 12 children all of whom lived to maturity.

5. Jasper Newton, who married Sarah Ratliff. Jasper was a farmer and also served one or more terms as Justice of Peace in Wolfe County. His home was on the head of Chambers Fork of Stillwater.

List of their children: Elisha, married a Sebastian. Callie married Joe Cundiff. Monroe was killed by a train near Richmond. Jefferson married Hannah Blankenship. Cleveland married Francis Nickell. Eliza married Jerry Profitt, later died of T. B. Elizabeth married Henry Buchanan. Addison was married three times. Newton, Jr., died young.

5. Sallie married David Hogg, who served a number of terms as county court clerk of Wolfe County.

5. John married Francis Rose. Their home was on Stillwater Creek. Their children were: John, who married Margaret Brashears and Francis, who married Hiram Whisman.

5. Nancy married Bowen Rose. He was a successful farmer and lived on Stillwater. He was elected judge of Wolfe County and they moved to Campton where they lived until his death. He was a Republican. Their children were as follows:

6. Artie Rose, dead; Dora Bell married Thomas Hollon; Elisha married Mayme White; Millie married Walker Haney; Sallie died in infancy; Carl never married; Leona married Ceburn Allen; Gertrude married James Childers; Elizabeth married Kelly Combs; Jo Ann married George Haney.

5. William H., son of Elizabeth and Elisha Chambers, was born April 8, 1860 and died on Nov. 18, 1936. He was married three times: first to Rosalee Byrd, second to Rose Little, and third to Minerva Childers Shull. His home was on Stillwater. In addition to farming he taught school and was also a Hardshell Baptist preacher. He served a number of terms as superintendent of schools in Wolfe County.

Children of Rosalie Byrd and William H. Chambers were: Katherine, who married Bruce Rose.

7. Cecil, who married Martha Booth.

8. Rita Lee, who married Herschell Farmer and they have one son, Mike.

7. Frank, who married Ruth. Had one son, a student at the University of Kentucky.

6. Carrie, who married Roscoe Wells.

8. Children given elsewhere in history, under Rose family.

6. Zuda, who married Robert Rothman. She gave many years of her life as a missionary in a foreign land.

EARLY AND MODERN HISTORY

7. Robert, Jr., is a captain in the Army where he serves as a chaplain.

7. Richard Lee, a student in theological seminary.

Children of William Chambers and Rose Little:

6. Daisy Chambers, who is a school teacher. Never married.

6. Henry Clay Chambers, married twice. First, Martha Hollon and second Golden Bailey.

7. Children by both women.

5. Jefferson Davis Chambers, son of Elizabeth and Elisha Chambers, married twice. First to Francis Swango and second to Jessie Swango. No children second marriage.

6. Rhoda died at 12 years of age; Elizabeth married Hiram Whisman; Andrew Charlie died young; Elisha died young.

5. Dulcenia, daughter of Elizabeth and Elisha Chambers, was born on Jan. 3, 1864 and died on Jan. 10, 1936. Married David B. Rose. Their children were:

6. Lizzie Hane Rose, who married William Steele; Jefferson married Francis Taulbee; Granville married Nina Brewer; James married Etta Sweeney; Lillie married James Tester; Wayland married Claude Vest; Edna married John Rose.

5. Greenberry Chambers, son of Elizabeth and Elisha Chambers was born in Wolfe County in 1866, married twice. First to Ella Rose, who died without issue. Second to Martha Ann Chambers.

He moved to Texas in 1890 where he and his second wife had ten children, two of whom died when babies: Elizabeth, Lou Ethel, Elisha J., Sarah B., Cora, Minnie and Nancy.

5. Joseph Chambers, son of Elisha and Elizabeth Chambers was born on Dec. 29, 1867 and died on March 12, 1942. He married Louelen Byrd. They lived on Stillwater and he was a farmer. Their children were:

6. Loucinda, married four times: first to Courtney Rose, second to John Griffith, third to McDonald, and last to H. J. Good; Shirley married Marie Brandenburg; Sarah Ann married George Griffith; Joe Campbell married Garnett Brewer; Lillie married Steve Swango.

5. Elijah, son of Elizabeth and Elisha Chambers, was born June 30, 1869 and died Dec. 25, 1938. Was married twice. First to Nannie Tutt and second to Clara Cecil. He lived on Chambers Fork of Stillwater and was a farmer. His children by his first marriage were:

6. Lillie married Nathan Hatton; Elizabeth married Osa Wells; Lydia married Grover Flynn. He had no children by second wife.

5. Lydia Ann, daughter of Elizabeth and Elisha Chambers, was born Feb. 29, 1872, married twice. First to Kelly McClure, second to Logan Little.

6. Children by Kelly McClure were:
7. John Frank McClure, who married Alice Adams and Omer McClure, who married Effie Rose.
6. Children by Logan Little were:
7. Carrie Little, married Herbert Smith; Howard Little married Coreen Stevens; Elizabeth Little married Earl Lindon.
5. Esther Chambers, daughter of Elizabeth and Elisha, was born Nov. 1, 1874 and died on Dec. 17, 1927, married twice. First to Monroe Gevedon, second to Theopholus Cundiff. Children by Gevedon:
6. Estill Gevedon married Dora Gevedon.
6. Children by second marriage: Dulcenia married John Taulbee; Henry Clay Cundiff married Nora King, then Martha Hollon; Dan Cundiff married Elsie Cole; Brack married Wanda Evans; Lillie married Truman Perry; Logan Cundiff married Myrtle Taulbee; Marion Cundiff married Wilma Durbin.

Esther Hurst Welch

Esther, daughter of Samuel H. and Sally Hurst, was born on Oct. 5, 1835 on Frozen Creek, Breathitt County, died on March 3, 1874, married Oct. 16, 1868. Zera Welch.

After her marriage Esther moved to Stanton, then in Montgomery county, where she died. They had one son, William L., born Dec. 15, 1870 and married Oct. 14, 1925 to Mary Miller. Died on May 8, 1948.

Daniel Duff Hurst

Daniel Duff Hurst, son of Samuel and Sally Landsaw Hurst, was born on Stillwater in Wolfe County, Sept. 9, 1837 and died in Jackson, July 9, 1915. He was married at the close of the Civil War to Sarah Rebecca Ferguson, who died in 1880. He never married again.

5. Children of Daniel D. and Sarah Rebecca Hurst were:
5. Henry Hurst married Mary Kash.
6. Ethel married Hale Pearman.
6. Myrtle married Alex Crawford.
6. Dan married Frances Deep.
5. Florence, born in Wolfe County in 1867, married James B. Marcum, a prominent lawyer of Jackson, trustee of the University of Kentucky many years, and a U. S. Commissioner many years preceding his death. He was assassinated in the front door of the courthouse at Jackson, Ky., on May 4, 1903, by Curtis Jett and Tom White and their trial was one of the most famous ever held in Kentucky. This assassination was in connection with the famous "Hargis-Callahan-Cockrell feud," which was so well advertised over the entire nation. They had six children.
6. Nell, Tom, Alfred, Imogene, James B. and William Marcum.
5. Elizabeth, daughter of Daniel D. and Sara R. Hurst, was born in Montgomery County, married twice, first to Walter Boone, they

EARLY AND MODERN HISTORY

had two children: Henry and Dan Boone. Second to Lawrence Jones. They had two children: Rebecca and Clyde Jones.
  5. Fannie, daughter of Daniel D. and Sarah R. Hurst, was born in 1872 and married Talyrand Snowden. They had two children: Mabel and Edward Snowden.
  5. Maggie, born 1874, died in 1891.
  5. William Rupard, born in 1879, lives in Oregon.

Dulcenia Hurst Kash
  4. Dulcenia Hurst Kash, daughter of Samuel H. and Sally Hurst, was born on Stillwater, Wolfe County, Ky., Nov. 15, 1839 and died in Bourbon County, Jan. 15, 1907. She married James Kash of Breathitt County. After their marriage they began housekeeping on the Rock-house fork of Stillwater on a tract of land given her by her father. Here their oldest son was born.
  5. Samuel H. Kash, born in 1861 and died in 1922. He was married twice, first to Elizabeth Stoops, and second to Neta Johnson.
  6. One daughter by second wife, Frances, who married Henry V. Pennington.
  5. Mary Belle Kash married I. N. Phipps.
  6. Frances married Howard Miller.
  6. Harry Kipling Phipps married Minnie.
  6. Anna Mildred married twice.
  5. William L. Kash, born in Wolfe County in 1869 and died in 1911. He was an engineer for the C&O Railroad and was killed in an explosion at Bagdad, Ky. He married Julia Armstrong. They had two children: Jessie and Helen.

Henry C. Hurst
  4. Henry C. Hurst, son of Samuel H. and Sally Landsaw Hurst, was born on Stillwater on May 24, 1842 and died on August 9, 1930. He married Caroline Wilson, daughter of Shelby Wilson, whose home was on Red River in Wolfe County. After the Civil War he moved to Oklahoma where he lived until his death.
  5. Alice married D. W. Ball; Bruce never married; Clay never married; James married Jessie Patton and they had two children, live in Oklahoma; Bertie married O. Goodwin; Holt married Marie Jarrett.

Emily Jane Kash
  4. Emily Jane Kash, youngest child of Samuel and Sally L. Hurst, was born on Stillwater, in Wolfe County, Nov. 4, 1844, and died in Lexington hospital, Feb. 28, 1928. She married Alfred Cope Kash, Dec. 23, 1867. He was a brother to James S. Kash, who married Dulcenia Hurst, sister of James. After Jane's marriage they continued to make their home with her father until his death. In addition to farming, Alfred C. Kash was a school teacher. He also was storekeeper for a distillery for several years. A few years before his death they moved from Stillwater to Campton. After his death his

WOLFE COUNTY

widow moved to Hazel Green where she lived many years, then moved to Jackson.

5. Laura E. married H. B. McGuire. They had the following children:

6. Bruce married Nell Little; Everett (Ted) H. married Eula Hammonds.

7. Three children: Jimmy, and twins, a boy and girl.

6. Asher married Pearl Combs; Lindsay married Onie Sweeney, second time Leona Clapp (dead); Eugene married Kathleen Morgan; Trimble, single; Alfred married Mary Owen Lewis; Wendell married Geneva Rolph.

5. Samuel H., born Nov. 2, 1871, died Jan. 20, 1944. Married Bertha Samples. He taught school, kept a store in Hazel Green many years after he was married, also was post master for several years. Moved to Lexington where he had a farm, also held position as U. S. Deputy Marshall, later was working for the city of Lexington when he died suddenly of a heart attack.

6. Lucille married Charles Burton.

7. Son and daughter.

6. Maurine married Charles Edmons. No children.

5. Elisha Chambers Kash, born in 1874 and died in 1944. Married Anna Broaddus. Lived many years in Jackson where he owned considerable property. He was a traveling salesman for several years, served as Railroad Commissioner for the 3rd District of Ky. Later sold all his property in Jackson and moved to Lexington to educate his children. He died there of a heart attack.

6. Howard married Fannie Bell Perry.

6. Mary Jane married Abshear.

5. William L. Kash, born Jan. 15, 1877, now dead. He was an attorney at law for many years, practiced in Jackson and later in Irvine where he died. He served two terms as Commonwealth Attorney. He was also a Hardshell Baptist preacher. He married twice, first to Ollie Swango. They had two children: Charles married Helen Mauer. Died soon afterwards with peritontitis; Irene married Leonard Slusher. Had two children.

Second marriage was to Florence Chaney and they had twins: Mary Lee and William Everett Kash.

5. John Kelly Kash, born in 1878, married Nell White and lived many years in Jackson, where he served one six-year term as Commonwealth Attorney. Then he moved to Washington, D. C. where he spent many years working for the Government.

Kelly has served as a news reporter, school teacher, commonwealth attorney, and lawyer. Kelly says that he saw the celebrated Hargis-Cockrell feud in Breathitt County from beginning to end. This feud lasted ten years and during that time more than a hundred men died violently at the muzzle of a gun because of feuding. He was an eye witness to the slaying of J. B. Marcum.

While Herbert Hoover was president, Kelly went to Washington as legal counsel for the Bureau of Internal Revenue. Following this he went into private practice in Washington. Shortly before and at the beginning of World War II he served on a committee which made a survey of Military installations in the U.S.A. He was also a commissioner in the Foreign Economic Administration.

He was making plans to return to Washington again in the spring of 1954 when he took seriously ill and was confined to a hospital in Lexington, Ky. At this time he is still anything but a well man.

5. Daniel Hurst Kash, born August 17, 1881 and died July 19, 1927, married in 1910 to Loura Rose, daughter of Silas H. Rose. He (Daniel) was a physician and practiced his profession for many years in Wolfe County, later in Jackson, Ky., then moved to a mining camp near Jackson, where he was located as camp doctor when he died in a Lexington hospital following an appendectomy operation. He was buried at Hazel Green Cemetery. Children of Daniel and Loura Kash are:

6. Vernon, who made a doctor, served as a doctor during World War II overseas was ranked as a Captain. Married Wilma Hays. They have three children.

7. Danny, Larry and Becky.

Dr. Vernon O. Kash and children now reside in a recently built, and perfectly beautiful modern home in Winchester. Danny is a student at Millersburg Military Institute, and the other two children attend school in Winchester.

6. Mildred, the only daughter of Dr. Daniel Kash and Loura Rose Kash, married Robert Coleman Stilz, who is now president of Bank of Commerce in Lexington, Ky. They have four children: Alvin, Robert, Kash and Gayle.

5. Oliver, born May 22, 1887 to Jane and James C. Kash, married twice, first to Monnie McLin and second to Lena.

6. Children, all by first wife. Christine married.

6. Dorothy married a Reece and they live in Florida.

6. Oliver Kash Jr., is a chiropractor and lives in Grayville, Ind. He married Lavinna. They have two sons.

TRUE INCIDENT
(This interesting bit of material was submitted by
Mrs. Bess Hollon Gullett.)

Speaking of ancestors and history, there is a true story told me by my 93 year old aunt, Mrs. America Wilson Alexander.

Her grandmother, Easter Hurst Wilson, came from Virginia. A brother, Sam Henry Hurst, had drifted to Kentucky, married and settled in what is now Breathitt County.

Easter, when a young woman had her fortune told, as was a custom in those days and also served as a form of amusement for the young folks. Her fortune was very interesting. The fortune teller told her something like this, "You think you're going to be married to the young fellow to whom you're engaged; but you're not. You've never seen your husband to be. You're taking a long trip soon and there you will meet the right one."

Easter Hurst didnt wait long until she came to Kentucky to visit her brother, Sam Henry Hurst. A party was given in her honor after she arrived in Kentucky, and there she met Andrew Wilson, the man she married, and she remained in Kentucky to rear her family.

Of her grandchildren, only four remain, namely: W. C. Taulbee, formerly of Hazel Green; Jackson Wilson, Breathitt County; Frank Press Wilson, and Mrs. America Wilson Alexander, both of Helechawa, Wolfe County.

Many great and great-great-grandchildren live in Eastern Kentucky and refer to her as "Old Granny Wilson."

THE HORTONS
(Contributed by John White, August, 1954)

W. S. Horton was born in 1812 in Virginia and Martha Jane Richmond was also born in Virginia in 1812. They were married in Virginia and came to Kentucky about 1830. They had nine children hereafter designated as number one, or first generation in Wolfe County.

1. John W. Horton married Mary E. Shackelford.
1. Isaac Horton married Liza Shumaker.
1. Harvey married Amelia White.
1. Thomas married Anna Tyler.
1. Wm. Frank married in Campton, Ky., to Elizabeth Wills, daughter of Jordan Wills, born 3-3-1856.
1. Isabella married Perry Taulbee and they had two children.
1. Sarah married J. N. Vaughn. They had two sons and three daughters.
1. Mary Jane was never married.
1. John W. Horton and Mary E. Shackelford had five children.
2. Nancy Horton married W. E. White.
2. W. A. Horton married Lelia Evans.
2. Floyd Horton married Martha Bradley.
2. Eliza Horton married Cud Hanks.
2. Emma Horton married William Willis.
1. Iraac Horton married Liza Shumaker and they had four children: (2) Jesse, John, Clarence and Newt.
2. Nancy Horton, daughter of John W. Horton and Mary E. Shackelford Horton, married W. E. White. They had five children.
3. Mollie White married Willie Lacy.
3. John White married Mary Tyler.

3. Emory White unmarried.
3. Roscoe White married Samantha Hall.
3. Edna White married Shully Coons.
2. W. A. Horton, son of John W. and Mary E. Horton, married Lelia Evans and had three children.
3. Alpha married James Galbreath.
3. John Horton married and moved away.
3. Norah married Harris Arnett. She is now deceased.
3. Bufford married a daughter of Roe Patton.
2. Floyd Horton, son of John W. and Mary E. Horton, married Martha Bradley and they had six children.
3. William married and moved away.
3. Reece married and moved out of the county.
3. Rev. Z. A. Horton married an Osborne in Menifee County. He was a preacher for many years.
3. Vernon married away from here.
3. Ellis married Steve Bowen.
3. Martha moved away.
2. Eliza Horton, daughter of John W. and Mary E. Horton, married Cud Hanks. They had four children.
3. Seldon Hanks married in Ashland.
3. Beulah married Claude Stamper.
3. Emma never married.
2. Emma Horton married William Willis and they moved out of the county and had several children.
1. Harvey Horton and Ameila (White) Horton had five children.
2. Sarah married W. C. Smith, later known as Judge Bill Smith.
2. Dora married Gus Lykins.
2. Alice married J. D. Lacy.
2. Mary Jane married Mort Combs.
2. Newt married Nora Byrd.
1. Thomas Horton, son of W. S. and Jane Richmond Horton married Anna Tyler and they had nine children.
2. Frank (now dead) married Lula Tutt.
2. Eugene married Hettie McCoun.
2. Catherine married Charles Hieronymus.
2. Cora married Lee Congleton, both now deceased.
2. Richmond married Lillian Byrd. He is now dead.
2. Sarah (dead) married Wilson Hammonds.
2. C. B. Horton (dead) known as Corsie, married Gertrude Crawford.
2. Claude married away and lives in Mexico.
2. Herbert (dead) married Ethel McCoun.
2. Marion L. Horton married Luna Dell Horton.
Frank Horton, who married Lula Tutt had five children.
3. Avariel married Harold Barker.
4. Six children. See Barker family.

3. Beth married a Coffman and lives in West Virginia. They had three children.

3. Anna married Jimmy Adams. They live at Somerset, Ky., and have three sons. He has an important position with the State Department of Kentucky Highways.

3. Berta married Shirley Brown. They live at Owensboro, Ky., and have two children.

Eugene, son of Thomas and Ann Horton, married Hettie McCoun and has six children: (3) Robert, Eunice, Seldon entered the Air Corps and is stationed in the West in 1954, Allene and Theron (a girl).

2. Catherine married Charles Hieronymus and had eight children.

3. Wilmer married Genola Barker and they have two sons, Jimmy and Tommy. Wilmer is a graduate engineer from the University of Kentucky and holds a responsible position with Ford Motor Co., in Detroit, where they own their lovely home.

3. Grace is a teacher and is unmarried.

3. Jean married and lives near Somerset, Ky.

3. Jerome married and lives at Frenchburg.

3. Jack married and has one child and lives in Detroit.

3. Paul lives in Washington, D. C. and is in the Diplomatic Service.

3. Benjamin is married and lives in Somerset, Ky., and is a successful dentist.

3. Albert is married and lives near Beattyville with his parents, who are now elderly people.

2. Cora, daughter of Thomas Horton and Anna Tyler Horton, married Lee Congleton and they lived in Lexington. She is now dead. Lee Congleton gave to each of his children, $20,000 in money and they had six children.

3. Ethel unmarried and is a teacher in the Lexington schools. She teaches French. She studied in Europe, languages, and music lessons on the harp and also studied other things.

3. Dewey married and lives in Lexington. Has one daughter, Anne, who is married and has one child.

3. Herman is married and lives in Lexington.

3. Ralph is married and lives in Lexington and has two children.

3. Inez is married and they have two boys. She married a Dulaney and they live down south.

3. Virginia is unmarried. She is a doctor specialized in obstretics and is connected with one of the larger hospitals in Cincinnati, O.

2. Richmond Horton married Lillian Byrd. He is now deda. They had three children.

3. June Horton is unmarried and teaches school.

3. Hope is also unmarried.

3. Billy is unmarried and in the Service of his country.

2. Claude, son of Thomas Horton and Anna Tyler Horton, is married and lives in New Mexico. They have five children.

2. Sarah, daughter of Thomas and Anna Horton, married Wilson Hammonds. They had one daughter, Mabel.

3. Mabel Hammonds married Howard Wiles, a teacher at the University of Kentucky. They have one son, Howard, Jr., who was graduated from West Point Military Academy and is making the Army his career.

4. Howard, Jr., is married and is stationed with the Army Post in Virginia. (5.) One child.

2. Corsie (C. B.) Horton, now dead. Married Gertrude Crawford. He was graduated from the University of Miami, Ohio. They had six children.

3. Ralph is married and has two children. He runs a successful grocery and hardware store.

3. Maureen is now deda. She married.

3. Charles Horton, Jr., is married. He is studying to be a merchaical engineer. He has two children and they make their home in Flint, Michigan.

3. Evangeline is a nurse. She married a professor and lives out west. She and her husband spent three years in Ethiopia making an educational survey. They arrived back in the United States in August, 1954. They have three children.

3. Hazel is unmarried and lives at home.

3. Thomas is married and lives in Detroit. He is manager of one of Kressge's large stores there. They have three children.

2. Herbert, son of Thomas and Anna Horton, was married to Ethel McCoun. He is now dead. They had six children.

3. Raymond, married and lives in Louisville. He is in TV and Radio work. He has three children.

3. Glen is married and also lives in Louisville. He is a salesman. No children.

3. Wilson is married and lives in Louisville and has some children.

3. Herbert, Jr., and Samuel is married.

3. Virginia and Leona are married.

All of Ethel and Herbert's children were reared in the Children's Masonic Home, Louisville, after his death.

2. Marion Horton married Luna Dell Barker and they had three children.

3. Mabel married Robert (Happy) Campbell.

4. Gerald, 13; Lynda, 10; Richard, 8; Nancy, 4 years.

3. Kathleen married William E. Burch. They both attended Miami University where he received his degree. They now live in Minneapolis, Minn. He spent six years in the Navy as a Lieutenant.

They toured Europe rather widely while he was in Service.

3. Donnie married Kathryn Ann Bahl. They are both graduates of Miami U. Donnie is now in the Army and stationed in Washington, D.C.

THE TILMAN JOHNSON FAMILY
(Contributed by Mrs. J. B. Buchanan and other relatives.)

Tilman Johnson came to Wolfe County from North Carolina and married Mary Elizabeth (Betsy) Swango. They had eight children: Frank, Lou Ann, Debbie Ellen, Maria, Adeline, Ella, Nannie and Caroline.

1. Frank Johnson married Caroline James. They had 12 children: Willie, Ellis Alvin, Mollie, Fannie, Rettie, Lou, Myrtle and Pearl were twins, Joe, Callie, Frank and Emma.
2. Willie married Bell Fallen.
2. Ellis Alvin married Ida Taulbee and second Lou Ward.
2. Mollie married Porter Lacy.
2. Fannie married Willie Rice.
2. Rettie married Frank Sample.
2. Lou married Elmer Jones.
2. Myrtle married Forest Cecil.
2. Pearl married Will Davis. (Myrtle and Pearl were twins).
2. Emma died at 17 years, unmarried.
2. Joe died at an early age.
2. Callie married Boone Lacy.
Frank married Grace Lacy. No children.
Willie Johnson married Bell Fallen and they had four children.
3. Ova, son of Willie and Bell Fallen Johnson, married in Ohio where they live.
3. Charlie also married in Ohio.
3. Jess married in Montana where they live.
3. Louis is now deceased.
2. Ellis Alvin Johnson married Ida Taulbee and they had six children before she died and he then married Lou Ward. There was one child (died at birth) by his last marriage.
3. Ethel married John Beverly Buchanan and they had four children.
4. Ida Nell married Marvin Leo Mitchell. They live in Middletown, Ohio where he is employed at American Roller Mills. One daughter. (5.) Elaine.
4. George W. (Jack) Buchanan married Evelyn Hammond; both are graduates of Berea College. Jack served in the Army two years after their marriage. He is now Vocational Agriculture teacher near Frankfort, where they live. One son. (5.) David Scott.
4. Roger, graduate of Berea College where he was also President of the Young Men's Organization his senior year. He served in the

EARLY AND MODERN HISTORY

U. S. Army two years and was stationed in Germany for almost eighteen months of this time. He was honorably discharged from Service in June and is back home now (1956).

4. Kenneth attended Eastern State College, Richmond, Ky., one year. Then went into business working for a Road Contracting Co., in Dayton, Ohio.

3. Archie Tilman Johnson married Anna Rose. They had two children.

4. Ellis Alvin, named for his grandfather Johnson, married Frances Collins. She is working towards her Master degree at Columbia University, New York City. E. A. attended college two years, then went into business in Jackson, Ky., where he is a partnership owner of Dodge-Plymouth Garage.

4. Byron married Betty Byrd, daughter of Curt Byrd. He is working in Middletown, Ohio. They have one daughter. (5.) Patricia.

Archie and his first wife, Anna Rose, were divorced after his two sons were born and he later married Angeline Rose, daughter of Stevie Rose. To this union was born one daughter, Rosemary.

4. Rosemary married Raymond Harris, a graduate of the University of Kentucky in the College of Engineering. Rosemary attended Morehead College two years. They have two children. They live in New York where he is employed. (5.) Mary Diane and Paula Jane.

3. Bob Johnson married Mary Haynes.

4. Bobbie, their oldest son, lost his life while in the U. S. Navy during World War II.

4. Twins, Billy and Betty. Billy married Virginia Barker. Billy is an interior decorator. They have two daughters.

5. Linda Lee and Katherine Marie.

4. Betty married Ward Young. Ward and Betty are both school teachers. They are teaching in Algonac, Mich. They have two daughters. (5.) Diana Lynn and Carol Ann.

4. Norma married Joe Sharp.

4. Laura, while in college, married Ray LeCornic, who is a graduate Diessel Mechanic. They have one daughter. (5.) Cynthia Rae.

3. Mary Johnson married James S. Walker, who is now a retired fireman from the City Fire Department of Dearborn, Mich. They have one daughter. (4.) Beverly married Don Sutter while in college.

3. Gladys married Frank Franklin. They live in California. Have three children.

4. Joe, in college; served in the Navy 4 years. He is married.

4. Mary Ann was killed in a tragic car accident in Pamona, California at the age of 15 years.

4. Mike is about 13 years of age (1956). The Franklins live in Pamona, California.

3. Lillian Johnson married Ralph Cann and they live in Dear-

born, Mich., where he has been 25 yeras with the Traffic Department of Ford Mfg. Co. Three children.

4. Ralph, Jr., is a graduate of Law School and is practicing in Detroit. He married Eleanor Tappan. Two children.

5. Paul Brian and Karen Ellen.

4. Carolyn, daughter of Ralph and Lillian Cann, married Bill Wolf. Two daughters. (5.) Leslie Jane and Tracy.

4. Doris married Dick Kohyna. They are living in California. Have one daughter. (5.) Laura.

2. Mollie Johnson married Porter Lacy. Two children.

3. Flossie married Perry Swango. No children. Established a successful business in Lexington.

3. Courtney Lacy married Pearl Clark. One son.

4. William Earl married Edna Mae Emmel. He is a graduate of the University of Kentucky. Works in coal fields now at Pineville. Children: (5.) William Earl Jr., Kathy and Johnnie.

2. Fannie Johnson married Willie Rice.

3. Rollie Rice married Golden Taulbee.

4. Olin is married and has one child. Lives in Dayton, Ohio.

4. Dorothy married Delmar Strong and they live in Dayton, O. Have one son.

4. Anna Lou married Charles Strong. Live in Dayton, Have two sons and one daughter.

4. William married Wanda Graham. He is in the Army and they have one daughter.

4. Iva Nell is a waitress in a restaurant in West Liberty.

4. Merna married.

4. Austin at home in school age.

3. Beulah married Charlie Nickel.

4. Vernon married.

4. Fay married and has one daughter.

3. Marvin was accidentally shot while out squirrel hunting. He married Gladys at Salyersville.

3. Rella married Mort Lindon.

4. Eula Jean is a graduate of Berea College and teaches in Illinois. Now married.

4. Ralph was in Service a couple of years and since returning has been working for the State Highway Department. Married Wanda Hatton.

4. Alta is in college at Eastern State, Richmond, Ky., graduated.

4. Wanda is also at ESTC, Richmond, graduated. Now married.

4. Joe is in the Army.

4. J. C. is in school.

4. Carolyn also in school age.

2. Rettie Johnson married Frank Samples.

3. Pearl married Bruce Adams. They had twin boys.

3. Henry, James and Fuller, all died of Tb. before they were 21

EARLY AND MODERN HISTORY

years of age.

2. Lou Johnson married Elmer Jones.

3. Troy married in Iowa.

2. Myrtle married Forest Cecil.

3. Mara married Howard DeHart and they live in Ashland. No children.

3. Charles married Mary Catherine Nickell, the second time. He married before this and to the first union was born a son, Charles Cecil Jr.

4. Girl and boy to second marriage.

3. Helen married Robert King.

4. Robert Jr.

2. Pearl married Will Davis. He is now deceased. She lives in California.

3. Lucius.

2. Sarah Caroline (Callie) Johnson married Boone Lacy. They had six children, then he died. She later married Malcom Barker and they had two children and he died.

3. Oliver, married Jessie Gollege. They had three children and live in Columbus, Ohio.

4. Marjorie Ann married Johnny Gossman. They live in Columbus, Ohio. They have three children: (5) Jeffrey, Phillip and Timothy.

4. Norma Jean married Johnny Hicks and they have one son.

5. Steve.

3. Ollie died a young unmarried daughter at home.

3. Monnie is unmarried and lives at home with her mother in London, Ohio. Monnie is an operator for the Ohio Bell Telephone Company.

3. Devonia married Charles Cundiff. They live in London, Ohio and have one daughter: (4) Sandra.

3. Hallie married Blair Childers. They live on a farm on Johnson Fork of Lacy Creek, Wolfe County. No children; very active in community affairs. They serve as Worthy Matron and Worthy Patron of the Hazel Green Chapter No. 514 of OES. Mrs. Childers is also president of the Homemakers club at Hazel Green.

3. Sanford Lacy married Reba Tom and they live in Summer Ford, Ohio. They had three children. Mark died an infant.

4. Alan Lee and Joyce Lynn.

3. Minnie Ellen Barker, daughter of Sarah C. Johnson Lacy Barker and Malcom Barker, died when a small girl.

3. Frank Barker, son of Sarah C. and Malcom Barker, married Martha Davis. They live in Youngwood, Pa., and have three children.

4. Nedra, Susan Jessica and Sarah Caroline.

WOLFE COUNTY

GRANDPARENTS OF JEFFERSON JOHNSON
(Contributed by Mrs. Molly Johnson Rowland)

John Johnson was born 1742.
Ellen Johnson was born 1744.
John Siphers was born in Virginia.
Nancy Siphers was born in Virginia.
Parents, Elijah Johnson, born 1787, died April 30, 1863, in Ky.
Annie Siphers Johnson, born 1788, in Virginia, died May 15, 1863 in Kentucky.
Children of Elijah Johnson and Annie Siphers Johnson:
Louticia was born in 1814 in Virginia.
Jefferson Heldridge was born May 9, 1816 in Virginia. Died June 30, 1859, Hazel Green, Ky.
Elizabeth was born in 1820 in Virginia, came to Morgan County with her parents about 1840.
John Johnson was born in 1824 in Virginia. Came to Morgan County with his parents, and went on West.
George Johnson was born in 1827 in Virginia. Lived in Morgan and Breathitt Counties, Ky.
Ellen Johnson was born in 1830, in Virginia, died May 11, 1863 in Kentucky.

Jefferson H. Johnson married Dec. 25, 1845, Mary Swango in Wolfe County, (Morgan County then). He was a school teacher, according to Captain Bill Hurst, a prominent attorney of Wolfe County, he was one of the best teachers Wolfe County ever had. Capt. Hurst was an old man when he made the statement while addressing a Wolfe County teacher's Institute in the summer of 1910 at Campton, Ky. A granddaughter, Mollie Johnson, was then teaching her first school in Wolfe County.

1. Jefferson Johnson and Mary had six children:
2. Cleta, born Dec. 1846, Morgan County. Married 1871 to James Monroe Spencer.
2. Thomas Crittendon, born Jan. 21, 1849. Died Sept. 15, 1921 in Lee County.
2. Jessie Ann, born Oct. 26, 1851. Married June 20, 1866 to Wm. Hainline.
2. Ella Jane, born April 8, 1854, married 1873 to Amby Wimer.
2. Deborah A., born March 27, 1856, married Dec. 29, 1872 to William Tyler.

Mariah Jefferson Johnson, born March 17, 1858, married Dec. 17, 1874 to William Hainline at her home in Breathitt County. She was then living with her mother and step-father, Henry Combs. She went to Missouri to live as did her sisters, Ella Jane and Jesse Ann who died in 1872.

Cleta and Jim Spencer were married in Wolfe County and lived at Malaga. They had a daughter who married a Brooks. They had a son, Howard Spencer. The fourth child was Thomas C. Spencer. He married Laura Napier of Owsley County. They moved to Lee County where their three children were born. They now live in Jackson, Ky. Their daughter, Maurene Spencer, married a Waller. They live in Chicago and have no children. Elizabeth is married and has some children. Their son, William Spencer, is married, has children and a good job in Jackson, Ky.

2. "Debbie" Johnson married William Tyler at her home in Breathitt County. Judge E. W. Strong officiated.

3. Will Tyler was born in Lee County, Virginia, Oct. 4, 1852. He died April 21, 1920, in Wolfe County. He was a powerful Methodist preacher and reared a big family in Wolfe. Fifteen children were born to this union, 10 girls and five boys.

4. The eldest, Ella Jane, was born May 17, 1874. Married Jan. 17, 1895 to William Bumgardner of Wolfe County. They had one daughter, Lydia.

5. Lydia married and lives in Ft. Wayne, Ind.

4. Clara, Perla, Gale B., Maude and William Barron, Lennie Ruth and Hugh Bascom, all either died young or had no children.

4. Catherine, born Aug. 19, 1878, married Marion Faulkner and had several children.

4. Hersons, Willie and Carl Tyler are all preachers in Wolfe and Breathitt Counties.

For several years one daughter has been a missionary in India.

4. Mary Tyler was born June 14, 1880 and married John White of Wolfe County. They have several children. (See White family).

4. Daisy Tyler, born April 17, 1882, married Arthur Kincaid in Wolfe County. They lived in Wolfe County and reared several children. Daisy now lives in Middletown, Ohio.

4. Ursey Tyler was born Feb. 29, 1888. She married March 8, 1908 to Christopher C. Hanks of Wolfe County. He was born March 3, 1884, and died Nov. 28, 1938. They had five children: Eulah, Allene, C. C. Hanks Jr., Lyda Ruth, and Bessue Lee.

5. Eulah Hanks, born June 28, 1919, married Feb. 2, 1932, Cecil Mills.

5. Allene Hanks, born June 24, 1912, died June 23, 1935. Married March 13, 1929 to Jesse Curtis.

5. C. C. Hanks, Jr., born March 4, 1914, died Nov. 27, 1938.

5. Lyda Ruth Hanks was born April 7, 1916, married Dec. 30, 1951, Robert Lewis.

Bessie Lee Hanks was born Feb. 24, 1918, married July 1, 1950, Luther Hillard.

Ursey Tyler Hanks now lives in Middletown, Ohio.

4. Thomas Roscoe Tyler married Ethel Lykins of Wolfe County They had eight children:

5. Cecil; Ruth who married a Hughes; Blanche married a Rageland; Barnes; Elmer; Norman; Monical married a Nealy boy.

WOLFE COUNTY

5. Marcella married a Henry. They all now live in Clark County. Before moving to Clark, Roscoe was a prosperous merchant in Campton.

4. James Tyler was born April 6, 1894. He married Oct. 20, 1921, Rosella Wireman, Wolfe County. He was a farmer and also a judge of Wolfe County. They had five children:

5. James Kenneth Tyler, born Oct. 17, 1923. James is now a farmer near Franklin, Ohio.

5. Helen Louise, born Dec. 3, 1925.

5. Wilder Jean, born Feb. 16, 1928.

5. Doris Maxine, born Nov. 24, 1931.

5. Phyllis Linnet, born Sept. 1, 1942.

4. Cora Alice Tyler, was born Feb. 18, 1892. She married a Shull boy in Wolfe County and they had several children. The union was dissolved. Alice now lives in Dayton, Ohio.

2. Thomas C. Johnson was the only son of Mary Swango and Jefferson H. Johnson. He was only 11 years of age when his father died. He was the second of six children. After some years his mother remarried Henry Combs of Breathitt County. Mr. Combs had several boys by a former marriage who also lived with them and later became prominent citizens of Kentucky. Mr. Combs died and was buried in Breathitt County. Mary Swango Johnson Combs then made her home with her daughter, Debbie Tyler. She died June 5, 1897 and was buried in the Tyler graveyard at Vortex, in Wolfe County, Ky.

Thomas C. Johnson was Clerk of Wolfe County when he married Jan. 13, 1874, Eliza Jane Bowling of Laurel County, born Feb. 20, 1856 at Oakdale, Breathitt County. Tom was born at Hazel Green at that time in Morgan County.

Elzia died Feb. 4, 1943 in Lexington, Fayette County and was buried in the Lexington Cemetery. Fifteen children were born to this union: The first three were born in Campton:

3. Clara, born Dec. 1, 1874, died Jan. 7, 1875.

3. Allie May, born May 7, 1876, died June 7, 1941. Married Nov. 11, 1934, John Murphy.

3. Jefferson Heldridge, born Oct. 24, 1877, died Nov. 11, 1935, Jessamine County.

The next three were born at Stillwater:

3. Jesse B., born Feb. 28, 1879, died Nov. 8, 1918, Fayette County. Buried in family graveyard at Tallega, Lee County, Ky.

3. Richard Revel, born Oct. 28, 1880, died June 17, 1954 in Oklahoma. Buried in Fayette County Cemetery, Lexington, Ky.

Loretta Johnson, born May 17, 1882, died April 17, 1884.

Seven of the children were born at Flat, Kentucky:

3. John Elliott Cooper, born Jan. 23, 1884.

3. Minnie, born Dec. 19, 1885, died June 20, 1951, Fayette County. Buried in Lexington Cemetery.

EARLY AND MODERN HISTORY

   3. Clayborn Xenephon, born Oct. 25, 1887.
   3. Willie Johnson, born May 24, 1889, died June 25, 1889.
   3. Archibald Leonard, born July 30, 1890, died June 4, 1953. Fayette County. Buried in Lexington Cemetery.
   3. Mary Belle (Mollie), born March 15, 1892.
   3. America Marcella, born Dec. 20, 1893, died Nov. 1, 1898, Lee County.

Two were born after the family moved to Tallega, Lee County, Kentucky.
   3. Maxiline, born Nov. 27, 1895.
   3. Deborah, born Nov. 30, 1897.

Jefferson was a merchant at Malaga, Wolfe County, Ky., when he married on Feb. 25, 1903, Calla Abner, of Lee County, who was born Oct. 2, 1879, the daughter of John Abner. To this union were born four children:

   4. Lillie Pearl, born May 13, 1904 at Malaga. Lillie Pearl married William (Bill) Deaton, of Breathitt County, Sept. 20, 1924. He was born Nov. 7, 1905. Their children are:

   5. William Deaton Jr., born July 13, 1925, Dayton, Ohio. He married May, 1946, Dorothy Caino, born May 1926, Scott County, Ky., and they have two children: Patricia Lane, born Feb. 28, 1947. Billy Gene, born Oct. 1951, Troy, Ohio. Their father is a skilled tool maker in Ohio.

   5. Vernon Lane was born Feb. 16, 1928, Dayton, Ohio. He married Nov. 11, 1950, Thomas Hilma Barkley, born July, 1928, Scott County, Ky., and they have a daughter, Dane Lee, born Dec. 29, 1954, Lexington, Ky. Vernon Lane is a carpenter. Both he and his brother, Billy, served in the Armed Forces.

Lillie Pearl and Bill Deaton are propsperous farmers of Jessamine County. During the early thirties they operated a farm at Malaga, Ky., in Wolfe County.

   4. Eva Lee, the second child of Jeff and Calla Johnson, was born Nov. 6, 1905, Malaga, Ky. She married Dec. 1, 1926, Erie Pelfrey of Breathitt County. They had two children:

   5. Wanda Lee, born Nov. 19, 1927, Breathitt County. She married April 1949, James Daniel Green. They have one son.

   6. Anthony Green, born in Dayton, Ohio.

   5. E. C. Pelfrey, Jr., born July 13, 1929, Breathitt County. He married August 13, 1952, Bonna Rae Farmer of Montana. They have three children.

   6. Patricia Ann, born in Dayton, Ohio.
   6. Susan Gail, born in Dayton, Ohio.
   6. Deborah Fay, born in Dayton, Ohio. Their father served several years in the Armed Services overseas prior to their marriage. He is making Military Service his career.

September 1, 1948, Eva Lee Johnson Pelfrey remarried to Hugh Hardman of Fayette County.

4. Abner Johnson, the third child of Jefferson and Calla, was born at Malaga, March 5, 1913. He married Lucille. They have one son.

5. William Abner, who was graduated from Nicholasville High School, Jessamine County, Ky., in June 1956. The same year he won the State Public Speech contest with the Future Farmers and received an expense paid trip to the National Contest held in Mo. He will enter the University of Ky. this fall (1956). His father is a prosperous farmer of Jessamine County. A few years before his death Jeff and Calla Johnson purchased a good farm in Jessamine County. Lillie Pearl and Abner each bought half the farm.

4. Jeff, Jr., the fourth child of Jeff and Calla Johnson, was born Aug. 28, 1918 at Jackson, Ky. He died May 20, 1919.

3. Richard Revel, the fifth child of Tom and Eliza Johnson, was a doctor, living at Tallega, Lee County, when he married, Sept. 17, 1918, Fannie Glass at her home in Booneville, Owsley County, Ky. She was the daughter of Dr. Arch Glass. To this union were born three children.

4. Richard Chadwick, born March 19, 1920 at Tallega. Married Dorothy Bradstreet at Waterby, Conn. in 1943. She was born June 12, 1922. Chad is a doctor. He did Military Medical Service in the Eastern States. Now lives and practices in Sand Springs, Okla., where his father practiced about 35 years. Chad and Dorothy had three children:

5. Cindy, born July 3, 1944, New Haven, Conn.

5. Valery, born Feb. 16, 1949, Oklahoma.

5. Richard Chadwick, Jr., born Dec. 7, 1954, Okla.

4. Shirley, Chad's sister, was born Aug. 18, 1921 in Sand Springs, Okla. She married Oct. 7, 1948, Brown James Aiken II, born in Texas, Dec. 5, 1916. They have one son.

5. Brown James Aiken, the third, born Aug. 1, 1951, in Tulsa, Okla. They deal in the distribution of pure foods.

4. Archibald Lawrence Johnson, was born July 29, 1932 in Sand Springs, Okla. He was graduated from Washington-Lee University and is now studying law.

3. John E. C., the seventh child of Tom and Eliza Johnson, was married, June 5, 1912, to Nellie Tye. To this union were born three children:

4. Princess Lucille, born June 13, 1914. She married Alfred M. Reece Jr. They have two sons:

5. Jerry Tye Reece, born March 5, 1933.

5. Thomas Speed Reece, born Jan. 31, 1939. They live in Lexington, Ky. with their father, who re-married. Princess is now married to Tom C. Fleet. They live in Sinton, Texas where they operate their own radio station.

4. Thomas Crittenden Johnson, second child of John E. C. and Nellie Tye, was born Feb. 20, 1916. He married June 9, 1935, Alta

Mae Bowles of Hazard, Ky. To this union twin girls were born, April 7, 1936; Tommy Christine and Kathanne Earl.

Tommy Christine died at an early age.

5. Donald Clayton was born June 8, 1938. He is an invalid.

Kathanne, the other twin, is now a Junior at the University of Ky. She has the wide blue eyes of the Johnsons and beautiful blonde hair. Tom, the father of Kathanne, is in the express business between Lexington and Whitesburg.

4. John Elliott Cooper Johnson Jr. (Jack) was born Feb. 7, 1918. He married Feb. 7, 1948, Elizabeth Elwins Williamson, Louisville, Ky. They have no children. They operate a grocery business.

The union between John E. C. and Nellie Tye Johnson was dissolved and each remarried.

3. Minnie, the eighth child of Tom and Eliza Johnson, married Nov. 16, 1910, Douglas Kincaid at her home at Tallega, Ky. "Dug" was 32 years of age, a bridge foreman, born in Lee County, the son of Socrates Kincaid, Sr. His mother was Anne Trimble of Montgomery County. To this union were born four children. The first died in infancy.

4. The second was Garvice Delmar Kincaid (G. D.), born Aug. 9, 1912 at Tallega, Ky. He is a lawyer, banker and financeer of Lexington, Ky. He married Oct. 4, 1940, Nellie Wilson of Lexington, born Aug. 16, 1915. They have twin daughters: Jane and Joan, born Dec. 10, 1941.

4. Mildred Kincaid, the third child of Minnie, married Frank Richardson of Madison County. They have two daughters.

5. Ann, married Paul Craycraft of Paris, Ky. They have one child.

5. Emma Jean, who is about 18 years of age, lives with her parents in Miami, Florida.

4. Beulah Grace, the fourth child of Minnie, was born Sept. 3, 1917 in Richmond, Ky. She married Walter Norris, of Maddison County. They have one son.

5. Blaine (Button) Norris, about eight years old.

Grace and Walter operate Joyland Park, Lexington, Ky.

3. Clayborn, the ninth child of Tom and Eliza Johnson, was a practicing attorney of Lee, Wolfe and other mountain counties in Kentucky when he married, March 17, 1923, Cora Johnson Ward of Lexington, Ky. To this union no children were born. They live in Lexington where "C. X." practices law.

3. Archibald Leonard, the eleventh child of Tom and Eliza Johnson, graduated from Hazel Green Academy in 1912. He was a graduate of the University of Kentucky and Louisville Medical College. Did extensive interne work and specialization. Practiced his profession in Lee and Fayette Counties. Served in the Navy during World War II. He was married twice but had no children. He was subject to the drink habit. He died June 4, 1953, in Lexington, Ky.

3. Mary Belle (Mollie) the twelfth child of Tom and Eliza Johnson married March 31, 1923, Lester Ambrose Rowland of Owsley County, son of James Sherman Rowland and Florence Ellen Ambrose Rowland. They were married in the Christian Church at Beattyville, Ky., by Rev. Martin Roberts. Both were former school teachers. Lester has been in the Railway Mail Service since 1919. He was born May 13, 1896. He attended Eastern State Normal College at Richmond, Ky. Mollie was graduated from Hazel Green Academy in 1912 and the University of Kentucky in 1915. They have three children:

4. Thomas Sherman, born April 2, 1925, Lexington, Ky.
4. Julia Florence, born Nov. 16, 1928, Lexington, Ky.
4. Eliza Bowling, born Feb. 16, 1931, Lexington, Ky.

Tom was graduated at the University of Ky., has taught in high school and college. Now is employed as Mathematician by the Ames Auerenautical Laboratories, Moffit Field. Julia married March 19, 1947 in Lexington to John O. Breninger of Canton, Ohio. John works for Lockheed and Julia works for Bendix in California. They have two charming daughters:

5. Jacquelyn Ruth, born Jan. 3, 1948 in Lexington, Ky.
5. Jorj Allae, born Sept. 23, 1949 in Phoenix, Ariz.

4. The third child of Mollie and Lester Rowland, Eliza Rowland, was graduated from the University of Ky. in 1952, served in the Navy two years and four months, in the Reserves, is a Lieut. Jr. grade. Since March 1955 has been employed by Delta Air Lines, in Chicago.

3. Maxiline, fourteenth child of Tom and Eliza Johnson, was married Sept. 17, 1918 at Tallega, Ky., to Ozia Claud Mingledorff II, born Nov. 21, 1894, Marlow, Ga. They were married by Claud's father, Rev. O. C. Mingledorff. Following their marriage they sailed to the Korean Mission Field where they served six years. Since, they have pastored churches in the states. They are now employed as teachers in a Bible College in North Carolina. Born to this union were five sons and one daughter:

4. Ozie Claude III, born July 7, 1919, Choon Chun, Korea. He was killed in Service D-Day, Normandy Beach in World War II, June 6, 1944.

4. Harry Warren, born April 26, 1921, Choon Chun, Korea. He was married to Jean Elizabeth Stock, Toronto, Ohio on June 26, 1942. They were missionaries to Mexico and Peru, S. A. 1943-1949. They have three sons:

5. Dale Warren, born May 22, 1943 at Johnstown, Pa.
5. Byron Claud, born Nov. 4, 1947 at Lima, Perue, S. A.
5. Kenneth Ray, born May 13, 1950 at LaGrange, Ga.

5. Joel Phillip was born April 11, 1924, Choon, Chun, Korea. He married Feb. 16, 1951, Norma Lena Hambrick at Columbus, Ga. They have one son.

6. Lowell Phillip, born July 19, 1952, Hamilton, Ga.

5. Stanley Peyton, the fourth son, was born March 19, 1928 at Douglas, Ga. He married June 28, 1952 at Kankakee, Ill. They have one daughter:

6. Renee, born Sept 6, 1953, Kansas City, Mo. The locations of marriage and birth were places where Stanley and Rachel Lillian Watrous (his wife) were in school.

5. Walter Russell, the fifth son, was born Feb. 6, 1932, White Oak, Ga. He married Maurine Burton at Chicago Heights, Ill. April 1954.

5. Edith Maxiline, the only daughter, was born June 4, 1939 at Toronto, Ohio. She is a senior in High School. She is an Honor student.

3. Daisy, the fifteenth child of Tom and Eliza Johnson, had her name legally changed to Deborah at Newport, Campbell County, Ky., in Feb. 1954. On Dec. 24, 1923, she was married to Jouett Chelby Boone of Stanton, Ky. They were married in Lexington, Ky. To this union were born four children.

4. Emilee, Sept. 12, 1924, Stanton, Ky. She married Dr. Harold G. Murphee of South Rhodesia at Ft. Thomas, Ky. on Sept. 10, 1944. They have four children:

5. Aweyneth Elizabeth, born May 30, 1946 in New York City.
5. Threce Ilene, born Feb. 8, 1948, in Monterey, Calif.
5. Harold Mark, Jan. 11, 1952, New York City.
5. James Thomas, born Jan. 11, 1952 in New York City.

Emily was graduated from Asbury College, Wilmore, Ky., where she met Harold, whose parents were missionaries to South Rhodesia. While Harold was a medical student in Cornell University, Emilee was in nurse's training in a hospital there. One of Harold's military assignments was Frankfurt, Germany. His family accompanied him.

4. Ada Bowling Boone was born Oct. 30, 1925 at Stanton, Ky. She married June 18, 1948, Ft. Thomas, Ky. to Richard Rex Sandburg of Cincinnati, Ohio. They have two children:

5. Nils, born Feb. 22, 1954, Cambridge, Mass.
5. Nancy Howe, born April 24, 1956, Cambridge.

Ada and Rex were graduated from the University of Cincinnati and did graduate work in New York. Rex is an accountant.

4. Clara Lyle Boone was born Sept. 6, 1927, Stanton, Ky. She has been a music teacher for the past six yeras. She was graduated

from Centre College, Danville, Ky. and did graduate work at Radcliff.

4. Daniel Boone, the only son and a distant relative of the Pioneer by the same name, was born Feb. 28, 1929, Lexington, Ky. He was graduated from West Point in June and married July 19, 1952, Nancy Belle Colley of Covington, Ky. Later they found themselves to be distant cousins through their Crawford ancestors in Breathitt County. They have two children:

5. Cheryl Teressa, born May 16, 1953, Biloxi, Miss.
5. Daniel Morgan, born Jan. 13, 1955, Fairbanks, Alaska.

OUR FIRST KASHES OF KENTUCKY
(Part from Caesar Hurst's book and other sources.)

James and Caleb Kash were the first two by this name to come to Kentucky from Greenbriar County, Va.

1. James Kash married Phoebe Lacy (sister to Lucy "Lacy" Trimble. See Trimbles.) Children:
2. Rachel Elizabeth.
2. Caleb married Polly Wilson.
2. James married.
*2. William married Sally Cope.
2. Lucretia married.
2. Nancy married.
2. *William Kash married Sally Cope. Children:
*3. Levi married Molly O'Rear of Montgomery County, Ky. Captain C. S. A.
*3. James married Dulcenia Hurst, settled in Montgomery Co.
3. Alfred married Emily Jane Hurst (see the Hurst family).
3. Caleb married Miss Strong (daughter of Ned), Breathitt Co.
3. Priscilla married John Strong, Breathitt Co.
3. Phoebe married Robert Barnett, went to Kansas.
3. Polly Ann married Stephen Carpenter, Breathitt Co.
3. Elizabeth married Green Williams, to Oklahoma.
3. Miranda married John C. Calhoun (See Wm. Day Family). Had three sons and two daughters.
3. *Levi Kash married Molly O'Rear.
4. Children: Lee, Luther, Letcher, Lillie, Laura and Lula.

*3. Levia Kash was a Captain in the Confederate Army and he was the only one of the Wm. Kash family to belong to the Confederate side. On one or two occasions during the Civil War, Levi met his brother, who was fighting on the Union side. They warned each other of dangers.

2. Caleb Kash married Polly Wilson, (daughter of Andrew), born 1800 and died 1873 — strange his wife's birth and death date were the same as his. Children:

*3. Levi married Mary Ann Pieratt (sister to Eli Pieratt).
*3. Miles married Elizabeth Dennis.
*3. Mason married a Goodpasture first, then married Eliza Maxey second. Lived at Hazel Green.
3. Shelby J. married an Adams.
3. James married.
*3. Joe married Sarah Ellen Swango (daughter of Harrison).
3. Reece married.
3. Evalina married Samuel Swango.
3. Elizabeth.
5 sons and 1 daughter. (See Abraham Swango Family.)
*3. Levi married Mary Ann Pieratt. Three sons and one daughter.
4. H. B., Caleb, Franklin, Howard married Nannie Mapel (see George Mapel Family), Anna married a Collinsworth, moved to Mo.
3. *Mason Kash married a Goodpasture. Two children. Married second Eliza Maxey. Two sons and three daughters:
4. J. Frank Kash married Ducia Belle Salyer (lived in Ohio).
4. Dr. Silas Kash married Maggie Pieratt.
4. Roscoe Lee Kash married Floyd Day (See Wm. Day Family).
4. Emma Kash married Wiley C. May (moved to Okla.).
4. Marjorie (Maggie), now dead, married Price Sewell (died Feb. 1955). Had two sons:
5. Franklin Sewell, M. D. married Corine Bach (Mt. Sterling, Ky.).
5. Price Sewell, M. D. married and lives in Jackson, Ky.
3. *Miles Kash married Elizabeth Dennis. Children: 5 sons.
4. Samuel, William, Stephen, Ova married Ora Cecil (daughter of J. B. and Angie Cecil). Children.
3. *Joe Kash married Sarah Ellen Swango (daughter of Harrison). Children, two sons and four daughters:
4. Rollin married Lula Day (See J. T. Day Family).
4. Bonnie married Will Jones.
4. Lula married Noah Ciscoe (graduated and taught at HGA). Graduated with the class of 1896, HGA. Won one of the first scholarship medals offered at HGA.
4. Stella died at 16 years of age.
4. Ella married S. E. Fishbach. No children. Live in Kansas City, Mo.
1. Caleb Kash married Elizabeth Trimble, married second Cenia Wilson. (brother of the first James Kash). Children by 2nd wife. Settled on Gillmore.
2. Sallie and Fanny.
2. Andrew married. Two sons, Arburry and McClellan; one daughter, Frances.
2. Caleb married a Campbell. Settled on Ky. River and reared a large family.
2. William married.

Among the early families which settled in Wolfe County was Alfred and Jane Kash, to whom were born a large family, mostly boys. The daughter, Mrs. Laura Kash McGuire, now of Jackson, is still living though in her eighties. Three of the sons: Dr. Daniel Kash, Rev. Will Kash, and Ely Kash and Sam Kash are dead, though they lived illustrious lives and were well known all over Wolfe, Breathitt and Estill Counties.

Oliver Kash, the youngest son, who sells insurance, lives at Fulton, Ky., and Kelly Kash lives at Irvine, Ky.

Kelly Kash was an attorney; but has been a newspaper reporter, school teacher, commonwealth attorney and lawyer. He was born in Wolfe County and entered upon his career during the turbulent feuding days of Eastern Kentucky. Being an apprentice lawyer under the late Judge J. J. C. Bach of Jackson at the time, he did not take any active part in the litigation resulting from the feuds until the latter part of the internecine wars which ended about 1912. Rather as a means of financing further study of law, he turned to newspaper reporting and wrote of the deeds and actions of the feudists instead of being connected with their prosecution or defense in the court trials which resulted.

Kash says he saw the celebrated Hargis-Cockrell feud of Breathitt start and end. This feud lasted ten years and during that time, more than 100 men died violently at the muzzle of a gun. As a reporter for the Lexington-Leader, Lexington Herald and Louisville Evening Post, Kash was of a necessity in the thick of things and was an eye witness to the slaying of J. B. Marcum, a leading lawyer of Eastern Kentucky.

In his capacity as a reporter he led an exciting and somewhat dangerous life during this period of time. Kash gave up his work as newspaper reporter during the administration of Gov. Augustus E. Wilson. He was appointed Commonwealth Attorney of the Judicial District made up of Lee, Wolfe, Breathitt and Estill counties and served in that position for eight years. He said that his first and last case as attorney involved patricide.

Kash met and fell in love and married Miss Nell White, a beautiful and talented Estill County lass.

While Herbert Hoover was president, Kash went to Washington, D. C. as legal counsel for the Bureau of Internal Revenue. Following this he went into private practice in Washington. Shortly before and at the beginning of World War II he served on a committee which made a survey of Military installations in the United States. He was also a commissioner in the Foreign Economics Administration. Although very active in the courts of the 3rd Judicial

EARLY AND MODERN HISTORY

District and despite the fact that he has a good law practice in Estill County he planned to return to Washington to enter Government service.

Since this information was collected Mr. Kash has been very ill and in the hospital in Lexington for a long period of time. However, he is some better but we are wondering if perhaps this will not change his plans about returning to Washington. (Mr. Kash died in 1954.)

We might say here that his brother, Will, was also a lawyer and a preacher and made an illustrious career for himself. Daniel was a doctor who practiced widely in Wolfe, Breathitt and Perry counties and died at the height of his career.

MONROE LACY
(This bit of information was rendered by Mrs. Marie O. Steckley, 13 W. Court St., Cincinnati 2, Ohio.)

My father, Monroe Lacy, who will be 80 years old on Nov. 20, 1954, came to Ohio in March, 1929 and has been here ever since.

Dad has two sisters and one brother living. Grace Johnson, Columbus, Ohio; Mollie Rose, South Lebanon, Ohio; and James (Jim) A. Lacey, Leeco, Ky.

My mother, Margaret Ellen (Robinson) Lacey (nick name Maggie) died in March, 1919. She was the daughter of Greenberry and Florence Robinson, formerly of Hazel Green.

Dad never re-married and there are four of his children. I am the oldest and was only eight years old when my mother died and the baby was 17 months old. Dad kept us all together and was practically father and mother, both, to us and I just can't put into words how grand and swell he is. I'll just say this much, he is the finest Dad in the world.

He has eleven grandchildren and two great-grandchildren.

THE LACY FAMILY OF WOLFE COUNTY, KY.
(Compiled by Mrs. Wm. Everett Bach, Lexington, Ky.)

Mr. John Lacy of Greenbrier County, Virginia, came to Montgomery County, Ky., at a very early date. He moved to what is known as "Lacy Creek" (named for him) when possibly this was still Montgomery County. He married Sarah Porter and the name Porter was handed down through the generations. Their children were as follows: William, Marcus (or Mark), Alexander, Ambrose, Moses B., Harvey, Nancy, Pheby and Caroline.

Wilbourn and Elinor were half brothers and sisters.

Mark Lacy married Sally Huff and had the following children: John, Nancy, Green, Sanford, Eliza, Andy Porter who married Emily Trimble Cockrell, Alexander Preston, James and Perry Lacy.

Mr. Mark Lacy died at his home on Lacy Creek in Wolfe County, in 1885 at the age of 92 years.

John and Sanford Lacy went West. Alexander Preston Lacy married Polly Nickell; Ferry Lacy married and had the following children: John, Sally Jane, Edi Ellen who married Marion Vaughn.

William Porter Lacy married Mollie Johnson. Their children were Flossie Lacy, who married R. P. Swango; and Courtney Lacy married Pearl Clark and had one son, William Earl Lacy, married Edna Mae Immel and had three children: William Earl Jr., Katherine, and John Andrew. William Porter Lacy had one brother, Daniel Boone Lacy, who married Callie Johnson (sister to Mollie Johnson) and they had the following children: Oliver married Jess; Ollie, died young; Monnie, never married; Devonia married Charles Cundiff and had one daughter, Sandra Cundiff; Hallie married Blair Childers, no children; Sanford married and had two children: Allen and Joyce.

THE LANDSAW FAMILY
(Permission of Caesar Hurst from his book.)

The Landsaw family of Wolfe County was established by William, who was born in Greenbriar, Va. (now West Va.) about 1774 and who died on Stillwater Creek in Wolfe County in 1826. He was married to Elizabeth Murphy, a daughter of John and Nancy Ransome Murphy. Nancy Ransome claimed to have been a cousin of George Washington, our first president. She is said to have claimed she attended the same church as George in her early days; and that her father sold some of the land on which the city of Washington now stands, and received payment for it in gold.

Elizabeth and William eloped when they were married as she was only 13 and her parents objected to her marriage. They came to Fleming, Ky., and established their home there.

About 1808 Landsaw purchased a large tract of land on Stillwater, Wolfe County, Ky., and erected buildings and moved his family to it in 1809. This embraced all the land that is now on Murphy Fork and Landsaw. This was a fine farm and contained much bottom land.

In the meantime the Landsaws had been forgiven by the Murphys and to help seal the friendship, William Landsaw gave John and

Nancy Murphy all the land that is now known as Murphy Fork, if they would move on it. The Murphys accepted and moved to Wolfe County where they maintained a residence until his death at the ripe old age of 103. He and his wife are both buried near the mouth of Murphy Fork Creek.

Children of William and Elizabeth Murphy Landsaw were: Mary (Polly), Sara H. (Sally), John, James, Dow, Delilah, Malinda, Dulcenia, Albert and Julia.

After William's death his widow married a second time to Abram Phillips. She and her second husband lived at the old place until 1857 when they sold the residence and about 500 acres to Isaac B. Combs. The remainder of the Landsaw land was divided among the heirs. Elizabeth had one son by her second marriage, George W. Phillips, who was born about 1830 and died in 1867.

He was married in 1852 to Ellen Lacy, daughter of John and Axie Lacy, whose home was on Lacy Creek in Wolfe County, Ky. and after George's marriage he and his wife made their home on Stillwater on land purchased from Delilah Gibbs. His wife, Ellen Lacy, was a half-sister to George W. Carson, who was County Judge of Wolfe County for many years and a prominent man reported to have considerable wealth.

George and Ellen Phillips had the following children: Sarah, Mary, Frances, Lydia, Axie, Abram and John.

Mary married Jerry Gillmore nad they later moved to Illinois.

Sarah married Samuel H. Hurst and full particulars about her family may be found under the "Hursts of Wolfe County" elsewhere in this book.

John married Pamelia Hanks, whose home was near Campton. They had one child, then left Kentucky to make their home in Ill.

James Landsaw, son of William and Elizabeth Landsaw, was born in Wolfe County, May 15, 1811 on Stillwater Creek and died on May 28, 1895. He married Elizabeth Hurst, daughter of Harmon Hurst, of Breathitt County and they lived all their life on Stillwater and are buried in the old Landsaw graveyard.

They had nine children: Frances, Lourinda, Mollie, Esther, Jane, Harmon, William L., Daniel D. and Elizabeth.

Louranda and Esther lived in Wolfe County throughout their lives and were buried here. Frances, Mollie, Jane, Elizabeth, Harmon H., and William L. went to Buchanan County, Missouri where their grandfather, Harmon Hurst, lived. Daniel D., in his latter years, went to Oklahoma from Wolfe County.

4. Lourinda married Miles K. Wilson and they lived on Landsaw

of Stillwater near her father, James Landsaw. They later moved to Lacy Creek where they died.

Children of Lourinda and Miles K. Wilson:

4. George, who married Ann Gillmore, and they moved to Okla.

4. James R. married Mollie Tibbs first, then Amanda Brewer, then Emma Oldfields.

4. William Preston Wilson married Jessie Orr., moved to Okla.

4. Harmon Wilson was killed at the age of 23.

4. Elizabeth married twice, William Buchanan and then to William Tibbs.

4. Joseph L. married Georgia Byrd in 1896. They had eight children and lived in Middletown, Ohio.

4. Samuel H. Wilson married twice, first to Hattie Davenport, they had two sons; second to Fern Steele, they had one son. They live in Oklahoma.

4. Andrew T. Wilson, married twice, first to Nannie Townsend, they had one daughter, Gladys, who married Jesse Bohanan.

John Miles Wilson married Georgia Oldfield. They had one son and one daughter. After her death he married Nancy Day and they had one son.

3. Mollie, third daughter of James and Elizabeth Landsaw, married Preston C. Little and they moved to Missouri.

3. Esther, fourth daughter of James and Elizabeth Landsaw, was born on Stillwater in 1845 and died in Wolfe in 1878. She married Miles K. Little. They had two sons and then she died. The sons live in Kansas.

3. Jane, fifth daughter of James and Elizabeth Landsaw, grew to womanhood at home and entered the teaching profession. She went to Missouri to live with her grandfather where she continued to teach. She later married Joseph Cox. They had six children.

4. James died in 1900.

4. Carrie married Ivan Crabb.

4. Jonathon married Gertrude Blazard.

4. Tobitha married Crafton Jones.

4. Martha J. married Claude H. Redmond.

3. Harmon Hurst, son of James and Elizabeth Landsaw, was born in 1850 on Stillwater and went to the home of his grandfather Hurst in Missouri in 1871. From there went to Kansas and later to Texas. He married Tobitha Childers. They had two sons and five daughters.

3. Daniel D., son of James and Elizabeth Landsaw, was born on Stillwater, March 10, 1854, and died in Oklahoma in 1931. He married Rachel Combs, daughter of Isaac Combs. He taught school, then operated a country store at the old William Landsaw place. He purchased the old home place then later sold out and moved to Oklahoma. He served as County Judge of Wolfe County, was a Republican and had six children.

EARLY AND MODERN HISTORY

3. Elizabeth was born to James and Elizabeth Landsaw, May 11, 1856. Her mother died when she was only five days old. Her father and sister took care of her until she was 12 years of age. Then she went to Missouri to live with her sister, Mollie. She married Thomas H. Wright. They had seven children.

Lorenzo Dow Landsaw

Lorenza Dow, son of William and Elizabeth Landsaw, was born on Stillwater, in Jan., 1813. He died and was buried on Lower Devils Creek in 1874. He married Susan Maloney, 1832. He purchased a plot of land on Hunting Fork of Holly Creek, Wolfe County, a few years after his marriage where he lived until a few years prior to his death. Dow and Susan had the following children:

3. Levina married Joab Pence.
3. Mary married James Harvey Tyra.
3. Elizabeth married George Nickell, 1834.
4. William, James Buchanan, Isaac Elsberry, Eliza, Martha, Nancy, Timothy and Sarah B.
3. William married Sally J. Wilson.
3. Susan married Jack Pence.
4. Their children: Lourany, Sirena, John, George, Daniel, Malissa, Jackson, Polly, Sarah, Lou Ellen and Newton.
3. Nancy married Thomas Combs.
4. Dulcenia, Dow, Alice and Sally.
3. Sidney married Conrad Cable.
4. Susan, Henry, Cora, John and Dora.
3. McKinley, son of Dow and Susan Landsaw, married twice, first to Martha Raney. They had one son, William. Second to Parthena Wilson, who died in 1919. He moved to Oklahoma after her death where he died.
3. Sally, daughter of Dow and Susan Landsaw, born 1854, married Oliver King.
4. John, Clay, Pierce and Sarah B.

Delilah Landsaw Gibbs

Delilah, daughter of William and Elizabeth Landsaw, married twice; first to James Gibbs, 1836. They lived on Stillwater in Wolfe County for many years, on land inherited from her father. Later they sold this land to her half-brother, George W. Phillips, and moved to Dry Ridge, Menifee County where they spent the remainder of their lives. They had the following children: William, Cassindra, Samuel, John, Berthena, Nancy, Sarah, Richard, Oscar, Mary, Boone, Emily and Belle.

After her first husband died, Delilah married Henry Phillips in 1875. They had no children.

Malinda Landsaw

Malinda, daughter of William and Elizabeth Landsaw, married

WOLFE COUNTY

McKinley Maloney and they lived first on Stillwater, then bought land on Cave Branch of Holly Creek in Wolfe County, where they lived until her death.

3. Eliza married Tolbert Vancleve.
3. William married Gincy Ann Kidd.
3. Ellender, married Green Stamper then William Eversole.
3. Susan married twice, Jesse Dunigan and then George Wadkins.
3. Elizabeth married John Roberts.
3. Loucinda married John Perdue, both of them were born in 1848.
3. George W. married Elizabeth Faulkner.
3. Nancy married Logan Rose. They lived on Holly Creek.
3. McDonaldson married Salincy Bryant.
3. Sally never married.
3. Rosaline married John Taulbee.
3. Greenberry married twice, first to Rachel Bryant, then to Ida Pugh.

Dulcenia Landsaw
2. Dulcenia, daughter of William and Elizabeth Landsaw, married Hardin Hurst and they lived in Breathitt County.

Albert H. Landsaw
2. Albert H., son of William and Elizabeth Landsaw, married Celia Combs. They lived on Stillwater until 1867 when he sold his interests in his father's old home to Samuel H. Hurst. He then moved to Marion County, Ill. He died in Little Rock, Ark.

Julia Landsaw
2. Julia, youngest daughter of William and Elizabeth Landsaw, was born in 1825, married John Washington Childers, 1847 and died in 1921.

They lived on Stillwater Creek in Wolfe County until about 1857, when he purchased land on Little Black Water Creek in Morgan County. He also purchased land on Long Branch and here he erected his home on the old state road between Maytown and Mariba. Living near him was his sister, Esther, who married James Gibbs.

3. Samuel Henry, married Jane Collins.
3. Richard Apperson married Almedia Tutt, then Ella Hill.
3. Rudolphus married Elizabeth Nickell.
3. Dulcenia died in 1872 at 16 years of age.
3. Elizabeth married L. C. McGuire.
3. Archibald married Dora McGuire.
3. Lyle married Jeff Oakley, then Owen Lawson.

EARLY AND MODERN HISTORY

THE MURPHY FAMILY
(This was taken from Caesar Hurt's book with his permission.)

John Murphy, Sr., was the grandfather of the Landsaws and the only Murphy who ever settled in Wolfe County. He brought with him to Kentucky two children, and two granddaughters. His children, Elizabeth and William, and his granddaughters were named Ripley.

William Murphy, son of John Murphy, Sr., married Tilda Biles, and had 21 children: Miles, Tilda, John, Lewis, Ward, Frank, Loge, Mike, Isaac, Nelly, Patsy, Lucretia, Nance, Elizabeth and Dink. Others all died in infancy.

Miles Murphy, son of William Murphy married a daughter of William O'Hara, moved to Illinois and is reported to have become very wealthy.

John Murphy, second son of William Murphy, married Sally Rose, a daughter of old Davey Rose, who reared a large family.

The other children of William Murphy married as follows:

Lewis Murphy married a Long. They had six children: Silas, John, Sug, Mary Ann, Lula and another girl.

Ward married a Hensley.
Dink married a Nichols.
Logan married a Yoken.
Mike married a Wilson.
Frank married a Marrs, settled on Blackwater.
Isaac married a Elkins.
Bill married a Bryant.
Tilda married an Osborn and settled on Holly.
Cretia married a Havens and settled on Grassy.
Lizzie Murphy married a Ward.
Nellie Murphy married a Rose, a great-grandson of Davey Rose, Sr.

Patsy Murphy married an Oldfield.

The Ripley girls, granddaughters of John Murphy, were reared on Stillwater, and married Ambrose and John Craig and they moved to Illinois where they reared large families.

(This information was contributed by Harry W. Murphy.)

John Murphy, the second son of William Murphy, who was married to Sally Rose, was my great-grandfather. I can't tell you the names of all his children but I will start with the one son which was my grandfather.

My grandfather was James Harry Murphy, who was married to Martha Baker, daughter of Benny Baker of Devils Creek and they resided at Murphy Fork in Morgan County. To this union was born two sons:

1. Frank Murphy, who married Ella Cardwell and they resided at Landsaw until 40 years ago when they moved to Chandler, Okla., where he was in the grocery business until retirement. He is residing at Chandler at the present. They had no children.

2. Benjamin Sherman Murphy, who married Elizabeth Vest and they resided at Murphy Fork until death. He was the post master at Murphy Fork until retirement. To this union was born 7 children:

1. Golden Murphy married J. Curren Nickell of Murphy Fork and resides at West Liberty. To this union was born 6 children:

A. J. Wendell, post master of West Liberty and he married Ella Turner and has two sons, Bobby and Herman.

B. Herman Volney Nickell was killed in action during World War II.

C. Virginia Nickell married Coy Hibbard and resides at London, Ky., and has three daughters: Linda, Donna and Marilyn.

D. Lucille Nickell married Denzil Haney and resides in Lexington, has one son, Sidney.

E. Geraldine Nickell married Charles Cunard and resides in Texas and has two children.

F. Imogene Nickell married Hobart May and resides in West Liberty, has one son, John Allen.

2. Harry Woodson Murphy married Ruth B. Henry of Ezel and now resides in Dayton, Ohio. To this union were born three children: Harry is a successful real estate dealer there.

A. Nellavene Murphy married Richard Austin and resides in Dayton, Ohio. No children.

B. Harry M. Murphy married Janie Schuler and resides in Dayton, Ohio. One son, Michael.

C. Larry D. Murphy still at home.

3. Courtney Murphy resides at Murphy Fork on the Murphy home place and is unmarried.

4. Martha Murphy married Victor Nickell of Ezel and resides in Lexington. Has two children:

A. Carol Nickell married Eugene Walter and resides in Lexington. No children.

B. Allan K. Nickell still at home.

5. Charles W. Murphy married Minnie Ingram of Wolfe County and resides in Campton where he owns much property. He has been County Judge of Wolfe County two terms and made a good judge. His present term expires January 1, 1958. He has two children:

A. J. B. Murphy married Mary Callahan and resides in Lexington. No children.

B. Mary Elizabeth Murphy is unmarried. She is a student at the University of Ky., where her brother, J. B., also is a student.

6. Earl F. Murphy married Irene Barber of Dehart and resides

in West Liberty, Ky., where he operates a store. They have one child: Patricia Murphy, still at home.

7. Raymond B. Murphy married Edna Wright of Neon, Ky., and resides in Lexington, where he practices law, as he is a graduate of Law school of the University of Ky. They have no children.

Louis Murphy, son of William Murphy and a brother of John Murphy, married a Long.

2. Silas, son of Louis, married a Swango girl at Maytown, Ky.
2. John Tom Murphy, who died at Mt. Sterling, married a Halsey.
2. Sug Murphy married Nosey John Rose of Lacy Creek, Ky.
2. Mary Ann Murphy married Press Elkins, father of Clifford Elkins.
2. Lula Murphy married James Little of Mize, Ky.
2. One girl married a Culbertson of Valeria, Ky.

THE PERKINS FAMILY OF WOLFE COUNTY, KY.
(Compiled by Mrs. Wm. Everett Bach, Lexington, Ky.)

Thomas Perkins, born October 15, 1823, in Virginia, died August 15, 1875, married Nancy Ferguson, born May 17, 1820, died January 7, 1901.

They were the parents of several children: Louisa; Elizabeth; Mary; William; Wiley C.; and Sanford Reed Perkins, who died at Hazel Green, Ky., January 28, 1936. His wife, Fannie Carolyn Hollon, died in Lexington, Ky., March 11, 1941. (There may have been other children but I do not have the names.

Samuel H. Perkins, (son of Sanford Reed) married Nora Stamper in Campton, Ky., April 28, 1915. They are the parents of four children: Franklin Reed Perkins, who married Ruby Wilson; Samuel H. Perkins, married Chamie Ann Beam of Bardstown, Ky.; Ada Carolyn Perkins married Buckner Woodford Hamilton, at Lexington, Ky.; Wendell G. Perkins married Doris Jean Doty of Lexington, Ky. Reed Perkins lives in Mobile, Alabama; Ada C. who married Buckner W. Hamilton, a Civil Engineer, also lives in Mobile, Ala., and has the following children: Bucky Hamilton, born June 16, 1943 in Mobile, Ala.; Carolyn Hamilton, born March 23, 1945, in Lexington, Ky.; Sam Perkins Hamilton, born Feb. 16, 1951, in Mobile, Ala. Samuel H. Perkins Jr., and his wife, Chamie Ann Beam, have the following children: Mary Beam Perkins, born in Louisville, Ky., Nov. 26, 1952; Laura Ann Perkins, born in Louisville, Ky., July 12, 1956. Wendell Guy Perkins, died January 22, 1950, in Lexington, Ky. Mrs. Samuel H. Perkins (Nora Stamper) is the daughter of Thomas Franklin Stamper and his wife, Millie Adeline Hanks; Millie Adeline Hanks was the daughter of Cudmillion Hanks and his wife (2nd) Armida Evelyn Hackney (See Hanks Family), also (See Stamper Family).

WOLFE COUNTY

THE PROFITT FAMILY
(Submitted by James Profitt, 1806 Woodland Ave., Middletown, O.)

When I was young, too young to remember, my father, Jerry Profitt bought a farm on Lacy Creek in Wolfe County, about three miles from Hazel Green. This land adjoined the Charles Sample farm. Steve Sample and I were school mates.

There were eight children in my father's family: Edward, who married Rose Cox. John married May Ridelle; Alice married Edward Terrel; James married Ethel Shelton; Emma married Oscar Hatton; Rebecca married James Shortt. All are now dead save Emma, Rebecca and James.

Jerry Profitt and neighbors raised flax and sheep and converted it into clothes for the family. Raised geese for feather beds. They cut timber and rafted logs. Run them down the Kentucky River. Bought green coffee and roasted it in skillets. They would take the Logs down on stream and walk back home by way of Lexington, which in those days was only a few houses huddled together.

My father, Jerry Profitt, taught Blab Schools. My Uncle John C. Profitt also taught Blab Schools. Blab Schools was where they all would speak out very loud.

P. S. I am sending you a $2 donation to help defray the expense of publication of your book for the Woman's Club.

Sewell Profitt, grandfather of James Profitt, a native of North Carolina, moved from North Carolina to Kentucky Territory in 1843. Together with my maternal grandparents, Albin Whisman and families settled on the Kentucky River near the mouth of Devils Creek, now known as Big Andy. (This community took its name from a conversation between Dr. Brack Cox and Andy Spencer. Mr. Spencer wanted to donate a portion of his land for a Community Church and name it Spencer. Dr. Cox suggested he donate the land and he would call the settlement, Big Andy.)

My grandparents moved to Kentucky by horse and wagon. Grandfather was a surveyor and a record of his work is now in the State Capitol, Frankfort. He surveyed for state and county. They brought their skillet and lid for cooking, sheep for their clothing. Raised flax and converted it to "Linsey" shirts, which he wore till we were about 12 years old. Mother made my first trousers of linen when I was very small.

My grandmother, Albina, was a heroine. She saved my mother from a bear by slaying it with a pine knot, when it came into her home when my mother was a child.

My dad, Jerry Profitt married Lavina Whisman and built a log house which was later known as Green Valley Jonio Hall, where I was born. The house still stands. Later he and Whig Cable sawed lumber and floored and sealed the house.

EARLY AND MODERN HISTORY

W. O. MIZE FAMILY OF H. G. A.
(Information supplied by Mrs. Carl Mize.)

William Oldham Mize was the son of Johnny A. Mize and Marium (Oldham) Mize.

Johnny Mize was born in Kentucky on Jan. 17, 1820 and died in Independence, Mo., on Dec. 21, 1847, and was buried there. During his lifetime he was a prominent merchant there. His wife was the daughter of William Oldham of Richmond, Ky.

1. One son, William Oldham (called Billie).

After Johnny Mize's death his widow married again to Johnny Blakemore. Prior to her second marriage she had returned to her folks in Richmond, Ky. Her second husband did not live long. They had one son:

1. Johnny Blakemore, who returned to Independence, Mo., to make his home after his mother's death on March 17, 1858.

After the second marriage of his mother, Marium (Oldham) Mize, W. O. (Billie) came to Hazel Green, Ky. to make his home with his aunt and uncle, J. G. Trimble and Nancy (Mize) Trimble. Billie was six years old at this time. He had polio when he was small which left him a cripple.

Billie made his home with the Trimbles until his marriage to Lou Ellen Cockrell, April 27, 1874. She was the daughter of the Christian preacher, Rev. McKinley Cockrell. Rev. Joe Nickell, pastor of the Hazel Green Christian Church at that time married them.

"Uncle Billy" as he was called by all who knew and loved him, was a member of the Hazel Green Christian Church 52 years, where he served as elder as many years. He was also Sunday School Supt. and teacher of the Beginners Sunday School class, (ages 1-10 years then), until two months prior to his death, August 19, 1915 when he sent in his resignation.

W. O. Mize was one of the founders of Hazel Green Academy and it was through his untiring efforts that legislation was passed while he was serving as State Senator from Kentucky, that a law was passed making it illegal to sell liquor or any intoxicant within three miles of the incorporation limits of Hazel Green. This was done for the protection of the town and the Academy.

W. O. Mize named Hazel Green Academy, which was conceived in honor of his son, Carl Mize. His wife, Lou Mize dreamed of a school like Hazel Green for many years prior to its realization. She was a great influence in helping to get the school.

W. O. Mize served two terms as State Senator from Kentucky and then stayed on four years longer as Clerk of the House. His first term began in 1880. He was State Senator from the 34th District composed then of Wolfe, Morgan, Menifee, Lee, Magoffin, Breathitt,

Owsley, Powell and Johnson Counties. At night, while Clerk of the House, he would write speeches for the Governor, Lieut. Governor and Senators, or anyone who needed his help. He was paid well for his services in this respect.

W. O. Mize made many substantial gifts both to Hazel Green Academy and to the Hazel Green Christian Church, which are mentioned elsewhere in the history. He built the only brick dwelling house in the town of Hazel Green on State Street and it still stands in good condition. W. O. Mize and Lou Cockerell Mize had one son.

2. Carl B. July 23, 1875. Carl was graduated from HGA in 1896, from Centre College in 1897 and from the College of Commerce, University of Ky., in 1897. He owned and operated a drug store in Indianapolis, Ind. for several years, then due to ill health had to sell out and come home to Hazel Green. He had a general store and a movie house in Hazel Green for several years, prior to his death. Carl Mize married Carrie Lee Rose, daughter of John M. and Sara Elizabeth (Swango) Rose on April 10, 1910. To them were born two children.

3. Marium Elizabeth, born Jan. 11, 1913 and died two days later, Jan. 13, 1913.

3. William Oldham II was born May 23, 1915. He is called "Bill" by most of his closest friends. He was graduated from Hazel Green Academy, attended Ky. Wesleyan College and the University of Ky.

Bill married the lovely daughter of Jim Swope and Zetta (Williams) Swope, Evelyn. They had one child which died in infancy, a little girl. During World War II Bill volunteered for the Air Force and served as pilot four years; part of which was in the European Theater of War. He also received his commission as Glider pilot. While in training he was given the coveted number "13" in the 13 Club for pilots at Avon Park, Fla. Only 13 pilots can belong at one time and the number 13 is always given to the most promising pilot in the bunch. Since Bill's marriage, he and his charming wife have established two successful restaurants in Florida. One, "Bill's Drive-In" at Jacksonville Beach and the other "The Chateau" on Atlantic Beach, Fla. The latter is considered one of the most beautiful such places in Northern Florida and is open from 5 p. m. until 12 for dinners only.

Recently, Bill was awarded one of the highest honors that the Chamber of Commerce in Jacksonville Beach, Fla., can confer upon a member for his outstanding community service. At the same time they also gave him a lifetime membership in the Jacksonville Beach Chamber of Commerce.

Bill has played Santa Claus for the children of Jacksonville Beach for 10 years. He always flies onto the beach in his private plane.

EARLY AND MODERN HISTORY

Mr. and Mrs. W. O. Mize donated the beautiful copper tower for the new Hazel Green Christian Church which was recently erected. Mrs. Mize, Bill's mother, is very active in the affairs of the Hazel Green Christian Church; having served as chairman of the official church board now for several years.

PENCE FAMILY ONE OF OLDEST IN WOLFE COUNTY
(Contributed by Boone Pence.)

Andrew Pence, grandfather of Boone Pence, married Rebecca Hollon Pence, who was the first child born in Wolfe County in 1802.

Boone Pence was born in Wolfe County (at that time a part of Breathitt) on Jan. 4, 1860 and if he lives until Jan. 4, 1955 will be 95 years of age. He is the son of Jack Pence and Susie Landsaw Pence. His father, Jack Pence, was also born on Pence Branch. Jack's father, Andy Pence, came to Kentucky from Illinois. Susie Landsaw was the daughter of Mr. and Mrs. Dowl Landsaw of Stillwater. Her parents were born in the county, too, but her paternal grandfather, G. G. Landsaw and wife came to Kentucky from Virgina. So, Boone Pence, who is still active at 94, comes to Campton frequently, recently climbed the stairs to the News office, lays claim to having ancestors from Illinois and Virginia.

Jack Pence and Susie Landsaw Pence had six sons: Boone, John. George, Jack, Newt and Billy; also five daughters: Melissa, Polly, Sally, Renie and Lula.

Boone married Hettie McDaniel and they lived all their married life on Pence Branch. She has been dead now for several years and they never had any children.

Boone says he can remember coming into Campton when a very small boy. He says there were only two stores in Campton back in those early days of his; Sewell Combs operated one general store and Newt Vaughn another one. The old courthouse which burned was here, the log one. There was no bank in those days, the Farmers and Traders being established in 1902.

Mr. Pence says he can remember that George Carson served several terms as County Judge back in those early days and that he was a prominent land owner then. Daniel Bruce was the name of the first sheriff he can recall almost 90 years ago.

His nearest neighbor was his grandfather, Andy Pence, who lived about one-half mile distance. His family lived on Pence Branch about nine miles out of Campton. Pence Branch is named for the Pence family. Land was real cheap then.

Mr. Boone Pence says he can remember seeing only one wild deer but the wild turkeys were plentiful. He says that he recalls attending the hanging of Floyd Williams and that "old" Taylor Center was sheriff at that time. There was a church back in those days near Bethany, operated by the Missionaries. There was also a free school across the branch from his boyhood home, but it only operated three months out of the year and only taught the elementary grades. There was no high school in the county until Hazel Green Academy was established about 1880. This part of Breathitt was cut off and attached to Wolfe about 1887.

One of the earliest families of Wolfe County was Michael O'Hair, who came from Ireland about the beginning of 1800. He moved to what is now Hazel Green with his large family of 13 children, then known as Montgomery county. One of his daughters, Eleanor B. married William Trimble in 1787. Another daughter, Sibby B. married William Lacy in 1790. All four of these persons are buried in the Hazel Green Cemetery.

Other first families of Wolfe County was Andrew Pence, who paid taxes on 640 acres of land on both sides of Holly Creek in 1830, and which the deed books say were purchased for $125. John Hollon, William and Ambrose Hollon had a deed for 2500 acres of land on Holly, bought for $150. These are no doubt the ancestors of Captain James I. Hollon, of Hazel Green, who is a son of the late J. B. Hollon, County Court Clerk for many years.

ROSE FAMILY
(This information through the cooperation of Mrs. Julia Tyra and Mrs. O. D. Rose.)

Dulcina Combs, daughter of Henry and Tempe Combs, was born on August 15, 1839 and died on Feb. 6, 1910.

She was married to Robert Jefferson Rose in 1863. Robert Rose and Dulcina Combs Rose had five children, namely:

John H. Rose, born Dec. 28, 1864. Died on April 14, 1947.
Joseph A. Rose was born Nov. 13, 1866, now dead.
Sewell C. Rose was born on Dec. 22, 1877.
Miranda Rose was born on July 16, 1873.
Jefferson D. Rose was born on May 27, 1889.

1. John H. Rose, son of Robert and Dulcina Rose, was first married to Sarah Edwards to whom was born one son, Charlie E. Rose.

2. Charlie E. Rose was married and had a large family, then he died in 1935. Next John H. Rose married Virginia James of Hazel Green and they had one daughter, Angalyn.

2. Angalyn married Courtney C. Wells and lives at Hazard, Ky. Only one of their four children is living. His name is Garland. (For further information see the Stephen Porter and Angeline Trimble James family).

John H. Rose was married a third time to Frances Ann Spencer, called Fannie, who is still living, now in the Masonic Home at Louisville, Ky.

1. Joseph A. Rose, son of Robert and Dulcina Rose, was born in 1866. He married Sylvania Campbell. They had three children. Bertha, May and Ova Dewey.

2. Bertha Rose married Boyd Lawson. They had two children. Paul Frederick Lawson and Helen Mae Lawson.

3. Paul Frederick Lawson married Theresea Chapman. He is a major in the U. S. Army and works in the Pentgaon in New York City. He and his wife have four children. Diana, Linda, Terry and Lawrence.

3. Helen Mae Lawson married Dr. Howard Morgan and they live in Nashville, Tenn. They have three children: Stephen, Patsy and Howard Lawson Morgan.

2. Mae Rose was married to Stephen James about 1920. They now live in Silver Springs, Maryland. They have four children.

3. Alice, Shirley, Judith and Hugh.

3. Alice married Armin Meyer and they live in Beruit, Lebanon, near Jerusalem. Mr. Meyer is in the Diplomatic Service, sent there by the American Embassy. They have two children.

3. Shirley and Judith attend college in Beruit. Shirley will graduate in June.

3. Hugh, son of Mae and Stephen James is the only son. He is now a Captain in the U. S. Army. He is married to May Hall, who is a daughter of a Commander in the American Army and they are stationed at LaJune, N. C. They have two small children, (4.) Stephan and Susan.

Stephen James, the husband of Mae Rose, visited in Hazel Green with his wife in the summer of 1954 for the first time in many years; but he is a native of Hazel Green. He released the information given below about himself with reluctance.

Mr. James is a former president of the American Public Relations Association and now is chairman of its committee on Ethics and he is co-chairman of the Farm Hands Club in Washington, D. C. He is consultant to the National Committee on Safety Education; he is Director General of the Pan American Highway Confederation. During the last war he organized and directed the Pan American forum.

He is the author of certain monographs and booklets including, "The Pan American Highway, Artery of Commerce and Culture," "A Safety Lesson For Each Grade", "A Finance Program for the

Pan American Highways," "The Most Important Highway in the World," and sundry booklets and magazine articles.

He has for many years been director of Education for the Automotive Safety Foundation. Among the National Professional Associations of which he is a member are: National Education Association, American Association of School Administration, The Adult Education Association, The Foreign Policy Association, The American Economic Association, The American Geographic, American Association of Learned Societies, Pan American Society, Association for Supervision and Curriculum Development, American Society for Public Administration, National Academy of Economics, and Political Sciences and the National Press Club.

2. O. Dewey Rose is the only son of the late Joseph E. Rose. He married Tennie Lou Coldiron, daughter of the late Crockett Coldiron and Ella Brooks Coldiron of Hazel Green. They have two children.

3. Josephine married Ralph Brewer.
4. Two children: Brenda Lou and Scotty.
3. Scotty, who gradauted with honors at Millersbrug Military Institute in 1955. He is now married to Jacquline McGuire of Grayson, and they are both attending the University of Ky. (1957)

O. Dewey Rose is maintenance foreman for the Kentucky Parks Association which position he has held and filled with skill for several years.

1. Miranda Rose, daughter of Robert and Dulcina Rose, was born on July 16, 1873 and married Boone Tyra, Sept. 14, 1893. They had two children, Erna E. Tyra, born Dec. 21, 1896 and Herman Tyra, born Aug. 3, 1894.

2. Erna E. Tyra, born Dec. 21, 1896, married Julia Robbins.
3. Pauline Tyra married James Cable, August 8, 1941.
4. Jimmy Wallace Cable.
3. Monnell married Bert Bumgardner.
4. Darrell and Sheila Jean.
3. Marcella Tyra married Harold Tutt.
4. A daughter, Julia.
3. Marcus married.
3. Erna Buel served in Korean War over two years, then came home and entered a Barboring college in Louisville, graduated, now barboring in Campton.
3. Danny Ellis is a student at the University of Kentucky.
2. Herman Tyra, second son of Miranda Rose Tyra and Boone Tyra, married Debbie Rose. To this union were born eight children. Herman died in 1936.
3. Reed Tyra, born Aug. 1, 1916 and died.
3. Blanche Tyra married Goble Buchanan.
3. Mildred Tyra married Marvin Stamper.
3. Erna Clifford Tyra married Blanche Cox.

3. Mabel Tyra married Edgar Buchanan.
3. Herman E. Tyra.
3. Herbert Tyra.
3. Lingle Tyra married Cecil Ward.
1. Sewell C. Rose, son of Robert and Dulcina Rose, was born in 1868. Married Polly Brewer second time. His first wife was Celia Sample and they had no children.
2. Elsie Opal.
2. Daisy Mae.
2. Everett.
2. Elmer, Millard, Ned, Hazel, Eugene and June were born to the second marriage.

THE JOHN AND REBECCAH ROSE FAMILY
(Contributed by various members of family.)

Recently in "Believe it or Not" column in a daily newspaper, this statement appeared:

The castle of Kilravock, Scotland, has been inhabited by the same family of Rose's of Kilravock for 661 years.

John Rose was born in 1761 and died in 1843. Rebeccah, his wife, was born in 1763 and died in 1830. They were both born in Ireland.

1. John Rose, son of John Rose and Rebeccah Rose, was born on May 1, 1791 and died in Sept. 1843.

John Rose married Pollie Morrow Rose (she was born Feb. 23, 1794) on March 10, 1814. To this union were born the following children:
2. William B. Rose, born Dec. 1, 1814.
2. Joseph Rose, born March 14, 1819.
2. Rachel Rose, born Nov. 7, 1822.
2. John D. Rose, born Dec. 21, 1825.
2. Robert J. Rose, born Feb. 28, 1828.
2. Elijah C. Rose, born Dec. 29, 1830.
2. Polly Rose, born June 26, 1837.
2. Jeff M. Rose, born Feb. 15, 1846.
2. William B. Rose, who was born on Dec. 1, 1814, married Nancy Williams. They had nine children: Elizabeth, Powell, Sally, Isaac, John M., Silas H., Polly Ann, Gillie Ann and Arzelia.
3. Elizabeth Rose married Milbourne Linkous, May 29, 1896.
4. Their children were Tom, Richmond, Nannie and Sarah.
3. Powell Rose, born Dec. 19, 1842, married Margaret Cundiff, Aug. 18, 1867. To them were born nine children: Nannie, Sarah, Rinda, Dora, Sam Chandler, Isaac, Lizzie, Arzelia and Lula.
4. Nannie married Grant Brown.
4. Sarah married Will Lewis and they had three children.
4. Rinda Rose married Will Collins and they had three children.

4. Dora Rose married Richard Elkins. They had one son, Willie.
5. Willie never married.
4. Sam Chandler Rose first married Cora Brewer and they had several children, then he married again.
4. Isaac Rose, second son of Powell Rose, married a Collier and they had one child.
4. Lizzie Rose married Bud Chrisman and they had five children.
4. Arzelia married Robert Hobbs and they had three children.
4. Lula Rose, seventh daughter of Powell Rose, married a Wentworth and they had one child.
3. Sallie Ann Rose married David Hogg and they had one child which died in infancy.
3. Isaac Rose, born May 4, 1847, married Darinda Pieratt, Jan. 18, 1871. They had six children and then his first wife died and he married Anne Wells and they had one child, a boy. Mrs. Isaac Rose is still living in Middletown, Ohio and is almost 94 as this is being compiled in 1955.
Children by first wife were: Tom, John, Raleigh, Florence, Ollie and Henry.
4. Tom died in 1886 unmarried.
4. John married a Womack. They had two children, William Allen and Kent. John and his wife are both dead.
5. William Allen Rose is married and lives at Prestonsburg, Ky.
5. Kent Rose is married and lives at Prestonsburg, Ky.
4. Raleigh married Addie Stamper. They are both now dead. They had four daughters and one son: Rinda, Myrtle, Florence, Roxie and Ike.
4. Florence Rose married Frank Fugate. They are both now dead. They had one son, Carl and one daughter, Stella.
4. Henry was the youngest son of Isaac and Darinda Rose. See attached pages.
4. Ollie married Elza Haney. They are now dead. They had one son, Tom Haney, who lives in Middletown, Ohio.
Isaac Rose married for his second wife, Anne Wells, and they had one son.
4. Collier, (Bill Dick), who married away. He is now living in New York City.
Henry Clay Rose, son of Isaac and Darinda Pieratt Rose, was married twice. He first married Nanny Cole, daughter of Henry Cole and they had two sons, Henry Carl and Homer S.
5. Henry Carl married Leona Henry. They had one son, Herbert Lawrence.
6. Herbert Lawrence married Billie Nell May, a daughter of Bill May. They live in Ashland where he is an attorney.
5. Homer S. Rose, second son of Henry Rose and Darinda Pieratt, married Cleo Burrows, daughter of Fred Burrows. They had three sons, Homer B., Harold S., and Robert Lynn.

6. Homer B. Rose works at West Liberty Funeral Home. Not married.

6. Harold S. Rose is a student at Morehead College.

6. Robert Lynn Rose, is a student in Morgan County Hi School.

Henry Rose married Nell Franklin, the second wife, daughter of Wally Franklin and they had three children: Chester, Jerry Nell and John Randolph.

5. Chester Rose is not married. He is a teacher in the Louisville school system.

5. Jerry Nell is married and lives in Lexington. She married a Morris and they have no children.

5. John Randolph Rose married a Faulkner. They have one daughter and live in Richmond, Ky.

3. John M. Rose, born Oct. 4, 1849, married Lizzie Swango, Sept. 15, 1881. They had three children.

4. Curtis Bowen Rose married Margaret Sewell. Curtis was a coal broker in Hazard for many years and was very successful. His wife was a daughter of Captain George Sewell of Jackson, Ky. They had three children. Curtis died recently.

5. Elizabeth Rose married Garnett Cloyd. They had two children.

6. Betty Cloyd, who married William Marshall of Covington, Ky.

6. Curtis Elmer Cloyd, who married.

5. Laura Jo Rose, second daughter of Curtis and Margaret Rose, married Robert Mitsler and he is in the hardware business in Hazard, Ky.

5. Ben Rose, only son of Curtis and Margaret Rose, attended Morehead College and the University of Kentucky. He is a successful coal operator at Hazard, Ky. He married Martha Ann Naylor.

4. Charles Rose, son of John M. and Lizzie (Swango) Rose, married Rose Jewell. They had three children. Charles made a successful stock broker in Lexington, Ky., where he and his wife made their home until his death in the summer of 1956. They had three children: Charles Jr., who died in infancy, Maurine and Mildred.

5. Maurine married Dr. W. C. Robinson, who is both doctor and surgeon. They live in Lexington, Ky., and have an adopted daughter, Dana.

5. Mildred married Maurey Rappert. They also live in Lexington and have one daughter, Renie.

4. Carrie Lee Rose married Carl Mize. (See Mize family).

3. Silas Hogg Rose, son of William B. Rose and Nancy Williams Rose, married Loma Goodwin, daughter of Robert Goodwin, who lived to be nearly 94 and had his picture made with his children and grandchildren up to the fifth generation. Silas Hogg had three daughters, Lillie and Lula (twins). Lillie died in a few days after birth. and Loura. Silas was a successful merchant on Stillwater for many years. His father, William Rose, brought the first grist mill into Wolfe County and erected it at the falls near Stillwater bridge.

WOLFE COUNTY

4. Lula Rose married Charles Samuel Cecil. (See Cecil-Sample genealogy.)

4. Loura married Dr. Daniel Kash, (see Hurst history).

3. Polly Ann, seventh child of William Rose, married Bill Elkins, and had three children: Jim, Myrtle and Howard. The last mentioned is now dead. The others are married and live in Stonewall, Okla.

3. Gillie Ann Rose, eighth child of William Rose, married George Buchanan and had eight children: Bill, Henry, Edward, John Beverly, Myrtle, Pollie, Hattie, and Hazel.

4. William married Loura Shull and had four sons and three daughters: James, Carl, Charlie, John (dead), Ruth, Mary and Esther.

5. James married Jean Sewell. They live in Waynesville, Ohio and have two children.

5. Carl married Edith Terrill. They live in Franklin, Ohio and have three children.

5. Charlie married Blanche Helton and they live in Dayton, Ohio and have one child.

5. John never married, is now dead.

5. Ruth married Oral Sewell and they live in Dayton, Ohio and have one child.

5. Mary married Jesse Campbell and they live in Waynesville, Ohio and have three children.

5. Esther married John Wyatt and they live in Louisville. No children.

4. Henry married Lizzie Chambers and they had two daughters, one of which is dead.

4. Edward married Stella McClure. He has operated a successful shoe repair shop in Hazel Green for about 25 years. They have three sons and two daughters.

5. Edward Jr., served in the Army four years during World War II. He married Blanche Hale and they live in Middletown, Ohio. They have two children.

6. Paul Douglas is seven years of age.

6. Francis is six years of age.

5. George Lavaughn Buchanan married Margaret Nevius. They live in Lexington, Ky., where he is an executive in the field of Insurance.

George L. has won many top awards in the field of insurance. They have two children. He was in the Army during World War II and then attended college at the University of Ky. a couple of years.

6. Elnora, five years old.

6. Gregory Lynn, three years.

5. James Bernard Buchanan married Billie Wray Hammonds. They live in West Liberty and she works for REA and Bernard is on the state highway department staff for Wolfe County with his offices in Campton. Bernard attended Lee's College at Jack-

son, two years after his years of service in the Army during World War II.

5. Eulah Mae attended Berea College and then married Jack Hutchins, a graduate of Berea College. Jack has a job as genealogist with the State of Ky. and they live in Frankfort. They have two little girls. (6.) Pamela and Peggy Ann.

5. Betty Lou, youngest daughter of Ed and Stella Buchanan, is a graduate of Hazel Green Academy and is attending Berea College.

4. John Beverley Buchanan married Ethel Johnson, eldest daughter of the late Ellis A. Johnson, who was a successful merchant in Hazel Green for a number of years prior to his death. They had four children, Ida Nell, George W., Roger and Kenneth.

6. Ida Nell, was graduated from HGA and attended Eastern State College at Richmond, Ky., after teaching a couple of years was married to Leo Mitchell, who is employed at Armco Steel in Middletown, Ohio. They have one daughter and a son.

7. Elaine is in kindergarten.

6. George W. (Jack) was graduated from HGA, then Berea, and served in the Army two years. He specialized in the field of Agriculture, which he teaches in one of the high schools near Frankfort. He married while in school at Berea and they have a son, David Scott.

6. Roger graduated from Berea College and then volunteered for the Army and is now in Germany where he is serving with the Adjutant General's Division. He is working in the office.

6. Kenneth attended Eastern State College one year and then entered the highway depratment, working for the state.

4. Myrtle Buchanan married Millard Burcham. They had no children.

4. Pollie married Nick Center. They had two children. She is now dead.

5. Elwood married Regina Taulbee, youngest daughter of Wesley Taulbee. Elwood served in the Air Corps four years and then attended the University of Kentucky where he graduated. They have three little boys.

5. Dale lives in Dayton, Ohio where he is a barber.

4. Hattie married a Musgrave and they live in Middletown, Ohio. No children.

4. Hazel married Green Berry Combs. They have two sons. They live on a farm near Stillwater Bridge.

5. Millard lives in Middletown, Ohio where he is employed. Not married.

5. Harry married Mollie Spaulding. They live in Middletown, Ohio and have one child: Peggy Ann.

3. Arzelia Rose was born on April 14, 1864 and married John C. Barker, who was born on Nov. 14, 1869. Johnnie was a Baptist

preacher for many years prior to his death. He and his good wife contributed untold help and goodness to the community in which they lived through their church work and neighborly kindness. They had six children, Elmer, Harold, Luna Dell, Garland, Rodney and Genola.

4. Elmer was graduated from the University of Kentucky and taught school several years. Then he became a staff member of the Book publishing co., out of Chicago, Ill. He married Mary Wynne Hampton, who is also a graduate of the University of Kentucky and who teaches school near Winchester, where they live. They have two children, Anne Wynne and John.

5. Anne Wynne was graduated from the University of Kentucky where she majored in music. She is now instructor of music at Clark County High School, Winchester, Ky.

5. John is a student at Clark County High School, Winchester.

4. Harold married Avariel Horton. Harold followed the oil business for several years, then went to Colon, Mich., where he is employed. They have five children. (See Barkers for their lineage.)

4. Garland unmarried at this time.

4. Luna Dell married Marion Horton and they have three children. (See Horton's for full story.)

4. Rodney married Jean Cable and they have three children. Rodney has a successful career in the art department with Armco Steel, Middletown, Ohio.

4. Genola married Wilmer Hieronymus. Wilmer is a graduate in Civil Engineering from the University of Ky. He holds a responsible position with Ford Motors in Detroit, Mich., where they own a lovely home. They have two sons, Jimmy and Tommie, both students in school.

3. Robert Rose, fourth son of John Rose and Polly M. Rose, married Fannie Nichols and had three children. When she died he married Dulcenia Combs and they had four children.

3. John Rose, second son of John Rose and Polly Morrow Rose, married Nancy Nichols and they had eight children: David, Joe, Steve, Rachel, Lu, Sarah, Elizabeth and Molly.

4. Dave Rose married a Hollon. They had two sons, both of whom made preachers. (5.) Floyd and Roxie.

4. Joe Rose married Nancy Cecil. They had the following children: Ida, Lillie, Stella, Curtis, Dorsey and Lou.

5. Ida married Charlie Samples. They had two children, William and Nancy.

6. William married a music teacher from Morehead College, Emma Shader. They make their home in Morehead. William was elected as State Senator for Kentucky for one term and plans to run again. They have no children.

6. Nancy was graduated from the University of Ky., and taught school and then married A. C. King, a civil engineer. They have

one son. A. C. is now dead.

5. Lillie Rose married L. E. Smith and they made their home in Lexington, Ky., until their deaths. They had four children: Virginia, Cappie, Kermit and Reba.

6. Virginia died at 19, unmarried.

6. Cappie married Frank Tache and she died soon afterwards leaving no children.

6. Kermit Smith died in the Battle of the Bulge in France during World War II.

6. Reba married Chester Cecil and they live in Lexington, Ky. They have two children: Rose Ann and a boy, both small.

5. Stella married Caesar Lindon, who was cashier of Farmers and Traders Bank, Campton, from 1925 until his death in 1933. They had two children: Charles Edward and Rosalyn.

6. Charles E. Lindon attended Jefferson Law School in Louisville, where he met and married China Cundiff, who was also a law student at the same time. He has been cashier of the Farmers and Traders Bank in Campton for several years. His wife operates a department store in Campton, known as Fletcher and Lindon.

6. Rosalind Lindon attended the Conservatory of Music in Cincinnati, Ohio and later married Bill Emerick. They moved to West Liberty and there had two daughters, Sally and Linda. They operated the Bus Station in West Liberty until Linda was about five, then Bill died. Rosalind leased the Bus Station and became music teacher at Morgan County High School.

7. Sally is a graduate of Morgan County High School, West Liberty and is now a Freshman at Eastern State College, Richmond.

7. Linda is in grade school.

5. Maggie died in early years.

5. Mattie Lee died in her teens.

5. Curtis O. Rose married Elizabeth Sample. They made their home in Paris, Ky. Curtis died several years ago. They had four children: Maurice, Joseph P., Mary Elizabeth and Curtis O., Jr.

6. Maurice died at eight years of age.

6. Mary Elizabeth married Kenneth Hopperton. They have two children: Kenneth and Mary.

6. Joseph P., attended the University of Ky., and later married Dixie Combs. He entered the Army which he is making his career. He is now a Major in the Army and is stationed in Germany where all of their children have been born. He will return to the United States this fall and be stationed at Atlanta, Ga. They have three children. Pamela, Joe Jr., and Margaret.

6. Curtis O. Jr., is at home. He attended the University of Ky., a couple of years and accepted a job with Kentucky Finance in Paris, Ky., where he and his mother live.

5. Dorsey C. Rose married Miss Maude Martin of Indiana, who

was head of the Music Dept. at Hazel Green Academy when they were married. Dorsey was cashier of the Hazel Green Bank for many years. Later he was bank inspector working in Kentucky and in Pa. He has served in recent years as post master of the Hazel Green post office and has done a very efficient job. They had twin daughters first which died at birth. Then Jean and Emma Lee.

6. Jean was graduated from the University of Kentucky and then worked a couple of years with Proctor and Gambol Soap Co. as an executive. Then married Bob Bingham. Bob is a successful attorney in Cleveland, Ohio where they make their home. Jean and Bob took an extended tour of Europe a few years ago. They have three children and lost one of the twins which were born last. Bob is a graduate of Harvard Law College and served four years in the Army as an officer.

Bob and Jean Rose Bingham had four children, the last two being twins, but the little girl to the set of twins died: Bobbie, Jr. and Sallie.

6. Emma Lee was graduated from HGA and attended Morehead College, then married Jack Friedman. Jack served in World War II and was taken as prisoner of War and held in Germany for over two years. After he returned he and Emma Lee moved to Owingsville and he went into the store business with his father. Emma Lee continued to teach and went back to Morehead and received her degree. She still teaches in Owingsville. Jack operates a store there. They have one daughter, Jean Anne, nine.

5. Lou Rose married Stanley Ward and they had four children: Madge, Kenneth, Nancy, and Lois. Lou and Stanley are both now deceased. Madge married and so have all the others.

6. Madge married Kenneth Smith. They are now divorced. No children. She works in Winchester.

6. Nancy married Paul Richardson and they live in Winchester.

6. Lois married Francis Hamilton and they live in Washington Courthouse, Ohio.

6. Kenneth lives in Dayton, Ohio. Not married. He works for Portland Cement Co.

4. Jeff Rose married a Miller first, then Bessie Cecil and had children by both his first and second wives.

4. Steve Rose married Rosie Little and they had eight children; all of whom are living save one: John Herbert, Angeline, Edna, Steve, Inez and Charles and a son who died in his early years with diptheria.

5. John married Lillian McClure and they had one daughter. John is in the grocery business in Huntington, W. Va., where he has been very successful. They had one daughter, Era Nell.

6. Era Nell Rose married Bill Bryant and they have one son and one daughter. Their home is in Lexington and they spend most of their time there; though his work takes him to Harlan,

frequently.

5. Herbert married Angeline Cox. They have two sons, Volney H. and Bill. Volney was graduated from Morehead College and entered the Navy where he served for several months, then was released on a medical discharge. He is married and he and his wife live in Ohio where they both teach.

5. Bill was graduated from Berea College and enlisted in the Navy and is still in Service at this time. He is a Lieutenant J. G. and is now stationed at the naval base in California.

5. Angeline married Arch T. Johnson and they have one daughter, Rosemary. Angeline attended Eastern and is a teacher at Hazel Green Academy where she has been teaching for several years.

6. Rosemary married Raymond Harris, who graduated from the University of Kentucky in electrical engineering. He is now employed in New York State. They have one daughter.

5. Edna married the late Dr. John Cox of Campton, who was County Health Doctor for many years. (See his life story under Cox). He is now deceased. They had no children. She is a teacher and has been for several years. She is presently teaching in Ohio.

5. Inez married Graydon Walters and they have one son, Graydon Jr. Graydon and Inez live in Charleston, W. Va., and have a successful grocery business.

6. Graydon Junior is also married and lives in West Liberty. They have a child. Graydon Jr., works in a grocery store for his uncle, Andy Walter.

5. Steve married Babe Hanks. They have two children. Steve attended the University of Kentucky and also Kentucky Wesleyan College. He operates a successful grocery store in Campton.

6. Steve, Jr.

6. Sharon. Both children in grammar school.

5. Charles married Violet Williams and they live in Campton where they both teach in Wolfe County High School. Charles is Vocational Agriculture teacher. They have two children.

4. Rachel married C. S. Samples. They had five children: Steve, Bertha, Nancy, Sarah and Denzil. (See Samples family for full particulars).

4. Lou Rose married Ed Cecil. They had Mort, John, Arlie, Clay, Ethel and Ella.

5. Mort married.

6. Andrew married Mary Havens and they live on a farm near Ezel. No children, Successful farmer with a modern home.

6. Vernie married Marie Shockey and they live on the farm on Murphy Fork. They have several children.

6. Orbin studied engineering and works in the State Highway Department at Frankfort. He married there and they have one child.

5. John Cecil out of the county and reared his family in Fayette. He is now deceased. (See Samples and Cecils).

5. Arlie married Bertha. They had three daughters, Mildred, Louise and Marcella.

6. Mildred married Fred Rose and they live in West Liberty where he has a successful business. He owns and operates "Rose's Chevrolet." They both attended college and taught school for several years, then he became manager of the REA which position he held until he resigned about two years ago. They have three children: Two daughters and a son. Patricia.

6. Louise married Earl Miller (now deceased). They had one son, Winston Earl Miller.

Louise lives with her parents near Mt. Sterling. She and Earl operated the Miller Mines near Helechawa prior to his death and did a successful business. Earl had his degree in law from the University of Kentucky.

6. Marcella married. They live near Camargo where Marcella teaches and her husband operates a dairy.

5. Clay was married twice but both of his wives are now dead. No children by either one. He is in very poor health and makes his home with Arlie.

5. Ethel married a Hurt, who was killed in the log woods when a tree fell on him. They had one child, Willie Helen. Willie Helen had two years college and taught school awhile, then married Marvin Bush; but due to her health condition they were later separated.

5. Ella married Jim Perkins, who is a successful farmer near Charleston, Ill.

4. Sarah Rose married Jim Elkins. They had four sons, Lexie, John, Steve and Mort, and one daughter, Lula, who married Asa Little.

4. Elizabeth Rose married Oscar Cecil (See Cecils).

4. Molly Rose married Sewell C. Combs. They had one child, Alice, who married a Pieratt.

Sewell married twice. He married a Swango the second time. They had three children: Harry, Courtney and Anna Bell.

3. Jeff Rose, fourth son of John Rose and Polly Morrow Rose, married Susan Samples and they had six children: Monroe, Sarilda, Mort, Robert L., Kelly and Mary.

4. Monroe never married.
4. Sarilda married Fred Stamper.
5. Susie married a Taulbee.
4. Mort married in Texas where he made his home. Now dead.
4. Robert L. Married Bertha Brewer at Stillwater, Ky., in Wolfe County on Dec. 24, 1902. He has the following children:
5. Carrie Rose, born 1903, married Ollie Patrick.
6. M. C. Patrick, Dayton, Ohio.

6. Bill Patrick, Dayton, Ohio.
6. Ruby Patrick married R. T. Eddy, Dayton, Ohio.
6. Bobby Patrick, U. S. Army.
6. Mary Patrick was accidentally killed in a train and car collision at a railroad crossing in Ohio when she was 16. Killed at the same time were her two sisters, Shirley 11, Romie Jean 8, and her brother, Mikie 3 years of age. This was at Gettysburg Crossing in Ohio in 1948.
6. Davie Patrick stayed with his grandmother until he was of age.
5. Morton Rose married, but no children. He is now dead.
5. Golden Rose married Dave Bowman of Middletown, Ohio. Her husband got killed.
6. Jewell was her only daughter. She is now about 30 years of age. She has been married twice. Her last husband got killed.
5. Sadie Rose married Bert Conley and lives in Los Angeles, California. Address is 1666½ E. 84th St., Los Angeles, California.
5. Lemuel Rose married a Combs first, then married again. He is now dead. Children by both wives.
5. Fannie Rose died at the age of two years in 1913 in Middletown, Ohio.
5. Rudolph Rose married Mable Spencer. They had three children.
5. An infant was born to Robert Rose and Bertha Rose, which died and was buried in Swango graveyard.
4. Kelly Rose married in Texas. Lives on Stillwater in Wolfe County.
4. Mary (dead), married Henry Garrison. One daughter.
3. Joe Rose, fifth son of John Rose and Polly Morrow Rose, married Polly Ann Nichols, and they had two sons and a daughter.

EASTERN KENTUCKY ROSE FAMILY
By E. T. Rose

John Rose and his wife, Rebekah (Bowen) Rose are buried in the old original "Rose Cemetery" on the headwaters of Main Lacy's Creek in Wolfe County, Kentucky, and their gravestones are inscribed as follows:

"John Rose, Born 1761, Died 1843."
"Rebekah Rose, Born 1763, Died 1835."

The above are the oldest definitely known "Rose" ancestors of E. T. Rose of Edna, Texas, who is now seeking further information concerning his said ancestors. It is definitely known that they settled in Eastern Kentucky about 1802 and shortly thereafter they began to buy land in Breathitt County, Ky. They reared seven sons, Namely:

1. David Rose, born in Va. in 1785, died in Ky. in 1871.

2. John (Jack) Rose, born in Va. in 1791, died in Ky. in 1843.
3. Robert Rose.
4. Samuel Rose.
5. Israel Rose.
6. Bowen Rose.
7. Powell Rose, born June 8, 1802, moved to Powell County, Ky.

There are different family traditions concerning the State from which said Rose family emigrated to Kentucky. One names Virginia, another Ohio and a third names Pennsylvania. As above shown, the two oldest sons of said original John Rose claimed to have been born in Virginia, as shown by U. S. Census Reports of 1850 and 1860. There is an unverified tradition that said original John Rose was the son of David Rose and his wife, Martha, who came to Pennsylvania from England in the colonial days with the ancestors of William McKinley, our late martyred President, and that later the McKinley and Rose families moved from Pennsylvania and settled near each other in the vicinity of Canton, O., and thereafter said original John Rose moved from Ohio and settled near Old Fort, Va.; where a number of his children were born, and from which they emigrated to Kentucky as above mentioned. If the above can be confirmed by dependable records, then said various traditions will be harmonized and proven substantially correct.

Said E. T. Rose of Edna, Texas, has ascertained from two biographies of President McKinley that the McKinleys and Roses were closely related and that the President's grandmother was Mary Rose, a daughter of Andrew Rose, Jr. and his wife, Hannah C. Rose, and that said Mary Rose married James McKinley, who was the second son of David McKinley, who was the great-grandfather of the President. Said biographies state in part concerning the ancestry of President McKinley as follows:

"President McKinley came from Crawford County, Ohio, stock, his grandfather and great-grandfather having been leading pioneer citizens. Strange to say, they lived in the Banner Democratic township of this rock-ribbed Democratic county, and, what was more, the old gentlemen voted the Democratic ticket. In a little German Lutheran cemetery, a few miles North of Bucyrus, on the State Road, can be found a modest gravestone, on which is the following inscription:

David McKinley
Revolutionary Soldier
Born 1756, Died 1840

The mound is neatly kept, and from the nearby corners of the old rail fence nod wild roses in fragrant profusion. Just beyond runs the Columbus and Sandusky Short Line Railway, with its stream of commerce; but few of the passengers know that in this little cemetery rests the original stock of the Nation's late President.

Beside the grave of McKinley is a companion mound with a similar headstone, on which is inscribed:
Hannah C. Rose
Born 1757, Died 1840.

These are the graves of the predecessors of the President, and throughout this county there still reside a number of their descendants."

Said James McKinley and his wife, Mary Rose McKinley, reared large family, and their second son, William McKinley Sr., who was born in Pennsylvania was the father of President William McKinley Jr. One of the President's biographies states in part:

"On his grandmother's side McKinley comes of equally good and sturdy stock, Mary Rose, who married James McKinley, the second, having come from Holland, where her ancestors had fled to escape religious tyranny in England. The first of the Rose family to emigrate to America was Andrew, who came with William Penn and was one of the representatives of the thirteen colonies before the rebellion against Great Britian. He owned the land on which Doylestown stands today. It was his son, Andrew Rose, who was the father of Mary Rose, the mother of William McKinley, Sr. This Andrew Rose did more than double duty in the war for freedom against Great Britain. He fought and made weapons to fight with."

Copies of the above information are being forwarded by said E. T. Rose to one or more parties in Ohio, Virginia and Pennsylvania, who may be able to show the relationship, if any, between said original Kentucky John Rose and said Rose family from which President McKinley was descended. It is suggested that this might be accomplished by checking the U. S. Census Reports of 1790 and 1800 for the States of Ohio, Virginia and Pennsylvania, or through the U. S. War Department records or through Probate or other public records in said three states, or through local family histories or through other sources of information best known to genealogists and historians of said stated.

Copy Of Census Reports

1850 — Rose David, 66 Va.; Sarah 58, William 15, Robert 14.

Rose John, 59, Va.; Mary, 59, N. C.; Robert 22, Elijah 19, Mary 12, Jefferson 10.

1860 — Rose David, 76, Va.; Sarah 68, Robert T. 25, Eliza Hogg 33, (perhaps a daughter); James Hogg 12, Elizabeth Hogg 8, William Hogg 3.

WOLFE COUNTY

Rose John, 69, Va.; Mary Ann 67, Frances 20, Jefferson 19.

Rose James, 42; Henrietta, 42, (Haney) (Dau. of Alex McQuinn); Benjamine F. 19, Robert E. 16, John 14, William 13, Allison 12, Martha 10, Mary J. 9, James B. 4, Charles W. 1, Alex McQuinn 76, (Father of wife).

1870 — Rose David, 86, Va.; Evoline, 40, Va., (wife); Wm. T. Halsey 17, Susan Halsey 11, James Halsey 9, Sarah B. Hasley 6.

I have given you an exact copy of census, to prove the Rose family came from Virginia.

When James Kash moved to Montgomery County, he sold his home farm on the head of Stillwater to David Rose and his wife, Evoline. She was a widow Halsey and had four children by her former marriage. I remember her very well as her home was near the school where I first attended. Her daughter, Sarah, married Jack Russell. His wife got the farm for keeping the old lady till her death. After she died Russell sold the farm and moved to the Chambers Fork of Stillwater. Jeff Johnson later purchased it and operated a store at the mouth of the creek below her house.

James Rose, son of Robert Rose and Mary Moore, married Henrietta McQuinn, daughter of Alexander McQuinn and was the father of all the Roses at Lee City. McQuinn gave him 5,000 acres where Lee City now stands. I have volumes of Census reports; but have not had time to look them over carefully.

Ask Steve Samples if Washington and Abram Swango were brothers. I will soon have a complete Rose history.

The following Wolfe County families came from the Greenbriar River in W. Va.: Trimble, Kash, Nickell, Wilson, Lacy, Swango, Landsaw, etc.

I find that a number of McQuinns who were named Henrietta were all called "Haney". I am hardly able to sit up, therefore this disconnected letter. If I ever get to feeling better I, perhaps, can give you a better report. Yours truly,

J. C. Hurst.

You might be interested in some of the following items taken from "Annals of Southwest Virginia — 1769 to 1800" — Botetourt, Montgomery, Washington and Wythe Counties.

Botetourt County

1773, March 12th — Charles Rose was a member of jury in case, James Buchanan vs: Edward Hill.

1789, January 5th — Bowen, Bathia, married John Plymill.

1794, February 24th — Bowen, Charles, married Elizabeth Shaver.

1795, February 24th — Bowen, William, married Elizabeth Smith. Bowen, Moses was Revolutionary Soldier.

1778, August 12th — "Court ordered that agreeable to an act of the Assembly, Sarah Chambers draw from the Treasurer of Virginia, whose husband is a soldier in the Continental Army, the sum of 10 pounds for the support of herself and child."

1780, March 10th — "Ordered that the sum of 35 pounds be allowed to Andrew Henry for his trouble for keeping a child of Alex Chambers, a soldier, and boarding his wife eight weeks and five days and that he draw on the Treasurer for same."

Fincastle County

1773, November 2nd — "Ordered that the Church wardens bind William and Nancy Rose to William Henley, their grandfather, according to law. Rose Andrew, Revolutionary Soldier, in company of Col. Peachey.

1773, November 8th — Deed from James Hollis to Daniel Chambers (late of York Government) 226 acres on branch of Reed Ck.

1778, February 20th — Daniel Chambers and wife, Abrigail, deed to 226 acres, to Joseph Hildrith.

Montgomery County

1785, February 9th — Rose, Israel, married Elizabeth Stephens. (The name looks like your folks.)

1796, January — Rose, Edward, witnessed Will of Joshua Pittman.

1798, April 4th — Rose, Robert was licensed to retail merchandise.

1794 — Chambers Moses, married Jane Mairs.

Washington County

1790, June 6th — Bowen, John, married Margaret Williams.

1798, November 22nd — Bowen, Bettie, married Drury Reed.

1792, January 3rd — Chambers, Ann, married Jack Anderson.

1799, December 28th — Chambers, Hannah, married Elijah Dugan.

1778, November 17th — "Court ordered that Mark Chambers be Constable in the bounds of Capt. Thomas Caldwells Company."

Albemarle County

1794, March 8th — Thomas Walker stayed at the home of Rev. Robert Rose on Tye River, on the east side of the Blue Ridge, (see Journal — Thomas Walker's trip to Kentucky.)

Bowens Who Were Revolutionary Soldiers

Arthur was a Captain.
William was a Captain.
Reese was a Lieutenant.

Charles, John, son of Reese, Henry and Robert were privates or not commissioned officers. All the above were in the battle of Kings Mountain and Lieutenant Reese was killed there.

Large numbers of Bowens were shown in Botetourt, Washington and Fincastle Counties.

WOLFE COUNTY

Mr. J. C. Hurst,
642 Central Avenue, Lexington 7, Kentucky
Kind Friend:

Thanks for your recent letters giving me further information concerning my Rose, Bowen and Chambers ancestors, etc. The copy of the census reports on my great-grandfather, David Rose, and his brother John (Jack) Rose, definitely show that they were both born in the State of Virginia and also that David Rose was the older fo the two brothers. In my recent letter to you, I took the position that said John Rose was the older, but said Census reports clearly show that David Rose was seven years older than his brother, John. You gave me my first information concerning said David Rose purchasing the James Kash farm on Stillwater Creek and residing on same with his second wife and her four children by a former marriage. I had been informed that he married the second time when he was 77 years of age and that his second wife was a young widow with four children, the youngest being named Sarah B., who married Jack Russell. The children of said Sarah B. and Jack Russell attended what is known as the Chambers school situated at the mouth of the Chambers Fork of Stillwater Creek, which I taught during the year 1901. At that time said Russells owned and lived upon a small farm on what is known as the Swango Fork of Stillwater Creek, which joins the Chambers Fork of Stillwater Creek near said school house. Believe that my said great-grandfather was the first white man to establish a homestead on Stillwater Creek, when he settled on his "Sugar Orchard" farm. Believe his brother, John, settled there a short time later and from the information I have, it appears that the Hursts, Chambers and Swangos first arrived on Stillwater Creek about 10 years or more later. I do not have anything very definite about this. Said David Rose reared 11 children by his first wife, Sarah or Sally Nickell, and also helped rear the three children of his daughter, Eliza Hogg, who became a widow while quite young, and, as above indicated, he married his second wife at the age of 77 and helped rear her four children and died at the age of 87. Long after said David Rose established a home on said Sugar Orchard farm, he purchased a 400 acre tract of land from the famous Henry Clay of your State, as is shown by deed dated March 28, 1828. Said 400 acre tract of land was situated on the Trace Fork of Stillwater Creek and in said deed from Clay, it was mentioned as "running on the war tract" or war path. I have been informed that Daniel Boone's trace or trail passed up the Trace Fork of Stillwater and for that reason the Creek was so named. In this connection, I have heard it said that the Boone Fork of Frozen Creek was so named because the name of "Daniel Boone" was found inscribed on a Beech tree on said Creek by the early white settlers. It is possible that this Beech tree was on the land that you inherited from your father. If any reliance could be placed in the above statements, it would seem that Daniel Boone came up the Boone Fork of Frozen Creek and also traveled up the Trace Fork of Stillwater Creek on his way toward the Blue Grass region. Said 400 acre tract of land on the Trace Fork became the property of my grandfather, David Rose, and my father and I were both born in the same log cabin on said land. Said deed from Henry Clay to David Rose was witnessed by Thomas Hart, John Rose, Bowen Rose and John Rose, again, Abraham Swango and William Murphy. I know nothing about said Thomas Hart. I assume that one John Rose who witnessed the deed was the father of the grantee therein, and that the other John Rose was the brother of said grantee and that Bowen Rose was another brother of the grantee. Said Abraham Swango, sometimes called "Abram" and also "Abe" was probably the original Swango to settle on Stillwater and owned the farm adjoining said Sugar Orchard farm. Harrison Swango, the son of said Abram Swango, married Annie Rose, the daughter of said original David Rose and became the grandparents of Courtney and Henry Combs. I cannot definitely place William Murphy, who witnessed said deed, but he was probably the father of John Murphy, who married Sally Rose, another daughter of said David Rose. I am giving you all this dope as it may come in handy in some line of your investigation.

You requested me to ascertain if S. G. Sample knows the relationship between Washington Swango and Abram Swango. He informed me that he did not know whether or not they were brothers but that he had heard the name "Wash" Swango mentioned frequently. I have never made any effort to work up a Swango family tree, as I do not have any direct kinship with said family. Sample suggested that you might contact Mr. Charlie Duff and his wife of Mt. Sterling, Ky., who are related to the Swango family and probably have a lot of family information. I would also suggest that you contact Harry Combs of Lexington or C. F. Combs of Cuero, Texas, or Bill Kash of Irvine, as they are all related to the Swangos. I have always understood that said Abram Swango donated two acres of land at the mouth of Meeting House Branch of Stillwater for church and school purposes and particularly as a site for a Hardshell Baptist Church. I am sure that you know the location of this two-acres at the old Beech Grove nera the Roscoe Wells home. A church building was erected on the site in the early pioneer days and during the week days the building was usde for school purposes and your father and my grandmother and other members of their family walked daily to said school from their old home on the head of Stillwater Creek. If I remember correctly, your grandfather, Samuel Henry Hurst, was elected clerk of said church in 1844 and continued to hold that job until his death in 1888. I do not know the names of all the children of said Abram Swango, but do understand that he was the father of Samuel Swango, who was the father of Bud Swango, Dr. Ova Swango and Elizabeth Swango, who married John M. Rose of Hazel Green, and the said Abram Swango was also the father of "Chap" Swango, who was a well educated man for his day and who erected and operated the old "Seminary" school on his father's land and near said Sugar Orchard farm. This school caused the nearby creek to be called the Seminary Fork of Stillwater. Said "Chap" Swango participated in the Civil War and was killed during the war, but I am not certain whether he fought for the North or the South. My great uncle, James Rose, married a Miss Fannie Swango and my uncle, Campton Rose, married a Miss Alice Swango. As I recall, there were four brothers connected with the Swango Fork of Stillwater Creek. John lived on the head of the Creek and operated a grist mill. Harry lived further down the Creek and operated a small farm, and Hiram lived near the mouth of the Creek and was also a farmer. Believe the fourth brother was Green Swango, who married Leatha Brashears of Whitesburg and they lived in the Calaboose section until Green died and then his widow married his widowed brother, said Harry Swango and lived with him until he died and Leatha died a few years ago at the ripe old age of about 100. I also understand that said Abram Swango was the grandfather of Greenberry Swango, who was at one time County Judge of Wolfe County, but neither Sample nor I know the name of the father of said Greenberry Swango. I did become acquainted with Greenberry's son, Jim Swango, many years ago. I met him while on a business trip to Terre Haute, Indiana. He went to Terre Haute from Kentucky as a lawyer, but at the time I met him he was devoting practically all of his time to the operation of a sand and gravel pit that he owned and out of which he seemed to have made a comfortable fortune.

You asked me what information I have concerning Elisha Hurst living near the mouth of Holly Creek. The only information that I have was furnished to me by your father in 1913 and I gave it to you in my last letter in connection with the Rose Family history that I obtained from your father. In naming the children of the original John (Dad) Rose for me, your father mentioned that Samuel Rose, one of such children, bought the Elisha Hurst farm at the mouth of Holly Creek. I then confined my inquiry particularly to my direct ancestors, but I am sorry now that I did not avail myself of that golden opportunity to obtain much other valuable family history from your father, who was so well posted concerning the pioneer citizens of Wolfe and adjoining counties. Believe that said Elisha Hurst was an older brother of your grandfather, Samuel Henry Hurst.

The information that you sent me concerning the Roses, Bowens and Chambers who lived in Virginia, along the East side of the Blue Ridge, is very interesting to me. The Rose names that you mentioned are family given names of my Rose family and I am inclined to believe that my Rose, Bowen and Chamber ancestors were closely related to the families mentioned by you who lived in the five mountain counties running along the East side of the Blue Ridge in Virginia. You stated that the following Wolfe County families came from the Greenbriar River in West Virginia: Trimble, Kash, Nickell, Wilson, Lacy, Swango, Landsaw, etc. You understand that the Greenbriar River area mentioned by you was in old Virginia until the Civil War and that such area was along the West side of the Blue Ridge Mountains. Your other information indicates that the Roses, Bowens and Chambers hailed from the same mountain range, and, as I understand, the Samples and Cecils also came from the Blue Ridge area of Virginia. The Stamper family came from Ashe County, North Carolina, which occupies the Northwest corner of said North Carolina, and also in the Blue Ridge Mountain area. You may have learned that the Stamper family were the first white settlers on Grassy Creek in Morgan County, Ky., and that they named the Creek where they settled after Grassy Creek, in Ashe County, North Carolina, from whence they came. I have not recently checked up on the matter, but as I recall, the Hurst family lived for a long time in Culpepper and Shennandoah Counties, Virginia. Sorry to bore you with so many rambling observations, but thought that I might say something that would be of interest to you. I was particularly interested in the following statement in your letter: "Thomas Walker stayed at the home of Rev. Robert Rose on Tye River, on the east side of the Blue Ridge (see Journal — Thomas Walker's trip to Kentucky)". Said Rev. Robert Rose was then living in Albemarle County, Virginia, which bounders on the East side of the Blue Ridge, and said Thomas Walker was the distinguished Dr. Thomas Walker who is credited with having been the first white man to explore Kentucky. He and his small party discovered and named the Cumberland Gap and they erected the first white man's residence in Kentucky on the Cumberland River, near Barbourville, on April 30, 1750, about 25 years before Daniel Boone estbalished Boonesboro. Dr. Walker served under Washington during the Revolutionary War and Washington once said to him: "If you have something to do and want it done now and well, get Dr. Thomas Walker."

I am inclined to think that you are correct in your statement with reference to the two Israel Roses. That is, one was the brother of the original John (Dad) Rose and the other was the son of said original John (Dad) Rose. Hope I have given you as much information as I have concerning the inquiries you made and hope that I have not burdened you too much with this long rambling letter. Hope you do not work too hard in assembling your historical data and that you will be able to make satisfactory arrangements to produce your Hurst family history in the near future. With kindest personal regards, I remain,

Very sincerely yours,

E. T. Rose.

ETR:1b

P. S.: Was interrupted so much after starting this letter that I have done some repeating and also omitted some things that I wanted to mention. Believe said "Abram" Swango was buried in the cemetery on his Stillwater farm, now owned by S. B. Allen. I am quite sure that I examined the monument at his grave. Charley Rose of your city, son of said John M. and Elizabeth Swango Rose should be able to aid you in lining up the Swango family. Note that you find in the "Annals of Southwest Virginia — 1769 to 1800" that Israel Rose of Montgomery Co., Va., married Elizabeth Stephens on Feb. 9, 1785. It is very probable that said Israel Rose was a brother of the original John (Dad) Rose, who named one of his sons "Israel", who was a brother of my great-grandfather, David Rose, who was born in Virginia in 1785, the same year that said Israel Rose married in Montgomery Co., Va. I am guessing that said David Rose was born in or near said Montgomery Co. I plan to check the early Virginia Census Reports on this point.

It appears that all my ancestors are natural born "Hillbillies". They passed up the Blue Grass, the plains and the prairies and chose the cool shady hills. I really have a longing for them myself. The Hursts lived on both sides of the Blue Ridge in Va. Notice that the Virginia Bowens distinguished themselves during the Revolutionary War. Maybe that is the reason my grandfather named his oldest son David "Bowen" Rose and his next son "Bowen" David Rose.

E. T. R.

EARLY AND MODERN HISTORY

SKETCHES OF EARLY FAMILIES
By E. T. Rose
Edna, Texas,
June 18, 1954

Mrs. Roy M. Cecil,
Editor, Wolfe County News,
Campton, Kentucky
Kind Friend:

Glad to get your letter of June 11th indicating that as Chairman of the Committee of the Wolfe County Woman's Club you are collecting valuable data concerning the early history of Wolfe County and that you would appreciate receiving appropriate information from me, particularly in regard to the Rose, Nickell and Hurst families. Sorry that I have been delayed in replying on account of having been away from my office so much the past few days, but I will now endeavor as best I can to furnish you some data that may be of assistance in your very valuable and commendable undertaking.

Nickell Family

I am handing you herewith copy of a letter that I wrote to Miss Annie Belle Combs of Richmond, Ky., under date of June 26, 1952 with particular reference to the Eastern Kentucky Rose and Nickell families, and I believe that such letter will give you some of the most dependable information that I have obtained concerning the Nickell family, and as you will notice I designed said letter with a view of proving as best I could that the Morgan County Nickell pioneers were closely related to a number of the Rose family pioneers of Wolfe County.

Hurst Family

For the most complete and reliable information concerning the Hurst family I will refer you to J. C. Hurst's history of the "Hursts of Shenandoah" and other related families that was prepared and published by said J. C. Hurst a few years ago after he had done an exceptional amount of research and investigation work. I purchased enough copies of said publication to distribute among my most immediate relatives, and in case you do not have easy access to a volume of this work I am sure that my sister, Mrs. J. W. Haney of Grassy Creek, Ky., or my sister, Mrs. H. K. Combs, of Irvine, Ky., or my sister, Mrs. Gertrude Childers, of Lexington, Ky., will be glad to lend you their copies for the purpose of your undertaking.

Rose Family

I have assembled a great deal of data from various and sundry sources for the purpose of preparing a small booklet concerning my Rose family, but thus far have not digested said material sufficiently to prepare such booklet in proper form, but I am handing you herewith some of my information and correspondence concerning the Rose family for such benefit as it may be to you, to-wit:

WOLFE COUNTY

1. A two sheet copy of information that I prepared concerning the original John Rose and his wife, Rebekah Bowen Rose, and you will notice that I have endeavored in such information to show a probable kinship between said Rose family and the McKinley family of Eastern Ohio of which our former President was a member. Since preparing said material I have not obtained further information to substantiate the old tradition that has been handed down in the Rose family concerning the Rose and McKinley relationships. This tradition has been perpetuated or kept alive by the descendents of Powell Rose, the youngest son of the said John Rose and wife, who was born June 8, 1802 and lived out his life in Powell County, Kentucky, where, I understand, he has many descendants and a great many descendants who have moved to other parts of our country. You will notice that said information only names the seven sons of said John Rose and wife but does not name any daughters, but I have been informed that said original Roses reared seven daughters as well as seven sons, but I have no detailed information concerning same.

2. I am handing you two pages of data submitted to me by said J. C. Hurst in April 1950 giving extracts from the U. S. Census Reports of 1850, 1860 and 1870 concerning my great-grandfather, David Rose, son of said original John Rose, and also concerning S. G. Sample's great-grandfather, John (Jack) Rose, who was a younger son of said original John Rose and wife. Along with said Census information supplied by Mr. Hurst, he sent other information concerning the Rose and Bowen families of Virginia as shown by a publication entitled "Annals of Southwest Virginia — 1769 - 1800". I wrote Mr. Hurst under date of April 29, 1950 acknowledging receipt of said information and also making various and sundry comments with reference thereto and with reference to other pioneer families mentioned by him in said information, particularly the Swango family. In my opinion you can obtain further information concerning the Swango family from the surviving children of Mr. John M. Rose. As indicated by the enclosed information, said original John Rose and his family moved into Eastern Kentucky more than 150 years ago, and I believe that the seven sons of said original John Rose are the ancestors of all, or practically all, the present day members of the Rose family who reside in Wolfe County and the neighboring counties. As you know, the living members of the Rose family in Wolfe County and the adjacent area are so numerous that it would require a large booklet to even list their names and addresses, and I have never tried to obtain further information concerning my collateral Rose ancestors in Eastern Kentucky but have confined my efforts to obtaining near relatives in my direct ancestral line. I give you briefly my definite Kentucky Rose ancestral line as follows:

EARLY AND MODERN HISTORY

1. My great great grandparents said original John Rose and his wife, Rebekah Bowen Rose.

2. My great grandparents David Rose (son of said original John Rose) and his wife Sally Nickell Rose.

3. My grandparents David Bowen Rose (son of said last mentioned David Rose) and his wife, Millie Stamper Rose. In this connection will state that said Millie Stamper Rose was a daughter of Hiram Stamper and his wife, Matilda Hogg Stamper, and that Hiram Stamper was sheriff of Perry County, Kentucky in 1829. Said Hiram Stamper was a son of Wm. Stamper and his wife, Emily Polly Stamper and he, said Wm. Stamper, was sheriff of Perry County in 1827 and 1828. Said Stampers moved frmo Grassy Creek in Ashe County, North Carolina to Perry County, Kentucky and settled in what is now Letcher County and later some of the family moved to Wolfe County and others moved to Morgan County. It is my understanding that the Morgan County Stamper family settled on and named Grassy Creek in Morgan County after their old home creek, "Grassy Creek" in Ashe County, North Carolina from which they had moved. Said Wm. Stamper was a son of James Stamper and his wife, Sarah Moore Stamper of North Carolina. Said Emily Polly, who married said Wm. Stamper, was the daughter of Edward Polly who was born in 1758 in North Carolina, and he served in the Colonial Army in the Revolutionary War.

4. My parents, Bowen David Rose (son of said David Bowen Rose) and his wife, Nancy Chambers Rose, reared ten children of which five now survive, including myself. If you need any further information concerning my branch of the Chambers family I shall be glad to furnish same to you upon request, but in my opinion, my cousin, Miss Daisy Chambers, a former President of the said Wolfe County Woman's Club, can supply you with what you may need.

I am not taking the time to check over the copies of data enclosed herewith, but hope that at least some of it will be of service to your club in the preparation of its brief history of Wolfe County. Do not now recall any historical incidents of particular importance concerning Wolfe County, excepting the traditional Swift Silver Mine, which may be entirely fictional. Hope some stories have been preserved concerning the early pioneer period of Wolfe County, but I do not have anything to offer along that line. I have heard fragments of interesting experiences of the early pioneers, including hardships and privations but not enough to formulate an interesting story. It seems to me that some mention should be made of the Civil War period during which the citizens of Wolfe County were greatly divided and during which time there was much lawlessness and ill feeling. I suggest that you contact Mr. J. C. Hurst of 642 Central Avenue, Lexington 7, Kentucky, and see if he will not supply you with some of his most important general information concerning Wolfe County. Believe he is now assembling data with a view of publishing one or more additional books concerning Eastern Kentucky, but that should not prevent him from being of great assistance to your club. I am pleased to hand you herewith my check for $25.00 drawn in favor of the Wolfe County Woman's Club to aid it in compiling and publishing its proposed Wolfe County History.

Very sincerely yours,
E. T. Rose.

AMERICA ELIZABETH NICKELL
(Contributed by Mrs. C. P. Gullet Sr.)

America Elizabeth Nickell (nee Davis) passed away at her home at Helechawa, Ky., in Wolfe County on Saturday, August 21, 1954 during her 91st year. She was born Feb. 12, 1863, a daughter of the late Willa R. and Elizabeth Wilson Davis, a pioneer family of Eastern Kentucky.

She was the last surviving member of a family of five children. Two brothers, James A. Davis and Henry Wise Davis and two sisters, Katherine Davis Gullett and Mary Davis Prater, preceded her in death.

Early in life she was converted, baptized and affiliated with the United Baptist Church at Insko, of which she remained a devout member throughout her life.

On August 1, 1879 she was married to James Harlan Nickell (deceased), and to this union were born four sons. The eldest, Boyd Nickell, died at the age of three years. Surviving are her sons: E. Morton Nickell, Milan, Ind.; John T. Nickell, Helechawa, Ky., and Dennie T. Nickell, Ashland, Ky. Also seven grandchildren and ten great-grandchildren.

She was known far and wide as "Aunt America" and everyone who knew her loved her.

EARLY AND MODERN HISTORY

ROSE AND NICKELL FAMILIES IN EASTERN KENTUCKY
By E. T. Rose

Edna, Texas,
June 26, 1952.

Miss Annie Belle Combs,
307, 5th Street,
Richmond, Kentucky
Dear Cousin:

I have less accurate information concerning our "Nickell" ancestors than any other branch of my family. I have picked up a little information from time to time during many years and filed it away for future reference, but have never taken the time to try to analyse same and produce a connected chain. Since time is rapidly running against the older members of our family and since you have written me about the matter, I will now review such information as I have.

We definitely know from family tradition and otherwise that our great-grandfather David Rose married Sally Nickell and settled on their "Sugar Orchard Farm" on Stillwater Creek in what is now Wolfe County, Ky., about the year 1810. There they reared eleven children as follows:

1. Nancy Rose, who married a Ward.
2. Sallie Rose, who married a Murphy.
3. Senia Rose, who married Pete Little.
4. Annie Rose, who married Harrison Swango, your grandparents.
5. Fannie Rose, who married a Hainline.
6. Eliza Rose, who married Silas Hogg.
7. Bowen Rose, who married a Henry.
8. David B. Rose, who married Millie Stamper, my grandparents.
9. James Rose, who married a Swango.
10. William Rose, who married Polly Christian.
11. Robert Rose, never married.

I have always been told by my said grandparents and my parents that my said great-grandmother, Sally Nickell Rose, was a member of the Morgan County Nickell family, and that we were related to Joe Darky Nickell's family through both the Nickells and the Stampers. Believe Joe Darky Nickell died about 25 years ago. Both of our said great-grandparents were buried on their said Sugar Orchard Farm and their monuments are inscribed as follows:

"David Rose, born March 20, 1785, died November 7, 1871."
"Sally Rose, born March 3, 1792, died November 15, 1861."

It is also a matter of record that three Rose brothers married three Nickell sisters about 100 years ago, such three Rose brothers being the sons of John (Jack) Rose, who was a brother of our said great-grandfather, David Rose, and the records of such three marriages as shown by the Morgan County Marriage Records are as follows:

(1) John D. Rose married Nancy Nickell on Feb. 3, 1848.
(2) Joseph Rose married Polly Ann Nickell on Feb. 25, 1852.
(3) Robert Rose Jr., (age 23) married Fanny Nickell (age 15), on Nov. 20, 1853.

S. G. Sample of Edna, Texas, is a grandson of said John D. Rose and wife, Nancy Nickell Rose, and S. G. Sample's mother, Rachel Rose Sample, told me in 1902 that after the death of her grandfather Nickell, her mother, said Nancy Nickell Rose, made her home with her Aunt Sally Nickell Rose and husband (our great-grandparents above named) for many years and until she married John D. Rose as above stated, such marriage taking place at the home of said Sally Nickell Rose and husband, David Rose, I do not recall that said Rachel Sample told me the given name of her grandfather Nickell, but at a later date she gave her son, S. G. Sample, the following information:

(Information given S. G. Sample by his mother, Dec. 30, 1930)

Robert Nickell, great-grandfather (maternal) of S. G. Sample, married Polly Nickell, probably a relative, and they reared the following named children, to-wit:

1. Perryander Nickell, married in Missouri, father of one child, Bell.

2. John Nickell, married Betsy Baker and they had the following children, to-wit: Henry, who married Orlean Wilson and later Miss Cable and died in Wolfe County; Andy Priscilla, who was burnt to death; Lizzie, who married Green Little; Pauline, Jane and Fannie, who each married a Shackelford, and one girl who married a Lyons; where John Nickell died.

3. Miles Nickell married Rosa Little and had six or eight children. Perry Ander, Robert and one girl married a Wilson. Miles died and the family went to Arkansas.

4. Joe D. Nickell married a Lackey and had no children. He died near Ezel, Ky.

5. Isaac Nickell married a Crain. Their only daughter was the first wife of Joe Wilson of Beattyville, Ky., and left two sons, Curry and Quillie, both living.

6. George Nickell married a Sorrel. They had a son and a daughter and lived on Blackwater in Morgan County, Ky.

7. James R. Nickell, a minister in the Christian Church, married a Gilmore. They were the parents of Berry, Enoch, Mrs. Carter, the mother of Mrs. Lon Hovermale and others.

8. Nancy J., at the age of 23, married John David Rose. They became the parents of nine children, who lived to become adults, to-wit: Joe P. Rose, Lou Cecil, wife of E. F. Cecil, Lizzie Cecil, wife of O. W. Cecil, Rachel Ann Sample, wife of Charles Smith Sample,

Jeff M. Rose, David B. Rose, Sarah Elkins, wife of James B. Elkins, Stephen Sewell Rose and Mary Rose, first wife of S. S. Combs, both now deceased.

9. Polly Ann married Joe Rose, brother of John David Rose, and they became the parents of John D. (Nosey), "Curly" Bob and Sarah McClure, wife of Ezekiel McClure. By her second husband, Alex Lacey, she became the mother of Porter and Boone Lacey.

10. Fannie married Robert Rose, brother of John David Rose, and they became the parents of Billy Rose, Mrs. Jeff Edwards, and Nancy Brown, wife of Tom Brown.

11. Lizzie married James Cox, son of Sol Cox. They became the parents of Emma Taylor and two or three other children. One child was blind, a girl. The Coxes lived in Indiana.

12. Jane married Rev. James Little of the Presbyterian Church, and they became the parents of Robert, who married Rosa Carson, Sophronia, Mrs. Nannie Graham, wife of Lilburn Graham, Sarah Ellen, Bruce, Polk and Clay.

The above information is substantially in keeping with the information given to you by our cousin, Mattie Hainline Amyx, who died in 1937, except that Mrs. Amyx stated that said Polly Ann Nickell's husband was named "Isaac" instead of "Robert" as above shown, and also that she had a son named Robert (Bob) instead of Isaac as above shown. Mrs. Amyx is a daughter of the above mentioned Fannie Rose Hainline, who lived to be 90 years of age and possessed good memory as long as she lived. Mrs. Amyx said her mother told her that Sally Nickell Rose and husband took into their home said Isaac Nickell, their nephew, and reared him until he was grown, and then gave him a horse, saddle and bridle as was the custom of that day; and that after the death of said Isaac Nickell, said Sally Nickell Rose and husband had the custody of and made a home for the three daughters of Isaac Nickell until they married the three Rose brothers as above stated. I am giving this detailed information to show the close relationship between said Sally Nickell Rose and the three Nickell sisters who married the three Rose brothers. If we can definitely connect any one of said four Nickell women with the "Morgan County Nickell family", then we will have them all connected.

About two months ago, you sent me a letter that you had received from Mr. H. H. Nickell of Daysboro, Ky., concerning the Nickell family. Mr. Nickell stated that he was about 84 years of age and was the son of Robert Nickell and that he had heard his father discuss the relationship between the Nickell and Rose families, but that he could not recall so as to give accurate details. He did give some interesting information, which I may hereafter mention. Probably the best informed living members of the "Morgan County Nickell family" with reference to the Nickell family history are as follows:

WOLFE COUNTY

1. Mr. H. H. Nickell of Daysboro, Ky.
2. Mr. Kelly Nickell of Mize, Ky.
3. Mr. S. H. Nickell of Lexington, Ky.

In view of the fact that we are all interested in keeping our family histories accurate, I am taking the liberty of mailing to each of the above named three parties a carbon copy of this letter and its enclosures, so that they may check the statements herein made for accuracy, if they can do so, and I request each of them to point out any errors they may notice and make such criticisms as they may see fit. We are all getting along in years and may not have much more opportunity to help obtain a better understanding of our "Nickell" relationships. I shall be glad to do all I can.

We have this further information: Some years ago Joe Nickell of Topeka, Kansas, claimed to have traced the Morgan County Nickell family back to Antrim County, Ireland, and he compiled a very interesting outline or chart of the Nickell family. S. G. Sample located a copy of this chart in possession of S. H. Nickell of Lexington, Ky., and made a few copies of same on June 21, 1938, and he gave me a copy for my file, and I have had other copies made and hand each of you herewith a copy excepting S. H. Nickell, who has a copy. In 1939 S. G. Sample wrote S. Monroe Nickell of Lexington, Ky., seeking information that might show the relationship of his grandmother, the said Nancy Nickell Rose, with the Morgan County Nickell family. I have a copy of Monroe's reply to said letter dated 3-9-1939, in which he stated that he was unable to give the direct connection, but was pretty sure that said Nancy Nickell Rose came from one of the three old Nickell brothers who first came to Morgan County, which then included most of Wolfe County. He said that John Nickell, one of said three brothers, was his ancestor, and that Isaac Nickell, another of said brothers, was the ancestor of said Joe Nickell of Topeka; and I am of the opinion that the third brother, known as "Big" Joseph Nickell, was the ancestor of said H. H. Nickell of Daysboro, Ky. Monroe Nickell further stated that it had always been his understanding that said Nancy Nickell Rose was a cousin of his grandfather Nickell, but he did not know just how it was. Monroe said he was planning to check upon his Nickell ancestors and write a pamphlet or book on it for the benefit of his interested relatives, but so far as I know he passed on without doing so. If Joe Nickell is still living in Topeka, Kansas, and if any of you know his street address, I would like to have it so that I can write him at once for further information. For your convenience in replying, I am enclosing self-addressed envelopes to each of you. Any information that you may give me will be highly appreciated.

I would like for all of you to study the enclosed Nickell Family chart carefully. You will notice that the original John I. Nickell came from Ireland and settled in Virginia in 1749 and that his six sons served in the American Revolution. One of said sons, Joseph Nickell, was born in 1750, married Elizabeth Fowler, and settled in Greenbrier, Va. and in 1788 removed to Kentucky. His family first settled on Lulbegrud Creek in Montgomery County, Kentucky, and later moved to Morgan County, Ky. Joseph and Elizabeth were the parents of the following named children as shown by said chart:

John b-1771 (Elsy Wilson) to Kentucky.
Isaac b-1775 (Priscilla Jones) to Kentucky.
Mary b-1778 (Andrew Wilson, 1796) Kentucky.
"Big" Joseph b-1790 in Kentucky.
Elizabeth (Samuel Francis).
James.   (Incomplete)

As above shown, the record of the children of Joe and Elizabeth Nickell is "incomplete", but I believe that if such record was complete, it would show Sally Nickell born in 1792. I submit that since the tombstone of Sally Nickell states that she was born in 1792 and since strong family tradition says she belongs to the Morgan County branch of the Nickell family, it would be logical and reasonable to believe that Sally Nickell Rose was a younger sister of said three pioneer Nickell brothers above named, and that the normal sequence of family births would place Sally next to and following "Big" Joe, who was born in 1790. I do not believe that Sally could have been the daughter of any one of said three pioneer Morgan County Nickell brothers. She was too old to be the daughter of Isaac or "Big" Joseph. If she was the daughter of John, the oldest brother, then she would have to be the twin sister of "Preacher" Joe Nickell, who was also born in 1792. Believe that all the circumstances indicate that she was the daughter of said first Joe Nickell and his wife, Elizabeth Fowler Nickell, and I have so indicated with ink on the enclosed charts.

Last year J. C. Hurst of Lexington, Ky., published a very complete history of the Hurst Family, in which he gave some information concerning the Landsaws, Wilsons, Murphys and other Hurst relatives. In speaking of his great-aunt, Esther Hurst, he stated that on Feb. 12, 1819, she was married to Andrew Wilson, Jr., who was a son of Andrew Wilson, Sr., and his wife, Mary Nickell Wilson, who was a daughter of Joseph and Elizabeth Nickell, as shown on said chart. He stated in said Hurst History that his investigations revealed that said Wilsons and the Nickells, Trimbles, Landsaws, Kashes, Lacys, Murphys and others came to Kentucky from the Greenbrier River section in what is now West Virginia, then Virginia. J. C. Hurst told me the last time I saw him that he was quite sure that Joseph and Elizabeth Nickell were the parents of said Sally Nickell Rose, and that he had found in making his research that said Joseph and Elizabeth Nickell were both born in Virginia. I will try to get more definite information from J. C. Hurst. If we are correct in assuming that Sally Nickell Rose is a daughter of said Joseph and Elizabeth Fowler Nickell, then it is evident that said Sally was born in what is now Kentucky in the year it became a State, as her parents had moved to Kentucky in 1788, as shown by said Chart. To be exact, she was born in Virginia on March 3, 1792 and Kentucky became a State on June 1, 1792. I point out that "Big" Joe named one of his daughters Sally Ann. It is probable that he named her Sally for his sister Sally. Both said Fannie Hainline and H. H. Nickell agree that the Nickells settled on Lulbegrud Creek when they first came to Kentucky. You probably noticed a recent article in the Wolfe County News which stated the Lulbegrud Creek, is about midway between Winchester and Clay City, and that it was explored and named by a party led by Daniel Boone and John Finley in 1769.

It is interesting to note that H. H. Nickell remembers when Matilda Nickell, second wife of "Big" Joe Nickell, visited the home of his father, Robert Nickell, when H. H. Nickell was seven years of age and he heard her tell about hearing a panther scream near "Tick Town" soon after her family arrived in Kentucky. According to said chart, "Big" Joe Nickell was married twice and his last wife was named Matilda, and I assume that said Matilda was either the mother or step-mother of said Robert Nickell, the father of said H. H. Nickell.

Pardon this long winded review, but I have tried to give you all the information I have that might be helpful. Don't hesitate to question any statement that I have made as we want only the facts. I do not question the correctness of the Chart prepared by Joe Nickell of Topeka, but I am trying to add to it where he states that it is incomplete. The compiler of this Chart seems to have overlooked or lost sight of the Wolfe County branch of the Nickell family.

I am handing you herewith the only picture I have of your class at the Hazel Green Academy. Believe it shows S. Monroe Nickell at the extreme right and you are next to him and Miss Mattie Quicksall (later Mrs. E. E. Bishop) stands in the center and Bill Quicksall is the third from the left. I do not know any of the others. You may keep this picture.

Very sincerely yours,

E. T. Rose.

EARLY AND MODERN HISTORY

THE SAMPLE FAMILIES OF MORGAN AND WOLFE COUNTIES
(By Steve Gibson Sample, 320 E. Main St., Edna, Texas,
April 25, 1954)

At an unguarded moment, in November, 1953, at the request of a relative, Mrs. Berta K. Cecil, of Hazel Green, Ky., representing a Woman's Club of Wolfe County, Ky., I promised to prepare for her a brief history of the Sample family of said county. She being a native Texan, the editor of the Wolfe County News, and the wife of Roy M. Cecil, himself a great-grandson of Celia L. (Sample) Cecil; (born June 9, 1842), it can all the easier be understood why I yielded to her request. Now, at the age of seventy, after having lived in Texas more than 41 years, I undertake this pleasant assignment, fully conscious of the fact that neither a fair memory nor incomplete files will prevent the inclusion of errors in this brief summary. The public and I will appreciate corrections from any having more accurate information as to any living or deceased members of these families.

The early members of these families came to Kentucky from Virginia. Their ancestors were originally Englishmen. There were relationships between all the Samples who came from Virginia into Morgan and Wolfe Counties. Most of them were direct descendants of William Sample and wife, Nancy (Wilson) Sample, who reared their family near Sword's Creek in Russell County, Va., in the late years of the 18th century and early part of the 19th century.

James Sample, born Nov. 8, 1829, died Nov. 8, 189-.

"Uncle Jimmie" as my father called this Virginian, was related to the other Virginia Samples who came into Morgan and Wolfe Counties, Ky.; but in what degree I am unadvised. Just when he came into Kentucky from Virginia is information not in my files. His first wife, by whom he reared four children, was a Miss Jones, whom he married in Virginia. His second wife was an Oakley, the widowed mother of George Robinson, and the former Mrs. J. H. Stamper (Lydia Ann), both now deceased and of Rich Elkins now deceased. He had no children by his second wife.

His children by his first wife were:

1. Sarah Susan (Sample) Rose, wife of Jefferson M. Rose, to who she was married Dec. 7, 1871. Reared by these parents, were: Serrilla E. Rose, b. 8-8-1874, who became the wife of Fred Stamper, but is now deceased; 1. James Monroe Rose, b. 8-8-1874. Living in the old (Jack) John Rose home on Stillwater Creek, which home is more than 100 years old; 1. John Morten Rose, b. 8-19-1879, now deceased; 1. Mary J. Rose, b. 9-21-1884, d. 3-3-1923, who married Henry Garrison and is survived by a daughter, Mrs. Thelma (Gar-

rison) Bach; Robert L. Rose, b. 1-26-1882, now residing at the old Rose farm on Stillwater; and Joseph Kelly Rose, b. 7-31-1887, formerly called by friends "Drummer" Rose as he was for many years a successful traveling salesman, living in his modern home near the old Rose homestead on South side of Stillwater Creek.

2. Mary (Sample) Hogg, who married David Hogg, a former county clerk of Wolfe County, Ky., and later a member of the Constitutional Convention of the State of Oklahoma. Her descendants are said to have been successful in Oklahoma.

3. Joseph Sample, who about 1871 emigrated to Arkansas, but I do not have at hand any data as to his wife or descendants. It is my information that he has been dead for many years.

4. Augustus Sample, who married Miss Ellen Day, an aunt of Messers. J. Taylor Day, Floyd Day, William Day and John C. M. Day, all now deceased. They moved to North Texas about 1871 and lived there until their deaths. They reared three sons, as I now recall the number, James, John Allen, and Lafayette. John Allen at the age of 85 is the only survivor of the three brothers. He and his wonderful wife, Ella (Tate) Sample, who died within the last year, were parents of an adopted daughter, Eva, now the wife of Thomas Keys and the mother of one child, John Thomas Keys, who recently joined up voluntarily with the Military Service. Through a mutual friend I first learned of John Sample twenty years ago. After the exchange of letters we and our wives met at Palestine, Texas, for a week end visit. At that time he and I were the same height and weighed exactly the same. Learning who his parents were and that he was born at Hazel Green, Ky., about 1860, it was easy for us to become and remain close personal friends, as well as blood relatives which we surely are. Like his Kentucky Day cousins he had already become interested in the lumber manufacturing business, in which he was successful, and in which business he continued more or less actively until about ten years ago. Since then his business has been to make a good garden and to take care of a small herd of cattle. Hunting and fishing are sports dear to his heart and as he is able he still spends much of his time in the woods or by the lake or stream. Not only I, but some twenty of my personal friends have him to thank for teaching us the way to hunt, kill and dress deer and have a good week's visit together around the camp fire on one or more of the Rose ranches about 220 miles from here. Because of the infirmities incident to his age he has not been able to go that far from home to be with us either of the last two years. He has been an outstanding descendant of the Day family as he is of the Virginia-Kentucky Sample family.

James Sample, the grandfather of John Allen Sample mentioned in paragraph last above was highly regarded by his neighbors and acquaintances, as a Christian gentleman. Those things I personally remember about him, though he died when I was a mere boy. With his grandson, Kelly Rose, above mentioned, I visited his grave, located about a mile from Stillwater Creek. In his early years he was recognized in both Morgan and Wolfe Counties as a skilled millright, and is said to have constructed and operated water mills, then very essential to the grinding of corn.

Sample The Confederate Soldier

Captain William P. Sample, b. March 30, 1830, after the Civil War, came from Virginia to Kentucky and settled with his family at Maytown, where he and his wife, Rhoda (Repass) Sample, continued to reside until his death. He was a Confederate Army Captain according to my information, who enlisted in Virginia and served there to the end of the war. Senator William Sample of Morehead, Ky., is one of his distinguished grandsons and the family name has been kept in good repute by the descendants of Captain Sample.

The Kentucky Samples abhorred war and its cruelties and so far as I know did not actively participate in the Civil War. They were probably considered as Confederate sympathizers. Sam Goodwin, step-son of my grandfather, Steve Gibson Sample, was with the Confederate Army in Virginia. My grandfather reared his family about three miles south of Ezel, in Morgan County, and his place was more or less frequently raided as I have heard my father, Charles Smith Sample, then a small boy, tell. On one occasion they took his rifle gun and bent the barrel around a tree.

They demanded his private papers and scattered them about the place. On another occasion one of the soldiers took his only family horse, and left a "jaded" cavalry horse, in its stead. Grandfather pursued on the horse left him and was able to overtake the officer in command, and upon entreaty being made the officer required the re-exchange of horses. On another occasion General George Morgan commandered what corn was in the crib for the feeding of horses, but paid for it in the type of currency his army used. My father has pointed out to me the stump of the three pronged tree where this General Morgan fed his horse on that occasion.

But according to Henry Hurst, an uncle of Hon. J. C. Hurst, of Lexington, Ky., about Feb. 25, 1864, while Henry was a member of the Union Army stationed at Mt. Sterling, Ky., their Big Sandy troops, patroling the Breathitt County and other areas near, "Brought in six guerrillas", one by the name of Samples. According to this letter written by Henry Hurst to his brother, W. L. Hurst, "Samples had served in the Rebel Army; but got out and joined the Guerrillas." The letter did not tell how Samples was disposed of. (See Hursts of Shenandoah, page 102.) I have no information as to the idenity of that particular Sample.

WOLFE COUNTY

Jackson Sample and Mrs. William Clark

Those were brother and sister and came with their families from Virginia into Kentucky during the last half of the 19th century. According to my information they were descendants of William Sample and wife, Nancy (Wilson) Sample, already referred to.

Jack Sample and family went on to Estill County, where he reared a large family. His son, William, later became prominent in local politics of his county. As I remember him in the early part of this century he was tall, wore long grey whiskers, was well dressed, and had a fine personal appearance. Prior to that time, during one of the Hazel Green Fairs, sometime in the 90's his father, Jack Sample, and a son-in-law, of the latter, Douglas Rogers, spent a night in our home on Lacy's Creek. Mr. Rogers was well and favorably known and at that time had heavy, black side burns. I have now no mental picture of the personal appearance of Jackson Sample. One of Jack's sons, Jesse, was killed by a young man named John Faulkner, with whom as a boy I worked on my father's farm. It has not been many years since I met Albert Sample, another son of Jack, at Beattyville, Ky. He has since died. Some of the third generation of that family still live in Lee and Estill counties. A son, Dave, lives at Austin, Ind.

William Clark and wife owned their home on the old State road between Hazel Green and Maytown.

Of course, I knew their sons, Rolie and William, but if there were other children in their family I have forgotten them. Both Rolie and his son, Elmer Clark, in comparatively recent years had public offices in Wolfe County. As I recall, Mary Clark, a sister, of the elder William Clark, was the wife of my great-uncle, Henry Sample, hereinafter mentioned.

William Sample and wife, Nancy (Wilson) Sample

I have no certain information as to the native home of either William Sample or his wife, Nancy (Wilson) Sample, daughter of Harris Wilson. Harris Wilson died in Russell County, Virginia in 1808, and the following October 2, his children, Richard Wilson, John Wilson, Rhoda Lawson, Harris Wilson, Elizabeth Wilson and Charlotte Barnette, conveyed their interests in 194 acres of land on the north side of the North Fork of the Clinch River in Russell County, Va., to the said William Sample. Strangely enough all these grantors signed by mark. (deed book No. 4, P. 381, Russell County.) William Sample on March 28, 1850, signed his will by mark. As the will was probated only five days later it is not improbable that his signing mark was made necessary by his last illness and the infirmaties of his age. Feb. 22, 1859, Nancy (Wilson) Sample also signed her will by mark. The will was probated June

9, 1859. By the terms of his will, William Sample gave to his daughters, Delila Hunt and Polly Sample, only "one negro apiece," assigning his reason that they had disobliged him so much. The mother, Nancy, took note that William had not taken care of Polly by his will and left all of the mother's property to Polly.

The earliest record I have found of William Sample in Russell County, Va., is a deed to him from Patrick Kendricks and wife, dated Sept. 24, 1804, of record in Vol. 3, page 521 of Deed Records. It conveyed to him 50 acres of land on Sugar Run, a branch of Clinch River (those who have traveled or lived in Virginia will know that "run" as used in this deed means creek or branch).

My father had the impression that William came to Russell County from Rotetourt County, Va. It has not been my privilege to check the records of that county. One William Sample, during the early days of Virginia statehood, was charged in court with counterfeitting. That was not in Russell County and may not have been our ancestor mentioned. Anyway, he was acquitted upon being tried. At the time of his death in 1850 William left 22 slaves, appraised at $6,100, and which sold for $5,427.39. Other unusual items of property were "One still and worm and three still tubs" which were bought by Jackson Sample at the sale for $16.80.

To offset any prejudice created by the above narrative of facts against the name "William Sample" I will recount that in the latter part of the 19th century another William Sample was one of the great preachers of Virginia. A former collector of Internal Revenue and Federal District Attorney, also an author of note, a Mr. Summers residing at Abingdon, Va., in 1937, told me of this great preacher. Within the last year in the public library in Houston, Texas, I read convincing accounts of his success as a preacher.

The children of William Sample and Nancy (Wilson) Sample were the following:

Patsy, born July 26, 1791.

Charles, born Nov. 19, 1793. (He went to Clay County, Missouri, and reared a family there.) He had one son, named William and one named John L., who while on a business trip through Mt. Sterling, Ky., suffocated from gas fumes in one of the Mt. Sterling hotels.

Sally, born July 8, 1797, married Enoch Pratt.

James, born Dec. 31, 1801, died in 1853.

Anna, born May 18, 1804, married Absolem Hurt.

Delila, born Sept. 24, 1806, married a Hunt.

Polly, born Dec. 4, 1808.

Lewis, born June 2, 1814.

Although an old record in my possession shows Patsy to have been the oldest of the children of William and Nancy Sample, and makes no mention of Martha, yet in the William Sample Will,

WOLFE COUNTY

Patsy is not mentioned and Martha Spratt is referred to as one of William's children.

James Sample, born Dec. 31, 1801, married Celia Fuller, born March 4, 1801, on June 16, 1825; She died on March 26, 1837. After Celia's death, he married Elizabeth Herndon.

Children of James Sample and wife, Celia (Fuller) Sample were:
Stephen Gibson Sample, born April 6, 1826.
Lucinda Catherine Sample, born Feb. 4, 1828. 1828.
William Patton Sample, born March 20, 1830.
James Frank Sample, born May 22, 1832.
Henry L. Sample, born Dec. 30, 1836.

Children of James Sample and second wife, Elizabeth Herndon Sample were:
Larken J., born June 30, 1840.
Celia L., born June 9, 1842.
Sofia Elizabeth, born March 16, 1844.
Elbert Sevior, Sarah Ellen, and Nannie J.

The above mentioned James Sample died shortly prior to becoming 52 years of age. Apparently all his life was lived in Russell County, Va., where he was a Lieutenant of Militia (1829).

Constable four or more terms, 1834-43, and a Commissioner of the Revenue in the Eastern District of said county for one term, 1848. His father, William Samples, named him Executor of the William Sample Will, but James, refusing to take upon himself the burden of the execution thereof, John F. McElhorny and William B. Acton were named administrators, James Sample being one of the sureties on their bond of $15,000. When James Sample died in 1853 his son, Steven G. Sample and son-in-law, James M. Cecil, became administrators of his estate. Among articles of personalty set apart to his surviving widow, Elizabeth Herndon Sample, were the following: seven beds, and clothes, 1 side saddle, 2 small wheels, 1 large wheel, one reel, 2 reap hooks, one hackel, 1 loom and appurtanances and grind stone, 2 hogs-heads, and 10 bushel wheat, ½ of sieve, cutting box and lot of oats, one yoke cattle. Steven G. Sample was charged with one bell, .37½. I am quite sure this is the bell used by said Steven G. Sample as a boy sheep herder, and worn by his dog. This bell was passed down to Charles Smith Sample, my father, and is now the prized possession of one of his descendants. Five bee hives were set apart to the widow and ten sold at prices ranging from $2 to $4. After paying all debts of the estate the Administration had left in their hands for distribution, from the sales of personalty, a net of $1,912.37. The lands were subsequently divided and conveyed.

A valued letter in my possession, written by Rachel Thompson Sample, widow of the Lafayette W. Sample, deceased, on August 12, 1937, gives the impression that when James Sample wooed

Elizabeth Herndon, for his second wife, he was in no romantic mood. Aunt Rachel says, "Yes, your great-grandfather's last wife was a Herndon. I can remember her. She wore a white frilled cap. I heard my mother say that she was bald headed, and before they were married he asked her how she thought old baldy would suit him. She said she told him she was a good woman. Her name was Betsy Herndon."

If still living, Cousin Rachel is 93 years of age. It was my privilege and that of my wife, my brother, D. S. Sample, of Kingsport, Tenn., and my sister, Sarah Sample Quicksall and her husband, to meet her at the home of her daughter, near Honnaker, Va., and visit with Aunt Rachel for a few minutes, in the summer of 1951. At that time one of her sons was sheriff of Russell County.

Shephen Gibson Sample, born April 6, 1826, married Louisa (Cecil) Goodwin, widow of David Goodwin, about 1850. Louisa was born Nov. 9, 1821, near Tazwell, Va.; and died in Morgan County, Ky., near Ezel, March 28, 1906. Steve (Uncle Steve, as his friends called him), died in the home of his daughter, Rebecca Sample Henry, wife of John D. Henry, about two miles south of Ezel. They were both buried on the farm of Miles Back, that being the place where they were first settled and bought a home when they came to Kentucky with their family from Sword's Creek, Va., in 1858. At the time they emigrated to Kentucky there came with them, James M. Cecil, brother of Louisa (Cecil) Sample, and Lucinda Catherine Cecil, sister of Steve Sample, and wife of James M. Cecil, and the Cecil children, born before that time. The Cecils bought a farm about a mile to the East of the Sample farm, another fork of Blackwater Creek, and there reared a large family and remained on that farm until their deaths. Their daughter, Angeline, and husband, James Cecil, lived on the same farm for some years after the death of the older Cecils.

Louisa, wife of Steve Sample, last above referred to, was a daughter of Samuel Cecil (River Sammy) and was reared in Tazewell County, Virginia, the county immediately East of Russell County. The old Cecil home was still occupied when I was in Tazewell County in 1935 and was said by William Cecil Pendleton, a noted historian of that area, to be the oldest occupied residence in Tazewell County. It was erected by James Cecil, father of the said Samuel Cecil. Louisa, as a young woman, and as an apprentice, learned to be a fine seamstress and tailor. Until her death she retained the very heavy pressing iron which she used in tailoring clothes while a young woman. She first married David Goodwin and as his wife became the mother of Samuel Goodwin, later a Confederate soldier, and who married a Miss Eliza Pieratt of Ezel, Ky., and became the father of Ollie Goodwin, later the wife of James Frank Sample, Asa Frank Goodwin, later a medical doctor, now deceased, and John Goodwin, a retired dentist now living in Mt. Sterling, Ky., where he successfully practiced his profession and reared his family. After the death of David Goodwin, Louisa married Steve Gibson Sample and to them were born the following named children, to-wit:

James Madison, born 1851, died 1868.

Charles Smith, born Feb. 12, 1854, died Feb. 26, 1943.

Rebecca, born June 8, 1856, died Oct. 1926; married John D. Henry, born Dec. 28, 1858, died Feb. 17, 1916, December 8, 1874.

Celia, died at age of twelve years.

Alice, born 1861, married James Archie Lacey, died 1885 without leaving living issue.

Kate, born about 1863, second wife of John Smith Nickell and mother of one child, Clifford Nickell, now living at or near Middletown, Ohio. She died at age of 22 years.

Frank, who died as a small boy.

After rearing their family at the old home on Greasy Creek in Morgan County, Ky., and after the marriage of their children, Steve and wife retired while still comparatively young, sold their farm and moved to Ezel, Ky., where they lived for a few years, and then sold their home there and during the remainder of their lives lived with their daughter, Rebecca Henry and husband, on the East side of Greasy Creek, within sight of their former farm home. After retiring, Steve Sample, with the sufficient capital they had acquired and saved, became a money lender and people in the general area of where they lived would come to him to borrow money and sell their vendor's lien notes. He was a comparatively good business man and so far as I ever knew did not lose any of his capital by making poor loans. He was exacting to the extent of expecting his obligors to make good on their promises, and valued very highly his income in the form of "intrust", as he termed it. I never knew of his fore-closing a lien or suing a debtor. It was my professional responsibility to probate his Will and assist in the settlement of his estate after his death, my father, Charles Smith Sample, and Uncle John D. Henry being the executors of his Will. The Will was probated at West Liberty, Ky., and, as I recall, the estate went equally to my father, the daughter, Rebecca Henry, and the grandson, Clifford Nickell. Both Steve and Louisa, his wife, became members of the Christian Church, probably under the preaching of Rev. Combs, the grandfather of Mrs. Beulah Thomas Bishop of Ashland, Ky., and Mrs. Roxie Daniel Long of Elizabethton, Tenn. Rev. Combs was their pastor for many years and had an enviable reputation as a minister in that area. Steve and Louisa lived up to their religious professions. I never knew either of my grandfathers (the other being John David Rose, living on Lacey's Creek in Wolfe County, Ky.) to use tobacco in any form, take a drink of intoxicating liquor, use profanity or tell a smutty joke. While the Samples lived in Ezel, Ky., about 14 miles from the home of my parents in Wolfe County, Ky., we spent at least one night in their home and I slept in the trundle bed, pulled out from under the larger bed. I recall scratching paper off the wall by the side of the bed, naughty grandson that I was. The Samples would drive their fat gray horse, Jeff, in the buggy and visit in our home for a few days at a time, usually once or twice a year, and on one of these occasions my grandfather gave me $5.00, half of which my father invested for me in a pair of boots and with the other half bought me two male calves and helped me to break them to the yoke and sled. Proceeds from that investment, and later accruals therefrom, were later used to supplement funds advanced by my parents to complete my high school education at Kentucky Wesleyan Academy, Campton, Ky. in 1900, and at Hazel Green Academy, Hazel Green, Ky., in 1900-1902. Grandmother Sample was an invalid, confined to her bed, during the last ten years of her life and the faithfulness of her husband in sitting by and attending her every want was indeed exemplary. He was about six feet, two inches tall and during most of the time I knew him must have weighed close to 250 pounds. Though in apparently good health at the time of the death of his wife, he did not survive more than two years after her death, making only one visit in the home of my father after her death.

Charles Smith Samples, born Feb. 12, 1854, at Sword's Creek, Virginia, died Feb. 26, 1943 at Lexington, Ky., married Rachel Ann Rose, born Feb. 3, 1860, died March 11, 1932, daughter of John D. Rose and Nancy Nickell Rose, Dec. 30, 1880.

For a short time after their marriage Charles and Rachel lived in the home of his parents on Greasy Creek in Morgan County, Ky. On Dec. 13, 1881, Harrison Swango and Nancy J. (Cecil) Swango conveyed to the said Charles Smith Sample a tract of land of 261.75 acres located on the head of the Johnson Fork of Lacey's Creek in Wolfe County, Kentucky, for a consideration of $1,100.00, of which $100.00 was at the time paid and the remainder evidenced by two notes for $500.00 each. My brother, Denzil Smith Sample, of Kingsport, Tenn., has the original of this deed and this farm is still owned by the children of the said Charles Sample and wife, although none of the family has resided thereon since Charles and wife moved to Lexington, Ky., about 1917. At one time there were, as I recall, 14 small oil wells on this tract of land and the accumulated royalties therefrom enabled Charles and wife to purchase a modern home with four acres of land in the suburbs of Lexington, Ky., where they resided from 1917 until their respective deaths. They were buried in the new Lexington

Cemetery located a few miles outside the city on the North side of the Lexington-Louisville highway.

There was an old log residence on the Lacey's Creek farm when the Samples bought it and they resided in that building until they could erect a more modern frame residence, one-and-one-half stories high, two rooms and hall and kitchen and dining room on the first floor and two bedrooms upstairs. This home, with some additions thereto, a stone chimney at each end of the main building and one for the kitchen, remained on the farm and was the residence of the family until the removal to Lexington. A few years later, while occupied by tenants, the old residence caught fire from the kitchen chimney and burned. Only a part of the stone chimneys now remain to mark the former happy home of this Sample family.

Five children were born to the Sample-Rose union, to-wit:

Bertha Florence, born March 10, 1882, now the widow of Sam Henry Kash, residing at 4628 Southern Parkway, Louisville, Ky., the mother of Lucile Kash Burton, wife of Charles Burton and grandmother of Jack Kash Burton and Sammy Burton, and mother of Maurine Kash Edmonds, wife of Charles Edmonds of Washington, D. C.

Steve Gibson Sample, born April 14, 1884, the author of this article, who married Edna Hurst, a daughter of Zachary Taylor Hurst, and Louisa Duff Hurst, on March 4, 1908, Steve and Edna being the parents of Charles Hurst Sample, born at Campton, Ky., Dec. 16, 1908 and Rachel Louise Sample Germer, born at Edna, Texas, Oct. 20, 1913 and of Steve Gibson Sample III, born at Edna, Texas, Sept. 15, 1917, died Jan. 8, 1921 of diptheria.

Nancy Louisa Heinrich, born Jan. 10, 1887, married Joe Frederick Heinrich of Mt. Sterling, Ky., June 12, 1913, resides with her husband in Mt. Sterling, Ky., and is the mother of Lt. Col. Charles Thomas Heinrich of the U. S. Army, born Jan. 5, 1915 and Joe Frederick Heinrich Jr., born Nov. 18, 1917. Both the Heinrich sons are married, Charles Thomas being the father of two sons and Joe Frederick Jr., being the father of one daughter.

Sarah Alice Quicksall, born Oct. 14, 1891, married Willie Wallace Quicksall, March 3, 1928, and residing with her husband at 111 W. Howry, Deland, Florida.

Denzil Smith Sample, born Nov. 28, 1901, married Lee Ottis Drury, Oct. 7, 1926, residing at Kingsport, Tenn., where he owns and operates at 201 Cherokee St., a large wholesale bakery and where he is at present President of the Kingsport Chamber of Commerce. Shirley Ann Sample Gunn, born Nov. 14, 1929, wife of Rev. James Gunn, Presbyterian pastor at Lebanon, Ky., is the only child of this union.

Our parents (Charles and Rachel) were typical farm people of their generation. Our father cleared the forests and tilled the soil, employing necessary labor for which he paid 50 cents per day, not usually cash but shelled corn at 50 cents per bushel or five pounds of bacon at 10 cents per pound. One of his most valued tenants was Ira Day, father of David Day, living at the old John D. Rose home on Lacey's Creek in 1953. Some of the hillsides were cleared by contract at a cost of $8.00 per acre. My father and neighbors would rotate with their "log-rollings," great neighborhood gatherings, the wife frequently having a "quilting" party on the same day, and "chicken and dumplings" always being in evidence as the noonday (dinner) meal. Like most farm homes the ox horn was used to call the workmen from labor to refreshments for dinner. A few homes on the creek, including the Wiley Perkins home and the Joseph P. Rose home, had large bells mounted for those purposes. William Lusk with his sawmill spent three years sawing the large poplar trees on the farm and he and his hands boarded in our home and paid 8 1/3 cents per meal for board and lodging. Our mother did the housework. She also assisted in the milking of the cows, the raising of the garden, the killing of the hogs and rendering the lard, making lye soap from ash lye and refuse meats, and usually did the washing and ironing. Our parents bought additional land on the Little Fork of Lacey's Creek and had coal mined therefrom, which my father delivered in his mule-drawn wagon to Hazel Green Academy dormitory and other customers for 8 1/3 cents per bushel, hauling 25 bushels of coal per load and making, by working from sunup to sundown, three loads a day. On the Charles Little farm which he purchased was an old apple orchard and over the protests of our mother he one year sold to some legally operating distillery apples from that orchard at 10 cents per bushel. Small strawberries and blackberries, sarvice berries, chestnuts, walnuts, hickory nuts, grapes, huckleberries and raspberries grew wild and our parents planted and maintained peach orchards and set out apple trees and had a very good apple orchard. They always kept a small flock of sheep, which they sheared in the early spring and from which our mother spun yarn, knitted socks and mittens therefrom and wove the remainder into blankets, carpets and jeans from which she made suits for her husband and the older son. The last home woven suit my father wore was brown in color, the yarn having been colored from boiled tanbark off the chestnut oak tree. My last suit woven by my mother was an indigo blue but she must have purchased a dye for the coloring from the J. Taylor Day store at Hazel Green, three miles away. My mother and her daughters in the earlier years also wore the necessary linsey dresses and underskirts, also woolen home knit stockings in the winter. At the time of the removal to Lexington, Ky., the three older children of the family were married and after going there Denzil completed his high school education and obtained his degree from the University of Kentucky in 1925. Our then elderly parents enjoyed their residence in Lexington as many of their former friends and relatives were living in Lexington or visited them from time to time. They with their five children were happy to celebrate the 50th wedding anniversary of the parents on Dec. 30, 1930. Porter Lacey, a first cousin of our mother, and Floyd Day, then living at Winchester, Ky., as I recall, were the only two guests present on the occasion of this anniversary who had witnessed the wedding ceremony 50 years earlier.

Our parents joined the Methodist Church during a revival meeting held at the old Rose log school house on main Lacey's Creek when I was a very small boy. Rev. Gardner, a Methodist minister, and Dr. W. L. Gevedon (a medical doctor residing in Morgan County), jointly conducted this revival service. Sister Bertha and I during the "shouting" at this meeting climbed on top of the benches, thinking someone was dead, as we had witnessed a short time before the shouting at the funeral of a neighbor girl.

Horseback riding, the woman on a side-saddle, was the customary way of traveling in Wolfe County during the 80's and 90's. Our father would ride a roan mare, Maude, with me behind him and my mother would ride a gentler horse, George, with Bertha on behind her and later Nancy in her lap, and together we would make most of the country Sunday meetings. After the family increased in numbers, we usually went in the farm wagon, with Barney and Henry, two old mules, pulling the wagon. When my father and I went muleback in those days he rode Henry, the more excitable of the two mules, and I rode Barney, the lazier of the two.

My father never sought or obtained elective office other than school trustee; but he was pretty continuously a school trustee in the Johnson District. Our parents were ambitious that their children get the best obtainable education and the five of us as the years went by were in regular attendance at this school. Some of the teachers in their order were James Swango, Charles Swango, Frank Creech, Mallie James, Ida Swango, Lula Kash, E. O. Taulbee and William L. Kash. In 1899 sister Bertha was sent to Kentucky Wesleyan Academy at Campton where she and Lillie Henry, Stella Rose and Ora Cecil roomed together and prepared their own meals. The following fall at the age of 15 years, my parents gave me the choice of a sizeable wooded tract of land out of the home farm on which I might begin work as my own, or of continuing my education, and I chose the latter and in the winter of 1900, Bertha and I again attended Kentucky Wesleyan Academy at Campton. That winter we joined the Methodist Church under the preaching of Rev. David May and Dr. J. J. Dickey, both of whom lived beyond the age of 90 years. After that we were sent to Hazel Green Academy, from which I received my diploma in the Class of 1902, under Professor William H. Cord. Bertha and I both taught in the public schools and in 1904 I studied law at Centre College and obtained my L.L.B. degree in the Law Department of Bowling Green Normal School, under Dr. H. H. Cherry, in June, 1905. Nancy, after the marriage of Bertha to Sam H. Kash, represented my father in the mercantile partnership of Kash and Sample at Hazel Green and in which store Sam Kash kept the post office until his removal to Jackson, Ky., sometime after I, with my wife and son, came to Edna, Texas, Nov. 27, 1912. Sister Sarah and brother Denzil in turn were students at Hazel Green Academy, Denzil, 17 years younger than I, being the help of our father and Sarah the help of our mother on the farm until the removal to Lexington about 1917. No parents ever had a more dutiful or helpful daughter than sister Sarah, who continued with them until her marriage in 1928, and thereafter, with her husband, and in later years jointly with sister Bertha and Sam Kash, until the death of our father in 1943.

Briefly, with the hope of charity from the readers of this article, I will review the course of my immediate family beginning with my admission to the Bar in 1905, law practice at Campton, Ky., from that date until 1912 during the last three years of which I was County Attorney of Wolfe County, covering the important event in my life of March 4, 1908 when Edna Hurst, then living with her parents in Breathitt County, became my wife. Before coming to Edna, Texas, in 1912, I bought and paid for a small residence $1,000.00 cash, and that, with additions thereto made over the years, is still our happy home. E. T. Rose and I had been law partners at Campton, Ky., for a time and again we became law and business partners at Edna, Texas, in 1912 and remained such until Jan. 1, 1945 when by agreement we partitioned most of our properties and dissolved the law partnership. He has continued active as a successful business man to the present time and I have continued, dividing my time between law and business and hope next year after fifty years of law practice to retire from that profession.

Charles Hurst Sample, our only living son, born December 16, 1908, was educated in the public schools of Edna, Texas, obtained his B. S. degree from the University of Texas and his Master's degree from Columbia University, majoring in Geology and from 1932 to the present time has been active and successful as a geologist at Houston, Texas. He was married Feb. 11, 1934 to a former high school classmate, Frances Billups, and they are the parents of Charles Hurst Sample, Jr., now a freshman in Texas Tech at

Lubbock, Texas, Edna Frances, a high school student in Lamar High, Houston, Texas, and John Steven, a junior high student in Pershing Junior High, Houston.

Rochel Louise Sample Germer, born Oct. 20, 1913, likewise was educated in the Edna public schools, taking piano lessons under Mrs. Mary Bronaugh, who now instructs Louise's three children in piano music, then obtained her B. S. degree, majoring in education, at the University of Texas in 1934. During the first year of her teaching at LaWard, Texas, she met Walter Frederick Germer, a teacher and football coach in the same school and they were married April 7, 1935. He continued his coaching, going to Port Lavaca and then to Refugio, Texas, where he successfully coached his teams in football and other school athletics, but about five years ago he decided to give up his chosen profession of teaching and coaching and go into the ranching and farming business and since then they have lived on and operated a ranch located about a mile North of Edna, Texas. Their three children are Marjorie Louise, now in Edna High School, Walter Frederick Germer, Jr., this year in the 8th grade and Edna Diana, in one of the lower grades. All three children, like their mother, who whistles as well as plays, are talented musicians as are also the grandchildren residing in Houston. Freddie and Charles Sample Jr., are outstanding athletes. The father of Charles, Jr., was a long distance runner on the University of Texas track team when he was in school there.

THE SWANGO FAMILY
(By Mrs. W. E. Bach)

William Swango, the emigrant, coming from Germany and landing in Philadelphia, was the father of Abraham Swango who married Ailsie Pyles in Wilmington, Deleware. William's wife, died and was buried at sea. There were other children besides this Abraham.

Abraham and Ailsie (Pyles) Swango came to Frederick County, Virginia, where he was a Lessee of George Washington. Their son, Samuel Swango, married Elizabeth Johnston (some thought she was Betsy Banyion or O'Banion) and they came to Mt. Sterling, Ky., where he left a Deed of Gift naming his children: Abraham, Sophia, Mariah and Milly Sommerville.

Mariah Swango married Thomas Wills (my great-grandfather).

Sophia Swango married Johnnie Wills and had the following children:

Jack Wills, Mart Wills, William Wills and Mariah Wills.

Mariah Swango married Thomas Wills and had the following children: Elizabeth, Samuel, Shelton, Deborah, Abraham, Jordan

EARLY AND MODERN HISTORY

(my grandfather), Armina, James Lemuel Wills.

The two Swango sisters, who married the two Wills brothers have many descendants.

(For further information — Mrs. William Everett Bach, Lexington, Ky.)

William Swango came from Germany before 1750. His wife died at sea and was buried at sea. They had three sons:

1. Abraham, who married Ailsie Pyles (Alice), 1760, in Wilmington, Deleware. They came to Berkley, W. Va., then to Kentucky.

1. Second son, Isaac, went to Pennsylvania.

1. Abraham Swango and Ailsie Pyles had four sons and three daughters: First son, James, no record. Second son, Samuel, had two sons and three daughters, (Samuel was born in 1767, married Elizabeth Johnston(O'Banion), born 1769, Va. Children of Samuel and Elizabeth were: Abraham, Mariah, Sophia, Richard and Milly. Mariah married Thomas Willis and Sophia married Johnny Wills.

2. Abraham, son of Samuel and Elizabeth Swango, was born in 1792, married Deborah Auglin (Ogden), born in 1798. They had six sons and seven daughters:

3. George Washington, born 1811, married Lucinda Hollon.

3. Harrison, born 1812, died 1908. Married Anna Rose, born 1816, died 1864. Second marriage, Nancy Cecil Steel, born 1829, died 1915.

3. Lydia, born May 2, 1817, died 1893. Married William Montgomery.

3. Stephen, born 1820, married Caroline Trimble.

3. Elizabeth (Betsy), born 1822, died 1893, married Tilman Johnson (see Tilman Johnson family.)

3. Mariah, born 1824, died 1959, called "Sugar". Married Shelton Trimble.

3. Samuel, born 1826, married Evaline Kash.

3. Mary (May or Pop), born Aug. 1, 1827, died June 5, 1897. Married Jefferson Heldridge Johnson, born May 9, 1816, died June 30, 1859. Mary remarried Henry Combs of Breathitt County.

3. Nancy was born 1829. She married Adam Harmon in 1851.

3. Jesse was born in 1831. He married Nancy Jane Hanks.

3. Ella Jane was born 1833 (Evaline). She married Jesse O'Hair, went to Coles County, Ill.

3. Emily Jane, born 1835, died 1837.

3. Chapman, born 1837, died 1863. He was never married. He was a teacher and served in the Civil War.

2. Samuel Swango and Evaline Kash Swango, daughter of William Kash, settled on Stillwater on his father's farm. He and his wife had five sons and two daughters:

3. Jessie M. (Bud), the oldest son of Samuel and Evaline Swango, married Emma Trimble, daughter of Shelton Trimble. Bud

died of a heart attack at the old home place. Jessie and Emma had two sons, and four daughters, Bufford, Robert, Ollie, Mary, Lillie and Emma.

4. Ollie Swango, first daughter of Jessie and Emma, married Will Kash, son of Alfred Kash. They had two children, then she died. A son and daughter. He then married a second time and had twin boys. He died.

5. Irene Kash married a Slusher. Lives at Jackson, Ky.

5. Charles married after he was graduated from the University of Kentucky and died.

4. Mary Swango, second daughter of Jessie and Emma Swango, married C. P. Hurst Jr. Had two sons, both are dead.

4. Lillie Swango, third daughter of Jessie and Emma Swango, married Granville Rose. They had no children. He died then she married a Burton.

4. Emma, fourth daughter of Jessie and Emma Swango married Caesar McCoun. They had three children.

3. William, son of Samuel Swango, died when a young school teacher. He died of pneumonia at the home of Mrs. Elizabeth Rose.

3. Lou Ellen, daughter of Samuel Swango, married Fletcher McGuire of Beattyville. They settled in Hazel Green where he was a successful merchant and land owner. Lou Ellen and Fletcher McGuire had two children, Courtney and Cora.

4. Courtney married Elisa Lee Lindsey of Maysville. He was a successful doctor and practiced for 35 years mostly in Maysville where he married. He died in 1949 of a heart attack. They had no children.

4. Cora McGuire married Charles Andre from Virginia. They live in Morristown, Tenn. Had several children, one son, Florian, became vice-president of the Kraft Food Co., and lives in Scarsdale, New York.

3. Sarah Elizabeth Swango, youngest daughter of Samuel Swango, married John M. Rose, a merchant, and lived in Hazel Green, Ky. Later moved to Clark County where she died in 1913. She is buried at Hazel Green and so is he. They had three children.

4. Curtis Bowen Rose, who married Margaret Sewell, daughter of G. W. Sewell of Jackson, Ky. He was a successful coal mine operator for many years prior to his death. They had three children: Elizabeth, Laura Jo, and Ben. (See Rose family.)

4. Charles M. Rose, stock dealer and business man in Lexington for many years. Married Rose Jewell. They had two daughters, Maurine and Mildred.

5. Maurine married Dr. W. C. Robinson, surgeon, son of Dr. B. F. Robinson of Lexington.

5. Mildred married Morey Rappert from Indiana and he is a prominent merchant in Lexington. They have one child.

4. Carrie Lee married Carl Mize, only son of the late senator

W. O. Mize and Lou E. Mize of Hazel Green. They had one son, William Oldham (Bill).

5. W. O. Mize married Evelyn Swope of Winchester and they have established a nice business in Jacksonville Beach, Florida. Their only child died in infancy. For further information see (Rose Family).

3. Chapman married Dora Lacy. He was jailor at West Liberty several years. They later moved to Dayton, Ohio. They had seven children: Stanley, James, Luther, Dewey (deceased), Archie, Evelyn and Stella.

4. Stanley is a successful businessman.

4. James (Jim) is an electrician.

4. Dewey Main (deceased) was named for the Ship "Main" and Admiral Dewey as she was born the day it was sunk. She married a Sebastian and died young.

4. Elizabeth Archie married and lives in Dayton, Ohio.

4. Evelyn married Dr. Corbett Coldiron. They live in Dayton, Ohio where he is successful as a doctor and surgeon. They have several children. He is the son of the late Crockett and Ella Coldiron of Hazel Green.

4. Stella Katherine married an artist and lives in New York.

4. Luther married and lives in Dayton.

3. Levi Kash Swango, fourth son of Samuel, became a doctor and settled in Morefield and later in Nicholas County, Ky., where he practiced until his death. He married Jimmie Branch. They had no children.

3. Ova H. Swango, fifth son of Samuel Swango, married Dora Crain. He was a successful doctor. They settled at Jackson, Ky. They were married Jan. 26, 1899. They had one daughter, Evelyn, who died unmarried at the age of 24. Dr. O. H. Swango died on August 14, 1937.

2. Harrison Swango, second son of Abraham, was born in Wolfe County. He married Anna Rose. Settled on Red River near Hazel Green. He lived to be past 90. They reared a large family of six sons and one daughter.

3. David Swango was a Captain in the command of raider John Morgan, during the Civil War. He was killed in action at Mt. Sterling, Ky. He was Captain of the same company that his Uncle Chapman Swango had commanded when he was killed earlier in the war.

3. William, second son of Harrison, was a Lieutenant in Morgan's Command and was killed in action in the State of Virginia. He was surprised and shot down but raised to his knees, emptied his revolver into the enemy and expired.

3. Calvin, third son of Harrison, served through the Civil War and married a Trimble girl and settled just below Hazel Green. Had a family of three girls and one son, Ida, Ava, Ora, and Herb.

WOLFE COUNTY

Herb was taken sick and died soon afterwards in Campton, Ky., before he could be taken home.

3. Newton, fourth son of Harrison, went to Coles County, Ill., when a young man. He married a Miss Craig and built a house just north of Charleston. He reared a family of three sons and three daughters: Fred, Tom, Don, Mrs. Zollie O'Hair, Mrs. Claud Newman and Mrs. Sam Talbot.

3. Arbury, fifth son of Harrison, went to Illinois with Newton and spent several years. Returned to Kentucky and married Fanny Kash, daughter of Dr. Miles Kash; settled near Hazel Green on Red River. They reared three sons and four girls: Curtis, Cletus, Oliver, Etta, who married Clay Little, Carrie, who married Henry Cecil, and there were two younger girls.

3. Harmon Swango, sixth son of Harrison, married Maggie Cecil, and lived on her father's farm near Hazel Green. He had three sons: Rush, Perry and Ernie, and one daughter, Mollie, who never married. She is now deceased.

4. Perry married Flossie Lacy, granddaughter of Betsy Swango, sister of Harrison. They live in Lexington.

4. Ernie married Nora Lovelace from Perry County. No children. Married second time and has two children.

3. Lizzie, a daughter of Harrison Swango, married S. S. Combs and had two girls and two boys.

4. Anna Bell never married. She now lives in Richmond, Ky.

4. Courtney went to Texas.

4. Harrison married a Tutt and is now deceased.

2. Stephen Swango, third son of Abraham Swango, was born in Wolfe County and married Caroline Trimble, sister to Green Trimble and settled near Hazel Green. (See Trimbles.) He was killed when thrown from a horse while driving cattle. He had two sons and five or six girls: Greenberry, William, Eveline, Rose Ellen, Lizzie, Clara and Alice.

3. Greenberry served in the Rebel Army under General John Morgan and had part of his ear shot off by a musket ball. He served as a page in the senate; was county judge of Wolfe County several terms; served as registrar of the Kentucky Land office at Frankfort one term; was a member of the Constitutional Convention of Kentucky (sometime during the 80's). He married Miss Eliza Young of Virginia and reared three sons: James, Charley and Morton.

4. James is a lawyer and business man in Terre Haute, Ind.

4. Charley died in Butte, Montana.

4. Morton died soon after he was married.

3. William T. Swango, youngest son of Stephen Swango, married Ellen Quicksall of Ezel, Ky. They lived several years at Hazel Green, then moved to Winchester where he engaged in farming and livestock dealing. They had one daughter, Dora.

EARLY AND MODERN HISTORY

4. Dora married Rev. George D. Prentiss, a Methodist minister. Lived in Florida in 1956.

3. Evaline, daughter of Stephen Swango, married John O'Hair of Paris, Ill., and moved away

3. Rose Ellen, daughter of Stephen, married Morton Pieratt and reared two sons, Stephen and Berry, and a daughter, Lizzie.

4. Stephen married Vic Kendell of Mt. Sterling and they have two daughters. He is president of the Bank of Mt. Sterling.

4. Berry married in Chicago and moved to Miami, Fla., where he now lives.

4. Lizzie, a daughter, who married Charley Duff of Mt. Sterling. They had one daughter.

3. Lizzie, daughter of Stephen Swango, married Renny Pieratt (brother of Morton), and reared one son, Bufford, who married Effie Maxey and had one daughter, Clara. Lizzie died young. Clara won the premium at the World's Fair in Chicago, Ill., for being the most beautiful woman there at that time.

3. Clara Swango married Asa Pieratt (brother of Morton and Renny), and they had two sons: Renny and another.

3. Alice Swango, daughter of Stephen Swango, married Tom Frazier, settled in Bushton, Ill. They had two children: Grace and William T.

4. Grace died as a young woman.

4. William T. married and had three children: James, John and Virginia.

3. Zerilda, daughter of Stephen Swango, married a Harmon and lived in Missouri. One daughter, Grace.

2. Jesse Swango, fifth son of Abraham Swango, married Nancy Jane Hanks and settled near Paris in Edgar County, Ill. They had a daughter, Lillie, and two sons, Harlem and Clarence.

2. Chapman Swango, sixth son of Abraham Swango, never married. He followed teaching profession. He founded a school on Stillwater known as the Ceminary. He fought under Captain John Morgan and was killed during the Civil War.

2. George Washington Swango, first son of Abraham Swango, was born on June 7, 1811 and married Lucinda Hollon (who was born on Oct. 30, 1813) in Wolfe County. They had a family of ten sons and three daughters:

3. Fanny, born Jan. 3, 1835, married James Rose.
3. Jane, born Nov. 29, 1847, married William Lawson.
3. Caroline, born Sept. 14, 1849, married Henry Shockey.
3. Abraham, born March 23, 1831, died in infancy.
3. Andrew, born Nov. 13, 1833, married Rhoda Ingram and had three sons and two daughters.

4. Stephen, son of Andrew, a doctor, married Belle Shackelford and had one girl, Ivy. He later married Mrs. Lizzie Ingram.

WOLFE COUNTY

4. Shilo, son of Andrew Swango, married Nora Halsey, who died leaving two sons and a daughter. He then married Ida Murphy and they had two sons and two daughters. He later married a Miss Stamper, who died soon and Shilo was killed in the State of Ohio when a train hit his car.

4. Mary, daughter of Andrew, married Henry Helton, a county school teacher and Baptist preacher and they reared a large family.

4. Francis, daughter of Andrew Swango, married Jefferson Chambers of Wolfe County and they went to Oklahoma and died leaving two sons and a daughter.

3. Stephen, third son of George Washington Swango, married Sarah Jane Shackelford on Jan. 6, 1859. They had five sons and six daughters. Sons: James C., William Washington, Andrew Chapman, Jessie and John B. Daughters: Julia Caroline, Lou E., Nancy Evaline, Mary Florence, Margaret Olive and Pearlie.

4. James C., son of Stephen and Sarah Jane Swango, married Rebecca Patrick, Oct. 14, 1883. They had Luther, who married Edith Points and settled in Oregon; Alma Lucille, who married Moses Henry Blankenship. They both died in Virginia, leaving no descendants.

Kate Cornelius, who married Earl B. Arnsparger on August 10, 1926, and they were divorced in 1935. She was a teacher in the Cincinnati, Ohio school system. She died Sept. 1946 leaving around $1500 to Hazel Green Academy to redecorate the chapel which was done.

4. William Washington Swango, son of Stephen and Sarah Jane Swango, married Telitha Halsey the first time. They had six children.

5. Claude living in the State of Oregon.

5. Bruce, who served in World War I as First Lieut. Afterwards returned to States and went into lumber business in California, was injured with a log and died on operating table. He left a wife, Jan Lynette Haynes and a child.

5. Clay Swango, son of William Swango, went to California when he was 15 years of age. He died while in the Air Force in World War I, Ft. Sill, Okla.

5. Floyd, fourth son of William and Telitha Swango, joined the Navy and was stationed for the duration of the war in English, French and Irish waters. He was on the battleship, "Utah", which went to meet President Wilson when he went to France to arrange the Peace Treaty after World War I.

5. Maude, daughter of William Swango, married Lona Henry and they live in Illinois.

5. Stella, daughter of William Swango, married Robert Tutt.

4. Andrew Chapman Swango, third son of Stephen and Sarah Jane Swango, born June 3, 1863, died Nov. 12, 1894. Married Rebecca Kash in 1886. Several children died in infancy. One son,

Lenix, survived him.

5. Lenix married Lizzie Wells, who died, leaving two children: Maurine and Bob. He then married Lucy Nickell Oldfield. He became a teacher and farmer and later entered the merchandise business in Illinois. He was postmaster and depot agent at one time. He had three children by his last marriage: Maxine, Harold and Lynn Clyde.

4. Julia Carolina, first daughter of Stephen and Sarah Jane Swango, was born on Feb. 26, 1865 and died on Nov. 11, 1918. She married Zack Halsey. They had the following children, Grover Chapman Halsey, Therman, Lillie and Azzie and Verna.

5. Grover Chapman Halsey married Lizzie Henry.
5. Azzie married Floyd Cannoy.
5. Lillie married Elmer Little.
5. Verna married Harry Cline.

4. Lou E., second daughter of Stephen and Sarah Jane Swango, was born Feb. 16, 1869 and died July 31, 1941. She married Edgar T. Kash. They lost three children in infancy, and reared four boys and three girls.

5. Arthur married Emma Lou Wells. They had no children but reared four.

6. Arthur Garrett Kash, a nephew, married Willa Rose.
6. Lula Kash, who married Hayes Nolan.
6. Elsie Little, who married Dan Horton.
6. Nancy Lee Kash, who is 15, a student at Hazel Green Academy in 1956.

5. Ottis, second son of Lou Swango Kash and Edgar T. Kash, was married twice; first to Arizona Rose and they had two children, Genoa Lou, who married a Schrader and has some children. Arthur Garrett, who lived with his uncle, Arthur, after his father's death. Married Willa Rose and they have two children.

Ottis married a second time to Lillian Dean Kash, a school teacher. They had four children, then he died. William Dean married a Rose and they have two children.

Robert Gene, who has just received his honorable discharge from the U. S. Army after serving two years at Ft. Knox, Ky. Maggie Lou, who was graduated from H.G.A. and later Lees College as Honor graduate. She plans to teach. Mabel Sue is a senior at Hazel Green Academy in the fall of 1956.

5. Rosie Clarice, first daughter of Lou E. and Edgar T. Kash, died in 1904 when she was about ten years of age.

5. Grace, second daughter of Lou E. and Edgar T. Kash, married Lee Rose Sr. Two daughters and two sons.

6. Marcille married Attorney Charles Dobbins and lives in Louisville.

6. Geraldine married Murrel Burkhart, who is a Captain in the U. S. Army.

6. E. Kash Rose, is a doctor and surgeon and specialized in cancer treatment. He married a girl from California where they now live. They have two children.

6. Lee Rose Jr., is youngest son of Grace and Lee Rose Sr., of Louisville. He married Christine Dunn, a Wolfe County girl and they live in Louisville and have one son.

5. Lucille, third daughter of Lou E. Swango and Edgar T. Kash, married R. C. Paige. They had two children: R. C. Paige Jr., and Sue Ann. R. C. was graduated from the University of Kentucky with honors recently. Sue Ann is about grown. Lucille, the mother of these two children, died Jan. 1, 1942.

5. Mabel, fourth daughter of Lou E. and Edgar T. Kash, married Volney Hollon and they live in Barstow, California, where they operate a lovely motel. They have one daughter, Patty K. She is a student.

5. Daisy Florence, fifth daughter of Lou E. and Edgar T. Kash, died when a small child.

5. Stephen Kash, third son of Lou E. and Edgar T. Kash, married Mabel Nickell, a girl from Morgan County, daughter of Mr. and Mrs. R. K. Nickell. They had one son, Stephen Neal.

6. Stephen Neal is a first Lieutenant in the Air Corps. He married a Detroit girl and they have one daughter. Stephen Neal is a talented musician and plays with the band in the Army. Stephen Sr., his dad, works in a bank in Detroit, Mich., where he and his wife, Mabel, have lived every since they were married.

5. Edgar T. Kash, Jr., fourth son of Lou E. Swango Kash and Edgar T. Kash, married Nora Miller, a Wolfe County girl. E. T. is clerk of the Draft Board and a farmer. Nora is a teacher. They live in Hazel Green. They have two children: E. T. III, and Thelma Jo.

6. E. T. III married Deloris Byrd, a Wolfe County girl. He was graduated from the University of Kentucky and served two years in the Medical Corps in the U. S. Army, stationed in Germany about 18 months. He is now out of the Army and plans to work on his M. A. degree at University of Kentucky this fall. They had one child and it died in infancy.

6. Thelma Jo Kash, daughter of Nora Miller Kash and E. T. Kash Jr., was graduated from the Home Economics Department of the University of Kentucky, in June, 1956 and was married the latter part of June to William McAtee, who works for a U-Drive place in Lexington.

5. Ada Thelma Kash, the last child of Lou E. Swango Kash and Edgar T. Kash, died at the age of ten years in 1918.

4. Jesse L., fourth son of Stephen and Sarah Ellen Shackelford Swango, was born Oct. 10, 1872 and died April 3, 1940. He married Rosa Kash, farmed in Kentucky until 1903 then moved to

EARLY AND MODERN HISTORY

Missouri and later to Miami, Okla. They had seven sons: Thomas, John, Gene, Steve, Emmet, Oliver and Albert A.; also two daughters: Orabelle and Olive.

4. Nancy Evaline, third daughter of Stephen and Sarah Ellen Shackelford Swango, was born May 31, 1875 and died on May 14, 1914. She married John M. Henry and they had two sons: Stephen and Asa; and four daughters: Ivory, Sylvia, Golden and Ruby.

4. Mary Florence Swango, fourth daughter of Stephen and Sarah Ellen Swango, was born on June 26, 1877 and died on April 2, 1881. She was accidentally strangled to death while playing with some children in a rope swing.

4. Margaret Olive, fifth daughter of Stephen and Sarah Ellen Shackelford Swango, was born Sept. 16, 1880 and died on June 10, 1924. She married Boyd Cannoy and they moved to Illinois in 1902. They left a family of four sons and four daughters: Jesse, Steve, Felix, Lee, Gladys, Opal, Lottie and Florence.

4. Pearlie C., sixth daughter of Stephen and Sarah E. Swango, was born on August 3, 1882 and died on Feb. 11, 1943. She married James Murphy and lived with her father until her death. They bought the old homestead in Wolfe County, Ky. and lived there until 1925 when they moved to Coles, Ill. They reared six sons and four daughters: Stephen, Vernon, Glen, Wendell, Leland, Robert, Lula, Ruby, Ausley and Genevieve.

4. John B., fifth son of Stephen and Sarah E. S. Swango, was born October 18, 1870 and died May 31, 1938. He married Lydia Ann Maxey on Feb. 12, 1891. They were both school teachers and farmed in Kentucky until 1903 when they moved to Coles County, Ill., to farm. They had three sons: Omar, Olive and Stephen Ottice.

5. Omar married Fern Nixon, Dec. 25, 1923. They had two daughters: Geneva Ruth and Mary Virginia. The latter married Ralph Eugene Dare.

5. Oliver, second son of John B. and Lydia Maxey Swango, married Lela Richie, the first time, and they were divorced. Then he married Lorel Gross. They had two daughters, Stella Marie and Dorothy Ann.

5. Stephen Ottice, third and last son of John B. and Lydia Swango, married Estelle Jones and they had two boys and two girls.

3. Green, the fourth son of George Washington, born June 11, 1839, married Miss Rhoda Clark, but they soon parted. He later married Elitha Brashears and became a farmer and county school teacher.

3. John, fifth son of George Washington Swango was born on April 10, 1841, married Sarah Lewis and settled on Swango. They had five sons and four daughters. He died in 1925.

4. Jane, daughter of John Swango, married Jona Taulbee.

4. Cynthia, daughter of John Swango, married James Whisman.

4. Lou, daughter of John Swango, married James Hobbs.

4. Josie, daughter of John Swango, married Jeff Chambers and later Badway George.

4. George Washington Swango, son of John Swango, married a Miss Buchanan and became a doctor and had a son, Jeff Davis Swango, who was also a doctor.

4. Benjamin Franklin Swango, son of John and Sarah Swango, born June 12, 1874, married Deborah Taulbee, May 6, 1896. They had two children: America and Alfred Henning.

5. America Swango, daughter of Benjamin and Deborah Swango, was born April 5, 1897 at Campton, Ky. She married Alphaeus Ray Appenheimer at Leoti, Kansas. They had seven children.

3. William, sixth son of George Washington Swango and Lucinda Hollon Swango, was born July 19, 1843. He married Polly Smith. Settled on Blackwater near Maytown, Wolfe County, Ky. He became one of the leading doctors of his time. He never attended a medical college; but learned at home. Medicine was second nature to him. The college graduates often called on him for assistance and consultation. They sought his advice and said he knew things that were not found in books. Until his health failed him he enjoyed a large practice; often saying he had more practice than he could do justice to. He had no sons, but five daughters.

4. Eletha married William J. Dennis and had three sons and two daughters.

4. Caroline, daughter of William Swango, married James Wilson. They had seven or eight children.

4. Emma J., daughter of William Swango, married Burns Kash and had two girls and two boys, Eliza, Grace, Percy and Roy.

4. Lou E., daughter of William Swango, married William Wilson, a brother to James, and they had one boy, Troy, and a girl, Leona.

3. Ambrose, seventh son of George Washington Swango and Lucinda Hollon Swango, married Nancy Gibbs. Settled on Buck Creek and later moved to his father's old home on Stillwater. He became a doctor and Baptist preacher. He had four daughters: South, Zulema, Alice and Lizzie and two sons: Harlan and Jesse. After the marriage of the three oldest girls they moved to Stanton in Powell County.

4. South married James Lacy, who died after a few years and she went to Ohio and married again.

4. Zulema married Robert Brewer and died when a young woman, leaving some small children.

3. Hiram, eighth son of George Washington Swango and Lucinda Hollon Swango, married Sarah Shockey. They bought a farm on Swango Fork of Baptist, and resided there all his life. They had a son and two daughters. After the children were grown, Hiram

and Sarah separated. Hiram then married Nancy Ratliff and Sarah married James Harris.

4. Henry Swango, son of Hiram and Sarah Swango.

4. Matilda, daughter of Hiram and Sarah Swango, married Joll Gevedon and had two sons and one girl: Henry, Hiram and Geneva.

4. Rosa Bell, daughter of Hiram and Sarah Swango, married Bowen Rose. They had one son, Robert, and one daughter, Arizona. Bowen Rose shot and killed two men, John Mays and Jake Wireman for stealing his mule. They were both riding his mule when he killed them. Bowen Rose was acquitted when he had his trial. Later Rose was shot by Bad Bill Tutt.

3. Harrison, ninth son of George W. and Lucinda H. Swango, was born Jan. 15, 1854 and died Oct. 21, 1934. He married Mary Hobbs and settled on Stillwater near his father's home. Their children all died in infancy. His wife died in Middle life and then he married Eletha Swango, widow of his brother, Green Swango. Harrison reared his nephew, Isaac Swango, son of Samuel Swango.

3. Samuel, tenth son of George W. Swango and Lucinda H. Swango, married Ellen Hobbs, who was a sister to Mary Hobbs, Harrison's wife. They had one son, Isaac. Then Ellen, Samuel's first wife, died and he married Catherine Taylor. They had two sons and two daughters: Taylor, Stephen, Caroline and Sarah.

4. Isaac married Caroline Lawson, who died after they had several children. He had a son, Samuel, and another son, Harrison.

THE SHEFFIELDS

(Contributed by information supplied by Mrs. Ruby Terrill, by Mrs. Dora Sheffield Wilder)

Charlie Sheffield when old enough, joined the Union Army, was chased by the rebels, and saw a boat empty which he used in paddling away from them. Later met a young girl in Montgomery County near Mt. Sterling by the name of Cynthia Adams, who later became his wife. He came from McGoffin County to Hazel Green to live. After some years, he moved to Campton. During this period a daughter was born by the name of Dora Sheffield.

She tells of her father being a shoemaker and when they lived in Campton there were four places of business: (1) Combs and Vaughn, (2) Williams, (3) Steele, (4) Elkins Store. Old Jonathan Elkins lived in a two-story white house up in a field out of town. Mr. Sheffield located in Uncle Cill Combs hotel and stayed eight or ten years.

Mrs. Wilder (former Dora Sheffield), lived in Campton for about ten years or until she was fourteen years of age. She states that the Sheffield, England was named for her grandfather. After going to Owsley County she met and married Will Wilder in Booneville.

She tells in her story that there was a big school taught in the Masonic Hall with a Professor Day teaching the larger children and his wife teaching the smaller ones. They had services on Sunday in the court house before building the old Methodist Church. Old Uncle Harry Little preached and it was a Union Church. Preacher Bill Childers took Dora into the church. Also visiting the town was a presbyterian preacher, Cooper, from Hazel Green. He may have come after they had church in the church house. She remembers church in the Masonic Hall and Sewell Combs was Superintendent. The services were held in the lower floor of the hall. There were Duff's there too.

The Masonic Lodge Bell was struck by lightning during a storm and two men ran from the court house, Mr. Bird and Mr. Hollon, to the hall and both men were killed.

She was again in Campton when Floyd Williams was hung. She also remembers Mr. Hughes, Cud Hanks, Boone Hanks, and Lump Hanks. She tells that they were known in her day as Big Cud, Little Cud, Young Cud and Old Cud. She remembers Uncle Cud Hanks' home place and gave a description of the yard and house as she remembered it.

She stated that Mr. Steve Tutt was sheriff when she was in Campton.

REUBEN AND SALLY TURNER SMITH GENEALOGY
(This information was contributed by Mrs. Jane Allison of Campton, Ky.)

Reuben and Sally Turner Smith were married in Virginia in the 18th century. They had four children:
1. Samp, who married Miranda Combs.
1. Hugh, who never lived in Wolfe County.
1. Lucy, who married "Old" Samp Cox.
1. Jim Smith, who never lived in Wolfe County.

Samp Smith married Miranda Combs and eleven children were born to this union.
2. Maggie, who married Bob Carroll (now dead).
2. Willie married twice, first to Sarah Horton and then to Maude Asberry.
2. Jane married Dr. J. R. Carroll.
2. Alice married Pryce Cole and they lived in Jackson, Ky.
2. Roy married Dora Lacy, now dead.
2. Malvery never married, died early in life.
2. Charlie married in California and reared his family there.
2. Grover also married in California.
2. Carl, who was a veteran of World War II and was lost trace of then.

EARLY AND MODERN HISTORY

2. Lucy Grace married Sterling Shull and went to Arizona to live.
2. Wallace married in California.
Willie Smith, oldest son of Samp and Miranda Combs Smith, better known in Wolfe County as "Judge Bill Smith," had two sets of children. By his first wife, Sarah Horton, he had three children:
3. Jack, who married Margaret Alley. They had four children, a daughter and three sons.
4. Jackie married C. J. Sebastian and they live in Lexington, Ky., and have two daughters.
4. J. B., John, and Bruce Alley Smith.
3. Verner Smith married Blanche Fulks and they had no children. They reside at 518½ Madison Ave., Huntington, W. Va.
3. Myrtle married.
The second set of children which were born to Judge Smith and his second wife, Maude Asberry Smith, are:
3. William, Jr., married Rowena Campbell. Have one child.
3. Irene married Ben Durham.
3. Sallie married Dallas Denniston. They have three children.

STEEL FAMILY
(Facts supplied by Mrs. Mattie Steel Sewell)

Robert Steel came either from Ireland or Scotland and settled in the U.S.A. Robert Steel married Rebecca Ora and they settled in Tazwell County, Virginia. They had a son, Ora Steel, who married Elizabeth Cook and they came to Wolfe County to settle in 1856. Ora Cook was killed while serving in the Army during the Civil War. He lost his life in the battle of Mud Lick Springs.

Ora Steel and Elizabeth Cook Steel had ten children: Thomas, Crockett, George, Robin, Lucinda, Louise, Emmaline (grandmother of Elizabeth Evans), William Wiley, Jane and Henderson.

2. Thomas never married. He died of measles at Irvine, Ky., while in the service of his country during the Civil War.

2. Crockett married Lillie Elkins and they had several children; two of whom are living in summer of 1955 when this material was compiled: Willie Steel and Jasper Steel, both of Campton, Ky.

George Steel died young. Robin also died young.

Lucinda Steel married Ingram Taylor and they had five boys, all of whom are now dead.

Louise Steel married a Bell and they settled in Virginia and have always lived there.

Emmaline married William Coons and they had one son, John Coons, and then William died.

3. John Coons married Mary Bell Center. They had seven children: Nancy, Bertha, Nick, Elizabeth, Shully, Jane and John.

4. Nancy married Crit Childers. They had three sons: Garrett, Ted and Calvin.

5. Garrett married Ethel Brown, daughter of Joe A. Brown. They had one child, Gerald. Garrett has served as Commissioner of Wildlife 15 years.

6. Gerald, after being graduated from Wolfe County High School, enlisted in the U. S. Navy for four years.

5. Ted married Thelma Adams, daughter of Jack Adams, and they live in Dayton, Ohio. Ted is a Baptist preacher. They have two sons: Phillip Neal 17, and Larry, 7 years.

5. Calvin Childers married Fay Ratliff and they live in Dayton, Ohio where he is a driver for Brink's Armored Truck Lines, which deliver currency to banks. They have one son: Michael, 6 years.

4. Bertie Coons married Ben Williams and they had five children: Ben Jr., Virginia, Jean, Paul and John.

5. All of the above family live in Michigan and married there.

4. Nick Coons married Nora Swope. They had five children: Clarence, Henry, Macy Francis, Betty and Jimmie.

5. Clarence married Brooksie Bevins. They have two children.

5. Henry married away.

5. Macy Francis married away.

5. Betty was graduated from Wolfe County High School last year and plans to enter college this fall.

5. Jimmie is unmarried.

4. Elizabeth Coons married Rush Evans. He died in 1948 and they had no children. He was cashier of the Farmers and Traders Bank, Campton, at the time of his death.

4. Shully Coons married Edna White and they had two children. They live in Louisville.

5. Nancy Bell Coons married in Louisville. Her husband is Byrl Franklin.

5. Leland married Virginia Evans. Lives in Louisville.

4. Jane married Carl Cundiff. They have one daughter, Marietta, who married in Norfolk, Va.

4. John Coons married Margaret Robbins and they had three children: Archie, Elizabeth Lou and another girl.

2. William Wiley Steel, son of Ora and Elizabeth Cook Steel, married Sarah Jane Lacy. They had eight children: Euroria, Emma, Porter, Bell, Clay, Ollie, Mattie and Amelia Price.

3. Euroria Steel, daughter of William Wiley and Sarah Jane Lacy, married Melton Potts and they had four children: Lula, Dixie, Carrie and Charlie.

4. Lula is now dead. She married Steven Netherly and they had one daughter, Enid.

5. Enid married Willard Alexander and they settled in Floyd County. They had four children.

6. Mildred, Ruby, Darrett and Stephen.

4. Dixie married Clyde Vice. She is now dead. They had no children.
4. Carrie married Jack Collier. He is dead. They had two children.
5. Marvin married Betty Adams.
5. Juanita married Truman Snelling. They had four children.
4. Charlie married Nancy Lane. They had four boys and a girl. He is now deceased.
3. Emma Steel married Robert Byrd and they had seven children: Shelby, Katherine, Mattie, Bonnie (dead), Nellie, Lillie and Ruth.
4. Shelby died in his youth.
4. Katherine married Agust Lohman and they had three sons.
5. Jack married and lives in Oklahoma.
5. William and James.
4. Mattie Byrd married Charles Williams. They have two sons.
5. Charles Williams married Irene Trivett and they live in Salyersville, Ky.
5. Robert Williams unmarried in 1955.
4. Lillie Byrd married Richard Horton. They had three children.
5. June married Bart Hake and live in Virginia.
5. Holt unmarried.
5. Richmond (Dickey), unmarried.
3. Porter Steel now dead, married Mabel McCormick. They had two sons.
4. Mofford, unmarried.
4. Mack married and lives in Florida.
3. Bell Steel now deceased, married Selby Palmer, who is also now dead. They had ten children, who were all born in Ohio where they now live: Maude, Carrie, Clay, Eva, Mattie, Edith, Ina, Sally, Marguerite and Gladys.
4. Maude married John Garrett.
5. Kenneth married Elsie Reed. Live at Bowen, Ky.
6. Brenda, a young girl.
5. Gertrude married Edd Bach in Ohio where they live.
6. Eddie and Debbie.
5. Arnica married Ova Blair.
6. Timothy and Darryl.
Maude's first husband, John Garrett, died and she married again. This time to Lexie Ellington. They had one daughter, Willa.
5. Willa, daughter of Maude Palmer and Lexie Ellington, married Dale Crabtree. They live in Washington, D. C. and have three children: Danny, Connie and Kathleen.
4. Carrie married Jeff Norris and they had four children: Shelby, Mildred, Gladys, and Dorothy.
5. Shelby, unmarried.

5. Mildred married a Robinson. They have one daughter, Karen.
5. Gladys married Bill Gilley and they have three children: Lonnie, Deanna, and Robia.
5. Dorothy married Bill Ray and they had two children: Gerald Ray and Gloria.
4. Elva married Roy Sallee and they had two children.
5. Paul, unmarried.
5. Virginia married Ed Sparks and they live in Ohio. Two children: Roy Lynn and Douglas.
4. Mattie Palmer married George Reed. They had two children. Sherwood, the elder son, is a doctor. He is a cancer specialist.
5. Dr. Sherwood Reed married Allie Carey and they live in St. Joseph, Mo.
6. Patricia and Cynthia, small daughters.
5. Moneford Reed is a University graduate and is in the Army. He married Margaret Roland.
4. Edith married George Halsey. They have three children.
5. Palmer, unmarried.
5. Imogene married Paul Campbell and they live in Ohio. One daughter, Charmayne.
5. Marjorie married Carl Heine. They have one son, Carl, Jr.
4. Ina married Ralph Downing. Now dead. Five children.
5. Ova, unmarried.
5. Sybil, unmarried.
5. Fay married Harley Williams.
6. One daughter, Donna.
5. Patty married Bob Valk.
5. Talmage married Betty. They have one child, Dennis.
4. Sally married Sam McQuinn.
5. Orvil married Mary Williams. One child, Sandra.
4. Marguerite married Omer Brewer and they live in Florida.
5. Ralph Brewer married away. Diane, Jimmy and Kenneth.
4. Gladys married Henry Raney. Live in Ohio.
5. Lois, Verla, and Jane, unmarried.
3. Clay Steel married Josie Johnson.
4. Clay Steel married Grace Milligan. No children. Lives in Tennessee.
4. Earl Steele married Marjorie, lives in Tennessee. A girl, Joan.
3. 3. Ollie Steel married Henry Reynolds.
4. Lyda, unmarried.
4. Mabel married Elwood Garrison.
5. Lionel married Martha Jensen.
6. Lionel Jr., Edward, Martha and Johanne.
5. Donald married Geneva Lewis.
6. Donnie Helen, Mary Jane and Calvin Lewis.
5. Mildred married Edward Cook. No children.

EARLY AND MODERN HISTORY

    4. Mabel's first husband, Elwood Garrison, died and she married John Bryant. They had six children.

    5. Jean Bryant married Herbert Gibson. They had 3 children.

    6. Gary Lee, Connie Lynn, and Craig Anthony.

    5. John D., Jr., married Lucy Smith. They had two children. William and Virginia Ruth.

    5. Zelma married Lloyd Dyer and they had two children: Richard and Robert.

    5. Sadie married Porter Tolson and they have one child, Diane.

    5. Victor, unmarried, 16 years of age.

    5. Martha Ann, a young girl.

    4. Vernice married George Stevens.

    5. Faye married Ernest Johnson. They have two children: Randy and Connie lives in Pennsylvania.

    4. Shelby married Gloria Huff. Three children: Donald and two others.

    4. Clay married Zelma Bowen, three children born to them: Fred, Allie and Corie.

    4. Lena married Breck Cornett. One child: David.

    3. Mattie Steele married Taylor Sewell. Sewell is now deceased. They had no children.

    3. Amelia Price married John Garrison.

    4. Earl married Lucy Ford. No children.

    4. Glen, unmarried.

    4. Earnest died at eight years of age.

    4. Mabel died at the age of three years.

    4. Edith married Ray Williams. One child.

WOLFE COUNTY

TUTT FAMILY

The genealogy on the Thomas K. Tutt family was submitted by Mrs. Flossie Shackelford, Mrs. W. W. Abel and some of it by Mrs. J. B. Tutt.

Thomas Kelly Tutt, my grandfather, was born in Perry Co., Ky. and I cannot find out when he moved to Wolfe Co., but he died there in Sept. 1902 and his children were born and reared in Wolfe Co. He married Leodicea Stamper April 24, 1854, but it is possible that Wolfe Co., was at that time a part of Morgan County. I am pretty sure that they were married in Morgan. I think Mrs. W. E. Bach, of Lexington has a record to that effect. If Wolfe was then a part of Morgan his oldest children might have been born there but you may know more about the counties than I do.
Anyway, here are the children:

  Melissa, married Charles Gosney.
  Matilda, married Sherman Shackelford.
  Belle married Chambers Manker, 1st. marriage.
  Belle married Chambers Manker 1st marriage —Frank Thomas 2nd marriage.
Thomas K. Jr., Louellen Crawford.
  Rausie married John Phillips.
  Sarah married Howard Fulks 1st. marriage, Morton Phillips 2nd. marriage.
  Melissa's children:
  Benjamin Gosney (deceased)
  James Jackson
  John B. (deceased)
  Pearl
  Charles Sherman
  Sullivan
  Inez
  Sarah
  Woodford
  Mamie
Matilda's children:
  Flossie Shackelford
  Edna Shackelford
  Samuel Shackelford
  Fred Shackelford
  Benham Shackelford
  Sallie Willard
Thomas K. children:
  Leah Tutt
  James Tutt
  Ruth Tutt
  Robert Tutt

EARLY AND MODERN HISTORY

May Tutt (deceased)
Edith Tutt
Benjamin Tutt (deceased)
Thomas Hoy Tutt
Belle's children:
Stella Manker
Frank Thomas Jr.
Gertrude Manker
Seitz Manker
Rausie's children:
Gladys Phillips
Mollie Phillips
Sarah's children:
Ella Fulks
Elsa Fulks
Olive Fulks
Flossie Fulks

Thomas Kelly Tutt Sr.

Sarah Leah (Tutt) Abel, received education in public schools of Wolfe County, Kentucky, Kentucky Wesleyan Academy and Wilbur R. Smith Business College, Lexington, Ky. married to M. Wright Abel, a native of Dayton, Tenn. lives in Lexington where her husband has been associated with C. S. Brant Seed Co., for 46 years.

One daughter, Susan Jean (Abel) Adams, has A. B. and M.A. degree in psychology from the University of Kentucky. She married Richard Terrill Adams, native of Harward, Ill., who holds the A.B. degrees from the University of Illinois, and his Phd. degree from Columbia University, New York. Jean lives with her three children, Lucy Lee, Ellen Wright, and Thomas Perrill in New Orleans, La., where her husband is teaching at Tulane, University.

James B. Tutt, second child of Thomas Kelly Tutt Jr., and his wife, Laodecia Stamper Tutt, married Ella Center, daughter of "old" Doctor G. M. Center and Rausline Creech Center, Hazel Green, Ky.
They had five sons:
Pryce E. Tutt married Kathleen McLin, daughter of the late Robert J. and Lillie Day McLin of Hazel Green, Ky.

Pryce received his education at Hazel Green Academy, Berea College, Morehead, and Richmond State Teacher's College.

Kathleen was graduated from Hazel Green Academy and has studied some Library Science courses at the University of Kentucky, Lexington.

They are both staff members of Hazel Green Academy.
They have one son, Lynn Alan Tutt. He is seven years old at this

time (1955). Bert Tutt married Ruth Clark, daughter of Cud Clark and Mary Rose Clark of Campton, Ky. Bert received his education at Alvin Drew School, Pine Ridge, and Berea, Kentucky. Bert served in World War II in Germany. He finished a course in agriculture after the war ended. Ruth is a graduate of Alvin Drew School, Pine Ridge, Ky. They have one daughter, Carol Faith Tutt who is 13 years old now. (1955). They are farming their own farm about four miles east of Campton, Ky. They also farm 100 acres of land which belongs to Luther Ambrose, Gosneyville, Ky.

Harold Tutt married Marcella Tyra, daughter of the late Ernie Tyra and Julia Tyra, Campton, Ky.

Harold received his education at Hazel Green Academy, Ky. and at Berea, Ky. Marcella graduated from Wolfe County High School, Campton, Ky. Harold served in World War II in Germany.

He is now employed at Chrysler Air Temp -- Dayton, Ohio. Where he owns his own home. They have a daughter, Julia Clara Tutt who is eight years old.

Marion K. Tutt married Oleda Risner, daughter of Harry Risner and Loura Dunn Risner of Burkhart, Ky.

Marion received his education at Hazel Green Academy and Lafayette Vocational School, Lexington, Ky. Marion served in World War II in Germany. Oleda is a graduate of Woodford High School, Cincinnati, Ohio. They have a daughter, Diana Sue Tutt who is seven years old.

Marion is now service manager at Kinkead Wilson's Motor Co., Lexington, Ky., where they live and own their own home.

Robert K. Tutt married Geneva Mulcahy, daughter of Harry Mulcahy and Nannie Miller Mulcahy, Nicholasville, Ky.

Robert received his education at Hazel Green Academy, Hazel Green, Ky., and Wilmore, Ky. Robert joined the Air Force in 1950 for three years later he served one year with occupational troops in Korea. Geneva is a graduate of Wilmore High School. Robert is now stationed at Orlando, Fla., where they live and own their own home. They have a son two years old, Johnnie Bert Tutt.

Alice Ruth Tutt,, third child of Thomas Kelly Tutt Jr. and Laodecia Stamper Tutt, received her education in the public schools of Wolfe County and at Berea College. She taught school in Wolfe County for several years. She married Daniel Hayden Center, son of Dr. G. Marion Center and Rausline Creech Center. They live near Berea, Ky. and her husband has a position with Berea College.

They have five children as follows:

Bernice Center Robertson, has her A. B. degree from Berea College, has done Social Service work in Clay County, worked in the auditory department at Blue Grass Ordinance, taught school one year in Heidelberg, Germany, (in the American school there) while her husband was studying in Heidelberg University. She is now teaching in Berea College. Marvine D. B. Robertson, who has an A. B. degree from Berea College and an M. A. and D.D. from Union College, New York and his Phd. from Columbia University, N.Y. He is now teaching at Berea College, Ky. They have two young sons, Donald and Bruce.

Vivian Marie Center Landis, second daughter of Alice Ruth Tutt Center, has a A. B. degree from Berea College, she married Phil Landis, a chemist from York, Pa., Vivian held a job as chemist at Lake Charles, La. before her marriage. They have been living in New Jersey where Phil is a chemist for the Sonoco Oil Co. but are now in Chicago, Ill. where Phil is working on his Phd. degree at Northwestern University. They have two sons, Bryan and Michael.

Mabel Center Bochm, third daughter of Alice Ruth Tutt Center, also has an A. B. degree from Berea College, She married Heinz Bochm, who has an A.B. degree from Berea College. They live in Peaceful Valley, Colorado, where they own and operate a vacation resort; swimming, horse back riding, skiing, square dancing and many other sports are conducted at their resort, Mabel is also teaching school there. They have two children, Paul and Kathleen. Daniel Hayden Center, Jr. fourth child and first son of Alice Ruth Tutt Center, attended Berea College three years. He is now employed by the United States Government in the Pentagon building in Washington, D. C. He is married to Nancy Henderson, of Bay City Mich., Nancy is also working for the government in the Pentagon building. Danny plans to enter college in Washington, D.C. next year and get his degree.

Luther Willis Center, fifth child and second son of Alice Ruth Tutt Center, is living at home and attending Berea College, where he is a senior in the Argiculture department. He is not married has served two years in the United States Army; saw service in this country and Korea and Japan.

Robert Bruce Tutt, fourth child and second son of Thomas Kelly Tutt Jr., served in World War I, was wounded in the battle of Chateau Thiery, France, later married Stella Swango of Maytown, Ky. now lives in Effingham, Ill. has four children.
Children as follows:

Roberta, first child, of Robert Bruce Tutt and Stella Swango Tutt married James Gibbons of Mattoon, Ill. Roberta received her education in the public schools of Illinois and at Illinois State teacher's college. She taught school for several years. She is with her husband in Germany where he is with the U. S. Army as a warrant officer. He is making a career of the Army. They have one son, Richard.

Thelma Tutt, second child of Robert Tutt, received her education in the public schools of Illinois. She is married to Charles U. Bartimus and they live at Seward, Ill. where her husband is principal of a school. They have a son Teddy. Her husband has his A. B. degree and working on his M. A. degree at this time.

Juanita Tutt Gray, third child of Robert Bruce Tutt, married Revel Gay from North Carolina, they live in Matoon, Ill., where she has a position in the auditing department of a large furniture mfg. Co., They have one daughter, Judy.

Thomas Wright Tutt, fourth child of Robert Bruce Tutt, married Jane Hall from Paris, Ill., they live in Matoon, Ill., where he is employed by a large trucking Co. They have one son, Timothy Thomas.

Minerva May Tutt Smith, fifth child of Thomas K. Tutt Jr., has an A. B. degree from Berea college, was graduated with highest distinction, taught school several years in Wolfe County, Powell and also in Rockcastle Counties. Married John W. Smith also a graduate of Berea College (he was a native of Jackson county), who lives at Anchorage, Ky. and is personnel direcor at the Quartermasters Corps, Jeffersonville, Ind., May died Aug. 31, 1951. Their two children are:

Jean Margaret Smith Miller, who received her education in Louisville Public Schools, Berea and Georgetown, colleges. Married Joe M. Miller and they have three daughters: Nancy, Michelle and Malinda. They all live in Anchorage, Ky.

Thomas Meredith Smith, also has his A. B. degree from the University of Louisville, M. A. from the University of Montana and is now employed by the United States Government in Forestry at Flagstaff, Arizona. He married Jean Graham, of Frankfort, Ky. who was also graduated from the University of Louisville. They have one daughter, Julia Lynn.

Orena Florence Tutt Aug. 29, 1900 and died Aug. 4, 1901.

Lenore Edith Tutt Ambrose, sixth child of Thomas K. Tutt Jr. was graduated from Berea College with an A. B. degree with highest distinction. Married Luther M. Ambrose who holds an A. B. MA and Phd. degree and has taught in Berea college for 35 years. Edith is now in Bangkok, Thailand with her husband, who is on an educational assignment for the government. Edith is also teaching in a school in Thailand for American children.

Dr. and Mrs. Ambrose have four children, namely:

Ellen Ambrose Bleecher, first child of Dr. and Mrs. Luther M. Ambrose, received her education at Berea College. Married Harry

Bleecher of New York City, N. Y. they live in Philidelphia, Pa. they have three children, a daughter, Carol and two sons, Dale and Robin.

Frederick Ambrose, second child of Dr. and Mrs. Luther Ambrose, served in World War II and in Korean War. Married Ethel Pearson, native of North Carolina. They now live in Tuscon, Ariz., where Fred is a senior in College majoring in Agriculture. They have no children.

Thomas Barton Ambrose served in World War II and Korean War. He is now a senior at the University of Kentucky, where he is majoring in psychology. He married Helen Cooney, a native of Ireland, whom he met in England while serving there during World War II. They have two daughters, Coleen and Kathleen.

Luther Martin Ambrose, fourth child of Edith Tutt Ambrose and Dr. Luther M. Ambrose, received his education in Berea College, is now employed in a music shop in Lexington.

Martin is a musician and has had an important role in the play "Wilderness Road", which was given in 1955 in the Berea Amphitheatre. He sang sereval solos in the play. Also played an important character part.

Benjamin Curtis Tutt, eighth child of Thomas K. Tutt Jr., was born March 10, 1904 and died April 24, 1935.
He married Ethel Burton and they had one daughter, Virginia who died in babyhood.

Thomas Hoy Tutt, ninth child of Thomas K. Tutt Jr. served four years in the United States Navy, first marriage to Daisy Crawford, who died June 25th. 1942. Two children by first marrige; Stella Florence, who married George Ashton of Clairton, Pa. She has one son, George Jr. they live in Dravosburg, Pa. and received education in public schools of Jefferson County and Berea College. Thomas Hoy Jr. who isattending Fern Creek High School, lives at home.

Thomas Hoy Tutt's second marriage was to Ruby Summer and they have two daughters; Betty Lou and Libby. They live in the surburbs of Louisville. Tom works for Duponts, where he has been employed for 16 years.

Thomas Tutt Jr. was born in July 1831 and died in Sept. 1902. He was the son of John Jacob Tutt and Jane (Kelly) Tutt.

Thomas Kelly Tutt was married to Laodicea Stamper in Perry County on April 24, 1854. They had five daughters and one son. The daughters were Melissa, Nellie, Matilda, Rausie, and Sarah and the son's name wah Thomas Kelly Tutt Jr.

Thomas Kelly Tutt Sr. lived most of his life at Bethel, Ky. post office was Gosneyville, Ky. The children were reared there. Thomas Kelly Sr. owned several hundred acres of land, and was considerde a philanthropist of his day; gave ground and helped build school buildings, church buildings and ground for cemetery where his father and mother and his wife are burried. He gave his children each a good sized farm and was always generous in everything that would help the community in which he lived.

Thomas Kelly Tutt Sr. was a man of high christian ideals-a man of prayer; for many years before his death, he would slip quitely away every day to a small thicket of young trees near his home, where he crawl under their protecting branches and kneel in prayer, holding two young saplings as he prayed.

He was a happy christian, always cheerful and looked on the bright side of life. Laodicea Tutt was also a woman of strong character and convictions. She had belonged to the Baptist church prior to her marriage, when she joined the Methodist church with her husband. When she was dying her husband asked her if she were afraid and she replied, "No, I have enough of that old Baptist in me that I am not afraid."

Thomas Kelly Tutt Jr. was born May 12, 1865 at Bethel, Ky., which is located several miles from Campton, Ky. He is the son of the late Thomas Tutt Sr. and Laodicea Stamper Tutt. He was married on April 26, 1888 to Lou Ellen Crawford, who was born at Holly, Ky. in Breathitt county but who resided at Bethel at the time of their marriage. She was a teacher in the public schools of Wolfe County for many years. She died at the home of her daughter, Edith Tutt Ambrose, Berea, Ky. on Oct. 21, 1955 and is burried in the family cemetery at Bethel, Ky. They had nine children, six of whom are living. Names as follows:

Matilda A. Tutt, daughter of Thomas Kelly and Laodicea Tutt, married Sherman Shackelford, Feb. 11, 1886.

Children of this marriage:

Flossie, married Frank H. Rieke, Paducah, Ky. (deceased) No children.

Edna, married (1) Frank Collins, New York, (deceased) no children.
(2) Henry N. Price, Middletown, Ohio. no children.

Samuel E., married Viola Center, Hazel Green, Ky. 2 children.

Maybel, deceased at age of seven.

Fred T., married Fae Green, Pomeroy, Ohio, 2 children.

Benham B., married Iva Flack, Middletown, Ohio, 2 children.

Sally Willard, married Corbet Lindon, Bethel, Ky. no children.

Children Of Samuel And Viola Shackelford

Lawrence E., married Grace Whitt, Middletown, Ohio 2 children, High School graduates.

Virginia Hazel, married Edward J. Hogan, Col. O. 2 children High School graduates.

Children Of Lawrence and Grace Shackelford

Lawrence David, Linda Kay.

Children Of Edward And Virginia Hogan

Richard J. (College student, Ohio State University), Sharon Lee.

Children Of Fred And Fae Shackelford

Marilyn Ann, A. B. Ohio State University (2 children) married Robert Scott, Providence, R. I., A. M. Ohio State University.

Children Of Marilyn A. And Robert Scott

Stephen Alan:
Roger Lynd:
George S.: A. B. Ohio State University 2 children Lieutenant, J. G. U. S. Navy, married Shirley Morris, Middletown, Ohio.

Children Of George S. And Shirley Shackelford

Richard Allen, Saundra Lynne.

Children Of Benham And Iva Shackelford

Vernon B. high school graduate and served in U. S. Navy 1 child, married Lorraine Richard, Middletown, Ohio.

James S. high school graduate, served in U. S. Navy, 3 children, married Lois Irons, Middletown, Ohio.

Children Of Vernon And Lorraine Shackelford

Douglas S.:

Children Of James And Lois Shackelford

Three children: Katherine, Patricia, and Susan.

TAULBEE FAMILY
By Mrs. Paris Rose

Son of Wm Taulbee, Samuel Taulbee married Ellen Davis. They had four children. Mary, Blanche and R. B. George (deceased)
1. Mary Taulbee married Paris Rose. They had five children.
2. Pearl (deceased)
2. Myrtle (deceaesed)
2. Earl married Beuna Craig. They had seven children.
3. G. C. married Maxine Faust.
3. Don married Jane Kettering.
3. Mary Margaret married Russell Watson.
3. Elizabeth Ann
3. Johnnie and Sue.
3. Carolyn.
2. Edgar Rose married Katy McCoy. They had six children.
3. Edgar Jr. married Vergie McCoy.
3. Mary Esther married Donald Liggett.
3. Joan at home.

Taulbee—Rose

3. Michael.
3. Peggy Sharon.
3. Gary.

WOLFE COUNTY

*2. Ida Rose married Everett Lawrence and they live in Xenia, Ohio. They had four children.
3. Thomas is a senior in high school.
3. Doris deceased.
3. David.
3. Donald.
*1. Blanche Taulbee married John Anderson of Insko. They have one son.
2. Elmer Davis Anderson who married Elizabeth Carpenter. Teaches in West Liberty school.
*1. R. B. Taulbee married Mae Anderson. They had four children before his wife died.
2. Straughton married Ruby King. Several children.
2. Bill married Elizabeth Cole. Four children.
2. Ettie married.
2. Edith married in Indiana.
After R. B.'s first wife died he married Cora Stidham. They had one daughter.

TYLER FAMILY

James Tyler and Katherine Barren Tyler were married in Virginia. They moved to Wolfe County, Kentucky about 1830. They had nine children.
1. W. T. Tyler married Deborah Johnson. He was a preacher for 30 years.
1. Hughie married Cammie Osborne.
1. John married Laura Faulkner.
1. Robert married Liza Shepherd.
1. Melvin married Nan Chambers.
1. Lawrence died when a young boy.
1. Jane Tyler married C. C. Hanks.
1. Mahala married Boone Hanks.
1. Anna married Thomas Horton -(see Hortons).
W. T. Tyler and Deborah Johnson Tyler had nine children.
2. Ella married Willie Bumgardener.
2. Katherine married Marion Faulkner.
2. Mary married John White.
2. Daisy married Arthur Kincaid.
2. Ursey married Lump Hanks.
2. Alice married Plummer Shull.
2. Ruth married Clarence Hoopengarner. — Moved to Indiana.
2. Roscoe married Ethel Lykins first time.
2. James married Rose Wireman. He was county judge.
3. Helen.
3. Phyllis.
3. Another girl.
3. Kenneth.

EARLY AND MODERN HISTORY

1. Hughie married Cammie Osborn and they had eight children.
2. Willie Tyler married Pearlie Taulbee.
2. Melvin Tyler married after he went to Mexico.
2. Charlie moved away and married out of Wolfe County.
2. Jimmie never married.
2. Lula Tyler married Washington Faulkner.
2. Nettie married after he moved to Winchester.
2. Anna married away out of the county.
2. Deborah married Richmond Roberts.

*1. John Tyler, son of James Tyler and Katherine Tyler, married Laura Faulkner. They had several children and then moved to Winconsin.
2. Beverly, John, Tom, and two or three girls.

*1. Robert M. Tyler, son of Mr. James Tyler and Katherine Barren Tyler, married Nannie Allen. They had two children.
2. Willie married Mae Lykins the first time then later married Liza Shepherd.
2. Kernie married and moved to Indiana.

*1. Melvin Tyler, son of James and Katherine Tyler, married Nan Chambers. They had two children.
2. Bessie.
2. Shafter.

*1. Jane Tyler, daughter of James and Katherine Tyler, married C.C. Hanks. They had five children.
2. James Hanks, who married Ida Catron first then Lida Stamper Taulbee.
2. C.M. Hanks never married.
2. Bob Hanks, who married Myrtle Catron.
2. Alice Hanks who married Kelly Fulks.
2. Bertie Hanks who married Reece Catron.

*1. Mahala Tyler, daughter of James and Katherine Barren Tyler, married Boone Hanks.
2. Willie who married Zerilda Miller.
2. C. M. Hanks who married Florence Tutt.
2. Fred Hanks married Bess Tutt.
2. Finley Hanks married - - - - -
2. Lucy married Jim Drake.
2. Vernie Hanks married Van Elkins.
2. Millie Hanks married Letcher Byrd.

*1. Anna Hanks married Thomas Horton (see Mortons).
*2. Ella Tyler, daughter of W. T. Tyler and Deborah Johnson Tyler, married Willie Bumgardner. They had five children.
3. Lida B. who married Lumm Williams.
3. Ella married Frank Bolen.
3. Ray.
3. Rollie.
3. Ernest.

3. Carrie.

2. Katherine Tyler, daughter of W. T. Tyler and Deborah J. Tyler. Married Marion Faulkner. They had nine children.
    3. Gerald who married a Drake.
    3. Willie - - - - - -
    3. Carl married a missionary named Sophie - - -
    3. Another son was killed in the mines.
    3. Flossie who married George Oliver.
    3. Alice - - - married - - -
    3. Ruth.
    3. Margie.
    3. Esther.

2. Mary, daughter of W. T. Tyler, and Deborah J. Tyler, married John White.
    3. Deborah married John Miniard.
    3. Emma married Al Goodson.
    3. Edwin single.
    3. Bertie married W. G. Lockhart first and had one son, Billie, who is a student in LaFeyette Trade School, Lexington. Then she married Dr. Rex Center after her first husband's death.
        4. Rosemary, a little daughter.
    3. Mattie never married. (Minister).
    3. Ethel married Albert Thompson.
    3. Raymond White married Elizabeth Taulbee.
    3. James White married Velma Motter.

2. Daisy Tyler, daughter of W. T. and Deborah J. Tyler, married Arthur Kincaid. They had four children.
Kincaid. They had four children.
    3. Ora, never married.
    3. Anna never married.
    3. Ophelia never married.
    3. Roscoe Tyler married - - - -

2. Ursey Tyler, daughter of W. T. and Deborah J. Tyler, married Lump Hanks. They had four children.
    3. Lida who married in Tennessee.
    3. Arlene (now deceased) married Jesse Curtis.
    3. Bessie married - - - - -
    3. Eula married Cecil Miller.

2. Alice Tyler, daughter of W. T. and Deborah J. Tyler, married Plummer Shull. They had several children and then moved to Mich.

2. Roscoe Tyler, son of W. T. and Deborah J. Tyler, married Ethel Lykins. They had four children.
    3. Cecil, married Bertha Cundiff the second time.
    3. Barnes not married.
    3. Elmer not married.
    3. Norman not married.

Roscoe married Hazel Lumpkins the second time and they had two children, Glenn and a gilr.

EARLY AND MODERN HISTORY

Mrs. Roy M. Secil,
Campton, Ky.
Dear Mrs. Cecil:
 I read your statement in a recent issue of the "News" that you thought that I could, if so minded, contribute some material which could be used in the forthcoming book "The History of Wolfe County." As you may know, I have not been a resident of Wolfe County for more than fifty-two years. Therefore, I do not feel qualified to write intimately about places and persons I have not seen and had little personal contact with for so long.
 Maybe I can re-write, or copy something others have written and come up with an idea which can be utilized in the much needed and over-delayed history book. Accordingly. I have "lifted" from my files and arranged some material which I am sending to you for consideration-hoping it will be interesting--if not usable.
 If you are contemplating inclusion of some genealogical records, perhaps I can contribute something helpful on that subject, as I have some information on approximately five thousand decendents of Hollons and Related Families," some of whom long ago, gave up the ghost; some moved away; some ran away; some escaped; some still live in Wolfe County; and as far as I know some may have been sent away - - for safe keeping.
 Having seen so many names in the "News" that are familiar to me, in relation to Wolfe County, I got to reminescing and began to write down the names of families I knew" way back in the fall of the 80's" and ended up with 126, most of whom probably were born in the generation of my grand-fathers who were born in 1816 and 1820. Of these 126 families, 58 -- or 46% were my kin by blood or marriage. As to the multitude of their decendants, the Lord only knows. The few thousand I have on record would be as a tiny drop of water in Kentucky Lake.
 Wondering about the ancestry of those family names, I wandered into the archives and consulted authentic records. I came out with 48 names that had Coatslof-Arms granted to them in their home countries --mostly English? ! Someone OUGHT to write a book.
 If you wish to use some of my genealogy of "Hollon and Related Families," please advise and I will arrange it in order and in a style to conform to your history book.
Sincerely Yours,
Clay Hollon

Mrs. Berta K. Cecil,
Campton, Ky.
Dear Mrs. Cecil:
 In answer to your letter of Dec. 2, 1954, am at a loss just what to say, as well as how to say it, in regard to including some of my genealogical material (Vital Records) in your history of Wolfe County.

WOLFE COUNTY

All my records pertain to people who lived in or were born in Wolfe County and their Decendants, beginning with my great grandfather, John Hollon and his brother George) who settled there in 1804. It has been my purpose not to deal with ancestry beyond that period, although I do have some that goes much further back.

There are two branches of Hollon, other than the Wolfe County Hollons, who claim relationship, but that has not been proved and are not included in the lay-out of my Hollons of Wolfe County, but are kept in a separate section in as much as they bear the same name.

Am enclosing a folder showing the first two pages of the John Hollon line, and two pages showing my mother's line--Elkins-Richmond. They show the manner in which more than 600 families are arranged in direct line in order of birth, making it easy for any individual to trace his parentage back to the first Kentucky ancestor. Only names, ages or birth, death, marriages, etc. are recorded, covering a period of 150 years.

Eliminating all families not related to the direct line of Hollon, Elkins-Richmond, shown on the four pages, it would require 40 pages of this style, size and arrangement.

To use only enough of my material to fill five pages, of the size mentioned, would not be advisable, owing to the fact that it would eliminate all now living generations – the only persons who might be interested in a book of this kind.

I have done a tremendous amount of research, was actively engaged in the printing business for more than 50 years, and have it published is a nefarious, laborous, time-consuming and costly business. What do you think?

I had planned on a 64-page booklet, limp cover with plastic binding similar to the Ky. Mountain Club Annual, of which you are no doubt familiar.

Will be glad to have any comments or suggestions you wish to make.

Sincerely Yours,
Clay Hollon

KASHES

Dr. John Mason Kash married Nancy Goodpaster by whom he had three children. Two died before they were married.

The oldest daughter married a Craycraft and had two sons, Edward and Fred. Dr. Kash then married second, Elizabeth Carter Maxey (Eliza) daughter of Dr. (Renny) or Raney or (Renee) Maxey of Ezel. They had five children: namely: 1. Rosalie, whose history is found under the Day section.

2. Emma who married Wiley May of White Oak, Ky. They had no children. They moved to Oklahoma and lived there several years until his death about 26or 27 years ago; after which she came and

lived with Mrs. Price Sewell at Jackson, Ky. until her death in 1946.

3. Silas--a doctor, who was graduated from the University of Louisville in the same class with Dr. Reese Kash of Frenchburg. Silas lived in Missouri at Burdette and married a widow Mag Pieratt Cassidy and they had one daughter, Yvonne who lives in Missouri yet.

4. John Frank Kash lived at Roch Camp, Ohio. He married Belle Salyers and they had two daughters, Elva and Thelma.

1. Elva married Fred Lyons and they had three children. One of whom burned to death with Elva. (The child either caught on fire or fell into the fire and she tried to extinguish the fire and lost her life.) Mrs.Sewell says she thinks there is a daughter and a son, Claude Franklin.

2. Thelma married Charles Brace and they had two children, Thelma, Margaret and Charles Gill. The daughter, Thelma Margaret is married and has a family; the son is in business (Dairy) there with his father.

5. Margaret Ann died in 1950, the youngest of Dr. John Mason Kash's children, married Price Sewell (he died 1955) of Jackson, Ky. They had four children, two of them died young. George Mason and Mildred. The two remaining children are both M. D.'s.

1. Dr. Frank Kash Sewell of Mt. Sterling, Ky. who married Carmie Bach of Jackson. They have two children: Frank Jr., a Junior a Pre-Med. Student at Vanderbilt University and Martha Ann, a senior at Mt. Sterling High School. (Recent picture in Leader for D.A.R. citizenship award.)

2. Dr. Price Sewwell Jr., of Jackson, who married Juliet Rumph of Perote, Ala., (Met her while in Medical school at Vanderbilt, where both of the Dr. Kashes received their M.D.'s) They have two children, Price Sewell III, a sophomore at Jackson High School and James David Sewell, a seventh grade student at Jackson City School.

"THE GRAHAM FAMILY"

Three young brothers left their home in Scotland and came to America about the year 1805. They were:

1. Thomas Graham birth and date and place not sure.
2. Jesse Graham born in Scotland in 1792-Married Milly Spencer.
3. William Graham born in Ireland in 1795.

These boys migrated to South West Virginia, and settled in Powell Valley, Lee County, Virginia.

No. 2—Jessie Graham married Miss Milly Spencer, and to his union was born five children: 1. Joseph Douglas Graham; 2. Jane; 3. Pauline; 4. Elizabeth; 5. William Graham.

No. 2—Mr. Jessie Graham was a farmer with fruit orchards and bees. He died young around 1836. His wife followed him in death a few years later.

No. 2-1: Joseph Douglas Graham (oldest son of Jessie Graham and wife) was born in Jonesville, Virginia, 1-16-1827 and he was educated in Jonesville, Va. About 1844 he came to Kentucky to visit his Mother's brother Jessie Spencer, who lived near the mouth of Quicksand, Breathitt County, Ky. At that time there were no free schools in the mountains of Kentucky. Jessie Spencer, the Coxes and a few other families got together, and organized a subscription school, and employed Joseph D. Graham as the teacher for the consideration of ..30.00 per month and board. They built a crude log school house with puncheon floor and hewn seats—one of the first in the mountain section. After teaching a few years in Breathitt County, he came to Wolfe County to teach and met and married Jane Little, daughter of Phillip Little, a large land owner of near Daysboro, Kentucky.

No. 2-1: Joseph D. Graham and his wife, Jane Little Graham, settled on a farm first at Jonesville, Va. Three years later moved back to Gilmore, Ky. He spent his entire life serving in educational work, as a teacher, also served one term as School Superintendent.

Joseph D. Graham and his wife, Jane Little, had ten children as follows: 1. Napoleon Boneparte (Boney); 2. Thomas; 3. Elizabeth; 4. Douglas; 5. Lethia; 6. Marild; 7. Dillard; 8. Luther; 9. Sarah; 10. Lilbern; and one daughter, 11. Nannie by his second marriage.

2-1: Joseph D. Graham married Jane Little.

2-2: Jane Graham came to Ky. as did her brothers and sisters, later married a Presbyterian minister. After marriage they settled in Virginia. Do not know if any children.

2-3: Paulina Graham married Jack Williams and settled in Bath County, near Salt Lick, Ky. They reared four children: 1. Joe 2. Lillian; 3. Pearl; 4. Scholar Williams.

2-4: Elizabeth Graham married a Mr. Ledford—they settled in Montgomery County, Ky. We have no further record of them.

2-5: William Graham married Sarah Terrill. Born 1830—Children: 1. Amos married Mary Graham; 2nd: Lucinda Rose; 3rd: Addie Prater-lives in Cynthiana, Kentucky. He is now in his 90th year. 2. Timothy married Ellen McPherson; 3 Margaret married Henry Dunigan; 4 John married Lou Hollon; 5. Fanny married Jack Brewer.

1. Amos Graham has three children.

2. Timothy Graham married Ellen McPherson. Children: 1. Bill Graham; 2. Douglas Graham married Laura Brewer; 3 Tim Graham; 4. George Graham; 5. Sarah Graham.

2-1 Joseph Douglas Graham and his wife, Jane Little, had the following children: 1. Napoleon Boneparte (Boney) Graham, born in Jonesville, Va. Sept 1, 1850. He married 1st: Hannah Lacy, daughter of Moses B. Lacy, of Lacy Creek, Ky. and they settled on a farm at Gilmore, Ky. He served thirty years at Demund, Ky., as Post Master. They had six children as follows: 1. Martha and 2. Mary, both died in infancy; 3. Paris Morton Graham, born Nov. 30, 1876. He married Elvira Spencer, March 25, 1897.

4. Celso born to Napoleon ond Hannah Lacy Graham.

5. Seward Graham born Oct. 24, 1879. Died at six years of age.

6. Rebecca Jane Graham born Dec. 6, 1883. Attended rural schools and Hazel Green Academy. Married Erasmus Moore Russell who was a lunmberman, grain miller and a good mechanic. He died as a result of an accident while running his machinery at his mill in Hazel Green on Dec. 10, 1938. Mrs. Russell taught school in both Morgan and Wolfe Counties and is now retired and living in Hazel Green, Ky.

1. Napoleon Boneparte Graham, married 2nd; Angeline Lacy, a sister to his first wife daughter of Moses B. Lacy - Nov. 29, 1888. To this union was born seven children: 1. Arthur; 2. Dillard; 3. Berlin; 4. Victor; 5. Ada Rice; 6. Virgil; 7. Thelma.

1. Arthur Graham, born 1889 attended school at Hazel Green Academy. Taught school in Morgan and Wolfe County. Then went to Benson, Vermont and worked in a dairy and was promoted to Superintendent of a dairy and show cattle business. He never married - died 1934.

2. Dillard R. Graham, born 1890. Attended Hazel Green Academy, entered the Army in 1917, had a disability discharge in 1918. Married Exie Fields, to this union was born three daughters: 1. Wanda Lee; 2. Dixie Carolyn; 3. Marcella Graham.

3. Berlin Graham attended H.G.A. and went to Benson, Vermont, to work in a dairy. Became Superintendent of fine show cattle. Married and to this union was born two girls: 1. Dorothy Graham, now in Benson, Vermont: 2. Frances Graham, now in Louisana. She married Joe Coppinger from Mass.. 4. Virgil Graham attended H.G.A. and is a farmer - never married. 5. Ada Rice Graham attended H.G.A. and Eastern State College. Taught several years, and married M. A. Mann and settled at Dan, Ky. To this union were born four children: 1. Elenor; 2. Majory 3. Randolph; 4. Aleta Jane Mann. 6. Victor Graham died in childhood.

7. Thelma Graham attended H. G. A. She married Tinsley Walters. To this union were born five children.

No. 2-1: Joseph Douglas Graham and Jane Little Graham's children:

1. Napoleon Boneparte   M. 1st Hannah Lacy
2. Thomas   M. Zarilda Fallen
3. Elizabeth   M. Matt Bowman
4. James Douglas   M. Miss Mary Graham (Daughter Thos)
5. Lethia   M. Charles Pratt
6. Merrill (Dr.)   M. Miss Walker-Went to Texas

7. Dillard   M. Mattied Pennington, 2nd America Kelly
8. Luther (Martin Luther)   M. Julia Williams (Widow of Ely)
9. Sarah E.   M. Granville Bach-To Texas
10. Lilbern   M. Nannie Little (Daughter of Rev. James Little)
11. Nannie (by 2nd wife)   M. Dan Stamper-2nd Grant Dennis

We have already given part of the family of Boneparte Graham so will begin with:

No. 2 — Thomas Graham (Son of Joseph D.) Married Zerilda Fallen. They settled on Gilmore Creek and reared ten children: 1. Buren; 2. Moody; 3. Bertha; 4. Alice; 5. Maud; 6. Rosco; 7. Joe; 8. Edgar; 9. Virgil 10. Fannie.

In 1894 they moved to Lancaster, Texas. Their five daughters were teachers and home makers. Buren and Edgar were graduates of the St. University of Austin, Texas. Buren served 14 yrs. as Supervisor of Education in Phillopine Islands for U.S. Government.

3. Elizabeth Graham married Matt Bowman and settled at Athol, Ky. They were farmers and raised a family of six children as follows: 1. Alice Bowman, a teacher, married Squire Kash, a farmer and from this union there were five children: Roscoe; Beatrice; Homer and Matt. Roscoe Kash was the youngest graduate at the University of Kentucky at the time of his graduation and completed his medical college and is now a Physician in Tennessee. Homer Kash is a county officer in Lee County. 2. Calla Bowman, a teacher, married Elisha L. Noble, a teacher and farmer. To this union were born six children Livingston and Virginia are both graduates of the University of Kentucky. Other children are farmers.

3. Lela Bowman, married Roy Hurst both of them are teachers and also do some farming. They both attended H. G. A. and they live at Hurst, Wolfe County, Kentucky. They have two children.

4. Bedford Bowman married Mary Creech and settled at Athol, Ky. and reared five children and moved to Michigan where they are in the Insurance business.

5. Joe Bowman married and has a family residing at Athol, Ky.

6. Charley Bowman, a farmer married — Lovelace and they had two small children, he died when the children were very young. Homer Bowman.

4—James Douglas Graham (Son of Joseph D. Graham) was born at Gilmore, Ky. Te attended grade school and H. G. A. He taught school in Wolfe County for a time, then went to Virginia to continue his education He met Miss Mary Graham and married. They both taught in Virginia then moved and settled in Hunt County, Texas. To this union were born three children:

1. Olen graduated from Kansas State Agricultural College. He was employed by the government in agricultural work for several years, and is now in the gas business in Wharton, Texas.

2. Era Graham graduated in a college in Greenville, Texas, and married and raised two children.

3. Henry G. Graham (son of James Douglas and Mary Graham) was educated in Greenville, Texas and has not married.

5. Lethia Graham (daughter of Joseph D.) married Charles Pratt and to them were born two children: Clarence and Mary Pratt.

1. Clarence Pratt married Mohalia Rose. They were in the Mercantile business and raised a family—now live in Cleveland, Texas.

2. Mary Pratt married and raised children but no further record.

6. Merrill Graham (Dr.) (son of Joseph D.) attended school and went to Texas where he married—no further record of him.

7. Dillard Graham (son of Joseph D.) attended school at H.G.A. He taught school in Wolfe County, Ky., awhile then went to Virginia. He married Mattie Pennington and settled in Pennington Gap, VaA. Dillard Graham went into the mercantile business. After his first wife died, he married America Kelly, a teacher to them were born four boys: 1. Bordon; 2. Edd; 3. Roy; 4. ———————?

1. Bordon Graham married and has one son. They now live in Pennington Gap, Va.

2. Edd and Roy are in business. They were all educated in Pennington Gap, Va.

8. Luther Graham (son of Joseph D.) attended school and married Julia Williams. They had one son: James Graham who died very young.

9. Sarah (daughter of Joseph D.) Graham, born on Gilmore, Creek, Ky. and attended grade school. Then went to Virginia after the death of her Mother, stayed with her brother and attended high school. She taught school in Wolfe County. She married Granville Bach and moved to Texas. She hadone son, Edwin Bach, who served in the U. S. Army in World War I. He is now employed in the United States Postal System in Dallas, Texas.

10 Lilbern Graham (son of Joseph D.) was born at Gilmore, Ky., and attended school at Hazel Green Academy, taught in the rural schools in Wolfe County. He married Nannie Little, daughter of Rev. James Little, a Presbyterian Minister. They both taught school and settled on a farm at Gilmore, Ky. He later moved to Lancaster, Texas, where he was PostMaster for fourteen years. They are both living—she is about 83 years of age and he is 91 years of age. To them wer born five children: Edna; Mattie; Mickel; Elsie and Flora Graham.

1. Edna Graham graduated at Lancaster, Texas High School and attended College in Dallas, Texas. She taught school a few years and married James Fitzpatrick. They had no children.

2. Mattie Graham graduated in Lancaster High School and attended College. She married but reared no children.

3 Mickel Graham graduated at Lancaster High School and was in the lunmber business. Married and had a son and a daughter.

4 Elsie Graham graduated in high school and attended business college. She worked in Postal Service. Married and had one son.

5 Flora Graham graduated in high school and Teachers College taught several years.

11. Nannie Graham (by 2nd wife) married Dan Stamper and they had one daughter born after her father's death. Named Dannie Stamper. Nannie later married Grant Dennis and died leaving small children.

10. Lilbern Graham is the last of Joseph Douglas Graham's children living. He is now ninety one years of age.

To return to the family of Napoleon Bonepart Graham's family— we will continue to list the children and bring them down to date.

By his first wife, Hannah Lacy:

1. Paris Morton Graham, born November 30, 1876 attended grade school. He married Eivira Spencer, March 25, 1897 and settled on a farm. To them were born ten children:

1. Maud Ethel Graham, born February 27, 1898, married Stewart Phelps and live in Lexington, Kentucky. Maud is Chief Operator of the Traffic Department of the General Telephone Company of Kentucky, having served with this Company for 42 years. They had two children: 1. Harold Porter Phelps, born November 4,1918, married Lillian Adams, January 6, 1946, and have one child, Barbara Allen Phelps—now living in Idaho. Harold Porter Phelps was a Prisoner of War under the Japs during World War II for about 3 years.

2. Earl Allen Phelps died at the age of thirteen months. He was born April 9, 1921 and died April, 1922.

2. Winnie Christine Graham, born May 20, 1899, married David Massie and they have three children: Cora Bell Massie married Paul Martin; Mildred Massie married Paul Locknane; Buddy Massie died at age of 3 years.

3. Della Leona Graham, born August 13, 1900, married Joseph M. Hillard and have one son: George Elmer Hillard, after one year in college enlisted in the Air Force and was killed during World War II.

4. Flora Etta Graham, born February 12, 1904, married William Couch no children.

5. Fairliee Graham, born May 7, 1909. Died at age of 6 years.

6. Mattie Lee Grahm, born March 22, 1817, married John F. Berry and had one son, Mark Spencer Berry.

7. Allie Lee Graham, born March 22, 1917, (twin to Mattie Lee) Died.

8. Troy Graham, born May 8, 1902, married Nannie Venable— no children.

9. Paris Graham, born November 8, 1906, married Sadie Howard and have one son, Michael Graham.

10. Rebecca Russell Graham, born March 30, 1920, married William Walk and have one daughter, Mary Alice Walk.

Dillard R. Graham (son of N. B. Graham) married Exie Fields and had the following children:

EARLY AND MODERN HISTORY

1. Wanda Lee Graham attended H.G.A., married William Rice, a farmer who served two years in Military training. To them was born one daughter; Linda Kay Rice.
2. Dixie Carolyn Graham, a graduate of H.G.A. and attended Morehead State College. Married Talmadge Lee Davis, who is now serving Military training.
3. Marcella Graham is now a student at Hazel Green Academy.
1. Eleanor Mann (daughter of Ada Rice Graham and M.A. Mann) attended H.G.A., later attended Lee's Junior College at Jackson, Kentucky, and Morehead State College. Taught school and married Troy Bach, Jr., and they have one son; Mical Steven Bach; and one daughter; Rice Bach.
2. Majory Mann attended Frenchburg High School. She was married to Clarence Wells and from this union wer eborn a daughter, Brenda Lou Wells, they now live in Ohio.
3. Randolf Mann (son of M. A. Mann and Ada Rice Graham) a graduate of Frenchburg High School and Morehead State College has just completed two years Military Training, and is now working on his Masters Degree.
4. Aleta Jane Mann (daughter of Mr. ad Mrs. M.A. Mann) is now a Senior in Frenchburg High School.
1. Thelma Graham married Tinsley Walters. To this union were born five children:
1. Kenneth Walters attended High School and Industrial Training. He is married and has three children.
2. Milicent Walters (daughter of Thelma Graham and Tinsley Walters) attended High School and is married and has one daughter.
3. Alegra Walter, a graduate of Frenchburg High School. She married Phillip Mitchel. They have one daughter.
4. Lenore Walters, a graduate of Frenchburg High School and married a Soldier of the U. S. Army.
5. Arthur Walters in Grade School in West Manchester, Ohio.

Compiled and copied by Mrs. Wm. Everett Bach, Lexington, Ky. from Data submitted by Mrs. Phelps and Mrs. Rebecca Russell. July 6, 1956.

Three brothers Jessie Graham, Tom Graham, and William Graham came to America from Scotland in 1805. Jessie was born in Scotland in 1792; William in Ireland about 1795; and Tom's birth date and place of birth is unknown. Two of the brothers Jessie and William upon their coming to America settled in the Powell Valley. Lee County, Virginia. Jessie Graham married a Spencer, as a result of this marriage five children were born, Jane, Paulina, Elizabeth, Joe and William. Shortly after William was born about 1832, Jessie and his wife both died. The family migrated to eastern Ky.

William Graham volunteered for service in the Civil War and served with the 8th Kentucky Volunteer Infantry Division. About

1860 he married Sarah Terrill a daughter of Hazekiah Terrill who was an early survey in Kentucky. As a result of this marriage Timothy Graham, John Graham, Fannie Graham, Jane Graham, and A.R. Graham were born and each living to be of old age and reared large families. Timohty Graham married Ellen McPherson and they had 10 children. He died in July, 1910. Their children were: Bill, George, Sarrah, Lillie, Bertha, Amos, Pearlie, Taylor, Rich and James Douglas. A.R. Graham married Addie Williams. They had three children —Golden, Opsa, and Orphas. Both of the girls attended the conservatory of music in Cincinnati, Ohio, and Golden graduated from this institution. Elmer Graham was born to Amos by previous marriage. Amos is the only son of William and Sarrah who is living. At the present time he and his wife are residing in Cynthinana, Kentucky. Jane Graham married a Dunnigan and reared a large family. They are living in Ashland, Kentucky. John married a Holland but there were no children. He died several years ago at Mt. Sterling, Ky. Fannie married a Brewer and they had several children.

William Graham, one of the three brothers who came directly to America from Scotland, settled near Rose Hill, Lee County, Va. Several hundred of his descendents continue to occupy this area due to the work of them The Rose Hill School was established which is now known as the Rose Hill High School.

William was married to a Duff and later a Newland. There were children in both marriages, but I was unable to get and account for them. The descendents of Henderson Graham evidently are among the Graham's who are living in Virginia. John, another of the son's of William, married America Pennington and they had ten children: Mary Pennington, Henry B., Tmohas P., Joseph F.,

Sarrah, Martha, R. L. Charles Madison, John Patton, and America Jane. Several of these children left Virginia and came to Ky.

One of Henry's sons is teaching French at the University of Virginia. Joseph was a Methodist preacher; Thomas a teacher in Rose Hill School; Ether Hamilton was a teacher at Lincoln Memorial University; and Paul Graham a physician in Cincinnati, Ohio. Palmer Graham is Dean of Mathmetics in New York University.

The other of the original sons from Scotland Tom Graham went to North Carolina and settled there about 1810. I know nothing of his family.

J. Douglas Graham youngest son of Timothy and Ellen Graham, is a graduate of the law school at the University of Kentucky. He married Laura Brewer and they have four children.

Joyce who is a senior at the University of Kentucky.

Jean, who is a junior at the University of Kentucky.

Faye and Patty are both small daughters in grade school.

Mrs. Graham is a teacher in the grade school at Campton where she has taught for several years. Mr. Graham is Commonwealth attorney for this District and has been practicing law since he was graduated from law school in 1939.

EARLY AND MODERN HISTORY

FOREWORD

"Yes," I wrote Mrs. Cecil, "I will submit material for the Wolfe County History on the O'Hairs, Trimbles, Mizes, Gibbses, Days, McLins, and other related family branches."

At that time I did not realize what lay ahead of me; soon I found out! My search has taken me from Massachusetts to Florida, through Virginia and Kentucky, across the Middle West, to California and the coast of Oregon. Truly, it has been a labor of love for my people -- those who have gone on before, those who are, and those to come.

Throughout this compilation I have tried to eliminate inaccuracies. I shall be grateful to be informed of any that exist.

I wish to thank all who have helped along the way; indeed, the tie of kindred love is great.

This section of the Wolfe County Woman's Club book is dedicated to the precious memory of my beloved parents, Robert Joseph McLin and Lillie Day McLin.

Sincerely submitted,
Irene McLin Keller

THE O'HAIR FAMILY

In the fall of 1956 the following information was received for The Wolfe County History.

1. "My great grandfather was Michael O'Hair. He came from Ireland. He was born on September 11, 1749. He died in 1813."

This statement was submitted by James S. O'Hair of Laurel through Mrs. Rollie Gibbs, the former Rausa O'Hair, of Gillmore. No longer do the decendents of Michael O'Hair need to wonder about the date of his birth. This 1749 date is substantiated; it is correct.

One family record says, "Michael O'Hair came over from Ireland in 1757." If so, he was, at that time, eight or approximately eight years old. I do not know. However he did spend some of the formative years of his life in Virginia.

During this pre-revolutionary period there appears to have been a first marriage. To Michael O'Hair and this wife whose name has not been established there were born, according to at least two family records four children.

2. Michael — 1774; John — 1778; Jes — 1780; and Elsbery — 1782. All of these sons may have been dead by 1810. Whether they played any part in the history of Wolfe County is unknown. Apparently the first wife passed away soon after the death of the last son.

While the Revolution was in progress, Michael O'Hair enlisted with Virginia troops. Records of the military payments which were made to him show that he was in service during the time of some of the decisive battles of the war. (Records – National Archives and Record Service, Washington, D. C.; also War Paper 5, page 27 and page 148–Virginia Historical Society, Richmond, Virginia.)

In the summer of 1783 Michael O'Hair was either the Michael Oharro or the Michael Oharrow who collected the balance of his army pay in Virginia. At different times each of these two men used still other spellings for his Irish surname. Our spelling of the word O'Hair is an Americanized form of these Irish variants of this name.

Michael O'Hair was a taxpayer in Botetourt, County, Virginia in 1784. By then he was the husband of Elinor Hawkins. Both had been residents of the same parish in that county.

This couple yielded to the come-hither of the transylvanian call and emigrated to what is now Jessamine County, Kentucky. Some of their four children — Sarah, Betsy, Thomas, and Katy — may have been born in Virginia.

2. Sarah (Sally) married James Miller and located near Hazel Green, Kentucky, where they lived for a number of years before moving to Edgar County, Illinois in 1834. There were ten children

3. Daniel, Robert, and William Miller died before marriage.

3. James (1825-1906) married Cerilda Sims (1840-1899) of Montgomery County. They settled in Lllinois. Their son James William (1862-1934) married Belle Turner, the daughter of James S. and Lizzie Trimble Turner. (See the William Trimble family.)

3. Betsy married James Nickell, a brother of Andy Spaniard, who lived near Hazel Green. (Andy Spaniard Nickell was the father of the late Mrs. Hollis Gibbs of Gillmore.)

3. Patsy married Isaac Ellenge, a minister of the Christian Church.

3. Eliza married Mr. Porter.

3. Evaline may not have married.

3. Mary Ellen married a Mr. Sims.

3. Silby married a man from West Virginia.

2. Betsy, daughter of Michael O'Hair married William (Billy) Cree. His surname may have been spelled Crea. This couple lived in the neighborhood of Hazel Green and had two children.

3. Thomas, their son, died without issue.

3. Sally, their daughter, married a James Kash on March 20,1827. (Marriage Book 1—Morgan County, Kentucky.) They lived on Black Water Creek in Morgan County and reared a large family. They moved to Missouri about 1865.

2. Thomas, the son of Michael O'Hair, was the husband of Rachel Janes (or Rachel James.) She was born in 1790 and died in 1835. Their marriage date was October 24, 1810. (Floyd County, Kentucky.) After a time they moved to Illinois to take up a land claim, which Thomas O'Hair had previously surveyed. Their seven children were

EARLY AND MODERN HISTORY

Mary (Polly), Eleanor, Lydia (or Dydia), William, Jonathan, John and Clarisa. After the death of his wife, Thomas O'Hair moved to Texas. He was quite a horseman; as a surveyor and marksman in the wesetrn wilds, he enjoyed life immensely. He died in 1851.

2. Katy (or Caty) O'Hair at the age of thirteen married James Campbell and went to the Purchase Territory of Kentucky. Michael O'Hairs signature—Mical ohare—appears on her marriage permit at Nicholasville, Kentucky. This document was located by Adin Baber. (Conversational record of Nelson T. Jones with J. Green Trimble; Adin Baber: Ruth Frey).

Following the death of his second wife, Michael O'Hair married an orphan, Elizabeth Tribett, who had previously come from Virginia with a Mrs. Cooper, a widow. This woman and Elizabeth lived about four miles south of Mt. Sterling on Green Briar Creek. The O'Hair wedding took place on April 4, 1793. This Clark County record, which was discovered in a book of early Kentucky records by Nelscn T. Jones in 1928, was located at Winchester by Jesse D. Kash, formerly of Hazel Green. On this marriage rite Michael O'Hair's name appears as Mihal OHorow.

After living near Mt. Sterling for a few years Michael and Elizabeth O'Hair moved their growing family to a log cabin, which was situated on a tract of their mountain land at the mouth of Lacy Creek near Red River in the vicinity of the present town of Hazel Green. At that time only a dozen families were living in a radius of twenty miles. In later years a grandson, J. G. Trimble, wrote, "I remember well the location of the house and its surroundings and equipment including a little spinning wheel and big wheel, warping bars, reels, handloom, winding blades, trackle spools, and wool cotton cards." These necessary articles were used in every well-organized home "in the manufacture of tow and flax linen, blankets, linsey, flannel and jeans which were converted into clothing for the family." An old well that was dug by the O'Hairs still marks the site of their mountain home."

In 1813 a homemade coffin was lowered into a tree-shadowed grave on a "then beautiful and elevated eminence" across from Swango Springs in the vicinity of Hazel Green. Michael O'Hair, the Revolutionary Soldier, had passed into the Great Beyond.

His wife and ten children survived him. Another child had died in infancy. From morning until night Elizabeth O'Hair labored diligently for her family. Her later marriage to Josiah Bryant was not successful, so she resumed the name of O'Hair.

In her last years she made two horseback trips to Illinois and Indiana. Even as far back as 1894 J. G. Trimble said that he knew not any of her female decendents would even think of performing such a feat!

In 1839 this woman, who had known in her seventy-one years

every hardship of mountain living, passed away at the home of her son, James, in Putnam County, Indiana. She was interred at Brick Chapel Cemetery near Greencastle. Some year ago three of her decendents, Frank Trimble O'Hair, Jim Swango, and Fred O'Hair, were instrumental in having a suitable monument placed at her grave. On this great rough boulder with its stern type of rugged beauty are two plaques. One honors Elizabeth the Pioneer Mother; the other pays tribute to her husband, Michael O'Hair, Soldier of the Revolution, who died at Hazel Green, Kentucky.

In 1956 another decendent, Mr. Karl O'Hair of Paris, Illinois, conceived the idea of honoring Michael O'Hair in an appropriate monumental way. Through his efforts, the remains of the Revolutionary soldier were removed to the Hazel Green Cemetery. Assisting Mr. O'Hair in his project are two other O'Hair decendents—Myrle Lycan O'Hair (his wife) and Mr. Adin Baber of Kansas, Illinoiis.

On May 26, 1957, a memorial service for Michael O'Hair will be held at Hazel Green, Kentucky. At that time there will be a dedication of the revolutionary monument which has been given by the Government of the United States of America. By this stone will be a family plaque of honor. The original sandstone marker, which was found in a pile of discarded stones by Adin Baber and taken to Illinois in 1940, will be brought back to Hazel Green to become the footstone for the new grave of Michael O'Hair.

THE MICHAEL O'HAIR FAMILY

To Michael and Elizabeth Tribbett O'Hair were born eleven children, -- Sibby, John, Eleanor, Nancy, Michael, James, Washington, Harrison, Mary, Rose Ann and William.

2. Sibby, who was born on February 4, 1794 on Slate Creek in Montgomery County, Kentucky, was about six years old when she moved to Lacy Creek with her parents. She became the wife of William Lacy, who was an elder in the Hazel Green Christian Church for over fifty years. This couple made the confession of their faith during a revival which was conducted at Hazel Green around 1829 by the Honorable Raccoon John Smith, that great evangelist of the Christian Church. They were among the first converts to this faith in Eastern Kentucky.

Aunt Sibby was a mid-wife, and for a time she was the only general doctor for miles around Hazel Green. Most of her medicinals were made from her own boiled concoctions of native herbs. She made "her incessant missions of mercy without money and without price."

William and Sibby Lacy had no children but they took into their home a number of orphans-possibly ten or twelve-and were loving parents to them.

William Lacy, who was born on May 29, 1790, passed away on June 2, 1878. Aunt Sibby followed on June 20, 1881. (References—Ruth

Frey; Adin Baber; James I. Hollon).

2. John O'Hair (September 25, 1796,—June 17, 1886) married Eliza Hardwick on October 20, 1830. According to J. Green Trimble her parents lived in the vicinity of Hazel Green. John and Eliza moved "west" and settled in Edgar County, Illinois. They had nine children.

3. John Henry, Michael Elsberry, Wiliam Henderson, Mary Florence (called Polly), James Junior, Sarah, Calvin, Nelson, and Jesse Ogden.

The late Frank Trimble O'Hair, a son of John Henry and Nancy Evaline Swango, was an eminent attorney and congressman. (See the Caroline Trimble Swango Family.)

Louanna Frazier, a daughter of Mary Florence, who was called Polly, married John F. Jelke, the oleomargarine manufacturer, of Chicago. She made one of the largest contributions for the Elizabeth Tribbett O'Hair monument in Lndiana.

Karl O'Hair who is sponsoring the Michael O'Hair memorial at Hazel Green is a great grandson of John and Eliza Hardwick O'Hair. His grandfather was James Jr. ("Little Jim") and his father was the late Herschal O'Hair. Mrs. Karl O'Hair is also an O'Hair decendent. (See TheMichael O'Hair Jr. Family.)

Mr. Karl O'Hair is manager and part owner of the Motor Finance Company of Paris, Illinois. Since 1948 he has been president of the school board in that city.

Grady O'Hair, the present postmaster of Paris, Illinois, is also a decendant of John and Eliza O'Hair.

2. Eleanor, another daughter of Michael and Elizabeth O'Hair, was called Nellie; she married William Trimble. (See "The Trimbles").

2. Nancy (1798-1872) married Jesse Ogden, a Kentucky relative of Mrs. Abraham Swango, the former Debbie Ogden, of Stillwater. The Ogdens settled near Paris, Illinois and became prominent cattle people. Jesse Ogden's motto was "Buy stock and let it grow." He also "grew" children—thirteen of them!

3. Jonathan, Stephen, John Preston, William, Sarah, Elizabeth, Lydia, Mary, Michael, Rosanna Sybira, Jesse and ——————.

Two present decendants of Nancy O'Hair Ogden are Mr. Robert Ellege of Paris, Illinois and Mrs. Jesse Carnes, who lives on a farm near that place.

2. Michael, son of Michael and Elizabeth Tribbett O'Hair, was born on July 10, 1801 and grew up on Lacy Creek. On November 16, 1820 he married Lucretia Boyles (Kentucky Record--Floyd County) After a time they followed the O'Hair trail to Illinois and helped to settle Edgar County. Here Michael established the first school and the first church. He "maintained a blacksmith shop at the side of the road where hundreds of movers stopped going west." (Adin

Baber) Michael passed away on March 16, 1875, and is buried in the old Swango graveyard in Edgar County. Michael and Lucretia Boyles had nine childrne.

3. James, Jack, Jesse William S., Daniel Boone, Eleanor, Elizabeth, Caroline, and Sibby.

Frank S. O'Hair, a grandson of the said James O'Hair (3) lives in Paris, Illinois, where he conducts a wholesale business centering around the selling of oil and gasoline. He is also a director of a bank and serves as on official of the annual Edgar County Fair. His late father, the honorable Zollicoffer O'Hair, married Mary "Mollie" Swango of Wolfe County descent.

A present day decendant of the said Jack O'Hair (3) through his daughter Ella is Myrle Lycan, now Mrs. Karl O'Hair of Paril Illinois.

2. James Edington, son of Michael and Elizabeth Tribett O'Hair was born on July 5, 1804 on Lacy Creek and passed away on July 24, 1899 in Putman, County, Indiana. When he was about fifteen he went to stay with a Mr. James Montgomery, who lived in a more settled part of Montgomery County. He fell in love with his foster father's orphan niece, Margaret (Peggy) Montgomery, and married her on March 5, 1825. Until the fall of 1829 they lived in a one-room cabin on a little hillside farm near the mouth of Frozen Creek, which was then in Estill County. Then J. G. Trimble says, "James and Peggy O'Hair moved to Illinois on horseback carrying all their worldly possessions and one child each—Asbury and Ellsberry." From Illinois they moved on to the wide open spaces of Indiana. Here James Montgomery became a successful farmer. He had Kentucky blue grass brought to Putman County; cattle grazers threatened to do something about it. "Well", says Adin Baber, "You know how much that bothered an O'Hair!"

By his first wife, Peggy Montgomery, James E. O'Hair had eleven children.

3. William Asbury, James Ellsbury, Greenbury Montgomery, John Tribbit, Eliza Jane, Bascom, Sarah Elizabeth, Robert Simpson, Celina Gibson, Sylvester Greenville, and Leroy Taylor.

By his second wife, Permelia Lockeridge, James E. M. O'Hair had two children:

3. Robert Leroy and Margaret Permelia.

Mr. Fred L. O'Hair, a son of **Robt. Leroy**, helped to sponsor the O'Hair memorial in Indiana. He served as president of the Central National Bank in Green Castle, Indiana for many years. When he retired his brothers, Robert, a former New York banker, became president.

2. Washington, another son of Michael and Elizabeth Tribbett O'Hair, went first to Illinois in 1836 and then on to the wilds of Texas. He was married twice. (Trimble Record) One of his children was named Robert; for a time he was in a store business in Illinois. The West agreed with Washington; when he died in 1910, he was

EARLY AND MODERN HISTORY

over a hundred. (Adin Baber).

2. Harrison, a twin brother of Washington, died in infancy. (Trimble record—N.T. Jones.)

2. Mary (Polly) O'Hair was born on July 25, 1809 near the present town of Hazel Green. When she decided to marry William Hanks, who lived in the same county, members of her family objected. William Trimble, her brother-in-law, offered to give her one of his most valuable slaves if she would call off her marriage. Polly married William Hanks on October 6, 1827; William Trimble sold Nigger Bo b for one thousand dollars!

About 1829 William and Mary (Polly) Hanks took up a claim of government land in Edgar County, Illinois. They farmed for a living; one cash crop was maple syrup and sugar. In later life William Hanks became a money-lender and at his death was the largest land-owner in Edgar County. Mary O'Hair Hanks passed away on August 26, 1901. William and Mary (Polly) Hanks were the parents of fourteen children.

3. Mary Ellen, Nancy Jane, J. E., Michael Asbury, Nelson Tribbett, Evaline, Caroline, Sibby Ann, Sarah Elizabeth, James Sylvester, William Washington, Henderson Jackson, Stephen Greenville, and Rosanna who died at age two.

Nancy Jane, the second child in the William Hanks family, married Jesse Swango, the son of Abraham and Debbie Ogden Swango of Stillwater, Kentucky.

Adin Baber who has given much O'Hair information for the Wolfe County History, was a son of Dexter Dole and Eva Parker Baber, a grandson of Adin and Mary Ellen Hanks Baber, and great-great-grandson of William and Mary "Polly" OHair' Hanks. He is a prominent cattleman in Kansas, Illinois. His wife was the late Lois Ann Shoot. Their two daughters are Nancy Shirley, now Mrs. John Kern of Bethesda, Maryland, and Alice Baber, who is on the artist's staff of McCalls magazine.

2. Rose Ann, another daughter of Michael and Elizabeth Tribbett O'Hair was born on June 9,1811. She became the wife of James Wells on September 5, 1829 (Morgan County record) They moved to Illinois. Rose Ann died there on November 18, 1894.

To James and Rose Ann Wells were born six children.

3. William, Frank, Nelson, Lucinda, Evaline and James.

After the death of her first husband, Rose Ann married Isaac Perisho. They had six children.

3. Emily J., John Ellsberry, Mary Eliza, Rosanna, Barbara, and Hiram.

One of Rose Ann's decendants through her daughter, Lucinda Wells Frazier, is Lawrence Frazier, an auctioneer. He operates the oldest community sales pavilion in Illinois.

2. William, the son of Michael and Elizabeth Tribbett O'Hair, was born on Lacy Creek in 1812. On September 2, 1830 he married Polly Nickell, who was born in the present county of Wolfe. She

was the daughter of John and Nancy Kash Nickell and the grand daughter of "the first" James Kash. (William O'Hair's decendants; a J. G. Trimble record.)

William and Polly O'Hair first located on Lacy Creek and then moved to Edgar County, Illinois. After three or four years William became so dissatisfied with prairie living that he traded his Illinois farm of one hundred and twenty acres to William Trimble, his brother-in-law, for a farm at Laurel Creek, Kentucky. In his leisure time William O'Hair enjoyed roaming over the hills with his hounds in quest of deer, fox, and other wild animals. This pleasant man of Union sympathy was assassinated in his front yard during the Civil War. The fatal shooting which was instigated by Southern bushwhackers, occurred at noon time on William O'Hair's fifty-third birthday in 1865. (A J. G. Trimble record.)

Polly Nickell O'Hair (1814-1895) was called "Aunt Pop." Most of the time after the untimely death of her husband, William, she lived on Laurel at the home of her son, Michael. James S. O'Hair, a grandson says. "Whenever Granny sat in a chair to comb her bright red hair it was so long that it would drop down and two inches of it would lay on the floor."

William and Polly Nickell O'Hair had fourteen children named Sylvester, Michael, John, Harlan, Sibby, Boone, Ella, Leyander, Houston, Eva, Green, William (called Will,) Marion, and Taylor.

3. Sylvester O'Hair married Lorena Combs of Kentucky and settled in Breathitt County. Because of his southern sympathies he fled from Kentucky to Illinois. He ran a store near the town of Paris and fiddled for many dances. He had two daughters, Rose Ella and Sibby.

4. Rose Ella was married twice. Her first husband was Walker Wallace; her second husband was a Mr. Doll. Several year ago she gave Adin Baber the correct date of Michael O'Hair's birth.

4. Sibby O'Hair, her sister, was also married twice. Charles Wallace was her first husband, and her second one was John Rahel.

3. Michael, the son of William O'Hair, was born in 1832. He was a member of the Christian Church. He lived on Laurel and did some surveying and school teaching. Wolfe County people called him "Uncle Mike." He spent the last ten years of his life in blindness; he died in 1923. Uncle Mike and his wife Victoria Conway, who passed away in 1946, had seven children.

4. Michael, Ella, John T., James S., Cleveland, Jackson and William.

4. James S. O'Hair, son of Uncle Mike, was born on Laurel on March 31, 1887. He married Emma, the daughter of John and Frances Hager of Trent, Kentucky on April 3, 1907. She was born on September 15, 1887. and died on October 21, 1941. James S. and Emma O'Hair had ten children.

5. John O'Hair was born on March 18, 1908. Dewa, the second

EARLY AND MODERN HISTORY

child lived from November 21, 1909 until September 11, 1910. Ola (April 29, 1912) became a Mrs. Lesley. Sarah, another daughter, was born on April 10, 1914; she married a Tibbs. May (June 6, 1916) is now a Mrs. Cundiff. Nora O'Hair Keeton, who was born on June 26, 1917 lives in Middletown. Martha (September 14, 1919) became a Mrs. Rhea. Priscilla (March 3, 1922) married a Curtis. Davie O'Hair liver from June 19, 1924 until May 20, 1927 Don O'Hair, a minister, was born on February 14, 1927.

Rev. Don O'Hair and his wife, Dorothy, live in Middletown; he broadcasts over W.P.F.B. each Sunday night. His sister, Nora Keeton, sings on the same broadcast.

4. Their father, James S. O'Hair, who had the exact date of Michael O'Hair's birth, married a second time. In July 1942 he became the husband of Ella Linkous of Wolfe County. They had one daughter.

5. Emma Jane O'Hair was born on June 16, 1943.

4. William O'Hair, another son of Michael and Victoria Conway O'Hair was born at Laurel on October 11, 1897. He married Jane, a daughter of Joe Lee and Rosann Ross of Wolfe County, on July 24, 1916. She was born on January 14, 1898 and died May 3, 1951. They lived on part of the old O'Hair farm at Laurel. William and Jane O'Hair had nine children.

5. Chester, an Ohio farmer, married Lizzie Lee Taylor. Robert, another son, is married and lives in Middletown. Hobert O'Hair became the husband of Lula Campbell Barnard O'Hair lives at Trent. Sibbie O'Hair is now Mrs. Frank Hobbs. Mary married Homer Lemley. Sarah became Mrs. Harrison Spencer. Vivian O'Hair works in Ohio. Opal, now Mrs. Jack Hollon, lives at Trent, Kentucky.

3. John, son of William and Polly Nickell O'Hair, was born in 1833. During the Civil War he was in Sherman's March. He married and lived on a dairy farm in Lincoln County, Kentucky.

3. Harlan O'Hair was born in 1835; he married Delia Chaney of Wolfe County and lived on Laurel. They had two daughters, Rausa and Eva.

4. Rausa married Rollie Gibbs, (See the Hollis Gibbs Family.)

4. Eva married Charlie Brewer, son of Newton Brewer of Rogers. Kentucky. He died in 1947. Charlie and Eva O'Hair Brewer had one son, Edward.

5. Edward Brewer lives in Middletown.

3. Sibby, the first daughter of William and Polly O'Hair was born in 1836. She took after her mother and had bright red hair. She left Kentucky to live with relatives in Illinois and Indiana. She married a Mr. Charles Leach. They are buried near Kansas, Illinois. Their three daughters were Grace Leach, Mrs. Robert Kennedy, and Mrs. Leonard Fuller of Terre Haute, Indiana.

3. Boone O'Hair (1838) went to Texas. He married and had a family.

3. Ella was born in 1839. At the age of thirteen she went to live with a relative in Indiana. She married a Mr. John Brewer.

3. Leander (1841) married and settled in Louisville, Kentucky.

3. Houston O'Hair (1842-1892) married and had one son, Ellsbery.

4. Elsbery O'Hair (1883-1955) is buried near Frenchburg, Kentucky.

3. Eveline (Evy) was born in 1844; she married Alec Baber and lived in Dow City, Iowa.

3. Green O'Hair, who was born in 1845, became a Southern sympathizer. He married and had one daughter. He died in Indiana.

3. William (Will) O'Hair was born in 1847. He married Susie Conway. She was a sister to Victoria Conway, who married his brother Michael. These O'Hairs lived in Wolfe County and had eight children:

4. Lizzie, Will Edward's wife; Willy who died at seven; Mary, James Risner's wife; John H. who married Lizzie Peck; Lula, the wife of Harsen Banks; Tom, who married Victory Hager; Boone, the husband of Kate Lawson; and Emma, who married Jack Hall.

3. Marion O'Hair, who was born in 1849, died when he was about twenty.

3. Taylor, the youngest child of William and Polly Nickell O'Hair was born in 1851. (References—James S. O'Hair, Mrs. Rollie Gibbs, Adin Baber.)

Irene McLin Keller, Compiler

Personal rights of all contributors have been respected.

The right to reproduce this chapter in printed form must be obtained through The Wolfe County Woman's Club with the permission of the said compiler.

THE TRIMBLES

Early in the eighteenth century—possibly in 1732—five Trimble brothers names James, Moses, John, David and Alexander emigrated from County Armagh, Ireland to America. They came over in their own boat and landed at Baltimore, Maryland. Established families appeared with some of these five imagrants, who may have settled in Pennsylvania, Virginia, Kentucky, and Ohio. The ancestors of these Trimbles had been Scotch Presbyterians.

The Wolfe County branch of the Trimble family is said to have been descended from David, one of the five immigrant brothers. Our Virginia ancestor, David Trimble (1760-1827), was the son of a James Trimble. I do not know what relationship existed between the said James Trimble (1735-1815) and David, the immigrant.

David Trimble, our ancestor, married Lucy Lacy, of Greenbrier County, Virginia (now West Virginia) on August 28, 1781. The county records of that period show the following marriages of four other Lacys ——

William Lacy to Martha Blankenship, July 3, 1786.

EARLY AND MODERN HISTORY

John Lacy to Sarah Porter, June 26, 1788.
Mark Lacy to Agness McDonald, November 21, 1785.
Pheby (Phoebe) Lacy to James Kash, December 17, 1791.

Some of these Lacys, if not all, played a part in the history of Wolfe County. (The given name "Lucy" and other Lacy data—Ruth Frey.)

In the fall of 1797 David and Lucy Lacy Trimble left Greenbrier County, Virginia (now West Virginia) to settle in the newly created county of Montgomery in Kentucky. Among the people in their traveling party were Lucy's sister, Phoebe, and her husband, James Kash, and James' brother Caleb. (See "Our First Kashes.")

The Trimbles located in the vicinity of Mt. Sterling, possibly near Jeffersonville (Ticktown). There they reared eleven children named Mark, William, Polly, Nancy, John Isaac, Lucinda, Louise, Jane Clark and Elizabeth. Three of these children who settled in the present county of Wolfe were Louisa, Elizabeth and William.

1. Louisa (1804-1890) married Solomon Cox. In 1837, according to J. G. Trimble, Solomon Cox brought five wagon loads of merchandise through Hazel Green on his way to Quicksand. His caravan created much excitement; some people viewed in amazement their first wagons!

Solomon and Louisa Trimble Cox are buried in the Hazel Green cemetery. (See "The Cox Family" by Mrs. W. E. Bach.)

1. Elizabeth, another daughter of David Trimble was, according to family tradition, the first wife of "the first" Caleb Kash. (See "Our First Kashes." Elizabeth and her husband lived at Daysboro, where she passed away at an early age. I do not know whether she left any heirs.

1. William, son of David and Lucy Lacy Trimble, was born in Greenbrier County, Virginia (now West Virginia) on January 12, 1787. At the age of ten he came to Montgomery County, Kentucky, with his parents.

When the War of 1812 came up, he enlisted and served as the bugller for his regiment. In later years he told his son, J. Green Trimble, that at the most crucial moment in the Battle of the Thames the silver tones of his bugle-horn gave his fellow soldiers encouragement and cheered them on to glorious victory.

On Novmber 15, 1814, William Trimble married Eleanor O'Hair, who was called Nellie. She was born on October 14, 1797, and was the daughter of Michael and Elizabeth Tribbett O'Hair (See "The O'Hairs.")

In 1815 William and Eleanor Trimble went to houstkeeping in a log cabin on a tract of land which he had previously bought for five cents an acre. This area embraced the lower part and about one third of the large bottom on Red River along with several thousand acres of hillside land. Between 1821 and 1823 he bought another tract of two hundred acres, which became the heart of the present town of Hazel Green, Kentucky. Here William Trimble built a large log house back in a pine grove across the street from the second site of the Hazel Green Christian Church on State Street. At a later date his house was weatherboarded. Today a lone pine marks the site.

William Trimble laid out thre village streets in his domain in 1825. Graduallly lots were sold and a town was built. In the interim the place was called Trimble's Store after its first business house. This log structure that was erected by William Trimble was on the Main and State Street corner, which is now the site of the May Restaurant. William Trimble finally named his town after Hazel Green, Alabama, and the luxuriant hazelnut bushes that covered a large part of the area.

He built up, according to J.T. Day, a lively trade in furs, peltries, and farm products. In addition he was a farmer, a cattle grower, a hog raiser, and a dealer in land and slaves. William Trimble, the founder of Hazel Green, was it sfirst postmaster. In this capacity he served for twenty-four years. By the time his village of twenty-seven lots had become an established town in 1849, he had amassed a fortune. William Trimble was not a churchman, but he donated land for the first churches in Hazel Green. The First Christian Church was located on a part of the Main and State St. lot which was used later for the J. T. Day Store. (Records—J.T. Day; J. G. Trimble.(

Thirteen children were born to William and Eleanor O'Hair Trimble. As they grew up, married each was the recipient of a handwoven coverlid. Some of these were made by slaves in the William Trimble spinning and weaving house. They carded the wool for the one that is called the Lizzie Trimble Turner coverlid. Later they tinted part of the wool with a blue dye, that had been made by "boiling down" certain berries. The center of this lovely old blue and white spread is a beautifully executed design of flowers, graceful leaves, and ferns. In between the year date of 1844 which is woven into each corner of the surrounding border is the respetitive pattern of a little church and a little school house with intervening trees. At least one of the coverlids displays the aristic handwork of Eleanor O'Hair Trimble, who passed away, on May 24, 1855. Ohers were woven by an old man who went through the country hauling a loom with seventeen treadles. Each of the existing coverlids is a prized heirloom of the descendant who owns it today.

The ravages of the Civil War, which spread over his little town, saddened William Trimble. He stooped with the years and walked more slowly.

On October 3, 1870, James Greenville Trimble wrote the following letter to his youngest brother, Frank, in Summerville Tennessee —

"It is my painful duty to announce to you the death of our father which occurred last night (Sunday) at a quarter before ten o'clock.

He suffered the most excruciating pain during the last three or four weeks; was conscious of his approaching dissolution, and was entirely resigned to his fate. He informed me nearly two weeks since that he would die on the day that he did. He will be buried tomorrow morning and his funeral preached at ten o'clock." (Letter —Ester Wilson.)

Thus passed away in his eighty-fourth year William Trimble, the founder of Hazel Green, Kentucky.

The thirteen children of William and Eleanor O'Hair Trimble were Evaline, Caroline, William Preston, David Shelton, James Greenville, Stephen Asbury, Emily Jane, Rose Ann, Louisa Jane, Mary Elizabeth (Lizzie), Nelson Harvey, Melissa, and Jay Franklin.

THE EVALINE TRIMBLE McGUIRE FAMILY

2. Evaline, the oldest child if the William Trimble family was born on January 14, 1816. She married James Felix, the son of James and Diadama Mann McGuire, on October 17, 1833. James Felix, who was called iJm, was born on November 17, 1804 and died in 1883. His father, James McGuire, had been the second settler in Lee County, and his Grandfather McGuire had been killed nithe Battle of Blue Licks.

Jim and Evaline McGuire lived for a time at Hazel Green; then they moved to St. Helens in Lee County. Evaline McGuire did all kinds of work in her marriage life. In 1846 when J. G. Trimble and his bride stopped to see her on their way to Hazel Green, they found her at her loom weaving a carpet.

As Aunt Evaline grew older she was not very steady on her feet so she made use of a walking cane. However, on each Sunday morning as she approached her church, she would pause, look around, and then hide her cane! She always hoped "her horse" would be waiting when she got back. (Laura McGuire).

Evaline Trimble McGuire died on February 20, 1899 and is buried at St. Helens in Lee County.

Jim and Evaline McGuire had eleven children—an infant who died; Greene, a confederate soldier, who was killed in battle; Simpson who died of injuries which he received in The Civil War; Felix; Fletcher; Bascom; Brutus, Cassisus; Caroline; Ellen; and Lou.

3. Felix, who was born on August 13, 1840 fought with General John Hunt Morgan in The Civil War. In 1871 he married Martha Payne Dixon of Maysville, and they lived at St. Helens. Felix died on July 19, 1911 and his wife passed away in 1929. They had seven children named George, Cassius, Walter Tearne, Simpson Kelly, Nellie, Roy Lee, and Sadie.

4. George W. McGuire, the son of Felix, lives in Denver, Colorado.

4. Cassius died in 1915.

4. Walter Tearne (called Turner) was born on December 7, 1876 and died August 18, 1952. He married Mary Graham Eaton, a daughter of J. B. and Lida Eaton of Clay City, on June 16, 1909. They had five children -- an infant son who died; Walter, a veteran of World War II and presently a resident of Denver, Colorado; James Felix (1918-1950); Kelly Martin, a veteran of World War II; and Ruth Graham McGuire, the wife of Lowell D. Puffenberger of Ashland, Kentucky and the mother of two children named Sue Graham and Lowell Dale, Jr.

Walter Tearne McGuire represented Wolfe and Powell Counties in the Kentucky Legislature in 1921. His wife, Mary Graham McGuire, who passed away in 1956, had been postmaster at Clay City.

4. Simpson Kelly, son of Felix and Martha McGuire, married twice. By his first wife, Bettie Cope, he had four children. By his second wife, Lillie Shockey, he had two children.

4. Nellie married a Mr. Craig and had three children.

4. Roy Lee died in 1931.

4. Sadie, the youngest daughter of Felix McGuire, married William E. Jackson and had two children.

3. Fletcher, another son of Jim and Evaline Trimble McGuire, was born on November 28, 1843 and died on December 2, 1895. He became the husband of Lou Ellen Swango. She was born on March 9, 1854 and died on July 30, 1890. (See "Our First Kashes—The Samuel Swango Family.") Fletcher and Lou Ellen McGuire lived on Broadway in Hazel Green. They had two children named Cora and Courtney.

4. Cora married Charles Andre, a native of Virginia and a bookkeeper in the J. T. Day store. After a time they moved to Morristown, Tennessee, where Mr. Andre engaged in a hardware business. They had eight children—Charles Junior, an infant who died; F. J. Andre, who became Vice President of the Kraft Food Company; Edward, a resident of Los Angeles; William, who lives in California; Robert F. of Clevelond, Ohio; Virginia and Evelyn, who died; Charles Jr. of Knoxville, Tennessee, and Katherine, now Mrs. N.H. Lewis of Glendale, California.

4. Courtney McGuire became a doctor; he practiced in Maysville, Kentucky for thirty-eight years. He married the former Lisa Lee Lindsay, a resident of Mason County, on December 6, 1911. Courtney McGuire, who was born on June 1, 1877, died on December 16, 1949. His widow, who was born on May 15, 1882, survives him.

Dr. McGuire gave a pulpit and altar set, which contains a pair of brass candlesticks, a flower stand, and a tall brass cross, to the Hazel Green Christian Church in memory of his parents, Fletcher and Lou Ellen McGuire.

3. Bascom, son of Jim and Evaline McGuire was born on March 9, 1848 and died on June 25, 1918. He married Laura Kash of Wolfe County on December 24, 1890. (See "The Hurst Family") She was

born on October 3, 1869. Laura attended Hazel Green Academy and began teaching school at the age of sixteen. For many years she has been a member of The Primitive Baptist Church. To Wolfe County she has been a loyal friend; to her family she has been a wonderful mother. Since 1918 she has been a resident of Jackson, Kentucky. Her eight sons are Bruce, Lindsay, Everett Hale (Ted), Wendell, Asher, Kash Trimble, Eugene and Alferd.

4. Bruce was born in Wolfe County on December 17, 1891. He is now a retired employee of The Carnegia Steel Mills in Pittsburg, Pennsylvania. On May 21, 1914, he married Nell Little of Jackson, Kentucky. They have three daughters—Elsie, Helen, and Nell.

4. Lindsay (December 12, 1893—February 28,1927) married Onie Sweeney of Prescott, Arizona on September 22, 1921. He died from liabilities incurred in World War I; his wife preceded him in death. Their only child, Evelyn Gene, was reared by her Grandmother McGuire.

4. Everett Hale (Ted) was born on August 22, 1896. He attended Hazel Green Academy and is Executive Vice President and Chairman of The Citizen's State Bank of Hazard, Kentucky. on May 1, 1923 he married Eula Hammons of Jackson and they have three children, Alice and E.H. Jr. (twins) and Jimmie.

4. Wendell (October 13, 1898) married Mrs. Geneva Rolph of Jackson in 1927. He has been a L.&N. Railroad Agent for many years. His four children are Mickey, Mary Jo, Laura Sue, and Bennie.

4. Asher (August 1, 1901) attended Berea College. He is a meat salesman for a Louisville Company and lives in Hazard. His wife, the former Pearl Combs, and he, are the parents of two children, Bobbie and Don.

4. Kash Trimble McGuire was born in Wolfe County on December 3, 1904. For the past twenty-five years, he has been employed in the Newport Steel Mills. He resides at Dayton, Kentucky.

4. Eugene, another son of Laura McGuire, was born in Wolfe County on Friday, June 28, 1907. He married Kathleen Morgan of Hazard and is a salesman for White Cross. He has three daughters, Mary Jean, Kaye, and Marcia.

4. Alferd Kash, the youngest son of Bascom and Laura McGuire was born on January 14, 1911 in Wolfe County. He graduated from Berea College and Georgetown College of Law in Washington, D.C. He is now doing research work in Arlington, Virginia. His wife is the former Mary Owen Lewis of Philadelphia.

3. Brutus, another son of Jim and Evaline Trimble McGuire, married Elizabeth Duff, a sister to the late Pocahontas Duff Combs (Mrs. A. T.) of Campton, Kentucky. They settled in Texas. Their six children were Ollie, now Mrs. J. P. Craig of Lexington, Kentucky; the late Brutus McGuire, a lieutenant colonel in Warld War II; Opehia (Hudgins) of Lexington; Henry (deceased); Hallie B.

McGuire of Cincinnati; and the late W. O. McGuire, who was a C.&O. railroad employee, of Ashland, Kentucky.

3. Cassius, a twin brother of Brutus McGuire, died at age eleven.

3. Caroline, a daughter of Jim and Evaline Trimble McGuire, married Captain Jim Beatty and lived at Beattyville. In 1877 Caroline Beatty passed away at the age of thirty-two. She left five small children named Hugh, Harlan Trimble, Lula, Lena, and Caroline, who died in early life. Lena, Lula (Blakey), and Harlan Trimble Beatty, a banker, lived in Beattyville.

3. Ellen, a daughter of Jim and Evaline McGuire, married Potter Duff. Carolee Duff Arnett of Lexington is a daughter.

3. Lou, another daughter of Jim and Evaline Trimble McGuire, never married. (References—Laura Kash McGuire, Mrs. Lowell Puffenberger, Carrie Mize, Mrs. Courtney McGuire.)

THE CAROLINE TRIMBLE SWANGO FAMILY

2. Caroline, the second child of William and Eleanor O'Hair Trimble, was born on October, 5, 1817 at Hazel Green, Kentucky, and died there on September 1, 1898. On March 5, 1840 she married a farmer, Stephen Swango (1818-1877). He was the son of Abraham and Deborah Odgen Swango of Wolfe County.

To Stephen (called Steve) and Caroline Swango were born nine children named Evaline, Emily Jane, Green berry, Zarilda, Rose Ellen, Elizabeth, Alice, Clara, and William Trimble. All were born at Hazel Green. Three of the Steve Swango daughters married three Pieratt brothers.

3. Evaline Swango (March 29, 1841) married John Henry O'Hair, a son of John and Eliza Hardwick O'Hair (See "The O'Hair.") Their marriage date was March 27, 1859. They settled in Illinois and had three children—Emeline (Emily) who married William Overstreet, Wigfall, and Frank Trimble O'Hair.

Wigfall's beautiful daughter Lucille made "the movies" and then married Mr. Albert Smith, the owner of the Company.

Frank Trimble O'Hair, a graduate of DuPauw University, became an eminent lawyer. He was the man who beat "Old Joe" Cannon for Congress.

3. Emily Jane, the second child of Caroline Trimble Swango, married W. F. Hanks in 1861. They moved to Missouri and had one son, James.

3.Green Berry Swango (1846-1926) married Eliza Jane Young (1846-1925) of Tazewell County, Virginia on August 26, 1869. They had become friends while Green Berry was recuperating, in the Young home, from wounds which he had received as a Confederate soldier. Theymad e their wedding trip on horseback to Hazel Green, Kentucky in five days.

Green Berry (Called G. B.) ran a store in Hazel Green; he served in th eKentucky Legislature; and later became Judge of Wolfe

County. In 1890 he was a member of the Constitutional Convention in Kentucky; from 1892 to 1896 he was a registrar in the State Land Officein Frankfort. In 1901 he moved his family to Montgomery County, Kentucky.

G. B. Swango was one of the three founders of Hazel Green Academy. Until the opening of this school his three sons, James Hugh, Charlie and Morton, had private tutoring.

4. James Hugh (1870-1937) was known as "Jim Swango" at Hazel Green Academy. While he was studying at Centre College, he won the National Oratorical Contest which was held in Chicago in 1893. He became a succesful lawyer and settled in Terre Haute, Indiana. Jim Swango and his wife, the former Elizabeth Williams of Paris, Illinois, had two children—James, a lawyer in Indiana, and Marion, who married a Mr. Johnson and lives in Florida.

4. Charlie Swango (1871-1901) died of pneumonia in Montana.

4. Morton Swango, who was born in 1872, married Miss Icy De Moss, an early music teacher at Hazel Green Academy, from Covington, Kentucky. They located in Butte, Montana. Some years later they sent Carl Mize of Hazel Green a picture of their three children, James Morton, Ann, and Jane. On the back was written, "Montana-Born but Kentucky-Bred!"

3. Zarilda, the fourth child of Stephen and Caroline Trimble Swango, married James Harmon in 1867 and moved to Warrensburg, Missouri. Their six daughters, Connie Roe, Myrtle, Stella, Grace, Alice, and Ethel, graduated from The State Normal College in Warrensburg.

3. Rose Ellen, the fifth child in the Steve Pieratt family, was born November 5, 1850. She married J. Morton Pieratt, son of Eli and Gilly Ann Pieratt of Ezel, Kentucky on September 18, 1870. They had three children—Steve, G. Berry, and Elizabeth.

4. Steve married Viccie Kendall and had two daughters, Gladys Pieratt White of Prestonsburg, Kentucky and Martha, who is now Mrs. James Nesbitt of Mt. Sterling, Kentucky.

4. G. Berry Pieratt married Annie Ross of Chicago.

4. Elizabeth (Lizzie) married Charles E. Duff of Montgomery County on September 24, 1900. They had met at Hazel Green Academy. "Lizzie and Charley" settled on a farm in Montgomery County. Their daughter Virginia, an honor graduate of the Mt. Sterling High School, graduated from the University of Kentucky with Distinction. She is th ewife of Sidney J. Calk of Montgomery County.

Charley E. Duff, a former student and friend of Hazel Green Academy, passed away on September 23, 1951. Not long before, this man and his good wife, Lizzie Pieratt Duff, had received the highest honor that can be bestowed upon a working farm family--The Master Farmer Award.

They had utilized a part of their 720 acres of farm land for high productive yields; they had developed a superior strain of cattle in their pure bred Whiteface Herefords and had sold breeding stock to customers all over the United States. They had shared their benefits with many people and with many organizations.

Today Hazel Green Academy looks at its herd of cattle; its ctation wagon; its scholarship fund; and remembers the gracious giving of The Charles E. Duff Family.

Through the years, The Hazel Green Churches also been a recipient of Duff generosity. The pews for the new auditorium are coming as a gift from Lizzie Pieratt Duff.

3. Elizabeth, the sixth child of Steve and Caroline Swango, was born in 1854 and passed away in 1831. Her husband, Raney M. Pieratt, died in 1888 while he was a member of the Kentucky Legislature.

4. Their daughter Clara, a graduate of DePauw University and the widow of John Levinge is presently in Mt. Sterling. Her daughter Ruth is dead. Her sons are Nelson Trimble Levinge and Colonel George Edward Levinge, a West Point graduate.

4. Buford, the son of Raney and Elizabeth Pieratt, died in 1910. He was the husband of the former Effie Maxey of West Liberty. They were the parents of two daughters—Elizabeth, who became Mrs. Charles Hawkins, and Lucille the wife of John D. Henry.

3. Alice, the seventh child in the Steve Pieratt family, married Tom Frazier in 1877 and lived in Illinois. They had two children named Will and Grace.

3. Clara (1858-1933) was the eighth child of Caroline Trimble Swango. She married Asa Pieratt in 1881. They lived at Mt. Sterling and had two sons, Raney and Dorsey, who are now dead. Asa Pieratt passed away in 1940.

3. William Trimble Swango, who was called W. T. and Willie, was the youngest member of the Steve Swango family. He was born in 1862 and died in 1934. W. T. married Ellen, the daughter of Jonathan and Annie Quicksall of Ezel, Kentucky, on January 1, 1885. They lived in or near Hazel Green until 1898. Their only daughter, Dora, married George Prentiss, a minister of the Methodist Church; they are now residents of Fort Meyers, Florida.

(References—Mrs. Charley Duff; Mrs. Carrie Belle Trimble).

THE WILLIAM PRESTON TRIMBLE FAMILY

2. William Preston, the first son of William and Eleanor O'Hair Trimble was born on October 6, 1818 and died March 15, 1905. He married Sarah (Sally) Kash on February 2, 1843. (Marriage date—Mrs. A. T. Stewart through Mrs. W. E. Bach). She was born December 11, 1821 and died September 16, 1895. One of Aunt Sally's Lacy Creek decendents has a pisture of her at her loom weaving. Several of her rare Adams' plates with red and green stylized leaves and flowers are still in existance. They came down through the Kash family and are now about one hundred and fifty years old.

EARLY AND MODERN HISTORY

The Preston Trimbles first lived on a Lacy Creek farm; later they moved to Hazel Green. Preston inherited nine farms from his father.

Just before the Civil War he bought a little colored girl, who was about four years old, for three hundred dollars. She continued to stay with the Trimbles after the War. They called her Nigger Ann. Her daughter, Kate, who lives near Mt. Sterling, came back a few years ago to visit the family.

Preston and Sally Kash Trimble had seven children named Angeline, Seaborn, Johephine, Mary Ellen, Rose, Frances, and Harlan.

3. Angeline, the first child, was born on March 3, 1844, and died on February 20, 1918. She married Stephen Porter James on June 29, 1865. He was born on October 25, 1840 and died on November 30, 1892.

Stephen Porter James was the son of Benjamine F. James, a Confederate soldier, who had fought with Lee at Appomatox, and his wife, the former Mary F. Scott. They came to Kentucky after the Civil War and were accompanied by their caravan of eleven children, of whom was Stephen Porter. A twelfth child was born in Wolfe County.

Stephen Porter James was killed by a falling piano, which he was helping to bring over the bad roads to Hazel Green Academy from the freight station at Torrent, Kentucky. Sometime after his death, Angeline and her children moved from Lacy Creek to State Street in Hazel Green.

The children is the Stephen Porter James family were Asberry Scott, James Foy, Mallie, Virginia, Shelly Preston who died in early life, Sheffie Porter, Howard, Eliza and Etta.

4. Asberry (Uncle Berry) was approaching his eighty-sixth birthday when he passed away in 1953. He was married three times; he had no children. After the death of his first wife, the former Mary Edwards, he married Rose Ellen Byrd. Fifty-three years later she was taken by death. Then "Uncle Berry" married Ella Caskey.

4. James Foy (Jim,) the second son of Angeline Trimble James was born on June 19, 1868. He married Alice Rose of Lee City and lived at Hazel Green. They had two sons, Stephen Porter and Cecil Cord.

5 Stephen Porter James married Mae Rose. (See The Joseph A. Rose Family.)

5. Cecil Cord James died in early life.

After his wife's death, James Foy James married Frances Sweeney and had two children—a daughter who died in youth and a son, Robert James.

5. Robert James married Estella Childress and lives in Middletown.

4. Mallie, the third child in the Stephen Porter James Family, was born on July 13, 1870 and died on April 25, 1939. She attended Hazel Green Academy and became a teacher. In 1898 she married C. E.

French, a former student of Hazel Green Academy, from Powell County. He was a minister of the Christian Church. Reverened and Mrs. French were residing in Illinois when he passed away. Their only son, Carlin Scott French, is a commercial artist in Chicago.

4. Virginia (Virgie), another daughter of Angeline Trimble James, was born on January 28, 1873 and died on May 16, 1917. On August 21, 1898 she became the second wife of John Henry Rose of Hazel Green. Mr. Rose was a carpenter and blacksmith; for many years he served as an elder in the Hazel Green Christian Church. (See The Robert Jefferson Rose Family).

5. Angalyn (Ann), their daughter was born on April 11, 1901. She married Courtney C. Wells, son of Benjamin Monroe and Martha Davis Wells of Morgan County on July 3, 1920. He was born on July 3, 1920. He was born on July 16, 1895. Courtney graduated from Hazel Green Academy with honor; he received his training in law at the University of Kentucky.

Angalyn and Courtney Wells have been residents of Hazard, Kentucky since 1921. Mr. Wells is presently a Circuit Judge. For twenty-five years Mrs. Wells owned and operated a retail wallpaper business. They had four children.

6. Edith D. and Courtney Juior died when they were small. John H. Wells (September 28, 1924-January 16, 1945) a soldier in the Infantry, Patton's 3rd Army, was killed in the Battle of The Bulge and is buried in the American cemetery at Luxenbourg. Harold Garland, their surviving son, was born on August 27, 1926. After military service in the Paficif area, re received his A. B. and L.L. B. degrees from the University of Kentucky. He has been a law clerk in The Court of Appeals at Frankfort.

4. Sheffie Porter, son of Steve and Angeline Trimble James, was born on November 7, 1878. He attended Hazel Green Academy and is a member of the Christian Church. He resides in Hazel Green at the home of his sister, Eliza James Arnett.

4.v Howard, the seventh child in the Stephen Porter James family, was born on April 17, 1880. After graduating from Hazel Green Academy, he worked in the Day-McLin Store at Torrent, Kentucky. Later he married Mary Brenamen and has been in a clothing store business in Charleston, Illinois for a long time. There are two daughters.

5. Gladys, now Mrs. Dale Armstrong, lives in Miami, Florida; Evelyn, now Mrs. Kenneth Wilson, resides in Charleston, Illinois.

4. Eliza, the eighth child of Angeline and Stephen James married E. A. (Coon) Arnett, son of Jeff and Rebecca Arnett of Salyersville. Kentucky on August 21, 1912. Mr. Arnett has been a carpenter and Hazel Green storekeeper. Mrs. Arnett assisted in the jot'em Down Store at Hazel Green Academy for twelve years. The Arnetts had four children—Leham, Lennis, Howard (1920-1921), and James.

5. Leham, who was born on January 12, 1914, is a graduate of Hazel Green Academy, a member of the Christian Church, and an Electronic Scientist at Wright's Field in Fairborn, Ohio. On February 5, 1943 he married Betty Lynch of Springfield, Ohio. Their daughter, Carol Louise, was born on December 18, 1945.

5. Lennis, a graduate of Hazel Green Academy, is the wife of Ralph Long of Middletown, Ohio. They live in Lexington, Kentucky where Mr. Long works in the field of air-conditioning.

5. James, the youngest child of Eliza James Arnett, married Adeline, daughter of Leonard and Ida Blankenship Neff, formerly of Hazel Green. They live in Terre Haute, Ind. where James has a dry-cleaning business. Their three children are Karen Sue, Jamie, and James, Jr.

4. Etta, the youngest child of Stephen and Angeline Trimble James, was born on April 11, 1884. She married James Amyx, son of Preston and Mary Ellen Hainline, formerly of Mt. Sterling, Kentucky on October 22, 1902. They live in Marshall, Illinois where Mr. Amyx works for the railroad. There are three daughters.

5. Virginia is now Mrs. Louils J. Doll of Marshall, Illinois. Mary Elizabeth, who married Carl Hutchings, lives in Martinsville, Illinois. Juanita Amyx is now Mrs. Keith C. Thomas of Whittier, California..

3. Seaborn, son of William Preston and Sally Kash Trimble, was born on November 24, 1848 and died on January 21, 1916. He married Emma, a daughter of Jordon and Juda Cox Wills, on February 8, 1871. (See The Willss Family by Mrs. W. E. Bach.) According to his decendents, Seaborn was a very humble man who never got in a hurry. He enjoyed deer and fox hunting and kept several hounds. Emma, his wife, who was born on January 31, 1853, died on April 20, 1929.

To Seaborn (W. S.) and Emma Wills Trimble were born five children names Sarilda Alice, Clarence, Jordon Green, Rose and James Calvin.

4. Sarilda Alice Trimble was born on January 6, 1872. She attended Hazel Green Academy; was a member of the Christian Church; and became the wife of James P. Lacy (1869-1953). Everbody called him Jim. He was the son of Green and Margaret James Lacy who lived on Lacy Creek. By trade Mr. Jim Lacy was a carpenter; by ability he was an exceedingly good one. Alice Trimble, his wife, was a fine seamstress; some of her "fancy work" took first prize at a Montgormery County fair. Her death occurred on December 3, 1896. Years later Mr. Jim Lacy became the husband of Josephine (Josie) Wheeler. Her father was Judge Wheeler of Hazel Green..

Jim and Alice Trimble Lacy had one daughter, Clemma Belle.

5. Clemma, who was born on August 26, 1894, attended Hazel Green Academy. On April 21, 1915 she married Alexander Thomas

(A. T.) Stewart, a son of William and Elizabeth Patton Stewart of Carter County. Mr. Stewart had formerly taught school and been police judge in Rowan County. He was a graduate of Bowling Green Law School; in 1910 he began his law proctice in Powell County. Mr. Stewart passed away in 1956 at the age of seventy-eight.

The Stewarts lived at Stanton, Kentucky where their six children, Virginia Alexander, Hazel, A. T., James (Jim), Ivan, and Hoover were born.

6. Virginia, who was born on February 28, 1916, is a graduate of Powell County High School and a member of the Christian Church. She had most of her college work at the University of Kentucky. From 1935 to 1941 she taught Home Economics at Hazel Green Academy. She is the wife of Charles Walker Prewitt. His parents Charles P. and Lora Walker Prewitt are now residents of Florida.

Charles Walker Prewitt hold an A. B. degree from Transylvania, a M. A. from the University of Kentucky, and an Ed. D. from Columbia. For some years the Prewitts have lived in Willimantic, Connecticut where Dr. Prewitt has taught Science Education at Willimantic State Teacher's College. In 1956 he received a Fullbright Lecture Scholarship for a year of work in Burma. His wife and sons, Charles Walker (Walkie) and David (Davie), are with him in Rangoon.

6. Hazel (May 14, 1917), the second daughter of Clemma Lacy Stewart, graduated with honor from Kentucky Christian College at Grayson, Kentucky. She is the wife of Thomas A. Dale, Minister and Professor of Speech at Kentucky Christian College. Their two children are Thomas and Dale. ?

6. A. T. Stewart (1918-1940) graduated with honor from Powell County High School. He was a senior at the University of Kentucky at the time of his accidental death.

6. James Lacy Stewart (April 26, 1920) is a licensed embalmer and funeral director. He married Elizabeth Hollon (See the Daisy Day Hollon family.)

6. Ivan Stewart (July 24, 1922) served as Second Lieutenant in Chemical Warfare Service in World War II. He received his B. S. and M. S. degrees in agriculture from the University of Kentucky and holds a Ph. D. from Rutgers University. In 1951 he joined the staff of the Lake Alfred Citrus Experiment Station. Since then he discovered that Yellow Spot, which caused decreased production in citrus trees, was due to a deficiency in molybdenum. "Not only did Stewart come up with a solution but he also discovered that a mere ounce of sodium molybdate in one hundred gallons of water would correct the condition." He has also found a corrective solution for iron chlorosis in acid, sandy soils. This specialized work in increasing the availability of fertilizer components to both soils and plants has made Dr. Ivan Stewart an outstanding bio-chemist.

He is the husband of the former Gladys White of Irvine, Kentucky, and the father of three children.

6. Hoover Stewart, who was born on July 18, 1928, was valedictorian of his high school class at Stanton, Kentucky. He received his B. A. degree with honor from the University of Connecticut and holds a M.S. degree from the same institution. At the present time he is working on his Doctorate in Science Education at Columbia.

On August 16, 1956 Hoover Stewart marrier Dorothy, the daughter of Henry Allen and Dorothy Skinner Stovall of Hazel Green, Kentucky. Dorothy is a graduate of Hazel Green Academy and Transylvania College; she has had special training in library science and is employed as a librarian.

4. Clarence, the second child of Seaborn and Emma Wills Trimble, wasborn October 17, 1874. He became the husband of Emma, a daughter of Newton Green and Susan Willis Maloney of Lacy Creek, an January 18, 1900. They live on a tract of a William Trimble farm. Clarence is a Democrat, a Mason, and a member of the Christian Church. Nine children were born at Lacy Creek, Kentucky to Clarence and Emma Trimble.

5. Emma Golden, the first child, was born on May 13, 1901. She married Jim Goin on June 15, 1918. They live at Irvine, Kentucky and have four chilldren—Howard, Virginia, James and Eddie Roy.

5. Beulah Fern, who became the wife of J. B. Hughes on November 26, 1932, lives in Florida. Her birth date was September 14, 1902.

5. Mazie, the third daughter, was born February 6, 1906 and married Evert Nickell in 1923. They had two children Evert and Margie.

6. Evert (Eddie) was killed in Germany in 1944 during the Battle of The Bulge.

6. Margie, his sister, docs missionary work in Texas.

Mazie Trimble's second marriage was to Lloyd McIntosh. She died on September 1, 1946 and is burried in the Trimble Cemetery on Lacy Creek.

5. Robert Bruce, the only son of Clarence and Emma Trimble, was born on January 25, 1909. He is a veteran of World War II. On December 18, 1948 he married Helen, a daughter of Alexander and Velma Kennard Davenport of Cincinnati, Ohio. Since 1950 they have lived on the Clarence Trimble farm, which was formerly an integrant of the Preston Trimble homeplace tract. Bruce is a Mason, a Democrat, and one of the progressive farmers in Wolfe County Helen, his wife, is his competent helper; she collected and assembled most of the family history for the Lacy Creek Trimbles. Bruce and Helen have one child.

6. Donna Sue Trimble was born on April 19, 1956.

5. Mattie Alice, daughter of Clarence Trimble was born on July 30, 1911 and died July 7, 1926.

5. Ruth Easter (April 4, 1915) married Carl Thomas, Gillen and lives in Cincinnati, Ohio. Their son is named Carl Thomas.

5. Ruby Christine Trimble, was born on November 18, 1916, married Harold Deatherage on May 31, 1941. They live in Erlanger, Kentucky and have two children, Carol Ann and Harold Bruce.

5. Marie (January 30, 1922) is now Mrs. Charles Edward Brown of Louisville. Her marriage date was December 1, 1942. The Browns have three children named Sandra Jean, Charles Edward, and Janet Marie.

5. Maxine, the youngest daughter of Clarence and Emma Maloney Trimble, was born on January 9, 1923. She is employed in Cincinnati.

4. Jordon Green, the third child of Seaborn and Emma Wills Trimble, was born on January 23, 1872 and died on December 20, 1930.

4. Rose, another daughter of Seaborn Trimble, was born on December 26, 1879. She married J. R. Brooks, whose parents were Erastus and Dorcus A. Brooks of Hazel Green, on September 6, 1918. They settled on part of a Preston Trimble farm on Lacy Creek. Their two children were India Alice and Robert Campbell.

5. India Alice Brooks (October 1, 1919) graduated from Hazel Green Academy. She is now Mrs. Kenny Moyer of Germanstown, Ohio. Her two children are Sharon Ann and Kenny Lloyd.

5. Robert Campbell Brooks (May 20, 1923) has been married twice. By his first wife Betty, daughter of Buford and Lula Brewer, he had one son, Michael. On September 10, 1953 Robert C. Brooks became the husband of Marie Center, a daughter of Fred and Mary Lou Center.

4. James Calvin (Jim) Trimble, the youngest child in the Seaborn Trimble family, was born on December 1, 1882 and died December 25, 1931. He married Lela, a daughter of Ira and Zarilda Proffit Day, and live on Lacy Creek. There were three children. On January 1, 1932, following her husband's death on Christmas Day, Lela Trimble passed away.

5. Toney (August 9, 1920), the oldest son, was reared by his aunt, Rose Trimble Brooks. His wife is named Josephine. They live in Middletown, Ohio.

5. James Ralph (September 1, 1929) was also reared by Rose Trimble Brooks. He married Gertrude, the daughter of Clarence and Ida Holland Cockerham, at Campton, Kentucky. They have one son, James Clarence.

5. Eunice, the youngest child of Jim and Lela Trimble, was born on September 8, 1931. She was reared in the Clarence Trimble home. On November 5, 1948 she married Austine Oldfield. They live in Middletown and have one son, James Bernard.

3. Josephine, daughter of Preston and Sally Kash Trimble, became the wife of Calvin Swango and lived at Hazel Green. They

had four children, Ida, Ava, Ora, and Erb.

4. Ida was the first wife of Will Cecil and had a daughter named Fern. Ava, the wife of a Dr. Fallen; Ora, who married Roy Finley, and Erb, who also married, settled in Texas.

3. Mary Ellen, a daughter of Preston Trimble, was killed at the age of fifty-seven in a home accident.

3. Rose Trimble, another daughter, was never married.

3. Frances Trimble, a daughter of Preston Trimble married Taylor Whaley, a carpenter, who had come from Cynthiana, Kentucky in 1884, to work on the J. T. Day home in Hazel Green.

4. Charles (Charley) Whaley, their son, is a veteran of World War I. He works in Perry County. His wife is dead. He has one daughter.

3. Harlan, the youngest child of Preston and Sarah Kash Trimble, became "Uncle Harlan" in Wolfe County. He was born on January 28, 1860. For about eight years in the last decade of the nineteenth century while Preston Trimble had the mail route from Hazel Green to Mt. Sterling, Harlan was his horseback mail carrier. Prior to this he had attended Transylvania College for two years; he had also taken time to make a covered wagon trip to Missouri with Jeff Nickell. Travel was a little slow; it took thirty days.

Uncle Harlan was a real fox-hunter and left many tracks on his farm. Time passed quickly for him for he liked to fiddle, play "setback," and relate mountain stories.

On April 14, 1888 he married Nannie, the daughter of Bennie and Polly Gilmore James. They lived on a Preston Trimble farm on Lacy Creek. Their only child Roxy Enith, who was born on October 1, 1891, died in 1906. Nannie James Trimble passed away in 1937 at the age of sixty-eight. Uncle Harlan followed in 1942. (J. G. Trimble, Jr., Mrs. E. A. Arnett, Mrs. Bruce Trimble, Mrs. A.T. Stewart, Mrs. Courtney Wells.)

THE DAVID SHELTON TRIMBLE FAMILY

In 1821 when the summer had come to Hazel Green, Kentucky, and the trees on Lick Branch stood like green soldiers high on the hill beyond Red River, another baby came to the William Trimble home. Yes, it was June—infact it was the twenty-third of June, and the baby was a boy—and the boy, perhaps on that very day, was named David Shelton Trimble.

The ways of the woods were in the heart of this hunter boy who grew up to be a farmer. On March 8, 1842 he went over to Stillwater and took Maria, a daughter of Abraham and Debby Ogden Swango for his wife. (See the Abraham Swango Family).

2. To Maria and David Shelton Trimble, who settled in or near Hazel Green, were born eight children.

3. Robert Letcher Trimble (November 30, 1842—April 24, 1909)

married Mary Ellen Honn of Illinois on September 9, 1875.

3. Mary Ellen, who was born on November 21, 1844, died on January 29, 1846.

3. William Taylor, another son, was born on December 22, 1846.

3. Kelsey Howard, who was born on October 7, 1849, died on October 27, 1850.

3 Henry Howard (1852-1941) lived in Missouri for many years.

3. James Jesse passed away in Missouri on February 21, 1879. His birthdate was September 5, 1854.

3. Daniel Boone was born on January 11, 1857. He settled in Middletown, Ohio and some of his decendants are living there at the present time.

3. Rosa Maria, the last child of David Shelton and Maria Trimble was born on December 14, 1858. She married Abraham Hybarger of Paris, Illinois on November 21, 1878 and lived there. She died on April 18, 1938.

After the death of his wife Maria, David Shelton Trimble married Thirza Matilda Catron, the daughter of Stephen and Emily Pool Catron on March 19, 1862. Thirza was born in Grayson County, Virginia on December 8, 1843, and died in Paris, Illinois on February 9, 1931. Her parents are buried in the Catron Cemetery near Pomroyton in Menifee County, Kentucky. She was a sister of William Catron, whose son Reece had a general store in Campton. Omer, Reeces' son is now a Campton merchant.

After the birth of their first child, Shelton and Thirza Trimble moved to the present county of Menifee where they had about a thousand acres of land rich with virgin timber. They lived near Marba and the place still bears the name of Trimble Bend.

According to Shelton Trimble's daughter, Nannie Frey, her father was fond of "water-melon-musk" melons and raised both. "He had two patches—one down under the hill in a sandy bottom for those who couldn't resist temptation and one down by the barn for his own use. Early every morning during the season it was his custom to pick the choice fruit, bring it to the house and cut it open for children to eat before they left for school."

A grand daughter, Ruth Frey, says, "Grandfather set out a large orchard of fruit trees on the hill behind the cabin, and when the apples were ripe, grandmother called in the neighboring women who peeled cut and dried apples for half of what they prepared." In Wolfe County terminology Ruth means "on the halves!"

Shelton enjoyed hunting and always kept a dog. He was a staunch Democrat and enjoyed a St. Louis paper which was sent to him by his son Franklin. At night "light was provided by a small brass lamp which he held as he moved it across the page as he read."

Shelton Trimble died on July 24, 1907 at the age of eighty-six and si buried at Hazel Green.

Of his eighteen children by his two wives, fifteen lived to be men and women. It has been said that David Shelton Trimble did not see all of the remaining together at any one time. Ten of "his eighteen" were by his second wife, Thirza Catron Trimble.

3. Mary Blanc (Blanche) was born in Hazel Green on November 30, 1863 and married John Bercaw on March 18, 1888 in Paris, Illinois. She died there on February 11, 1948.

3. Emma Jane Trimble (December 6, 1865—February 8, 1906) married Jesse, son of Samuel and Evelyn Kash Swango (See "Our First Kashes") and lived in Wolfe County. He was born on January 10, 1856 and died on October 15, 1917.

4. Ollie, the first child of Jesse ad Emma Trimble Swango, was born on January 1, 1886 and died on January 5, 1919. She married Will Kash and had two children—Irene, now Mrs. Leonard Slusher, of Jackson and Charles Kash, deceased. ("Our Firse Kashes"—The Hurst Family).

4. Mary, the second child of Emma Swango, was born on March 20, 1888, and was twice married. On March 15, 1937 her husband, Captain S. H. Hurst, passed away.

4. Lillie Swango (September 28, 1889) married G. B. Rose on March 6, 1908. They lived at Stillwater. After his death, which oc- March 15, 1936, she became the wife of Bill Burton of Magoffin County and lives near Campton. Lillie furnished the material on the Jesse Swango Family for this history.

4. Buford Swango, the first son in this family, was born on November 8, 1892.

4. Robert Swango was born April 11, 1897.

4. Emma, the youngest child in the Jesse Swango family, was born January 23, 1906. She married a Mr. McCoun but is now divorced.

3. Franklin Powell Trimble (1867-1946), the first son of David Shelton and Thirza Catron Trimble, became the husband of Eliza Bush in 1894.

3. Eliza Ellen Trimble died in 1883 at the age of thirteen.

3. Charles Nexbit Trimble who was born in 1872 died in California in 1946.

3. Nancy Elizabeth (Nannie) Trimble, the only living daughter of David Shelton Trimble, was born on March 27, 1874. She spent a part of childhood with her aunt, Lizzie Trimble Turner, at Mt. Sterling where she attended school. On May 1, 1895 she married Alfonso Frey. They live in Paris, Illinois and are the parents of four children— Leo, Marie Ruth and Raymond.

Leo, a wholesale groceryman and his wife, the former Dorothy Williams, live in Paris, Illinois. They have three children Robert

Allen, Elizabeth and Leo Shelton.

Marie, who had special training in music, served as a church organist for thirty years.

Ruth, who had her college work at Transylvania, is a former teacher and a complier of family history. She helped with the Catron branch of her family for the book **"The Kettenring Family in America."** She took the Wolfe County History "to heart" and contributed much helpful information.

Raymond, her other brother, married Virginia McKnight and lives in Chicago. He is the Treasurer of the Illinois Agriculture Association. His older son James graduated from Harvard College cum laude; his younger son Michael is studying in the same institution.

3. Thomas Turner, another son of Shelton and Thirza Trimble was born in 1876 and died in 1953. His wife was the former Lillian Henderson.

3. Robert Riddle Trimble (January 3, 1879) married Pearl Martin in 1908. They live in Colorado.

3. David Crockett Trimble (May 23, 1881) lives at Trimble Bend. He married Lula Kilgore who is now dead.

3. Bruce Harlan, the youngest son of Shelton and Thirza Catron Trimble, was born on December 23, 1883. His wife was Nettie Bowen. He died in 1933 and is buried near Slade, Kentucky. (References— Ruth Frey, J. G. Trimble, Jr., Lillie Rose Burton).

THE JAMES GREENVILLE TRIMBLE FAMILY

"If my coming child is a boy," William Trimble said to his Johnson County friend, Greenville Lackey, "you will have a namesake."

The son, who was born on June 15, 1823 did carry in his name the appelation of his father's friendship. He was called James Grenville, J.G. Green, and J. G.

In his youth, educational opportunities at Hazel Green were so meager that J. Green Trimble had only one to two months of schooling a year. Largely through his own efforts, he accumulated enough knowledge to become a versatile, well-trained man.

As a young man he hauled dry goods for his father's store from Maysville to Hazel Green in a wooden-wheeled wagon, worked for a time in Breathitt County and clerked in an Estill county store. For ten years during the postmastership of his father at Hazel Green, J. G. Trimble served as his deputy.

While he was employed in Estill County he fell in love with Isaac Mize's daughter, Nancy. (See "The Mizes") She was born on September 24, 1824. In 1841 she was baptized in the waters of the Kentucky River and became a member of the Methodist Church. On Monday evening April 27, 1846 she married J. G. Trimble. He had one horse, and a man whom he had befriended gave him another one, so Nancy the bride and he the groom rode horseback on a real bridle trip from Estill County to Hazel Green—a distance of fifty-five miles.

In 1847 J. Green Trimble's two-story log house, which was later weatherboarded, was ready for occupancy. It was located at Hazel Green in the pine grove across from the present J. T. Day home. The front yard gate was on State Street which had been named for the "Old State Road" that had been completed in 1836.

J. G. Trimble sold goods in a store which helped to build on the Main and State corner of his lot. Like his father he bartered abit—traded his brought-on goods for bee-tree honey, pelts, furs and ginseng roots. All he sold in Mt. Sterling at a profit. Land, stock, and slaves served as additional means of income.

Four of his house slaves were Julia Ann, Hannah, Julia, and Jane.

Julia Ann's daughter, Jane, who was born on August 17, 1875, died on January 9, 1858.

Hannah's son, Henry, was born on November 1, 1861.

Julia's son, Barney, grew up at Hazel Green.

Jane's son, Jordon, who was born on March 31, 1850, died November 30, 1850. (Reference—Mary Bruce Jones).

J. G. Trimble was a staunch Democrat and was naturally a Southern sympathizer. During the war his store was burned by Union soldiers.

Through the years the number of children in the Green Trimble family increased; in 1870 the ninth and last child arrived. Three orphan relatives, Willie Mize, Nannie Mapel, and Frank Trimble had also found companionship in the same home.

In 1876 J. Green Trimble "wound up" his mountain business and moved his family to Mt. Sterling in a covered wagon with a four-horse team. These Wolfe County Trimbles settled in a colonial brick house on East Main Street. Luzuries exceeded necessities in that home, and good old Nigger Jim and the other servants added a genial southern atmosphere to the house and grounds.

After a time J. G. Trimble became president of the Mt. Sterling State Bank, and in that capacity he served for many years. His wife, Nancy Mize Trimble, passed away on Christmas Day in 1891. Methodist Church. The silver communion set—a wine pourer, two goblets, and two bread trays—in the Hazel Green Methodist Chuch came as a gift from him.

This man of the mountains had a phenomenal, photographic mind for reverbertive details. In newspapers letters he related the experiences of his life. Some of these letters, which were written by him at the age of ninety-one for The Jackson Times in Jackson, Kentucky, were later compiled and published by that newspaper under the title **Recollections of Breathitt**. In recent years this little booklet enjoyed a second printing.

WOLFE COUNTY

James Greenville Trimble died on June 22, 1919 at the age of ninety-six. He was buried beside his wife in the Machpelah Cemetery at Mt. Sterling.

All nine of the J. Green and Nancy Mize Trimble children were born in Hazel Green, Kentucky, where they had private tutoring.

3. Mary Clark Trimble, the oldest child, was born on Wednesday, April 21, 1847. She married James Samuel Greenwade of Jeffersonville, Kentucky and had six children. In 1888 the Greenwades moved to a farm near Hunnewell, Kansas. Aunt Mary was embused with a quaint charm that went well with her hobby of crocheting. She passed away on July 27, 1931.

Her three sons Charley, Robert, and Clarence preceded her in death. She was survived by three married daughters, Nannie Belle Hiatt, Ella Lee Cady, and Cora Bruce Geislin, and a number of grandchildren and great grandchildren. At present the Greenwade daughters live in the vicinity of Hunnewell, Kansas. They still own the wheat farm which J. G. Trimble gave to their mother. (J. G. Trimble, Jr., Ella Cady).

3. Rowena Belle (Roe B.), the second daughter in the Green Trimble family, married Jessie Taylor Day. ("Turn to The Days.").

3. Nelson Harvey Trimble was born on Thursday, November 19, 1852. Once while he was spending several days on a hunting trip near Pine Ridge, he carved his name on one of the large rocks at Sky Bridge. It can be seen there today.

Uncle Nelson owned real estate in Mt. Sterling and was a wholesale grocer in that place for many years. He was a pleasant, little man who shuffled his feet as he walked.

After the death of his first wife, the former Eliza Howe of Mt. Sterling, he married a teacher, Minnie Butler Threkeld of Shelbyville, Kentucky on December 5, 1880. They had an adopted daughter Margarite who married a Mr. Paul Hooven, and a foster daughter, Julia Morris, who married Alfred Gerald Gates of Indianapolis. They live in St. Louis and have two daughters—Mary Albert, now Mrs. F. D. Bennett of Michigan, and Isabel, a librarian at the Missouri Historical Society.

In his later years Nelson Trimble built the Trimble Theatre in Mt. Sterling. His wife Minnie, who had been a cripple for many year, died in June of 1937, at the age of eighty. Nelson H. Trimble passed away that same year on the twenty-first day of July. (Julia Gates).

3. Robert Mize, another son of J. G. and Nancy Trimble, was born on Thursday, May 3, 1855. After leaving Hazel Green, he completed a commercial course in Cincinnati. He married Isa, the daughter of John W: and Mary E. White of Montgomery County. Their home on West Main Street in Mt. Sterling was beautifully decorated and elegantly furnished, but so genuine was their hospitality that

house guests had "the feeling of belonging."

Robert Trimble owned stock in a number of Kentucky firms. For many years he served as a director of The Louisville Gas and Electric Company. Uncle Robert was a member of the Christian Church; Aunt Isa was a Methodist. Each supported the church by regular attendance and generous contributions. The brass banisters for the outside steps of the present Christian Church in Mt. Sterling were bought with a Robert Trimble donation.

Isa and Robert Trimble had three children, John White, Mary Ray, and Robert Junior.

John White, a graduate of the University of Virginia, married Mrs. Emma Lee Hibler Reed and lived in Mt. Sterling. He operated a farm in Montgomery County. His widow now lives in Lexington.

Mary Ray Trimble married an Englishman, Mr. Thurman Lee. They live in New York where Mr. Lee is associated with The Dry Rock Bank.

Robert Trimble, Jr., attended Centre College and became a very successful business man in Florida. He was philanthropist and left many charitable bequests in his will.

3. Ella O'Hair Trimble was born on Saturday, August 22, 1857. She was a well educated and cultured woman. After the death of her mother, Nancy Mize Trimble, she became the efficient manager of the J. G. Trimble home. She passed away on October 2, 1931. (James J. Hollon, J. G. Trimble, Jr.).

3. Bruce Walker, the sixth child in the James Greenville Trimble family was born on Friday morning, August 31, 1860. After leaving Hazel Green at the age of sixteen, he attended Harris Institute in Mt. Sterling and later graduated as a Minister of the Christian Church from the College of the Bible at Lexington, Kentucky.

In 1887 he married Cora, a daughter of Judge M. M. and Martha E. Boyd Cassidy of Mt. Sterling. Upon the termination o fa church pastorate in California, Bruce Trimble returned to Mt. Sterling and for several years was editor and part owner of "The Mt. Sterling Advocate." Throughout the years of his life he assisted as a guest minister at many churches. He was a trustee of the College of The Bible at Lexington, and for thirty-two years he served as the recording secretary of the annual Christian Church convention.

In all his endeavors Bruce Trimble was aided and encouraged by his devoted wife. Together they worked in The Mt. Sterling Christian Church. For thirty years Bruce Trimble taught the women's class that bears his name. For even a longer period "Miss Cora" served as the teacher of The Baby Class. They were liberal supporters of The Midway Orphan School, Hazel Green Academy, Transylvania, and other institutions. Their efforts made college years easier for deserving young people, who sought richer attainment through higher education.

Certainly to his Wolfe County relatives, Bruce Trimble was a solace in hours of sorrow. Many times when he returned to assist with funerals, he spoke to the student body at Hazel Green Academy.

This noble man, who had walked with an ever-growing consecration to Jesus Christ, Our Lord and Our Master, passed away in 1932. His widow spent the remaining years of her life at their home on West High Street in Mt. Sterling. A bequest in her will, paid for the walk-in refrigerator at Hazel Green Academy.

3. Fannie Lee, the seventh child of J. G. Green Trimble, was born on Tuesday morning, March 10, 1863. At an early age she united with the Methodist Church. Throughout her life she was a religious and civic leader. On Monday evening, September 24, 1884, Fannie Lee became the bride of Thomas D. Jones of Clark County, Kentucky in the first formal wedding ceremony that was performed in the present Methodist Church in Mt. Sterling. Her husband's mother, Amanda, was the daughter of James Milton Plank of Flemingsburg. Her husband's father, David Badger, Plank, a Kentucky bank presinedt, was the great grandson of the Thomas and Priscilla Jones who had came through Cumberland Gap with Daniel Boone to Boonesboro.

While Fannie and Thomas Jones lived on a farm near Mt. Sterling, they became the parents of four children. Whenever they reutrned to Hazel Green to visit, Aunt Fannie went home and held cottage prayer meeting.

After serving as City Clerk of Mt. Sterling, Thomas Jones, a former graduate of The University of Kentucky, moved his family to Tampa, Florida where he engaged in a wholesale coffee and spice business. Here Fannie died on December 17, 1916.

On November 9, 1918 Thomas D. Jones, who was born on August 20, 1864 passed away in Washington, D. C., following his appointment as Reading Clerk in the House of Representatives. He was buried beside his wife in the Mt. Sterling Cemetery.

They were survived by their four children, Raymond, Nelson, Mary Bruce and Kelly.

4. Raymond, who passed away in 1952 at the age of sixty-five, had been employed in Florida for many years.

4. Mary Bruce spent much time at the J. G. Trimble home in Mt. Sterling and has given generously of her store of Trimble information for the Wolfe County History. In recent years she has become a registered practical nurse in Tampa, Florida.

4. Nelson Trimble Jones is a business analyst and consultant in Tampa, Florida. He is a member of The Sons of the American Revolution through Michael O'Hair. Nelson Jones and his wife, the former Mildred Kerr, are the parents of five children—Thomas

Nelson, May Nelson, David Nelson, Mildred Nelson, and Robert Nelson.

4. Kelly Jones, who was a lieutenant of the Naval Aviation Service during World War I, has been a real estate broker in Tampa, Florida since 1921. (The Thomas Jones Family).

3. Nannie Mize Trimble made her appearance in the J. G. Trimble home on February 12, 1866. She received her education in private schools at Mt. Sterling and became quite a traveler. She married Mr. William Holly and lived for a time in New York. When she passed away in Lexington, Kentucky on January 6, 1946, J. Greenville Trimble, Jr. fulfilled her wishes and had her body cremated.

3. James Greenville Trimble, Jr., the youngest child of J. G. and Nancy Mize Trimble, was born on August 16, 1870 and spent his first six years at Hazel Green. Her higher education was received at Transylvania College and the University of Virginia. Upon the completion of a commercial course in Cincinnati he worked in Wichita, Kansas.

Green Trimble, Jr. made one trip abroad and has travelled much in the United States. He has always been a constant reader. In 1941 he sold the J. G. Trimble home in Mt. Sterling, and since that time he has resided in a Lexington hotel He is now approaching his eighty-seventh birthday and is the only surviving member of the J. Green Trimble family. He has given time and thought to The Wolfe County History; he says he can remmeber anything that he wants to remember".

THE ASBURY TRIMBLE FAMILY

Stephen Asbury, the son of William and Eleanor (Nellie) O'Hair Trimble, was born on December 3, 1825. He became a Hazel Green landowner and farmer. In later years he served as sheriff of the county. Asbury fell in love at an early age but his Breathitt-born fiancee, Mary Elizabeth, the daughter of Jerry Weldon and the late Kitty Cockrell South, was true to a death bed promise she had made to her mother—to not marry until her baby sister was old enough to take care of herself.

Finally after thirteen years of waiting, Asbury Trimble and Elizabeth (Eliza) South were united in the bonds of holy matrimony on July 7, 1863, near the Forks of Elkhorn in Franklin County, Kentucky. They settled in Hazel Green.

On April 13, 1864 a grandchild was born in the William Trimble home. This little boy, who was the son of Asbury and Eliza Trimble, was named South. One day homeguards came to the Trimble house looking for Asbury, the Southern sympathizer, "Leave" the commanded Eliza Trimble, "leave now!"

She looked at the glaring captain and then moved towards the cradle where her son South lay sleeping. "Captain", ejected one of the soldiers, "let her take her baby."

"What's hom name?" growled the captain.

Eliza now holding her baby looked at the Union captain. Then she squared her shoulders and said firmly, "His name is South. He is named after my five brothers and every man in the Southern Army."

What a brave, what a courageous woman!

On the morning of October 15, 1864 while Asbury was hurrying to put some negroes to work at the vats in the Trimble tannery, which was located near the Red River Bridge on Main Street in Hazel Green, a shot rang out through the crisp, autumn air. Asbury Trible stumbled and fell; he had been assassinated.

Years later I heard J. Greene Trimble say to his daughter, Roe B. Day, "Eliza was so brave at the time. She was naturally one of the most intelligent women whom God ever made.'

When South was six, his widowed mother purchased a ble grass farm—Bells Grove—near the Forks of Elkhorn. Here South Trimble grew up. He received his education in a Franklin County public school, at Excelsior Institute in Frankfort, and at a Louisville business college.

On November 24, 1825, South Trimble married Carrie Belle Allan, who was born on June 1, 1867, at Houston, Texas. She was the daughter of Henry Lowndes and Fannie Bell Morgan Allan.

Mrs. Asbury Trimble, the former Eliza South, who was born on September 29, 1830, passed away on March 16, 1900. She had lived to see her son, South, become a Democratic member of the Kentucky Legislature. In 1900 as Speaker of the House, South Trimble helped to steer Kentucky through those dark temestuous days following Governor Goebel's assassination.

During the first decade of the twentieth century, South Trimble served for six years as a Kentucky representative in Congress. From 1911 to 1919 he was clerk of the House in Washington. Efficiently he met the needs of the nation in World War 1. Again in 1931 the Democratic caucus nominated and elected South Trimble as clerk of the House. In this capacity he served through the peace years, during the crisis of World War II, and until his death on November 23, 1946.

Oratory tributes in the House of Representatives were paid to the Honorable South Trimble on his eightieth and eighty-second birthdays.

On April 13, 1944 Mr. Ludlow of Indiana said, "South Trimble, the beloved clerk of the House is eighty years old today . . . His friends are legion. He has been in many a sharp political fight, but he had always managed to emerge without and scars of heartburnings, either his own or the other fellow, for he is a kind, un derstanding soul who binds mento him as with hoops of steel'."

On that same day Mr. McCormack from Massachusetts said "In pausing to congratulate this great man we should think of his dear mother who contributed so much in the moulding of his character, and we should also think of that dear girl of his—his wife—who for fifty-nine years has been travelling the journey of life with him .... Mrs. Trimble is entitled to more credit for the great progress South Trimble has made than South Trimble himself!"

On April 13, 1946 our Kentucky Senator, Virgil Chapman, spoke these words, "Mr. Speaker, I am commissioned to call the attention of the House to the eighty-second birthday anniversary of a great American, a beloved Kentuckian, a distinguished member of Congress, a devoted public servant, the cherished friend of the membership o fthis body, the venerable Clerk of the House, South Trimble ... "

Mr. Trimble is a scion of the hardy, sturdy race of pioneers, intrepid men and dauntless women, who, armed with the rifle, the ax, and the Holy Bible defied the perils of the treacherous trails through the trackless wilderness and over towering mountains into the Dark and Bloody Ground of Old Kentucky; braved the menace of wild beasts; cleared the forests, raised their cabins, tilled their fields, reared their children; built in the western wildwood the imperial commonwealth we love to call "Old Kentucky Home" and dedicated it as a sanctuary of liberty and justice.

Mr. Trimble was born at Hazel Green, Kentucky not far from the historic spot where Daniel Boone cast his enraptured gaze on the promised land of his dreams. . . .

Mr. Trimble is the typical Kentucky gentleman. He loves the history and tradition, the institutions, manners, and customs of his native State. He loves its land, its people, its scenic beauty, its historical shrines . . "more than a half century he has seldom missed that gala day in May when the band plays "My Old Kentucky Home" and some equine king or queen wears the floral wreath of the winner of the Kentucky Derby." . . .

Many times family papers assembled by South Trimble have been used for the Wolfe County History, and "that dear girl of his" —Carie Belle Allan Trimble—who will be ninety in June has been an unfailing source of helpful information.

South Trimble was proud of his Wolfe County ancestors and on each St. Patrick Day he paid Irish tribute to them by wearing a green necktie!

Six children were born to South and Carrie Belle Trimble—James Frank, Maria, Asbury, Margaret Allen, South, Jr., and Frances Marie.

4. James Frank Trimble, the oldest son, died in 1945 at the age of forty-nine. He married Mildred Hamie and lived in Kansas City, Missouri, where he was associated with Morris and Company, and

Armour and Company.

4. Maria, the first daughter of South Trimble, married Carlos Fish. She was left a widow in early life. For eighteen years she has been postmaster in Frankfort, Kentucky.

5. Her oldest son, Carlos, is a doctor in Louisville, Kentucky. South, her second son, is a lawyer in New Orleans. Helen, her first daughter, died in 1954. Carrie Belle, her youngest daughter, is now Mrs. C. T. Eddie of Lexington, Kentucky.

4. Stephen Asbury, son of South and Carrie Belle Trimble, died at age six.

4. Margaret Allen, now Mrs. David Lynn, lives in Washington, D. C., where her husband is archetect of the Capitol.

5. Their children are David, South Trimble, and Margaret Acheson.

4. South Trimble, Jr., i san attorney-at-law in Washington, D.C., he married Elaine Lazaro, the daughter of a Louisana Congressman.

5. Their five children are Elaine, SouthIII, Mary Stephen Asbury, and James.

4. Frances Marie (Fannie May,) the youngest member of the South Trimble family, married Mr. A. C. Wallace, a banker. They live in Chevy Chase, Maryland.

5. Their three children are named John, Mary and Carrie Bell.

EMILY JANE AND ROSE ANN TRIMBLE

2. The new baby daughter of William and Elanor O'Hair Trimble was called Emily Jane. By her name in the family Bible appears the date, January 4, 1828.

On July 27, 1847, she married McKinley Cockrell, a Minister of the Christian Church and a co-laborer at Hazel Green with Reverend Joseph Nickell. His parents, Simon and Polly Smith Cockrell, lived in Breathitt County.

At the early age of twenty-eight Reverend McKinley Cockrell passed away. His birth date was January 16, 1827; his death date was January 22, 1855.

Some time after his death Emily Jane Cockrell married a Mr. Lacy. This marriage was not successful. Emily Jane resumed the name of Cockrell and lived at the William Trimble house at Hazel Green.

Aunt Emily was an earnest member of the Christian Church and a regular attendant at the Sunday and mid-week services. Mrs. John M. Rose, who was the mother of Mrs. Carl Mize of Hazel Green, and Aunt Emily wove the first carpet for the Hazel Green Christian Church.

On December 12, 1897 Emily Jane Cockrell died at Hazel Green at the home of her daughter, Mrs. W. O. Mize, with whom she had lived for some years.

3. To McKinley and Emily Jane Trimble Cockrell were born four children, two of whom died in infancy. The others who grew up were Lou Ellen and Mary Belle.

3. Lou Ellen (Lou) Cockrell was born on June 15, 1848 and died on May 26, 1926. She received her higher education at Millersburg, Kentucky. Lou Cockrell married Willim O. Mize, an orphan, who had been reared at Hazel Green by his paternal aunt, Mrs. J. G. Trimble.

4. Carl, their only son, married Carrie Rose.

5. The two children of this union were Marriam Elizabeth and Oldham Mize. (See the W. O. Mize Family by Mrs. Roy Cecil.)

3. Mary Belle, the other daughter in the McKinley Cockrell family, was born February 17, 1850 and died June 24, 1927. She attended school at Millersburg, Kentucky Belle Cockrell married Drew S. Godsey (1848-1907) of Hazard, Kentucky. They lived at Hazel Green and had one son, Henry

4. Henry Godsey was born on September 11, 1868. While he was at Centre College he won the State Oratorical Contest. He became a lawyer and served as clerk of the House in Washington. His wife was the former Bertie Snail of Danville, Kentucky. Henry Godsey passed away in Washington on September 22, 1908, and his body was brought back to Hazel Green for burial.

In 1912 his Mother, Belle Cockrell Godsey, married William Mulhollon from Missouri. Something had caused him to lose the natural pitch of his voice, so he always whispered. Mr. Mulhollon ran a barber shop in Hazel Green.

"Aunt Belle" in her later years was a cripple; she always sat in her wheel chair when she entertained her guests. She was such pleansant company that one never thought about her handicap. (Day Records, Mrs. Carl Mize, Kathleen Tutt, Esther Wilson).

2. Rose Ann, the eighth child of William and Eleanor O'Hair Trimble, was born on January 3, 1830 and died on March 27, 1863. She married Edward A. Hensley and lived on a farm near Maytown. At her death she was survived by her husband and three sons, whose names are unknown to me. All left Kentucky; her husband spent the last years of his life in blindness. One son lived in New Mexico; another settled in Missouri; and the third went to Nebraska. (Mr. J. G. Trimble, Jr., Ruth Frey, Mrs. South Trimble).

LOUISA JANE AND MARY ELIZABETH (LIZZIE) TRIMBLE

2. Louisa Jane Trimble, another daughter in the William Trimble family, was born on October 16, 1831. In 1848 she married Preston Wilson. He was born on July 10, 1823 and died on January 7, 1862. Six children were born to Preston and Louisa Wilson.

3. Henry, Asberry, Elvin, Howard, Rose Ellen, and Elizabeth Ann, who became Mrs. Joe A. Stephens of Mt. Sterling, Kentucky.

3. Howard Wilson, (1853-1900) the son of Preston and Louisa Wilson married Mary Conroy (1857-1931), in 1875. They lived in Butler, Missouri, and had one daughter, Esther.

4. Esther Wilson was educated at private schools in Mt. Sterling, Kentucky, where she now resides.

After the death of his first wife, Howard Wilson, married Sarah Elizabeth Tipton of Mt. Sterling. They had one son, Tipton.

4. Tipton Wilson, is cashier of the Mt. Sterling National Bank. He married Laura Hutchings of Harrodsburg, Kentucky. They have one daughter, Betsy, who married and lives in Evansville, Ind.

Following the death of her first husband, Preston Wilson, Louisa Trimble Wilson married a Mr. John Wilson. He lived, I've been told, near Helechawa; he was not related to Louisa Trimble's first husband. John and Louisa Wilson had one son, Harlan.

4. Harlan Wilson lived at Daysboro; he inherited his farm from his uncle, Frank Trimble. His children were Howard, Ernest and Esther.

Louisa Trimble Wilson passed away at Mt. Sterling, Kentucky in February of 1922. She is buried by her first husband in the Hazel Green Cemetery. Esther Wilson, J. G. Trimble Jr.)

2. Mary Elizabeth (Lizzie), the daughter of William and Eleanor O'Hair, was born at Hazel Green, Kentucky on November 3, 1833.

On April 27, 1856, Lizzie married James Samuel (Jim) Turner of West Liberty, Kentucky. He was born on September 16, 1827. He was a wealthy landowner with a large number of slives. Jim and Lizzie Turner lived on a farm between Hazel Green and West Liberty. They became the parents of six children.

Soon after the close of the Civil War they moved to Covington, Kentucky, and Jim Turner became a wholesale clothier in Cincinnati, Ohio. He died on December 4, 1875, and was buried in Mt. Sterling, Kentucky. For a number of years after her husband's death, Lizzie Turner resided in Mt. Sterling, About 1889 she went to Paris, Illinois to spend her remaining years with her daughter, Belle Miller. On May 10, 1903 Lizzie Trimble Turner passed away. She is buried in Mt. Sterling, Kentucky. The Turners had six children.

3. Henry Harrison, their first child was born on February 13, 1859 and died on September 23, 1860. Rollie Frank Turner, who was born on February 17, 1863, passed away on September 13, 1863. The next children were Mary Belle, Harlan, and Clarence Reid; these grew up. Lillie Mae, the youngest child, was born on November 25, 1874 and died on January 6, 1875.

3. Mary Belle ("Belle") Turner celebrated her birthday on October the twenty-ninth, but she would never tell her age. She was a talented concert piainist having graduated from Hamilton College in music. Her third cousin, Will Miller, a merchant in Paris, Ill., became her husband. He was a decendant of Sarah O'Hair Miller,

who had lived in Hazel Green. (See Michael O'Hair's Jessamine County Family). Will and Belle Miller had no children but they reared an orphan niece, Josephine Turner, now Mrs. Rolla Ralston.

"Cousin Belle' was a very cultured and widely travelled woman, and yet she was very superstitious. One day upon opening a gift box she exclaimed with horror, "Peafowl feathers! Oh! what will I ever do with them? They're harbingers of bad luck!" Just then a telegram announced the sudden death of her brother, Harlan.

Will Miller passed away at Paris, Illinois in 1934 at the age of seventy-two. Cousin Belle died on February 13, 1948 at the home of Josephine Ralston in Albany, Oregon and is buried there.

3. Harlan, the son of Jim and Lizzie Turner owned and operated a Mt. Sterling hotel. After he separated from his wife, Gertrude, he bought a Missouri Ranch and raised much stock. His only son, John, who graduated from the Colorado College of Mines, married and settled in the West.

3. Clarence, the son of Jim and Lizzie Trimble Turner, was born On December 26, 1871 and died on July 12, 1915. He owned a jewelry store, in Paris, Illinois and operated a farm in Missouri. Following the death of his wife, the former Josephine LaGrange, his small daughter, Josephine, was taken to be reared by his sister, Belle Miller, of Paris, Illinois.

4. Josephine Turner, a graduate of Ward-Belmont, College in Nashville, Tennessee, is the wife of Rolla Ralston, who operates an automobile business in Albany, Oregon. Their three sons are William, John Reid, and Robert Turner Ralston. Josephine has the wedding coverlid that belonged to her grandmother, Lizzie Trimble Turner.

4. Josephine's father, Clarence Turner (3), by his second wife, Pearl Smith, had one son named Harlan. (Mrs. Rolla Ralston, Lizzie Duff).

NELSON HARVEY, MELISSA, AND JAY FRANKLIN TRIMBLE

2. Nelson Harvey, another son of William and Eleanor O'Hair Trimble, was born on December 4, 1836. He died at Owingsville, Kentucky, where he was attending school, on January 14, 1853. His body was brought back to Hazel Green for burial.

2. Malissa, an infant daughter in the William Trimble family, was born on January 20, 1839 and passed away on Sunday, January 27, 1839.

2. Jay Franklin (Frank), the youngest of the thirteen children of William and Eleanor O'Hair Trimble was born on December 29, 1840. After the death of his mother in 1855, he spent a large part of his time in the J. G. Trimble's home, first at Hazel Green and later at Mt. Sterling. He became a well educated man and amassed a large fortune through his real estate business in Tennessee. Miss

Lillian Shelton of Summersville, Tennessee became his wife; they lived in Memphis. Frank Trimble died on October 12, 1915 at the age of seventy-five.

In his will he left one thousand dollars to The Hazel Green Cemetery Association. He also set aside seven thousand dollars for the buying of suitable monuments for the graves of his beloved family at Hazel Green. "It is my desire," he added, "that an especially nice stone be placed over the graves of my mother and father."

Certainly, his parent's monument with its simple lines of classic beauty does dignify the graves of Eleanor O'Hair Trimble and William Trimble, th efounder of Hazel Green, Kentucky.

Irene McLin Keller, Compiler

Personal rights of all contributors have been respected.

The right to reproduce this chapter in printed form must be secured through the Wolfe County Woman's Club with the permission of said compiler.

Irene McLin, Keller, Compiler

THE MIZES AND THE MAPELS

Through their children Isaac and Nancy Mize, who lived near Irvine, Kentucky, were associated with Wolfe County. Isaac Mize, the son of Joshua and Mary Witt Mize, and the grandson of David Mize, an early settler in Estill County, was born on November 25, 1792 and died in 1882. He served as county judge in Estill and represented that county in the Kentucky Legislature. His wife, the former Nancy Walker, was born on July 20, 1798 and passed away on March 13, 1860.

Their eight children were Elizabeth, the wife of Sidney Barnes; John; Nancy; Roderick, who lived in Missouri; Susan, Isaac Mize, Jr., the husband of Edith Vaughn; Fanny, the wife of Birch Benton; and James, who married Elizabeth Redding after the death of his first wife, Sue Watts..

The three who played a part in the early history of Hazel Green, Kentucky, were —ohn, Nancy, and Susan.

John A. (Johnny) Mize was married twice. By his first wife he had one son, William O. Mize, who married Lou Cockrell of Hazel Green. (Turn to the Emily Trimble Cockrell Family; see also "The W. O. Mize Family" by Mrs. Roy Cecil.)

Nancy, the daughter of Isaac Mize, Sr., married J. Green Trimble of Hazel Green. (Turn to the James Greenville Trimble Family).

Susan (Sue), another daughter of Isaac and Nancy Walker Mize, married George Mapel of Estill County and lived near Irvine. George Mapel passed away at an early age leaving his widow and three children.

Iater his wodiw, Sue Mize Mapel, married Claiborne Eubank of Clark County. They lived at Old Furnace in Estill County. Their two sons were Rodney (Rod) and Grant. For a time Rod Eubank clerked in the Trimble store at Hazel Green and lived in the J. Green Trimble home.

Now the three children of Sue Mize by her first husband, George Mapel, were Nannie, Sid, and Isaac William.

1. Nannie Mapel was born on September 30, 1854. As a little girl she came to Hazel Green to live with her aunt, Nancy Mize Trimble, (Mrs. J. Green). She had private tutoring. When she was about twenty, she married Howard, the son of Levi and Mary Ann Fieratt Kash, who lived near Hazel Green. (Mr. Roy Kash).

Nannie and Howard Kash lived on a farm at Public Square and ran a country store. They had three children.

2. William, Robert, and Sudie were their names.

After the death of her husband in 1885, Nannie Mapel Kash taught school at PublicSquare. Little Sudie died on Friday, November 16, 1888 at the age of five years, seven months, and thirteen days. Upon reaching manhood, Sudie's brothers, William and Robert, passed away. Nannie Mapel Kash then lived at her cottage on Broadway in Hazel Green. Later she married J. M. Cravens, a widower with several children. Two of these were named Julia and Charley.

Nannie Mapel Kash spent her declining years at Mt. Sterling at the home of her uncle, J. G. Trimble. Her death occurred on September 8, 1917. She is remembered as one of the five women who formed the Hazel Green Cemetery Association.

1. Sidney (Sid), another child of Sue Mize Mapel, married Mary Ann Lyle and lived at Clay City.

1. Isaac William (Will), the youngest child of George and Sue Mize Mapel was born on February 25, 1848 in Estill County. When he became a young man he worked in Wolfe County and stayed in one of the first boarding houses in Hazel Green. It was located on the northwest corner of Main and Broadway and was operated by Tillman B. Johnson and his wife Betsy; the former Elizabeth Swango.

Will Mapel, the boarder, liked the Johnsons; he liked their boarding house; and on January 24, 1878, he married their daughter, Louann! Some of you may have heard of her brother; his given name was Abraham Frank, and he was the father of the late Ellis A. Johnson of Hazel Green.

Will and Louann went to housekeeping in town. Will Mapel was one of the first teachers in the old frame building on the Hazel Green Public School grounds. In W. P. A. days this structure was torn down for the erection of the present stone school building.

Will Mapel practiced law in the area now known as Powell, Wolfe, and Estill counties. After a time he moved his growing family to a farm below town. (Below town" means between Hazel Green and

Murphy Fork.) After his death on November 16, 1888, his widow, Louann, came back to Hazel Green with her six children, Minnie, G. T., Nancy, Ruther Nile, Sally and Will.

Louann Johnson Mapel, who was born on July 21, 1856, passed away on August 27, 1933. She was buried beside her husband in the Hazel Green cemetery. "Aunt Louann," was a straight little woman with lots of mountain dignity. She always whispered abit as she talked.

2. Minnie, the first member of the Will Mapel family, married Morgan French and had three children, Marion, Dan, and Fern. They lived in Powell county, but Fern, after the death of her father, stayed with her grandmother, Louann Mapel, at Hazel Green.

Fern French graduated from Hazel Green Academy and Hamilton College. While she was teaching at Livingston, Tennessee, she became the wife of Robert Mitchell. They reside in that place and are the parents of three children.

Following the death of her first husband, Minnie Mapel French married Butler Barnes and continued to live in Powell County. Their three children were Teressia, Lucille (deacsed), and Mildred.

2. G. T. (Bud) Mapel, Louann's second child, married Stella, a daughter of one of the John Gibbes of Wolfe County. After a few years they located near Hamilton, Ohio, and reared a family of nine children. Stella Gibbs Mapel is buried in Hamilton, Ohio.

2. Nancy, the daughter of Will and Louann Johnson Mapel, graduated from Hazel Green Academy. Later she taught school, completed a business course, and worked at the Hazel Green Bank. In 1920 she became the secretary of Hazel Green Academy and served in that capacity until she retired in 1950.

I quote, "The church and the missionary cause has had many faithful and consecrated souls who have given of their best and of their all to the work of kingdom building. The record of none, however, has exceeded the record of "Miss Nancy" Mapel, who for thirty years has been the faithful, accurate, and efficient secretary of Hazel Green Academy.

"Gentle and sweet spirited, yet business-like and exact, "Miss Nancy" Mapel has served through the years keeping books, writing the letters, being advisor to students and faculty, and winning a high and permanent place in the hearts and lives of all with whom she has dealt." (H.G.A. Yearbook–The Former Students Association).

2. Ruther Nile Mapel, Louann's fourth child, was married three times. By his first wife, Maggie French of Powell County, he had three children. By his second wife, Jennie Baker of Montgomery County, he had three more children, and by his third wife, Myrtle Johnson of Estill County, he also had three children.!

Ruther Nile died in Estill County and is buried near Irvine. He was never a resident of Wolfe after the death of his father, Will Mapel.

2. Sally another daughter of Louann, has always lived at Hazel Green. She has never been able to walk very well, but she has brought happiness to all of us, who grew up at Hazel Green, by waving to us from her rocking chair.

2. William (Bill), the youngest child of Will and Louann John son Mapel, married Pearl Troy, a nurse from Clark County, Kentucky. They settled in Hazel Green where Will engaged in store and farm activities. When Pearl Troy Mapel passed away on September 2, 1948, she was survived by her husband and five children

3. Pauline, the oldest daughter, lives at Hazel Green with her aunts, Nancy and Sally Mapel.

3. Billy, a veteran of World War II, is dead.

3. Helen, Eleanor, and Betsy are mirried. They live in Ohio.

(References—Mrs. Charles B. Nelson, formerly Dolly Locknane, a daughter of James and Florence Mize Locknane and a grand daughter of Isaac Mize, Jr.; Miss Nancy Mapel, Mrs. Carl Mize; also Day and Trimble records).

Irene McLin Keller, Compiler

Rights of said contributors have been respected.

THE GIBBS FAMILY

The Gibbses came to America from England in early colonial days. At the time of William the Conqueror the family seems to have come into the British Isles from France. One French spelling of the word was Guibe; one early English form was Gybby. The sheaf of wheat on the Gibbs coat-of-arms is an old English symbol of landownership.

1. Our Wolfe County progenitor was John Gibbs who was born on March 3, 1755 either in Burke County, North Carolina, or in Pittsylvanis County, Virginia. All examined records except one state the former. Traditionally, he made some trips into Kentucky before the Revolution; he witnessed the slaying of Daniel Boone's son by the Indians. John Gibbs was never a resident of the present county of Wolfe but his wife, the former Hannah Mason, Muchmore spent her last days at Hazel Green. She was born in Pennsylvania on February 8, 1759, and was a first cousin to Daniel Boone. Members of the Muchmore family moved from Pennsylvania to Virginia and later to North Carolina. According to one family record John Gibbs and Hannah Muchmore were married in Burke County, North Carolina. (The John C. M. Day records, Alice Gibbs Hartman, Golden Day).

For a time during the Revolution John Gibbs was a member of the North Carolina Legislature. He enlisted for service with North Carolina troops and served for a time in 1780, and again in 1781. (Revolutionary File Number 8556).

The five children of John and Hannah Muchmore Gibbs were Forest, a later resident of Texas; Polly, who married John Brown Saint in 1817; John Gibbs, Jr.; Sally; and Nathan.

2. John Gibbs, Jr., was born in North Carolina in 1786. He married Elizabeth Shepherd (1798-1878). Chronologically, they lived in three Kentucky counties—Garrard, Breathitt, and Wolfe. John Gibbs Jr. passed away after 1870; he is buried at Holly Creek, Kentucky.

The eight children in the John Gibbs, Jr., family were James, Ebeneser, Elizabeth, Sally, William Mason, Washington, and Eliza.

3. James Gibbs (1814) was born in North Carolina. He married Delilah Landsaw (1817), and they settled in what is now Menifee County, Kentucky.

3. Ebeneser Gibbs (1816), married Sibby Little who was born 1812.

3. Elizabeth (called Polly), the first daughter of John Gibbs, Jr., was born in Garrard County, Kentucky. She married John Hollon, Jr., and they settled in Wolfe County on Holly Creek. Polly was born in 1820.

4. James Buchanan (Uncle Buck) Hollon, one of their first sons, married Caroline Elkins.

5. James I. Hollon, Sr., of Hazel Green is one of their sons. He married Daisy Day. (See the J. T. Day family.)

3. Sally Gibbs (1822) was born in Garrard County. She married John Tyra and they settled on Holly Creek.

3. Mason Gibbs (1826) was born in Garrard County. He married Melvina Terrell.

3. Washington Gibbs, who was born in 1830 in Breathitt County, was twice married. Ellen McQuin was his first wife; Martha Ingram became his second wife.

3. Eliza, the youngest child of John Gibbs, Jr., and Elizabeth Shepherd Gibbs was born in 1832 in Breathitt. She married Alex Pelfrey; they settled in Breathitt. (James I. Hollon, Sr.).

2. Sarah (Sally), the daughter of John and Hannah Muchmore Gibbs, was born in North Carolina in 1791. During the Civil War her husband, Washington (Luke) Wood, was killed by home guards on Frozen Creek.

2. Nathan, another son of John and Hannah M. Gibbs, was born in Burke County, North Carolina on October 12, 1793. He married Nancy Lane Lipps, a native of the same county. She was born August 14, 1797. About 1818 they came on pack horses through Cumberland Gap into the verdant wilderness of East Kentucky. After spending about a year on Quicksand in the present county of Breathitt, they moved to Frozen Creek where Nathan Gibbs had bought land. Twenty slaves, whom he had brought from North Carolina, helped to cut the trees, clear this land, and build the log house for his family. Through the years Nathan Gibbs con-

tinued to acquire land in the vicinity of Van Cleve and Frozen Creek. By 1844 he owned three square miles.

That year his elderly parents, John and Hannah Muchmore Gibbs, who had been living at Bedford, Tennessee, came to his home to spend their remaining years. John Gibbs passed away on March 15, 1847 and is buried at Frozen Creek. In recent years a Revolutionary plaque of honor was placed at the stone-covered grave of this soldier.

Nathan and Nancy Jane Lipps Gibbs had nine children. After the death of Nathan's father, they moved to a large tract of William Trimble land just east of Hazel Green. The place still bears the name of Gibbs Farm. Here Nathan and his sons engaged in farming. At that time the present Hazel Green Academy campus was Squire Gibbs' best corn field. Nathan Gibbs biult and successfully operated a saw mill and a grist mill on the Red River section of this land.

On March 17, 1850, Nathan's mother, Hannah Muchmore Gibbs, passed away. She was buried in the family graveyard, which is now a part of Hazel Green cemetery. Only a few letters are legible on the little stone that marks her grave.

Nathan's wife, Nancy Jane Lipps Gibbs, died on April 4, 1867. After a time Nathan Gibbs married Mrs. Eliza Noe McQuin of Lee City, Kentucky. He was nearly eighty and she was about thirty-five. On December 25, 1872 their only daughter, Cora Alice, was born. She was the child of Nathan Gibbs' old age and he loved her dearly. She recalls horseback rides with her father; she sat in front of him on his saddle, and if it rained a buffalo robe protected her from the water. She also remembers 'Nigger Aggie" who helped to care for her in her early years.

Following the death of his second wife, Elizabeth McQin Gibbs, Nathan married Elizabth Miller of Wolfe County. Their wedding took place on January 31, 1878. Their only child, Daniel J. Gibbs, who was born in 1882, passed away in 1884.

On November 12, 1882, Nathan Gibbs died and was buried at Hazel Green. Later his widow, Elizabeth Miller Gibbs, married a Mr. Samuel Moore. (Papers of J. T. and John C. M. Day.)

When Cora Alice Gibbs was a small child she was taken to Mattoon, Illinios to be reared by a niece. There she attended school. Later Cora Alice married C. L. Hartman and lived in Kansas and New Mexico. They had a daughter and a son.

For a number of years Alice Gibbs Hartman, who is now a widow, has resided with her son in California. She is a member of both The Daughters of The American Revolution and The Daughters of of The Confederacy. At theage of eighty-four she is one of the few surviving grand daughters of the Revolution in the United States. Alice Gibbs Hartman was commissioned a "Kentucky Colonel" by former Governor Lawrence Wetherby.

Her two children, who were named Treasure Alice and Don C. Hartman, were born in Kansas.

4. Treasure Alice Hartman, who was the wife of Colonel W. B. Aren, is dead. They had two sons, Windon and Wade.

5. Windon Gibbs Aren is a veteran of World War II. Wade Hampton Gibbs, Aren, the other son, is in the Navy Reserve.

4. Don C. Hartman is a successful horticulturists and florist in Arcida, California. His mother resides with him. (References—Mrs. Alice Gibbs Hartman).

THE FIRST FAMILY OF NATHAN GIBBS

The nine children of Nathan Gibbs and his first wife, Nancy Jane Lipps, were named Milton, Elizabeth, Mary Popp, John, Phoebe Elender, Sallie, Hulda, Evaline, and Hollis. Some of these children may have been born in North Carolina; the last five were born at Frozen Creek, Kentucky.

3. Milton Gibbs married Jane McGuire on October 30, 1845. (See "The Caskey Family.") they lived in Wolfe County and reared a family. Years later Milton Gibbs married again; his second wife's surname was Pelfrey.

4. According to a J. T. Day deed, four children of Milton Gibbs were James, who married a girl named Fannie; Florence, the wife of Lee Ferguson; W. W. Gibbs, who had a wife named Alabama; and Hannah, the wife of W. F. Haven. I do not know whether these four children were by Milton Gibbs' first or second wife.

4. Two children of Milton Gibbs and his first wife, Jane McGuire, were named James Nathan and Adolphus D.

Here's a bit of Wolfe County in the wild. Milton Gibbs had built a house and moved into it. Just as he was starting to hang the door, a business matter made it necessary for him to leave home for a few hours. He hung a quilt over the opening to keep out the cold air; then he told his wife, Jane, and his infant son, James Nathan, good-by. While he was away, a big bear shoved aside the quilt and walked into the house. Milton's little dog which was in the room raised a commotion. It ran and it barked, and it barked and it ran! Finally it chased the intruder away. When Milton returned, he tracked the bear and killed it.

4. James Nathan, Milton's son, had "the awfulest time that ever was" when he decided to get married. His father, Milton, started to West Liberty with him to get the license. When they came to the Licking River, they found it was flowing "out of banks" over the bottoms. They took off their clothes, made them into bundles, threw them across the river, and swam to the other side. Then they dressed, walked on to the court house, and secured the license. When they returned, they had to go through the same procedure again. However, James Nathan was afraid to trust his license to the probobility of his being able to successfully throw his clothes a-

cross the Licking, so he held the precious document between his teeth, and in this manner swam "bareback" across the river. When his father, Milton, was half way over, he took water cramps and had to be rescued. Finally they reached home safely, and James Nathan got married according to schedule! (Bethel Huff).

To James Nathan and Mary Ellington Gibbs were born eight children:

5. Samuel Adolphus, Franklin, Howard, Thomas, Hannah Jane, Ranson, John William and Laura.

5. Samuel Adolphus and his wife, Litty Ann Gibbs, had five children—Lonus, Emmet, James, Bunie and Burt. These children live in Ashland, Kentucky.

5. Franklin, the son of James Nathan, married and settled in Ashland, Kentucky. Two of his children were Arzie and Harold.

5. Hannah Jane Gibbs married Henry Hitchcock, they had a daughter and a son, Claude.

5. John William, the son of James Nathan and Mary Ellington Gibbs was born on November 27, 1871. He married Melissa Elizabeth, the daughter of Green and Mary Ellen Pelfrey Spencer of Wolfe County. Their marriage date was April 17, 1895. John William Gibbs is still living. His wife, Melissa Elizabeth Spencer, who was born on August 20, 1881, died on April 20, 1955. Their six children were named Kelly, Russell, Troy, Sylvester, Irvin, and Virgil.

6. Kelly Gibbs married Millie Hatton and had seven children named Bethel, Clarence, Beulah, Clyde, Dorothy, Christine and Kelly Donald.

7. Bethel Gibbs married Lawrence, the son of John B. and Mary Elizabeth Wages Huff of Wolfe County, on January 3, 1949. They live on a farm near Hazel Green. Bethel Gibbs Huff furnished the material on the Milton Gibbs line for this history.

7. Clarence, the first son of Kelly Gibbs, married Georgia Watkins. They live in Louisville. Their three children are Charline, Gary Lee and Eugene.

7. Beulah Gibbs married Price Briscoe and has two children, Leslie and Roger Dale. They live in Middletown, Ohio.

7. Clyde Gibbs married Maggie———. They live in Middletown, Ohio and have two children, Clyde and Michael.

7. Dorothy, another daughter of Kelly Gibbs, married Harold Eugene Wilson. They live in Butte, Montana. Their children are named Patricia and Michael Larry.

7. Christine Gibbs married Virgil Norvel of Middletown. They live in Bangor, Maine, and have one daughter, Jacqulin.

7. Kelly Donald, the youngest child of Kelly and Millie Hatton Gibbs is seventeen.

Kelly Gibbs (6) married twice. His second wife was Betty Miller. They live in Jeffersonville, Indiana and have a son, Stephen Wayne.

6. Russell, the son of John William and Melissa Elizabeth Spencer

Gibbs, married Margaret King of Fleming County, Kentucky. They live there and have seven children:

7. Ethel (Mrs. Elmer Harris), Omer, Ruth, Russell Jr., Shirley, Jerry Ray and Alice (Harris).

6. Sylvester, another son of John William Gibbs, married Hattie Woodard and settled in Bourbon County, Kentucky. They had fifteen children:

7. William Delbert, Elsie, Haskel Eugene, Roger Delona, Gilbert, Elwood, Daniel, Hazel Irene, (Mrs. Brian Walters,) Wanda, Opal (Mrs. Oscar Ellis), Elmer, Mary Elizabeth, Bertha, Clayton, and Geraldine!

Mrs. Bethel Gibbs Huff said, "When Elmer was four and Mary Elizabeth was about three, their mother sent them to the field to take water to the older children who were at work, Elmer reached there first and the other children hid him. When Mary Elizabeth arrived, they told her the cow had eaten Elmer. They expected her to cry. She did look sad for a few moments. Then scanning the faces of her other brothers and sisters, she said convincingly, 'Oh well! We have plenty more!'"

6. Irvin, the son of John William and Melissa Spencer Gibbs, married Mimi Jean Salyers of Magoffin County. They had two sons, Jerry Blaine and Bridges.

6. Troy Gibbs is single. He has a farm in Montgomery County and runs a watch repair shop in Mt. Sterling, Kentucky.

6. Virgil, the youngest son of John William and Melissa Spencer Gibbs, married Hazel Stamper. They settled in Montgomery County and had four children, Franklin, Stanley, Carolyn, and Janice Clay.

4. Adolphus D. Gibbs, the son of Milton and Jane McGuire Gibbs, married Matilda Barker of Grassy Creek, Kentucky. They settled in Montgomery County. Two of their children were named Lila Mae and John.

3. Now, Elizabeth (Betsy) Gibbs, the daughter of "the First" Nathan Gibbs and his wife, Nancy Jane Lipps, married Samuel H. Holmes and moved to Illinois. They had a daughter who married a Stewart; two sons, Benjamin and Frank; and another daughter, Arminta, who married a Mr. Corder and lived in Mattoon, Illinois. Arminta Holmes Corder reared her aunt, Cora Alice Gibbs (Hartman) of Hazel Green.

3. Mary Popp (Polly) Gibbs married James E. Ramsey and lived at Emporia, Kansas.

3. John Gibbs married Elizabeth Newton. After the death of her husband, Elizabeth Gibbs moved to Ohio. Seven children were Lee, W. R., Tom, J. H., Lou (Blevin), Cora (Mrs Ed. Fleming), and Evaline (Mrs. Jeff Hawk).

EARLY AND MODERN HISTORY

3. Phoebe Elender Gibbs married William Day. (See the Jesse Day Family.)

3. Sallie, the daughter of "the first" Nathan Gibbs married Frank Coldiron.

3. Hulda Gibbs married Riley Coldiron. They lived at Rothwell, Kentucky. Three of their children were named Rosa, Eleanor, and Victoria.

3. Evaline Gibbs married John W. Day. (See the Jesse Day family.)

3. Hollis, the youngest son of Nathan Gibbs and his wife, Nancy Jane Lipps Gibbs, married Martha Nickell, the daughter of Andy Spaniard and Rachel Kash Nickell. Hollis Gibbs was born in 1830 and died in 1926. His wife, Martha Nickell Gibbs, who was born in 1838, died in 1914. They lived at Gillmore, Kentucky on a three hundred acre farm, which Nathan Gibbs gave them.

Aunt Martha did a lot of weaving and was one of the best fiddlers in Wolfe County. Uncle Hollis was a very energetic man. When folks told him that he didn't have a lazy bone in his body, he would smile and say, "Well, I take time out now and then to go hunting!"

To Hollis and Martha Nickell Gibbs were born thirteen children—Tom, Laura, Nannie, John M. Maggie, Emma, Josie, Eliza, Farland, Marion, Tilden, Matt, and Nathan.

4. Tom Gibbs married Mary Chapman of Breathitt County and lived in Wolfe.

5. Jeff, Hollis, Emma, Clyde, John, and Pearly were their children.

4. Laura, the first daughter of Hollis Gibbs, married Harris Wilson. They lived at Helechawa and had six children:

5. Curt, Courtney, Esther, Josie, Holt, and Cora, who married Mort Nickell.

6. Ova, a son of Curt Wilson (5) married Roxie Little. They lived on Gillmore and had a dozen children.

7. Coy, Shirley, Dewesse, Ralph, E. C., Russell (deceased), Jewell, Lena, Bernice, Thelma, Jean, and Janet.

4. Nannie, the daughter of Hollis Gibbs, married Joe Lee Wilson of Wolfe County. They moved to Texas and died there. They had five children.

5. Laura, Scott, Rosie, Rita, and Jent were their names.

4. John M. (Johnny), the son of Hollis and Martha Nickell Gibbs, was born on Feb. 9, 1850 and died Feb. 17, 1911. He married Frances Fallen. She had come from Va., with her father, Jeptha Fallen, at the age of ten. Her mother's family name was Higginbotham. Frances Fallen Gibbs, who was born July 31, 1859 died at her home on Sep. 9, 1927. The nine children in the John M. Gibbs family were Hixie, Ranson, Jeptha, Rennie, Rollie, Bernie, McFarland, Josie, and Ida.

5. Hixie Gibbs, who was born on July 2, 1881, died on November 2, 1944. He married Lottie, the daughter of John and Lou Christian

Carpenter of Morgan County. To them were born four children, Lula, Stanley, Denzil, and Juanita.

6. Lula Gibbs married Elmer Patrick of Daysboro, Kentucky. They live in Dillsboro, Indiana and have three children, Iona Fay, Lilla May, and Anna Kay.

6. Stanley Gibbs has been married twice. By his first wife, Lucille Cox, he had two children, Karen Sue and Sharon Joe. By his second wife, Robbie, he had two children, Elaine and William Joseph.

6. Denzil Gibbs (1914-1944) was the husband of Ruby Linden. They had two children, Mildred and William Stanley.

6. Juanita, the youngest child of Hixie Gibbs, is married and lives in Dayton.

5. Ranson Gibbs (1882—1938), another son of John M. and Frances Gibbs, married Winnie, the daughter of William W. and Rose Jane Carpenter of Morgan County. Their marriage date was December 8, 1904. Winnie Carpenter was born on March 7, 1887. For years Ranson Gibbs was a farmer and mail carrier in Wolfe County. Later he moved his family to Dayton, Ohio, where his wodiw is still residing. They had seven children:

6. Roy, Rosa, Alma, Lillian, Greta, Robert, and Ranson. The older ones attended school at Hazel Green Academy.

5. Jeptha, another son of John M. and Frances Fallen Gibbs, was born on February 10, 1886. He married Rebecca, the daughter of Nelson and Polly Nickell, on January 22, 1907. They lived on Gillmore, on a farm. Rebecca Nickell Gibbs, who was born on March 24, 1887, died on December 8, 1936. She was survived by her husband and five children— Ruth, Mae, John, Ruby and Frances.

6. Ruth Gibbs, who was born on November 1, 1908, attended Hazel Green Academy. For fourteen years she has been employed at Frigidaire in Dayton, Ohio.

6. Mae Gibbs married Denzil, the son of Miles and Euroia Fallen. Mae and Denzil live at Helechawa and have four children:

7. Jackie, Edna, Euroia Fay, and her twin sister, Wilma Kay.

6. John Gibbs, who was born on April 17, 1911, is a Gillmore farmer. He married Emma, the daughter of Rollen and Ida Turner Combs. They had two children—Robert Lee, and an infant who died. Emma Combs Gibbs, who was born on October 17, 1922 died on December 14, 1943.

7. Robert Lee Gibbs is a student at Hazel Green Academy.

On July 26, 1947 John Gibbs (6) married a second time. His wife, the former Mabel Spicer, is the daughter of Anderson and Emma Anderson Spicer of Breathitt County. She was born on April 24, 1923. Mabel Gibbs, a graduate of Hazel Green Academy, has had college work at Eastern State Teachers' College and the University of Kentucky. For several years she has been a teacher in Wolfe County, Kentucky. She collected much of the family material on the Gillmore Gibbses for this book. John and Mabel Spicer Gibbs

are the parents of one son.
7. John Michael is his name.
6. Ruby, the daughter of Jeptha and Rebecca Gibbs, married Judge Kash, a son of J. I. and Ida Hatfield Kash of Gillmore. They have three children named Bobby, Naomi, and Wanda.
6. Frances, the other daughter of Jeptha Gibbs, was the wife of McDaniel Francis (deceased). They had one child named Judith Ann.
5. Rennie Gibbs, the son of John M. and Frances Fallen Gibbs, was born on February 27, 1888. In 1907 he married Malvie, the daughter of Chrictopher Columbus and Mary Bell Nickell Gillispie. She was born on November 14, 1891. Rennie Gibbs was a Wolfe County mail carrier. He was killed in a car wreck on August 4, 1931. His widow resides in Hazel Green. The four children in the Rennie Gibbs' family were Chester, Robert (1914—1915), Reva, and Wardie.
6. Chester Gibbs, who was born on January 16, 1912, atended Hazel Green Academy. He has worked in Dayton, Ohio.
6. Reva Gibbs graduated from Hazel Green Academy and attended Lees College at Jackson, Kentucky. She married George Allen, the son of Grover C. and Mary Allen of Breathitt County. He is a veteran of World War II. For six years he served as Circuit Court Clerk of Breathitt County. At the present time Reva and George Allen are residents of Hazel Green.
6. Wardie Gibbs (1916—1949), the other son of Rennie and Malvie Gillispie Gibbs, was a veteran of World War II. He married Callie Robinson of Hazel Green. They had two children, Janet and Wardena.
5. Rollie, another son of John M. and Frances Fallen Gibbs, was born on November 27, 1889. He married Rausa, the daughter of Harlan and Delia Chaney O'Hair, on August 11, 1908. She was born on January 27, 1892. (See the William O'Hair family). Rausa and Rollie settled on Gillmore.

Rollie Gibbs is a Mason and a member of the Christian Church. From 1914 to 1921 he was a foreman for the Cumberland Pipe Line Company. For twelve years he served Wolfe County as Tax Commissioner; for four years he was County Sheriff. He was a guard at the State Penitentiary for one year, and for years he was a W.P.A. foreman. He operates his farm on Gillmore and owns a home in Dayton, Ohio.

To Rollie and Rausa O'Hair Gibbs were born ten children— Jesse Othis (1909—1912), Lexie, Maxie (1913—1915), Wendell, Hubert (1917—1918), Edward, Roy B., Drexel, Wilgus, and James Earl.
6. Lexie Gibbs (October 20, 1911), married Dora Howard of Breathitt County. They live on a Gillmore farm.
6. Wendell Gibbs, who was born on May 24, 1915, married Willa Mae, the daughter of Press and Versie Hale Brewer. (Versie Hale was the daughter of John and Sarah Hale who lived at Hazel Green for many years.)

WOLFE COUNTY

Wendell works at the National Cash Register Company, in Dayton, Ohio. He is a Mason and a member of the First Church of God. Wendell and Willa Mae Gibbs have four children.

7. Betty Lee Gibbs who is now Mrs. Frank Shutts; Christine, Barbara Jo; and David Wendell.

6. Edward Gibbs, who was born on February 5, 1918 married Carrie, the daughter of Monroe and Carrie Woods of Wolfe County. They live on a Lacy Creek farm and have six children.

7. Meritta, Henritta, Wanda Gean, Larry Edward, James Rollic, and Danny Winiford are their names.

6. Roy B. Gibbs (April 21, 1921), does industrial work in Dayton, Ohio. He married Marie, the daughter of Ben and Esther Van Cleve Dunn of Wolfe County.

7. Kenneth is the name of their son.

6. Drexel Gibbs married Burl Moss of Montgomery County, Kentucky. They live in Dayton, Ohio.

6. Wlgus Gibbs (February 2, 1931), married Wilma Stamper of Tolliver, Kentucky. They have on daughter, Debronka Ann.

6. James Earl Gibbs, the youngest child of Rollie and Rausa O'Hair Gibbs, was born on May 2, 1936. He married Ledlene Ellis. They live in Dayton.

5. Bernie, the son of John M. and Frances Fallen Gibbs, was born on July 2, 1892, and died on December 4, 1936. Me married Lydia Ann, the daughter of Herbert and Ella Caskey Nickell of Morgan County, on March 19, 1918. She was born on November 19, 1893. Bernie and Lydia Ann Gibbs lived on Gillmore and had four children— Carl, Beulah, Corbett, and Freida.

6. Carl, their oldest child, is single.

6. Beulah Gibbs married Lester Hart of Little Rock, Arkansas. They live in Dayton.

6. Corbett married Arzella Rose of Wolfe County. Her parents were John and Maggie Russell Rose. Corbett and Arzella Gibbs live on Gillmore. Their children are Flosie, Bernie, Glenda, Evelyn, and Ray Allen.

6. Frieda, the youngest child of Bernie and Lydia Ann Gibbs, married Peter Baldauf, Jr., of West Liberty, Iowa. They live in Dayton and have three children—Peter, Ronald, and William Joseph.

5. McFarland (called Farland) Gibbs, another son of John M. and Frances Fallen Gibbs, was born May 25, 1894. He married Rausa, the daughter of Sam and Rebecca Allen of Breathitt County, on December 25, 1913. She was born on June 10, 1888. McFarland and Rausa Gibbs had two children, Bernard and Evalee.

6. Bernard Gibbs married Marie Taylor of Parkersburg, West Virginia. They live in Dayton and have two children, Evelyn Jean and Wanda Louise.

6. Evalee Gibbs married Carl Picklesimer, the son of Bernie and Rowena C. Reed Picklesimer. They live at Gillmore. Their one child

is named Bernia Lee.

5. Josie, the daughter of Jomn M. and Frances Fallen Gibbs married Willie Lee Haven of Morgan County, Kentucky on December 25, 1916. They lived at Dayton, Ohio. Their two sons are Arthur and Winfred. Josie Gibbs Haven, who was born on August 23, 1897, died on January 23, 1947.

5. Ida, the youngest child of Jomn M. and Frances Fallen Gibbs, was born on June 6, 1901. She married Bert Witt, who was the son of Buddy and Ellen Toliver Witt of Magoffin County on September 25, 1887. Bert was born on September 4, 1901. (Mrs. John Gibbs, Mrs. Malvie Gibbs).

4. Maggie Gibbs, another daughter of Hollis and Martha Nickell Gibbs, married Wesely. They lived in Wolfe County for awhile. Later they settled in Texas. One of their children was named Della.

4. Emma, the daughter of Hollis Gibbs, married George Oldfield. After a time they settled in Madison County, Kentucky.

4. Josie Gibbs, married Hamilton Oldfield. For a time they lived in Arkansas. Their only son is named Denny.

4. Eliza Gibbs married Madison Hatfield of Pike County and lived in Wolfe.

5. Martha, Jettie, and Eppie were their three children.

4. Farland, the son of Hollis Gibbs, married Delora Fallen of Wolfe County and lived at Gillmore.

5. Ettie, Bessie, Ollie (deceased), Bonnie, Raymond (deceased) and Marie were their children.

4. Francis Marion Gibbs, who was born on February 17, 1873, married Sallie Tutt of Wolfe County. They lived in Wolfe. Marion wa sa member of the Campton Baptist Church. He passed away on December 23, 1947. Since then, his wife has died. They are survived by three children:

5. Daisy, their daughter, is now Mrs. Lenox Lawson, of Pine Ridge. Alene Gibbs, who married Byrl Rose, lives in Campton. Orville, their son, works in Dayton.

4. Tilden, another son of Hollis and Martha Nickell Gibbs, married Mertie Lykins of Morgan County. They moved from Long Branch, Kentucky to Illinois. Tilden is dead; Mertie is living. There were three children.

5. Okie, their oldest son, lives in Illinois. Ova Gibbs is a resident of California. The other son is dead.

4. Matt Gibbs, another son of Hollis, is buried in the Gibbs' cemetery on Gillmore. (Nathan Gibbs, Christine Howard).

4. Nathan, the youngest son of Hollis and Martha Nickell Gibbs, was born on August 30, 1881. He married Mertie Gillispie on March 25, 1904. She was born on January 5, 1884. Mertie was the daughter of Christopher Columbus and Mary Bell Nickell Gillispie of Morgan County. She has a sister, Mrs. Malvie Gibbs, and two brothers, Rodney and Henry Gillispie, living in Hazel Green.

Nathan Gibbs has engaged in farming in Breathitt and Wolfe Counties At one time he was Deputy Sheriff of Wolfe County. He is the only surviving member of the Hollis Gibbs family. For the past few years Nathan and Mertie Gibbs have been residents of Hazel Green. The ygave generously of their store of Gibbs' information for this history. Nathan has eyes and ears for seeing and hearing hants! He's a reay story-teller!

To Nathan and Mertie Gibbs were born eight children—Marvin, Ora,. Carl, William Clay, Edna, Olivetta, Martha, and Lucy.

5. Marvin Gibbs, who was born on February 15, 1905, passed away on July 3, 1955. He was buried in the Gibbs' cemetery on Gillmore.

5. Ora Gibbs, who was born on October 12, 1906, married Robert Privett. They live in Breathitt County and have a large family.

5. Carl Gibbs was born on February 26, 1911. He married Mary Privett. They live in West Virginia and have eight children.

5. William Clay (Willie) Gibbs, another son of Nathan Gibbs, was born on September 20, 1912. He attended Hazel Green Academy. On June 29, 1940 he married Marie Hill of Summers County, West Virginia at Catlettsburg, Kentucky. They live in West Virginia. Their daughter is named Carolyn Louise.

5. Edna Gibbs was born on November 26, 1914. She is a graduate of Hazel Green Academy and Lees College at Jackson, Kentucky. Fo rseveral years she has been employed as an inspector in the National Cash Register Company in Dayton, Ohio.

5. Olivetta Gibbs, who was born on Augnst 3, 1918, died on November 15, 1938.

5. Martha Gibbs was born on April 13, 1921. She married Walter Smith. They live in Dayton, Ohio.

5. Lucy, the youngest child of Nathan and Mertie Gibbs, was born on December 9, 1923. She married Orville Young of Breathitt County, Kentucky. They live in Dayton and are the parents of one child. (The Nathan Gibbs Family).

Irene McLin Keller, Compiler.

Personal rights of all contributors have been respected.

The right to reproduce this chapter in printed form must be secured throughout the Wolfe County Women's Club with the permission of said compiler.

THE CASKEYS

The Caskeys were of Huguenot orgin. Thomas Caskey, the ancestor of many Morgan and Wolfe County Caskeys, was born on April 1, 1766, probably in the present state of New York. He married Lydia Hopkins on December 19, 1790 in Orange County, New York. She was born on March 29, 1775. They left New York for Kentucky in a wagon soon after their marriage. Lydia was not quite sixteen at the time. They first settled on Flat Creek near Mt. Sterling. Lydia was so homesick that she would not let her husband build a log house for a year. In the interin they lived in a three-conered log shack, which may have been an improver's cabin on a claim of bounty land.

Thomas Caskey liked to hunt and fish. It is said he exchanged his first Kentucky farm for a piece of mountain land in the present county of Morgan. The Caskeys finally settled on the Licking River about one mile and a half from West Liberty. Here they reared their family. Lydia Caskey died on June 30, 1850. Thomas Caskey passed away on March 7, 1853. They had thirteen children.

2. Mary, John, Hannah, Gardner, Robert, Jane, Margaret Eleanor, Lydia, Thomas, Samuel, William, and Sally Ann were their names.

2. Mary Caskey, the first child, was born on October 7, 1791. She married a Joshua Day. Their marriage date was November 19, 1813. I have heard that they settled at Daysboro.

2. Hannah, another daughter of Thomas Caskey, was born on November 15, 1795. She married James McGuire on October 14, 1813. They lived on Lacy Creek.

3. Jane, one of their daughters, married Milton Gibbs. They lived in Wolfe County. (See the Nathan Gibbs Family).

2. Margaret (Peggy) Caskey married Jesse C. Day. She was the paternal grandmother of Jesse Taylor Day of Hazel Green. (See the Jesse C. Day family.)

2. William Caskey, who was born on January 16, 1816, married Rebecca Gillmore of Wolfe County. Their marriage took place on October 21, 1836. Their daughter, Evaline, married Joel Havens.

The other members in the Thomas Caskey family settled around West Liberty, Caney Creek, Helechawa, Gillmore, Lacy Creek and Hazel Green.

During my childhood, one of the desendants of Thomas and Lydia Hopkins Caskey lived in Hazel Green. His name was William Taylor Caskey. He married Angeline, the daughter of Jeff Stamper. About 1875 they built a large two-story house northwest of the second site of the Hazel Green Christian Church on State Street. This home is now owned by Mr. and Mrs. Carl Walters.

For some years William Taylor Caskey was a merchant in Hazel Green. He was a member of the Hazel Green Fair Association. Taylor and Angeline Stamper Caskey were zealous workers in the Hazel Green Christian Church. In his will, Taylor Caskey left a bequest for this church. Angeline Stamper Caskey, who was born in 1848, died in 1928. Her husband, William Taylor Caskey, passed away the same year; he was born in 1847. They are buried in the Hazel Green Cemetery. (Mary E. Day, James I. Hollon, Christine Howard).

Irene McLin Keller, Compiler

Personal rights of Miss Mary E. Day have been respected.

WOLFE COUNTY

THE DAYS

The Days were among the first people to settle in that section of Montgomery County, Kentucky, which is now Morgan and Wolfe. They came in family groups from Virginia and located between the present towns of Hazel Green and Caney. Daysboro in its early period was literally a borough of Days.

Our Kentucky progenitor, John Day, a Revolutionary soldier, was of English extraction. He was born in Lunenburg County, Virginia on June 28, 1760 and died in Morgan County, Kentucky on July 16, 1837. Not long before the Revolution, his mother, Susan Wyley Day, was kidnapped and massacred by Indians. Her body was found on land which was owned by Hannah Muchmore's father in Botetourt County, Virginia. (Hannah Muchmore, the wife of "the first" John Gibbs, is buried at Hazel Green.

John Day's wife, the former Rebecca Howe was born in Virgiana on October 11, 1765, and died in Morgan County, Kentucky on March 17, 1856. She was one of the flower girls at the inauguration of George Washington. The little glass bowl in which she carried her flowers is in the possession of the Floyd Day family at Winchester, Kentucky.

John and Rebecca Howe Day were married on September 10, 1782 and lived in Montgomery County, Virginia. Here their children were born. In 1810, John Day moved his family to the two hundred acres of Kentucky land which he had received in 1784, as a military warrant, for his services in the Revolutionary War. This tract of land was located in the present County of Morgan near Caney Creek. I think all of his eight children married and settled in the localities of Caney Creek, illmore, Lacy Creek, Daysboro, and Maytown.

2. Joseph, Daniel, William, John, Elizabeth, Allen, Anne, and Jesse were their names.

2. Jesse C. Day, the youngest child of John and Rebecca Howe Day, was born at New River, Virginia on January 13, 1802 and died in Morgan County, Kentucky on April 2, 1883. He was about eight years old when his parents moved to Caney Creek, Kentucky. Jesse C. Day married Margaret (Peggy) Caskey, a native of Morgan County, on August 24, 1820. She was born on May 11, 1802 and died in 1884. (See "The Caskey Family").

To Jesse C. and Margaret (Peggy) Caskey Day were born ten children:

3. William, Robert, Rebecca Jane, Lydia, Elizabeth, John W. Cynthia Anne, Allen T., Ellen and Trumbo. (Genealogy file of John C. M. Day).

3. William Day was born in Morgan County on August 19, 1821 and died at Frozen Creek on January 28, 1884. He married Phoebe Elender Gibbs, the daughter of Nathan and Nancy Jane Lipps

Gibbs of Frozen and Hazel Green on June 18, 1844. They first went to housekeeping on a land tract of fifty acres, which William Day had secured as a land claim. It was located between Helechawa and Caney Creek. After the birth of their first child, Nathan Boone, they moved to the Nathan Gibbs farm on Frozen Creek. Gradually William Day bought, as is shown by deeds, most of this farm from his father-in-law. Here he built a large two-story log house that was later weatherboarded. In later years when a land consession was given, the Day house became a railroad stop. It was called Homestead. Today, Homestead is the site of a modern East Kentucky dairy farm.

William Day, a Democrat, was a man of loftiest principles; he represented Breathitt County in the Kentucky Legislature from 1859 to 1861. Phoebe Elender Gibbs, his wife, who was born on JanuaryV 30, 1825, passed away on June 11, 1862. In her eighteen years of married life she had given birth to nine children.

After her death William Day married Louraney Cope, the daughter of William Cope, and continued to live in Breathitt. Their only daughter, Lou Ellen was a heroic woman in Breathitt's bloodiest feuding days. She was the wife of James Hargis and the mother of two children, Beach and Eva Lee. Eva Lee married a Dr. Hogg and had a son, James, and a daughter, Helen. Following the death of her husband, Eva Lee Hargis married Kash Williams, the son of Green Williams. (See "Our First Kashes.")

Now, the nine children who were born of William Day and his first wife, Phoebe Elender Gibbs Day were Nathan Boonne, Jesse Taylor, Margaret, Nancy Jane, Lucinda, Mary Elizabeth, Floyd, John C. M., and William.

4. Nathan Boone Day, who was born in 1845, was wounded by Home guards during the Civil War. By his first wife, Betty Cope, he had three children—Carl, who died at the age of twenty-six, while he was a member of the Kentucky Legislature, Clara (Williams), and Walter, who attended Hazel Green Academy. He married Bush, the daughter of Isaac and Edith Vaughn Mize, and moved to Arkansas.

By his second wife, Peggy Crawford, Nathan Boone Day had one daughter, Virginia May, who married John T. Hindman, a bank employee. He is dead; she lives in Lexington, Kentucky.

Nathan Boone Day ran a lumber, stave, and tie plant on White Oak Creek near Frozen. He served two terms as Superintendent of Schools in Breathitt County and one term as County Judge. He died on July 28, 1899, from injuries, which he received in a machinery accident at his mill.

4. Jesse Taylor, another son of William and Phoebe Elender Gibbs Day, was born on December 12, 1846, at Frozen Creek, Kentucky. He chose James Greenville Trimble's pretty little "black-

eyed" daughter, Rowena Belle, for his wife. She was born on June 10, 1850 at Hazel Green. (See the James Greenville Trimble family.) They were married on November 4, 1869 by Reverend Joe Nickell, one of the early ministers in the Hazel Green Christian Church.

For over fifty years J. T. Day was a merchant in Hazel Green. During part of this time he carried on a wholesale as well as a retail business with branch stores at Lee City, Torrent, and Frozen. From 1888 to 1890 his brother, Floyd Day, and his son, Kelly Bruce Day, were co-owners in the firm, J. T. Day and Company. At a later date his son-in-law, R. J. McLin, was his associate in business.

The J. T. Day store was located on the Main Street corner of Mr. Day's home grounds. For years the large rock which is now the J. T. Day yard was at the front entrance of the store. Almost everybody in Wolfe County has gossiped a bit at that rock.

Roe B. and Jesse Taylor Day took a great interest in their home and yard. Their house, which was designed by an architect, was built in 1884.

J.T. Day ran a grist mill on a tract of his Red River land. He carried on a live stock and a lumber business in connection with his store. He accumulated much land; his saw mill gave employment to many people. Coal mines were "opened up" on some of his farms.

About 1888 he organized The Hazel Green Fair Association. The Day "bottoms" on which annual fairs were held still bear the name "Fair Grounds". The Hazel Green Hotel was built and managed by J. T. Day. He also owned and operated the El Park Hotel at Torrent, Kentucky. It became a fashionable summer and hay fever resort. (Read El Park Hotel" by Mrs. Roy Cecil.)

Jesse Taylor Day, a Democrat and a Mason, was one of the founders of Hazel Green Academy. Through the years he was a benevolent member of the Hazel Green Christian Church.

J. T. Day was a man for his age—the age that centered around the first development of natural resources in the eastern part of Kentucky. He wanted to meet the needs of mountain people because he was one of them; he understood them; he had their weakness; and he had their strength.

He was a man with a tender heart; a hard-luck story invariably brought tears to his eyes. Generously did he give, and always did he remain the poor man's friend.

His stores are gone now and his accumulated land-holdings have passed into many hands, but the little remembered acts of his kindness live on as a social heritage of the people whom he loved the best, the mountain people, the people of Wolfe County, Kentucky.

EARLY AND MODERN HISTORY

On February 19, 1921 Jesse Taylor Day passed away after an extended illness. Roe B. Day, his wife, died on May 3, 1932. They are buried in the Hazel Green cemetery.

To Jesse Taylor and Rowena Belle Trimble Day were born four children, Kelly ,Bruce, Lillie and Daisy.

5. Kelly Bruce who was born on September 10, 1870, had private tutoring until Hazel Green Academy was established. In 1888 he graduated from the Commercial College at the University of Kentucky. That year his father gave him one half of his interest in the firm, J. T. Day and Company. On April 7, 1890 while he was on a train enroute to Cincinnati to buy merchandise and an engagement ring for his sweetheart, he became the innocent victim of a stray bullet that had been intended for another man. His fiancee, Miss Mary J. Daviess of Georgetown, Kentucky, had been one of the first music teachres at Hazel Green Academy.

5. Lula Day and her twin sister, Lillie, were born on March 31, 1873. They attended Hazel Green Academy and received their higher education in Lexington at Hamilton.

On October 21, 1891 Lula Day married Rollin Kash of Hazel Green. He was the son of Joseph A. and Sarah Ellen Swango Kash. (See "Our First Kashes") Rollin Kash, a lawyer, had graduated from Centre College cum laude. He practiced his profession in the courts of Morgan and Wolfe, and until his health failed, he was an attorney in Hazel Green. He died on April 17, 1901. His birth date was October 14, 1870. Rollin Kash was survived by his wife and three small children.

His widow continued to live in Hazel Green. Her home, a gift from her father and mother, was built on the Asbury Trimble lot near the corner of Main and State Streets. It is now the residence of Mr. Rodney Gillispie.

Aunt Lula "loved" her home, her garden, her cows, her chickens, and her flowers. Landscaping never bothered Lula D. Kash; whenever she found a space for another rose, she just went to work and set out! She was such a good cook that it was customary to overeat at her house. Lula Kash was a very jovial person and one who didn't hesitate to speak her mind, if an occasion demanded it. She shared her worldly goods with many people. Wolfe County lost an admirable woman when she passed away in November of 1935.

The three children of Rollin and Lula Day Kash were named Jesse Day, Rowena, and Dollie Ellen.

6. Jesse Day Kash was born on October 2, 1892. He received his secondary education at Millersburg Military School. In 1915 he graduated from the University of Virginia in Law. On the tenth of July in that year he married Mary, the daughter of William and Nancy Smith of Pikeville, Kentucky.

Jesse D. Kash became an attorney-at-law in Clark County, Kentucky. While living in Winchester, he served eight years as County Attorney. Upon becoming a Trial Attorney for the Federal Commission in 1938, he moved to Washington, D. C. When he retired from this position in 1955, he returned to Winchester, Kentucky, where he engaged in law practice.

To Jesse and Mary Smith Kash were born five children—Rowena, Jesse, Nancy, Helen, and Mary Jane.

7. Rowena Kash attended Stevens College in Missouri. By her first husband, Charles Stephenson, she had two children named Tommy and Marie.

In 1956 Rowena Kash Stephenson of Winchester became the wife of Floyd Day, Jr. (See the Floyd Day family).

7. Jesse Kash, Jr., a veteran of World War II, graduated from Riverside Military Institute in Georgia and attended Centre College at Danville, Kentucky. He is presently employed in Lexington, Kentucky. He married Pauline Shelton of Clark County. They live near Winchester and have two children, Jesse III and Charolette Ann.

7. Nancy, another daughter in the Jesse D. Kash family, attended Blackstone College in Virginia and married R. T. Keuren, a native of New Jersey. They live in Westfield, New Jersey and have two children, Carol Lynn and Robert, Jr.

Helen Kash is now Mrs. Ova Thomas of Winchester, Kentucky. By her first husband, Richard Carter, she had two children, Pamela M. and Richard.

7. Mary Jane, the youngest child of Jesse and Mary Smith Kash, attended Mary Washington College in Virginia and the University of Kentucky. She married Virgil Puckett. They live in Winchester; their three children are Rollin Kash, Owen Taylor and Virgil Tracy.

6. Rowena, the second child of Rollin and Lula Day Kash, was born on April 8, 1895. She is a member of the Christian Church. Rowena attended Hazel Green Academy and received her higher education at Danville, Kentucky. On July 14, 1915 she married Courtney Combs of Campton, Kentucky. He was the son of Aaron Thrasher and Pocahontas Duff Combs. His education was received at Hazel Green Academy and Fugazzi business School in Lexington, Kentucky.

For many years while Courtney Combs was engaged in oil business in Owensboro, Kentucky, Mrs. Combs was prominent in West Kentucky club work. Later they moved to Fort Wayne, where Mr. Combs was associated with the Kitchen Maid Corporation. Here they were very active in the church and civic activities.

Courtney Combs died suddenly on February 9, 1950. For the past two years, Rowena Kash Combs has been employed at Hazel Green

EARLY AND MODERN HISTORY

Academy as an assistant librarian for the Wolfe County Book Mobile.

6. Dollie Ellen Kash, the youngest child of Rollin and Lula Day Kash, was born on June 23, 1897. She attended Hazel Green Academy and is a member of the Christian Church. On July 14, 1915 she married Dorsey, the son of Reverend Frank Press and Anna Nickell Wilson of Helechawa. They lived at Hazel Green and ran a general store. Their two sons were named Wilburn Kash ando Dorsey.

7. Wilburn Kash Wilson attended Hazel Green Academy. On November 26, 1941 he marrier Alice Potts. They live in Ohio where Wilson does industrial work. Their daughter is named Beverly Ann.

7. Dorsey T. Wilson attended Hazel Green Academy. He does industrial work in Upper Sandusky, Ohio. On May 13, 1939 he married Helen Barnhardt. They have four children, Dorsey Lee, James Wilburn, Robert Courtney, and Brenda.

After the death of her first husband, Dollie Kash Wilson (6) married Lee A. Reed, a veteran of World War I. He was the son of William and Florence Burgett Reed of Grassy Creek, Kentucky. Their marriage date was May 6, 1928. They live on a large farm near Sabina, Ohio.

5. Lillie, another daughter of Jesse Taylor and Rowena Bell Trimble Day, married Robert Joseph McLin. (See "The McLins.")

5. Daisy, the youngest child of Jesse Taylor and Rowena Bell Day was born on October 3, 1886. While she attended Hazel Green Academy she was the recipient of two medals. Daisy Day was a member of the Christian Church. She was a very popular girl in Hazel Green; on numerous occasions her early twentieth century clothes have been used in school plays at Hazel Green Academy.

On August 21, 1911, Daisy Day married James I. Hollon, the son of James Buchanan and Caroline Elkins Hollon of Campton, Kentucky. He was born on October 4, 1883, at Hollonville. James I. Hollon attended school at Campton, Kentucky, and received his higher education at Centre College, Danville, Kentucky and Georgetown University, Washington, D. C. He is amember of the Catholic Church. From 1914 to 1917 he was the editor of the Hazel Green Herald; from 1913 to 1926 he was postmaster at Hazel Green. James I. Hollon (Sr.) is a veteran of World War I. In 1917 he was commissioned a First Lieutenant and in 1918 he was promoted to Captain.

Daisy and James I. Hollon lived in the J. T. Day home at Hazel Green. Aunt Daisy was a woman of quiet charm and gentle dignity. To her nieces and nephews she was a real storybook aunt. She passed away on December 15, 1947.

To James I. Hollon, Sr., and Daisy Day Hollon were born four children – Kelly, James I. Hollon, Jr., Elizabeth Trimble, and Raymond who died at birth.

6. Kelly Day Hollon, who was a very talented pianist, was born

on September 3, 1912. He was a senior at Hazel Green Academy at the time of his accidental death on September 4, 1930.

6. James I. Hollon, Jr., (Jimmy) was born on May 19, 1916. He is a graduate of Hazel Green Academy and a member of the Christian Church. On June 3, 1939 he married Edna Mae, the daughter of Alvin B. and Minnie Lunsford Hoover of Lexington, Kentucky. Since 1936 Edna Mae has been the music teacher at Hazel Green Academy. For the past eleven years James I. Hollon, Jr., has been employed at Hazel Green Academy as farm manager and basketball coach.

7. Connie Mae Hollon, their daughter, was born on October 12, 1945. Their son James I. Hollon III, was born on June 23, 1950.

6. Elizabeth Trimble, the only daughter of James I. and Daisy Day Hollon, was born on January 27, 1918. She graduated from Hazel Green Academy and has served as the organist in the Christian Church. On June 23, 1951 she married James Lacy Stewart, the son of Alexander Thomas and Clemma Lacy Stewart of Stanton, Kentucky. (See the Seaborn Trimble family.) James (Jim) is a graduate of Stanton High School and Cleveland College of Embalming at Cleveland, Ohio. He is associated with the Hearne Funeral Homes at Stanton and Campton, Kentucky. He is also the driver of the Wolfe County Bookmobile trucks and distributes books to thirty-two schools in the County. James and Elizabeth Hollon Stewart live at Hazel Green in the J. T. Day home. They have two sons.

7. James Ivan Stewart was born on May 18, 1952. KellyDay Stewart arrived on May 28, 1956.

The James I. Hollon family donated part of the land for the site of the new Christian Church in Hazel Green. One of the memorial windows in this church has been given in honor of Daisy Day Hollon by her children.

4. Margaret, the first daughter of William and Phoebe Elender Gibbs Day, was born in 1849. She married Captain Callaway Cope. They had three children -- Robert, who died while he was attending school in Virginia; Archie, who married and reared a family at Jackson, Kentucky; and Carrie Day (Hager), a resident of Fla. She had a daughter named Mabel.

4. Nancy Jane, Lucinda Caroline, and Mary Elizabeth Day died in youth.

4. Floyd Day another son of William and Phoebe Elender Gibbs Day, was born on Frozen on December 18, 1854. He lived in the J. T. Day home at Hazel Green from 1869 to 1888. For some years he ran a general store in the town; later he was a part owner in the merchantile firm, J. T. Day and Company.

On June 14, 1888, Floyd Day married a daughter of Mr. John Mason and Eliza Carter Maxey Kash, who were then residents of Hazel Green. (See "Our First Kashes.") The formal wedding of this couple typifies others which were performed in Wolfe County during the same period. The following account was written by Spencer Cooper, Editor of the Hazel Green Herald.

"At half-past eight o'clock on Thursday evening the Christian Church at this place was crowded with citizens of Hazel Green, invitations having been distributed during the day, to witness the marriage of Mr. Floyd Day and Miss Rosalie Du Pont Kash, both of this place.

"Promptly at the hour named someone whispered, 'Here they come!' and all eyes were turned toward the entrance of the church. Reverend D. H. Fallen, who was to perform the ceremony, preceded the bridal party until the thresold was passed, and then stood to one side. Then came the contracting parties. The bride, dressed in nun's veiling and white satin trimmed with silk lace and ribbons, looked like a fairy queen leaning upon the arm of the groom, who was dressed in regulation black customary to such occasions. They marched up the carpeted aisle and stood beneath a beautiful arch of evergreens and flowers from which was suspended a silver lined bell. The attendants, Mr. Kelly Day and Miss Lula Kash, and Miss Emma Kash and Mr. Rollin Kash, taking positions on either side.

"The bridal couple faced the large audience and seldom indeed has a handsomer couple been united in the bonds of matrimony. Reverend Mr. Fallen pronounced the marriage ceremony in an elo quent and impressive manner, and the bride and groom, preceded by the attendants, marched out. In carriages they drove to the residence of the bride's father, where a feast of good things was spread in honor of the occasion, and the happy couple received the congratulations of a host of friends.

"On Friday a reception was given the bridal couple, attendants, and some special friends at the residence of J. T. Day, brother of the groom. The table fairly groaned with both substantials and delicacies. It was a feast fit for the gods, and everyone present enjoyed the occasion.

"The Herald sends greetings and congratulations and wishes the couple a long, prosperous, and pleasant journey through life."

In 1892 Floyd Day sold out his merchantile interest in Hazel Green to J. T. Day. He moved his family to Clay City and later to Jackson, where he had retail and wholesale stores. He owned and operated the first light and ice plants in that town. Floyd Day organized the first bank in Breathitt County; it was called the Jackson Deposit Bank.

In 1898 he built the Mountain Central Railroad to help carry timber to his saw mills at Clay City, Beattyville and Natural Bridge. In 1903 when it was to have been abandoned as a logging road, Floyd Day met the request of Wolfe County people and extended the line as a freight and passenger carrier to Campton Junction. In this capacity the railroad functioned until 1928. (Read "The Mountain Central Railroad" by Mrs. Roy Cecil.)

From 1918 to 1922 Floyd and Rosalie Day managed and operated the El Park Hotel at Torrent, Kentucky. Later they moved to Winchester, Kentucky. Rosalie Kash Day, who was born on October 11, 1869 at Jackson, Kentucky, passed away on June 8, 1929. Uncle Floyd followed on August 11, 1936. Both are buried at Winchester, Kentucky.

To Floyd and Rosalie Kash Day were born six children: Golden, Margaret, Eleanor, Rosa, Phoebe, and Floyd Day, Jr.

5. Golden Day, who was born at Hazel Green, received her higher education in Lexington at Hamilton and Transylvania. For a time she operated selling booths at Natural Bridge and sold baskets which were made by Mrs. Bill Ross of Hazel Green. (Mrs. Bill Ross was the former Sarah Harvey. Her husband was the son of Mary Bell ("Aunt Pop") Ross, who for years did washing and ironing for Hazel Green families.)

For a number of years Miss Golden Day has been District Office Manager of District Office 7, Department of Highways, at Lexington, Kentucky.

5. Margaret, the second child in the Floyd Day family, was born at Hazel Green. She married Webb Johnson of Winchester, Kentucky.

6. Webb Day, Jr., their son, lives in Lexington. He married Sara Buckles.

5. Eleanor Day, who was born at Jackson, was the former wife of John F. Auxier. She is now employed at Winchester.

6. Jane Day Auxier, her daughter, received her Masters degree at the University of Kentucky. She does secretarial work in Winchester.

5. Rosa, another daughter of Floyd Day, was born at Jackson. She married Winston Prewitt; they live at Lost Creek in Breathitt County.

5. Phoebe Day, the wife of T. U. Sanders of Frankfort, Kentucky, passed away in 1951. Her husband is also dead. They had two daughters, Rose and Dorothy.

6. Rose Du Pont Saunders is now Mrs. John W. Emerick of Charolettesville, Virginia. Dorothy Saunders is secretary of The American Ambassador at Saigon. Her work has taken her to many far and distant countries.

5. Floyd Day, Jr., the youngest child of Floyd and Rosalie Kash Day, attended the University of Kentucky. He is the Office Manager of the Bogie Equipment Company in Lexington. On December 14, 1956, he married Mrs. Rowena Kash Stephenson of Winchester, Kentucky. (See the Jesse D. Kash family.)

EARLY AND MODERN HISTORY

4. John C.M. Day, another son of William and Phoebe Elender Gibbs Day, was born on June 3, 1859. He attended school in Virginia. On June 30, 1887, he married Margaret Charolette McLin. She was born on November 22, 1865. (See "The McLins".)

John Day was Vice President and General Manager of the Mountain Central Railroad, which was built by his brother, Floyd Day. He had other business interests in Kentucky and Mississippi. He enjoyed hunting moose, deer, and "ancestors"! Every Wolfe County Gibbs, Day, and Caskey owes him a debt of gratitude for the preservation of family history.

On August 18, 1915, John Day passed away. Maggie McLin Day died on October 1, 1921. They are buried at Winchester, Kentucky, where they had resided fo ra long time.

To John C. M. and Maggie McLin Day were born five children: William B., Mary E., Kelly B., Margaret Charolette who died in infancy, and Catherine.

5. William B. Day (1888-1948) was married twice. By his first wife, Blanche Wasson, he had two daughters: Margaret Catherine, now Mrs. Mose Alverson; and Gay Wasson, who married Roger Ruhlman. William B. Day's second wife was Ann Ross Baber.

5. Mary E. Day, who is a graduate of Mt. Holyoke College, is now a retired Civil Service employee. She lives with her sister, Catherine, at Winchester, Kentucky.

5. Kelly Day married Louise Cooper. Their only son, Kelly Day, Jr., a graduate of Georgia Institute of Technology, is an electronic specialist with International Business Machines in Poughkeepsie, New York. He married Jean Hensted and has two sons.

5. Catherine, the youngest child of John C. M. and Maggie McLin Day, is a graduate of Kentucky College for Women. She is the wife of Clarence Bloomfied, the owner of Vic Bloomfield and Sons Department store in Winchester, Kentucky. Their only son, Clarence Jr., a graduate of Centre College, is now his father's associate in business. He married Mary Swetman and has two little boys.

4. William (Will), the youngest child of William and Phoebe Elender Gibbs Day, was born on February 20, 1862. He was only a few months old when his mother passed away. As a little boy he spent part of his time in the home of his grandfather, Nathan Gibbs, at Hazel Green. Later he atended school in Virginia. He married Rowena, the daughter of John and Evelyn Young Marion of Rose Hill, Virginia, on September 15, 1883. They lived at homestead on Frozen. Rowena Marion Day who was born on August 30, 1862 passed away on February 9, 1930. William Day died in 1934. Their eight children were Luther (1884-1905), Carrie, Bennet (1886-1891), Nellie, Grace who died in early life, Mossie, Bessie, and William Day III.

5. Carrie Day (1890-1930), was the first wife of June Jett, a merchant in Jackson, Kentucky. They had two daughters - - Marion,

who died in infancy; and June Eloise, who is now Mrs. Stratton Miller, of St. Matthews, Kentucky. Her three children are Beverly Carolyn, Stratton Jett, and Harry David.

5. Nellie, another daughter of William Day, is buried on Frozen. She was the wife of Z. T. Hurst, Jr. Her only son, Albert Hurst, is an office employee at Veteran's Hospital, in Lexington, Kentucky.

5. Mossie Day, a graduate of Georgetown College, received her M. A. degree from the University of Louisana. She married Green Lee Surber, railroad employee in Hazard, and taught in the Perry County School System for years. Since the death of her husband, she has been teaching in Jefferson County. Her daughter, Nell Day Surber, is a graduate of Barnard College in New York and the Law School of the University of Cincinnati. She is now Mrs. Peyton Fitz. She practices law in Cincinnati, where her husband is a Personnel Analyst at Shillitos.

5. Bessie, another daughter of William Day, attended school at Hazel Green Academy. She is a graduate of the University of Kentucky. After the death of her first husband, Holmes Riffles, she married Stephen Taulbee, a furniture store owner, in Hazard, Kentucky. For a number of years Bessie was a high school teacher in Hazard. After the death of an infant daughter, Rowena Ross Taulbee, Stephen and Bessie Day Taulbee adopted two children, James Stephen and Christine Bess.

5. William Day III (Willie), the youngest son of William and Rowena Marion Day, is dead. He was the husband of Julia Jett. Their only son, William Overton Day, a graduate of Indiana University and a second lieutenant in the Marines, married Patricia Anne Price of Bourbon, Indiana.

3. Now, John W. Day (September 24, 1832), a son of Jesse C. and Margaret Caskey Day, married Evaline, the daughter of Nathan and Nancy Jane Lipps Gibbs of Hazel Green, on October 16, 1852. (See "The Gibbs Family.)" Three of their eight children were Boone, Capt. and Taylor. Aunt Evaline was real witty and always enjoyed her own jokes. She was born on February 19, 1836 and died in July 1931. She is buried in Morgan County.

3. Allen T., another son of Jesse and Margaret Caskey Day, was born on March 27, 1837. He married Lou Ellen Cox. (See "The Cox Family" by Mrs. W. E. Bach.) Aunt Lou was born in 1843 and died in 1919. Allen T. and Lou Day ran a hotel, The Day House, in Hazel Green. It was located on the site of the present May restaurant. After Allen T. Day passed away in 1884, Aunt Lou continued to run her boarding house. She had a parrot that always wanted a cracker. It lived to a ripe old age and should have been buried with honors. Allen T. and Lou Cox Day had one daughter, Emma Florence.

4. Emma Florence Day (1862-1931), married John Evans of Wolfe County. (See "The Evans Family.") He was born in 1856 and died in 1907. For many years he was a bookkeeper in the J. T. Day store.

After his death Emma kept boarders. Her hospitable house, which was located near the Masonic Lodge on the "Old State Road," is still in use.

To John and Emma Day Evans were born four daughters, Lillian (Lillie), Lula, Nellie, and Mattie.

5. Lillian (Lillie) was the second wife of Will Cecil. He had a daughter, farn by his first wife, Ida Swango, who died in early life Will and Lillie Cecil were in the mercantile business in Cedar Bluff, Va Both are dead. They had two children: Pat, who works in the shipyard at Norfolk, Virginia; and a small son, Russell, who died on November 7, 1905.

5. Lula Mae Evans was born in 1882. She graduated from Hazel Green Academy. For a time she taught privately in Hazel Green. On June 21, 1917, she married Henry C. Ward, a graduate of Hazel Green Academy. He was the son of Jonh and Juda Cox Ward of Hazel Green. His birth date was May 17, 1878.

After living in Virginia and Canada, this couple moved to Myton, Utah where Mr. Ward was a merchant; he also served as the Post master in that place for twevle years. Later he was associated with a construction company in the same state. When his health failed Henry Ward returned to Hazel Green. He died at the home of his sister, Lou Ward Johnson (Mrs. E. A.), on May 23, 1939. His widow, Lula Evans Ward, resides in Florida.

5. Nellie Evans, who was born in 1883, attended Hazel Green Academy. She continued to keep boarders after the death of her mother, Emma Day Evans. Many people, who came to Hazel Green to drink the water at Swango Springs, stayed at her house. Nellie was a member of the Christian Church; she died in 1946.

5. Mattie, the youngest child of John and Emma Day Evans, was born on December 5, 1886. She attended Hazel Green Academy. On January 21, 1906, she married Ellis Boyd of Gardener, Virginia They lived in Honaker, Virginia, where Mr. Boyd was a telegraph operator for the Norfolk and Western railroad. He is now dead.

To Ellis and Mattie Evans Boyd were born six children -- Raymond, Geraldine, Moran, Ellis Junior, Dorothy Nell and Frances Louise.

6. Raymond Boyd, a lawyer in Lebanon, Virginia, married Nancy Lee Grady. Their two children are R .J. and Betty Carol.

6. Geraldine, who is assistant cashier of the Taziwell National Bank in Tazewell, Virginia, is the wife of Dave Rowe. He is a foreman for the Power Company in Tazewell.

6. Moran Boyd does clerical work in Virginia.

6. Ellis Junior is the owner of a service station in Honaker, Virginia. He married Marguerite Miller, a music teacher. They have five children.

6.Dorothy Nell Boyd married Ralph T. Howard on June 19, 1946. They live on a farm in Virginia. Their two children are Larry Lynn and Janice Kay.

6. Frances Louise, the youngest child in the Ellis Boyd family lives in Honaker, Virginia, with her mother, Mattie Evans Boyd. (Mrs. E. A. Johnson, Christine Howard, Mattie Boyd).

Irene McLin, Keller Compiler

Personal rights of all contributions have been respected.

The right to reproduce this chapter in printed form must be secured through the Wolfe County Woman's Club with the permission of said compiler.

THE McLINS

The McLins were of Scotch-Irish descent. They came from North Ireland to America in colonial times. The parents of the late Robert Joseph McLin of Hazel Green were Captain John Blair and Mary Bales McLin of Rose Hill, Virginia.

1. Captain John Blair McLin (1883-1910), a soldier of the Confederacy, served in the House of Delegates and in the General Assembly of Virginia. He was the son of Joseph and Charlotte Blackmore McLin of Jonesboro, Tennessee and the grandson of Alexander and Anne Liard Blair McLin of Elizabethtown, Tenn.

His wife, Mary Bales McLin (1846-1923), was the daughter of Robert and Margaret Ewing Bales and the granddaughter of Samuel and Mary Houston Ewing of Lee County, Virginia.

To Captain John Blair and Mary Bales McLin, who were married on December 15, 1864, were born nine children: Margaret Charlotte, who was called Maggie; Robert Joseph; Adelia Ann; John Blair, Jr., who lived at Irvine, Kentucky; Caleb Cecil and James White who were twins; Harriet Catherine (Hatty); Mary Florence; and Elizabeth Isabel, who was called Lizzie.

2. Margaret Charlotte (Maggie) McLin married John C. M. Day. (See the William Day Family.)

2. Hatty and Mary Florence, the only surviving members of this Presbyterian family, still maintain their father's custom of having a period of daily worship in the home.

2. Robert Joseph McLin, who was named for his grandfather's was born on January 13, 1867 at Rose Hill, Virginia in the colonial brick house which his maternal ancestors had built in 1832. Here he grew up and studied at Cumberland College at Rose Hill. Here also followed the vocation of his father and became a merchant.

His first trips to Kentucky were made on horseback through Cumberland Gap. In 1886 he became acquainted with Lillie Day of Hazel Green. She was the daughter of Jesse Taylor and Rowena Trimble Day. (See The J. T. Day Family.)

Six years later on December 22, 1892 Robert Joseph McLin met her, a radiant bride in winter white--at the landing of the beautiful

329

stairway in the J. T. Day home. Together they walked on a carpet of white across the street to the Presbyterian Church where they were united in the bonds of holy matrimony by Reverend Eugene P. Mickel.

Lillie Day was born on March 31, 1873. While she attended Hazel Green Academy she won two medals – one in music and the other for her scholastic standing. Lillie and her twin sister, Lula, received their higher education in Lexington at Hamilton. They were members o fthe Christian Church.

After living at Winchester for a few years, Robert and Lillie McLin moved to Hazel Green. As the business associate of J. T. Day, R. J. McLin helped to manage several East Kentucky stores under the name of Day and McLin. He became the president of a mining company in Breathitt County. In later years he served Wolfe County as Master Commissioner.

Robert Joseph McLin was an elder in the Hazel Green Presbyterian Church. He took a great interest in his home and family.

At Hazel Green the McLins lived at Happy Hollow, sometimes called Hoot Owl Hollow by fleeing suitors! J. T. Day gave the house and grounds to his daughter, Lillie. In later years R. J. McLin had the house remodeled and added more land to the tract. The original house was built about 1886 by John M. Rose, the father of Mrs. Carrie Mize of Hazel Green.

Lillie McLin, lovingly called "Beauty" by her children, approached the Great Beyond with prayers of thanksgiving and unfaltering faith; with loving words of appreciation for those who administered to her physical needs; and with a deep, sustained insight into the spiritual brightness of a heavenly day. She passed away on her husband's birthday, January 13, 1951. A memorial window in the new Christian Church at Hazel Green is being given in her honor by her children.

Robert Joseph McLin died on March 28, 1955. He was buried beside his wife in the Hazel Green cemetery.

Eight of the nine children in the Robert Joseph McLin family were born at Hazel Green. At birth these eight babies were dressed by Mrs. Crock Coldiron, who lived in the same town. For over fifty years this good woman assisted doctors at many local deliveries.

Robert Joseph and Lillie Day McLin named their nine babies Mary Roe, Monnie Bell, Lula Mildred, Daisy Florence, Robert Bruce, Margaret Christine, Lillian Day, Ruby Kathleen, and Mamie Irene.

3. Mary Roe McLin was born on October 12, 1893. She was educated at Hazel Green Academy and Kentucky College for Women at Danville. At an early age she united with the Presbyterian

Church. On June 2, 1920 she married a Morgan County farmer, Bernard Clay Howard, who had attended Hazel Green Academy. His birth date was November 20, 1884. He was the son foHarris and Celia Lacy Howard of White Oak, Kentucky. The Howards were of English descent.

On August 12, 1925 Mary Roe McLin passed away at her home at White Oak, Kentucky, following the birth of her fourth child. "Her whole life had been filled with deeds of loving kindness." After her death her husband and children lived in the Harris Howard home.

The four children of Bernard Clay and Mary Roe Howard were Maurine Clay, Lillian Catherine, Bernard Eldon, and Robert Woodford.

4. Maurine Clay Howard was born at Hazel Green, Kentucky on September 27, 1921. She was in her Sophomore year at Hazel Green Academy when she passed away on February 27, 1936, with leukemia. During her extended illness one of the most God-like expressions of friendship was the donations of blood by her Wolfe County schoolmates for necessary transfusions. In his funeral message Reverend M. V. Roberts, pastor of the Hazel Green Christian Church said, "Her loved ones, her friends, her schoolmates will long hold in memory a sweet smile; a sunny disposition; a womanly radiance." Maurine was buried beside her mother in the Hazel Green cemetery.

4. Lillian Catherine, the second child in the Bernard Howard family, was born at Hazel Green, Kentucky: For a time she attended school at Hazel Green Academy. On January 30, 1943, she married Tommy, the son of J. A. and Cliffie May Oldfield of Mize, Kentucky. Tommy, a veteran of World War II, graduated from Ezel High School and attended the University of Kentucky. Lillian and Tommy live on the 950 acre Howard farm at White Oak, Kentucky, with Lillian's father, Bernard Howard.

By the annual state-wide committee of homemaker's organizations in Kentucky, Lillian Howard Oldfield was selected as one of the two Master Farm Homemakers of Kentucky for 1956.

One of her projects has been the modernizing of the ten-room house which her paternal grandfather built fifty-nine years ago. Lillian's farm work takes her from the house to the fields and back again! Besides growing a large garden, canning and freezing vegetables and fruits, she has built up a large market for cured hams selling over a hundred in a season. Butchered beef, lamb, pork, poultry, eggs, molasses, strawberries, beans, apples, and "sourwood" honey are sold on the farm to motorists.

Tommy and Lillian Oldfield are very active in church and civic activities in Morgan County, Kentucky. They had three children --

Tommy, a student at Morgan County High School; Patricia Ann who met with accidental death; and Brenda Sue.

4. Bernard Eldon Howard was born at Hazel Green, Kentucky. He atended Millersburg Military School. Eldon is a veteran of World War II and is presently an engineering aide with the Kentucky Highway Department. On July 10, 1950 he married Merita, the daughter of Clay and Elizabeth Elan Byrd. They live at White Oak and have three children, Anita Ann, Bernard Clay, and Mary Roe.

4. Robert Woodford, the youngest son of Bernard and Mary Roe McLin Howard, was born on August 1, 1925 at White Oak, Kentucky. He attended Millersburg Military Institute and graduated from Morgan County High School. Robert Woodford Howard, a veteran of World War II, has been a coal mine operator in Morgan County.

3. Monnie, the second child of Robert Joseph and Lillie Day McLin, was born at Winchester, Kentucky. She received her education at Hazel Green and Danville, Kentucky. She is a member of the Presbyterian Church. Monnie McLin was the first wife of Oliver Kash. (See the Alfred and Jane Hurst Kash family.) They resided at Jackson and Lexington. Later Monnie Kash and her children lived at Hazel Green for a number of years. She is presently employed in Tampa, Florida.

To Oliver and Monnie McLin Kash were born four children, Janie Christine, Dorothy Lillian, Oliver Kash, Jr., and Raymond who died at birth.

4. Janie Christine, their oldest child, is a graduate of Henry Clay High School in Lexington and a member of the Presbyterian Church. Prior to her marriage she was a Civil Servise employee in Washington, D. C. She married Donald Stowe Leecraft, a veteran of World War II, from Durant, Oklahoma. He is a graduate of George Washington University and Georgteown University in Washington, D. C. The Leecrafts live at Tulsa, Oklahoma, where Donald is an atorney-at-law. Their adopted daughter is named Donabell. One of Christine's most prized possessions is the old Hurst hymnal, which was one of the first Primitive Baptist song books to make its way into the Kentucky mountains. It was published in 1829.

4. Dorothy Lillian Kash is a graduate of Hazel Green Academy and Bowling Green Business College in Kentucky. She was credit manager of the Montgomery Ward store in Lexington, Kentucky for a number of years. On March 27, 1943 Dorothy Kash married Richard, the son of Ralph Allen and Jennie Newby Reece of Marengo, Iowa. He graduated from the University of Iowa in Art. He is a veteran of World War II. In 1956 Richard Reece received his M. A. degree from the University of Florida in Education. The Reeces live in Tampa, Florida, where Richard is a Civil Service em-

ployee with the United States Coast and Geodettic Survey. His work is the compiling of maps of the coastline of the United States.

Four of Dorothy Reece's short stories have won first prize in National Contests which have been sponsored by the National League of American Penwomen. Hazel Green is the setting of some of her stories.

Dorothy and Richard Reece are active members of the Christian Church. They have two little boys, Dick and Christopher.

4. Oliver Kash, Jr., was born on August 29, 1919. While he was a student at Hazel Green Academy, he married Lavinia Maddox from Sandy Hook, Kentucky. Their marriage date was November 25, 1939. Lavinia was the daughter of the late Joe and Allie Maddox of Fleming County, Kentucky. She was born on September 16, 1922. Her brother, Dr. Paul Maddox, lives in Campton, Kentucky. Lavania atended school at Hazel Green Academy.

Oliver Kash, Jr., served in Korea in World War II. He is a graduate of the Palmer School of Chiropractic at Davenport, Iowa. Dr. and Mrs. Kash live in Grayville, Illinois and have three sons, Robin, Tommy, and Bruce.

3. Mildred, the third daughter of Robert Joseph and Lillie Day McLin, was born on March 12, 1898. She attended Hazel Green Academy where she had training in music. With untiring service and devotion, she lovingly enriched the lives of her parents, Mildred is a member of the Christian Church. Since the death of her father in 1955, she has resided in the home of her sister, Mrs. Christine Howard, at Hazel Green.

3. Daisy Florence McLin, who was born on August 25, 1900, united with the Christian Church at an early age. In 1919 she was the valedictorian of her class at Hazel Green Academy. She completed her Junior College work at Kentucky College for Women at Danville. In 1924 she graduated from Transylvania College cum laude; in 1925 she received her M.A. degree from the same institution.

On June 2, 1924 she became the wife of Reverend Allen Reed Huber, a graduate of Transylvania and the College of Bible. His parents were Amiel and Leora Lauderback Huber. He was born on October 4, 1901 in Mason County, Kentucky. After their marriage Daisy and Allen Huber had some graduate work at the University of Chicago.

From 1926 to 1931 they served as missionaries of the Disciples of Christ in the Phillpines Islands.

Upon returning to the United States they lived at Frankfort, Indiana where Reverend Allen R. Huber was pastor of the First Christian Church for five years. During that time he helped to organize the first federal credit union among Protestant churches in the United States.

In 1937 Allen and Daisy rteurned to the Philippines. Here Reverend Huber helped to start the Credit Union Movement. He is a co-author of the **Credit Union Handbook.**

On December 10, 1941 Daisy and Allen Huber were interned in the Philippines by the Japanese. They were liberated from Bilibid Prison in Manilla on February 4, 1945. No doubt during those years of confinement, hardship, and privation, Daisy remembered many times the subject of her valedictory address at Hazel Green Academy--"Not By Bread Alone."

The Hubers spent the school year of 1946 and 1947 at Cornell University. In 1947 they returned to the Philippines and worked there until the spring of 1951. Since that time Allen and Daisy Huber have been serving as pastors of the Jackson Christian Church in Jackson, Ohio.

3. Robert Bruce, the only son of Robert Joseph and Lillie Day McLin was born on April 3, 1903. He attended Hazel Green Academy and Greenbrier Military School in West Virginia. For a time he was a professional left-handed baseball pitcher. On June 28, 1928 he married Hazel, the daughter of the late Edgar Howard of White Oak, Kentucky. They live in Hazel Green where R. B. McLin had a store for a number of years.

To Robert Bruce and Hazel Howard McLin were born seven children -- Lawrence Bruce, Jean Eloise, Robert Harris, Lois Anne, Roberta, Linda Sue, and Rita Kay.

4. Lawrence McLin graduated from Morgan County High School with a college scholarship in the field of basketball. He attended the University of Georgia and graduated from Marshall College in Huntington, West Virginia. He won thirteen medals for participation in intramurals at Marshall and several athletic awards while he served in the Army in World War II. He married Aerolene Ison, a graduate of Morehead State Teacher's College, from Ison, Kentucky. For five years they lived in McArthur, Ohio where Lawrence was a high school teacher and basketball coach. During that time Aerolene taught in an adjacent town. In the fall of 1956 they moved to Florida. Lawrence Bruce McLin is head of the Physical Education Department in the William Boone School in Orlando and serves as head basketball coach and End Footbal Coach. Aerolene Ison McLin is a physical education teacher in one of the city schools.

4. Jean Eloise, the second child in the Robert Bruce McLin family, was the salutatorian in her high school class at Hazel Green Academy. She attended Berea College for two years and then worked at Huntington, West Virginia. She married William Joseph, the son of John W. and Margaret Bondfield Gleason of that city. He is an engineer. They live in Huntington. Their son, William Joseph Gleason, Jr., was born on April 7, 1956.

4. Robert Harris McLin graduated from Hazel Green Academy in 1950 with an athletic scholarship in basketball. He attended Morehead State Teachers' College and is presently engaged in industrial

work in Huntington, West Virginia. He married Phyllis Jean Frazee of that city. Robert Harris and Phyllis McLin are the parents of two small children.

4. Lois Ann and Roberta, daughters of Robert and Hazel McLin, are high school students at Hazel Green Academy.

4. Linda Sue and Rita Kay, the youngest children in the Robert Bruce McLin family, are twins. They attended the Hazel Green Public School.

3. Margaret Christine, the sixth child of Robert and Lillie Day McLin, was born on May 13, 1906. Intermittingly, she has been a teacher since she graduated from Hazel Green Academy in 1925. She has had her college work in Kentucky at Richmond, Jackson, and Morehead. She was the first wife of Elmer Howard of Morgan County. He was the son of Daniel Boone and Rita Lovely Howard. They were married on January 6, 1928.

In 1937 Christine McLin Howard moved to Hazel Green with her three small children. For sixteen years she has been a saleslady for Avon Products Incorporated. During W. P. A. days she did Pack Horse Library work and visited sixty-seven Wolfe County families twice a month. On weekends she has assisted in the Jot 'em down store at Hazel Green Academy. She has been an elementary teacher in the Hazel Green Public School for the past eight years. Christine is an active member in the local Christian Church. She lives for others and shares what she has with them. Her three children are Elmer Gerald, Peggy Tine and Daniel joseph Howard.

4. Elmer Gerald Howard, who was born at White Oak, Kentucky, graduated from Hazel Green Academy in 1950. He was valedictorian of his class and a "high point man" on the Hazel Green Academy basketball team. Elmer Gerald served as a deacon in the Christian Church. He attended Lees College at Jackson, Kentucky and Morehead State Teachers' College. For the past three years he has been employed in the Engineering Department of Armco Steel Corporation in Middletown, Ohio. He Married Sophie Marie Wills who did secretarial work at Armco. Their little daughter, Christine Marie Howard, arrived on May 8, 1956.

4. Peggy Tine the only daugher of Christine McLin Howard, graduated from Hazel Green Academy and completed a secreterial course at the Spencerian Commercial School in Louisville, Kentucky. She was a secretary for the United Christian Missionary Society in Indianapolis, Indiana at the time of her marriage to Paul Campbell of that city. He attended Butler College and is now employed at the Armco Corporation in Middletown, Ohio. Paul and Peggy Tine Campbell have two little girls, Paula and Pamela.

4. Daniel Joseph (Danny Joe), the youngest child of Christine McLin Howard, was born at Ashland, Kentucky. In early life when he made the confession of his faith, he decided to be a minister. Throughout his childhood and youth he has worked to fullfill his

noble purpose. He has given himself in loving service to the Hazel Green Christian Church and to rural church organizations in Wolfe County.

In 1953 Danny Joe was the valedictorian of his class at Hazel Green Academy. He is now a senior at Transylvania College. For the past year Daniel Joseph Howard has been the student pastor of the Somerset Christian Church near Mt. Sterling, Kentucky. His cousin, Lizzie Pieratt Duff, is the organist in this church. (See the Caroline Trimble Swango family.)

3. Lillian, the seventh child of Robert Joseph and Lillie McLin, was born on August 15, 1909. She graduated from Hazel Green Academy and attended Lees College. For a number of years she was employed as a teacher in Wolfe County. On January 10, 1934 she married Robert David, the son of Walter and Grizella Robinson Hufford of Rossville, Indiana. By training he is a carpenter and building contractor. Robert and Lillian Hufford live in Rossville, Indiana where they are zealous workers in the Presbyterian Church. Their five children are named Shirley Ann, Patricia Jane, James Neal (Jimmy), Rebecca Sue (Becky), and Deborah Day (Debby).

4. Shirley Ann Hufford, now Mrs. Maurice Sharp, will graduate from Indiana University in Speech in June of 1957. Shortly afterward she will joinn her husband, who is in the military service in Japan.

4. Patricia Jane Hufford attended Indiana University and is an office employee in Lafayette, Indiana.

4. Jimmy Hufford was awarded the badge of Eagle Scout at the Central Indiana Court of Honor in 1956. He is in his senior year at the Rossville High School.

4. Becky and Debby, the youngest children of Robert and Lillian McLin Hufford, are in the elementary school at Rossville, Indiana.

3. Irene and Kathlene, the youngest children of Robert Joseph and Lillie Day McLin are twins. They were born on April 20, 1912. (This date is printed by mutual consent!)

We McLin twins grew up at Hazel Green. When we were in the fifth grade we joined the Christian Church and were baptized in Red River. Throughout the years of childhood and youth, Kathleen and I roamed the fields and woods together. I thank Wolfe County for the great overflow of natural beauty that she gave me to have and to hold. I can say unhesitatingly that this gift, which has been enhanced by study and further observation, is one of the most stimulating forces in my life.

In 1930 Kathleen and I graduated from Hazel Green Academy on its fiftieth birthday. The subject of my valedictory address was "Our Golden Anniversary." Kathleen's salutatory essay was entitled "An Education--Or Just a Diploma."

Like many other Wolfe County boys and girls, I helped to pay my way through college by teaching school. I graduated from More-

WOLFE COUNTY

head State Teachers' College with High Distinction.

On January 27, 1940, I married Dr. Wayne Hicks Keller, a chemist. He was the son of William Reece and Virginia Hicks Keller of Henderson, Kentucky. He has on A. B. degree from Georgetown, College; a Masters degree from the University of Kentucky; and a Ph. D. from Cornell University, Ithaca, New York. He taught Chemistry at the University of Kentucky and Morehead State Teachers' College at Morehead, Kentucky.

At the outbreak of World War II Dr. Keller joined some Iowa State College reasearchers who were working as a sub-contractor group with the Metallurgical Laboratory of the Manhattan Project at the University of Chicago on the production of atomic energy. During the war period Dr. Keller was a co-inventor of the process by which the uranium used at Hanford and other atomic piles has been made.

From 1945 to 1952 he was Assistant Director of Research at the A. E. C. uranium plant at Mallinckrodt Chemical Works in St. Louis, Missouri.

In 1952 Dr. Wayne H. Keller became head of the Chemistry Department of National Research Corporation in Cambridge, Mass. He is engaged in the development of methods for the production of titanium, zirconium, and rarer metals which may be used in jet aviation, nuclear energy, and other new fields.

Our home is near the Charles River in Wanban, Massachusetts.

On January 19, 1934, Kathleen McLin married Pryce Ellington, the son of Jim and Ella Center Tutt of Wolfe County. He was born on January 21, 1912 at Tolliver Kentucky.

Pryce's paternal grandparents were Thomas Kelly and Leuellen Crawford Tutt of Wolfe County. His grandfather's nicknames were old T. K. and Long Tom. For a time, Pryce's maternal grandparents, Dr. G. M. and Rausline Creech Center, lived at Hazel Green; later they moved to Campton.

Kathleen has had special training in Library Science at the University of Kentucky. Pryce has had most of his college work at Eastern State Teachers' College, at Richmond, Kentucky. They have been on the Hazel Green Academy staff since 1936. Kathleen is the school librarian and assists with the Wolfe County Bookmobile. Pryce teaches mathmetics, industrial arts, and folk dancing.

Pryce Ellington and Kathleen McLin Tutt had two sons, Pryce McLin and Lynn Alan.

4. Pryce McLin Tutt died at birth on November 25, 1942.

4. Lynn Alan Tutt, who was born on August 5, 1948, attends the Hazel Green Public School.

Irene McLin Keller, Compiler

Personal rights of all contributors have been respected.

The right to reproduce this chapter in printed form must be secured through the Wolfe County Womans Club with the permission of said compiler.

EARLY AND MODERN HISTORY

Index For Early And Modern History Of Wolfe County

	Pages
Wolfe County—By Berta K. Cecil	3-9
First White Settler—Mrs. Mazie Cox Read	9
Pages taken from Richard M. Collin's History of Ky.	9-11
Swift's Mine—Margaret Carroll	11-14
Cumberland Forest—Mrs. Roy M. Cecil	14-17
El Park Hotel—Information supplied by Mrs. Nora Horton	17-20
Mountain Central Railroad—from papers of Floyd Day	20
Historical Data on Hazel Green—taken from Old Records	21-23
Hisorical Sketch of Hazel Green Academy	23-28
Wesleyan Academy Established at Campton—Mrs. Bertie Catron and Rev. W. L. West	28
Swango Springs—Information supplied by Mrs. Rose Conlee	29
Farmers and Traders Bank	31
Swift's Camp Church—Mrs. W. E. Bach	33
Presbyterian Church at Hazel Green—Mrs. W. E. Bach	34
History of Hazel Green Christian Church—Information by Mrs. Carl Mize	37
The First Baptist Church in Campton—Information supplied by Mrs. Mida Wyant	43
The Campton Methodist Church—Miss Lillian Galbreath	44
The Wolfe County News—Mrs. Roy Cecil	45
The Hazel Green Cemetery—Mrs. W. E. Bach	47
Sketch of Bethany Children's Home—by the Staff	48
Dessie Scott Children's Home—Mrs. Esther Pushee	51
Wolfe County Had a Dr. Cox For Three Generations	53
Letter to Maranda Tyra	53
History of Wolfe County Woman's Club—Mrs. Robert Snowden	54
Kentucky—Origin, Formation, Growth—Clay Hollon	57
Early Families of Wolfe County—Clay Hollon	59
Asbury—Mrs. W. E. Bach	59
Byrd's of Wolfe County—Mrs. Nora Horton	60-67
Gabriel Conklin Banks, G. C. Banks	68
Children of Wm. N. G. Barron and Annie Barron—Mrs. Molly Johnson Rowland	69
Deborah A. Swango—Wm. T. Tyler	70
Booth—Taylor Booth	70

WOLFE COUNTY

	Pages
Carroll Family—Mrs. Dora Bush	71
Cecil and Sample Related Families—Steve Sample	75
Chambers—Mrs. Kate Rose	88
The Childer's Family—Mrs. W. E. Bach	88
Collier—Mrs. Taylor Booth	89
Creech Center—Mrs. Rausline Creech Center	90
Solomon Cox—Miss Anna Bell Combs	92
The Cox Family of Wolfe County—Mrs. W. E. Bach	95
The life of Dr. Braxton D. Cox—Mrs. Katherine Riggs	95
The Cruey Family—Mrs. Salley Cruey Miley	97
Congleton's—Mrs. Lee Congleton	98
The Family of Frederick N. Day—Mrs. W. E. Bach	103
The Dunn Family of Wolfe County—Dr. James H. Dunn	107
The Evans Family—Mrs. Ruth Athey and Others	108
The Gosney Family—Mrs. Mazie Cox Read	109
The Hanks Family of Wolfe County—Mrs. W. E. Bach	110
Hollon and Related Families in Wolfe County—Clay Hollon	115
Rev. Johnny Barker and Family—Mrs. Marion Horton	125
First Hollon to Settle In Wolfe County—Captain James I. Hollon	128
The Hursts of Wolfe County—by J. C. Hurst	128
A True Incident—Mrs. Bess Hollon Gullett	144
The Hortons—John White	145
The Tilman Johnson Family—Mrs. J. B. Buchanan	149
Jefferson Johnson—Mrs. Molly Johnson Rowland	153
Our First Kashes of Wolfe County—J. C. Hurst	161
Monroe Lacy—Mrs. Marie O. Steckley	164
The Lacy Family of Wolfe County—Mrs. W. E. Bach	164
The Landsaw Family—J. C. Hurst	165
The Murphy Family—J. C. Hurst	170
The Perkins Family of Wolfe County—Mrs. W. E. Bach	172
The Profitt Family—By James Profitt	173
The W. O. Mize Family—Mrs. Carl Mize	174
Pence Family—Boone Pence	176
The Rose Family—Mrs. Julia Tyra and Mrs. O. D. Rose	177
The John and Rebecca Rose Family	180
Eastern Kentucky Rose Family—by E. T. Rose	190

EARLY AND MODERN HISTORY

Pages

Sketches of Early Families—E. T. Rose 200
America Elizabeth Nickell—Mrs. C. P. Gullett 203
Rose and Nickell Families in Eastern Ky.—E. T. Rose 204
The Sample Families of Morgan and Wolfe Counties—Stephen G. Sample 210
The Swango Family—Mrs. W. E. Bach 223
The Sheffields—Mrs. Ruby Terrill 234
Reuben and Sally Turner Smith Genealogy—Mrs. Jane Allison 235
The Steel Family—Mrs. Mattie Steel 236
The Tutt Family—Mrs. W. W. Abel 241
The Taulbee Family—Mrs. Paris Rose 248
Tyler Family—Mrs. Molly Johnson Rowland 249
Letters by Clay Hollon 252-253
Kashes—J. C. Hurst 253
The Graham Family—J. Douglas Graham, and Mrs. Maude Phelps and others 254

Beginning with pages 262 and through the rest of the book to page 337, all material submitted was in a finished form, ready for the printers; through the untiring efforts of Mrs. Irene McLin Keller, who is related to the families, whose histories she has written up in such an interesting and enchanting manner.

Pages

The O'Hair Family 265
The Trimble Family 271
The Mizes and the Mapels 301
The Gibbs Family 304
The Caskeys 315
The Days 317
The McLins 329

This book was begun while Mrs. Roy Cecil was president of the club in 1952 and completed in May, 1958 while Mrs. W. P. Cecil was president.

www.ingramcontent.com/pod-product-compliance
Lightning Source LLC
Chambersburg PA
CBHW030050100526
44591CB00008B/82